EXCELLENCE IN COLLEGE JOURNALISM

WAYNE OVERBECK, Ph.D., J.D.
California State University, Fullerton

THOMAS M. PASQUA, Jr., Ph.D.
Southwestern College

Wadsworth Publishing Company
Belmont, California
A Division of Wadsworth, Inc.

Senior editor: Rebecca Hayden
Production editor: Judith McKibben
Designer: Cynthia Bassett
Copy editor: Mollie Hughes
Cover design: Vita Otrubova
Signing representative: Aline Faben

Printed in the United States of America
1 2 3 4 5 6 7 8 9 10—87 86 85 84 83

ISBN 0-534-01268-X

Library of Congress Cataloging in Publication Data
Overbeck, Wayne.
    Excellence in college journalism.

    Includes bibliographies and index.
    1. Journalism, College. I. Pasqua, Thomas M.
II. Title.
LB3621.6.O93 1983   378'.19897   82-13387
ISBN 0-534-01268-X

PREFACE

Excellence in college journalism. With this as our theme, we have endeavored to summarize the things a staff needs to know to produce an outstanding college or university newspaper.

Throughout the book, the emphasis is on doing the job right. As we talk about reporting and writing skills, editing, advertising, photography, design, production, student press law and, finally, ethics, we cite examples from outstanding college newspapers. Almost every sample story or photograph in the book is not only student work, but also award-winning student work. You will find stories and photographs that won both regional and national awards. Many of our examples were provided by the American Association of Schools and Departments of Journalism–Hearst Foundation Journalism Awards Program. The newspaper design examples were taken from college papers that won the American Newspaper Publishers Association's coveted Pacemaker Award.

When we researched our specialized chapters on such topics as staff organization and advertising, we sought the advice of some of the most successful college newspaper advisers in the country, and we offer some of their ideas along with our own on such problems as recruiting a staff, organizing a beat system and selling advertising.

Our focus is on college journalism, not the metropolitan newsroom. While we have a deep commitment to professional journalism (both of us have worked for daily newspapers, in capacities ranging from cub reporter to editor-in-chief), we recognize the well-documented fact that only a minority of the students who join a college newspaper staff will ever work for the paper downtown. Thus, we concentrate on the special problems of college journalism, emphasizing the things a new staff member should know right away.

We discuss many different aspects of newspaper publishing. The book touches on the basic principles that are taught in almost every journalism course, including advertising and media law. Because the law has become such an important force in journalism, we decided to devote three chapters to it. One chapter is an overview of the First Amendment protection available to student newspapers; the second summarizes the legal pitfalls that await unwary journalists; and the third discusses open-meeting laws, public-record laws and shield laws—the basic legal tools of newsgathering.

Finally, we address some of the troubling ethical questions that confront college journalists today. The ethics chapter is intended to stimulate debate, not to provide pat answers for students to memorize. In fact, as we chose materials for the law and ethics chapters we found ourselves caught up in some of the same troubling ethical dilemmas student editors face. For example, student newspapers sometimes must deal with difficult questions of good taste in deciding whether to publish offensive—but newsworthy—quotations. If we were to discuss this problem, could we do it without using some of the questionable words? Even the nation's highest court has dealt with this dilemma and has chosen to include in its official record the actual four- and twelve-letter words that were the subject of landmark decisions on the appropriateness of language. In the end, we chose to do the same thing in some instances where the issue could not well be presented without using the words.

Another dilemma we faced was choosing award-winning student journalism from the large quantity of material available. We readily acknowledge that our selection was by no means perfect. The fact that we have included a given story, photograph, or newspaper page does not imply that we think it's the best of its kind ever done. Rather, our inclusion of a particular item merely says we think it is one of many good examples—and that a group of professional judges agreed with us, choosing it for a respected award.

In short, our goal has been not only to teach journalism, but also to do it in a way that emphasizes excellence. We hope this book will provide some incentive for college journalists to set high goals as they pursue their craft.

In writing this book, we received much help and encouragement from many sources. A number of our colleagues offered valuable suggestions. We can't list all of them here, but we'd especially like to thank Ben Adelson, Los Angeles Pierce College (emeritus); Steve Ames, Pepperdine University; Richard Cameron, West Valley Community College; W. B. Daugherty, San Antonio College; Louis Inglehart, Ball State University; Stan Soffin, Michigan State University; Peter Townsend, Miami-Dade Community College; and S. Roy Wilson, College of the Desert. And finally, we'd like to thank the people whose patience and faith enabled us to see this project to completion: our families. To Donna and Lara, to Sandy, Geoff and Alexis, and to Thomas M. Pasqua, Sr., we offer our special thanks.

Wayne Overbeck
Thomas M. Pasqua, Jr.

CONTENTS

The Challenge of College Journalism

You've joined the campus newspaper staff. Yours may be a large daily newspaper at a major university, a paper so large it's hard to distinguish it from the newspaper downtown. The paper may have a million-dollar printing budget, with advertising revenue to match. The staff may be so big that it takes an organization chart to figure out who does what, and you may need a complicated flowchart to keep track of the route a story takes from your typewriter or video display terminal through the editors and into print.

Or you may have joined the staff of a smaller campus newspaper, perhaps a weekly published at a community college, a smaller state university, or a private institution. In that case, you probably don't need a road map to find your way around the newsroom. Nor does your advertising staff need a Brinks truck to take the ad revenue to the bank. Yours is probably nowhere near a million-dollar budget. In fact, a few hundred extra dollars here and there may make all the difference between fiscal solvency and a year's supply of red ink in the balance books.

In either case, you are probably enrolled in a class that gives academic credit for your work on the campus newspaper. It probably isn't your first journalism class, but it may have been a while since you took the last one. Perhaps you were a writer, photographer, cartoonist, advertising person or editor in high school or on a military base newspaper. You may have even served on another college newspaper elsewhere; these days most college students switch schools at least once while en route to a B.A. degree. In fact, you may already hold a bachelor's degree in something other than communications or journalism, but you've decided to return to school for specialized training in this field.

Whatever your background, you're on the college news staff now. Maybe you're there for no other reason than because it's required in your particular major. Perhaps you work off campus more hours a week than you really care to admit, and you're thinking this class will demand more of your limited time than you can possibly give it. But it doesn't have to be that way: if your staff is well organized and has a strong commitment to do things right the first time, the spirit of excellence tends to be contagious, and it isn't long until there are enough staff members that nobody has to make the newspaper a full-time job.

On the other hand, maybe you're on the newspaper staff just because you like to write, edit, sell and design ads, draw cartoons or take pictures. For you, this is a creative outlet for your work. The college newspaper is your showcase, and you enjoy those intangible rewards everyone in this field experiences when the paper hits the newsstands. For most of us, it's still a thrill to see our bylines or photo credit lines in print—or just to have our names in the staff box—even after years in journalism.

Then again, perhaps your main reason for being on the staff is that you like to be involved. There may be 30,000 students on your campus, and hardly any of them know each other, let alone know the college president or even the student body president. For many of them college means nothing more than accumulating enough units to graduate: it's sort of like spending four years in an Army boot camp, just serving time. But for you it's not that way at all. College life is important, and you want to be close to the action. You've already learned something of the clichés about the "power of the press," and you suspect that the student newspaper editor has more real clout than anybody over in student government. There is no faster way to get to know a campus—and to become well known yourself—than through the pages of the campus newspaper, and you want to be where interesting things are happening. It's probably hard for you to imagine just being an ordinary student who goes to classes and then disappears.

All of those may be important motives, but there's still another major reason students get involved in campus journalism: to prepare for a professional career in the mass media or a related field such as public relations. There are thousands of professionals in journalism who got their start on college newspapers. For many of them journalism on campus was excellent preparation for the real world, and it wasn't long before they were stringing (contributing articles) for local daily newspapers, radio or television stations, or the major wire services. It is not at all unusual for a student journalist to turn a job as a part-time stringer into a full-time career position long before graduation. Covering the college president's office or the board of trustees differs little from covering major government agencies downtown, and many a student journalist has moved quickly from a campus beat to a city beat.

Similarly, few things one could do in college are better training for a career in public relations than working on the student newspaper. Perhaps you're on the staff because you expect to write news releases or edit a company publication someday, and you know writing and editing on campus will prepare you. If so, you're not alone. There are numerous successful public relations practitioners—many of them right at the top of their field—who will tell you they learned the basic communication skills that are so vital in PR while they were campus journalists.

But whatever your motivation for joining the staff, you want to make your college newspaper experience worthwhile. This book is intended to help you make a smooth transition onto the staff, but our goal is to do much more than that. We don't think it takes much more effort to produce an excellent student newspaper than a mediocre one. Good writing, creative design, eye-catching photography, effective advertising and efficient staff organization all go together. Throughout this book we emphasize what the country's best student newspapers are doing.

We hope you will pattern your staff organization and production systems after those that work well, so you can publish a good newspaper—and still pass your other classes. And when you set out to cover the campus, we want you to know how award-winning student newspapers approach that job. When you make your basic design and style decisions and decide how to handle photography, you should know how other staffs have resolved these questions. Above all, we want you to pattern your writing after the best in campus journalism.

Whether you are on the staff to be involved, to prepare for a career, to find a creative outlet or just to meet a graduation requirement, we want the experience to be as valuable and painless as possible. We hope you'll find that, whatever else college journalism may be, it is also fun. We want you to leave the production class saying, "I'm glad I did that."

A Review of the Basics

I f you're on a college or university newspaper staff, you may have already taken a newswriting course. If so, this chapter will be a review. But if you're new to journalism, it will introduce you to the journalistic style of writing.

Like poets, journalists use words sparingly—but for a different reason. Poets are concerned about the rhyme, rhythm and imagery of their words; journalists want to communicate facts and ideas to busy people, providing the maximum information in the minimum time or space.

THE BASICS OF STRAIGHT NEWSWRITING

The Inverted Pyramid Style

Long ago, journalists developed a basic approach to straight newswriting that would help them communicate clearly and quickly. This approach, called the *inverted pyramid* style, is the foundation of the journalistic writing technique.

Picture a pyramid (or a triangle if you wish) turned upside down. That is how a news story is organized. The biggest things are on top. That means the gist of the story— the most important information—appears in the first paragraph, which is called the *lead*. Then the details are presented in subsequent paragraphs, and the story gradually tapers down to the information of least significance. Should it turn out to be too long, an inverted pyramid news story can be cut from the bottom. Since each paragraph is less important than the one that preceded it, all of the major facts will still be in the shortened version. If a story is written this way—and you can cut from the bottom without deleting anything important—the story is said to *meet the cutoff test*.

In the inverted pyramid style, the lead paragraph is considered all important. The traditional lead was supposed to answer six crucial questions, called *the five Ws and H*. The five Ws and H are *who, what, when, where, why,* and *how*. In the old days the lead paragraph (or *lead graf* in newspaper jargon) covered all of these details.

Unfortunately, that led to long, clumsy lead grafs, and today journalists rarely try to get all five Ws and H into the lead. Modern newswriters will more often settle for only the key facts, maybe just answering the questions "who?" and "what?"

Also, today's approach to the whole concept of inverted pyramid writing is more flexible than it used to be. While it remains the basic form of newswriting, many stories that appear in newspapers or are aired on broadcast news programs deviate from the inverted pyramid style. Many modern stories do not meet the cutoff test. In fact, the inverted pyramid style is not often used today for feature, analytical and opinion writing (these kinds of journalistic writing are discussed in Chapter 4).

Nevertheless, the starting point in journalistic writing—the style you will probably be expected to follow on many of your early newspaper writing assignments—is the inverted pyramid straight newswriting style. As we said, the key to the inverted pyramid news story is its most-important-things-first organization. However, there are several other important aspects of this basic journalistic style of writing, including the concept of objectivity.

Objectivity

The straight news style is as *objective* as possible. The newswriter presents the facts, not his or her opinions. The idea is that the readers, given the facts, can form their own conclusions. You don't normally say that something is good or bad or right or wrong in a straight news story. You may quote someone else who makes those kinds of judgments, but you don't do it yourself. There is a place for opinionized reporting or *editorializing*. But in the straight news story the writing is factual, not judgmental. You don't present your own views in a straight news story.

Similarly, you don't tell your readers what to do (or not to do), even indirectly. For instance, you would never tell the readers how to vote. Someday you might write a story saying that several student leaders who promised to reduce student body fees have instead voted for a fee increase. However, you would not pass judgment on those facts or tell your readers to vote against those leaders in the next election. Of course, one of the cardinal rules of objective newswriting is to cover all sides, so you would certainly explain why the student leaders changed their minds, but you wouldn't say what you personally think about the issue. Let the readers decide that for themselves.

The objective news style is also a *third-person* writing style. Avoid the words *I, we* and *our* in straight newswriting. You wouldn't even refer to the United States as "our country" in a news story. Similarly, you shouldn't directly address your reader. The words *you* and *your*, like *I* and *we*, should never be used except in quotes. In this book, we (the authors) have chosen to violate this rule from time to time. We use the first person, and we often directly address the readers as "you." A skills-oriented textbook is more like a feature article or an editorial than a news story; we decided at the outset not to follow the straight news style. Were this a textbook about communications law or the history of western civilization, we'd use another style.

Short Sentences and Paragraphs

Another cardinal rule of newswriting is to keep it short and simple. You should write short sentences, using the simplest words that convey the proper meaning. And you write in brief paragraphs.

The rule of thumb on paragraphing in news stories is that anything longer than four typewritten lines is questionable. Many paragraphs are just one sentence in length. Others may be several sentences, but only rarely should a paragraph be as long as six typewritten lines. The average graf should be four lines or fewer. Don't be afraid of a two-line, one-sentence graf. You should alternate between long (that is, four- and five-line) and short (two- and three-line) paragraphs.

The journalist's philosophy about paragraphing differs sharply from what you may have learned in an English composition class. Journalists make no attempt to write topic sentences, or to treat a subject definitively in one paragraph. Journalists use short paragraphs in the interest of readability and for typographic reasons. Paragraphs look longer when typeset in narrow newspaper columns than they do on a typewritten page.

NEWS VALUES AND NEWSWRITING

When you start to write a news story, the first thing to decide is what to include in the story and what to leave out. More to the point, you must decide what the most important aspect of the story is, since that goes into the lead.

"The hardest thing I had to learn," *New York Times* writer Russell Baker once said, "is what is news."[1]

Curtis MacDougall's classic newswriting textbook—a book that has been used by college journalism students for 50 years—itemizes five characteristics that make an event newsworthy.[2] MacDougall says an event is newsworthy if it involves: (1) prominence, (2) proximity, (3) consequence, (4) timeliness or (5) human interest.

Prominence refers to the idea that some people are more newsworthy than others. Once someone is well known, what he or she does is of interest to readers. What may be a common event in an ordinary person's life is newsworthy if it happens to someone famous. If you came down with mononucleosis, only your friends and family would be concerned; if the president of the United States had a bout with "mono," it would be front-page news. The same principle applies on a college campus. The campus paper probably would consider it newsworthy if the college president (or the starting quarterback) caught "mono."

Proximity refers to the closeness of a story to its audience. The classic test of newsworthiness is the presence or absence of a *local angle*. Newspapers cover news involving local people and local organizations. If someone is killed in an auto accident in your town, the local paper probably will cover the story, but the numerous fatal auto accidents that occur elsewhere every day rarely rate any coverage. Only if a faraway accident is truly unusual or spectacular will it be covered. Similarly, if a local person wins an award or runs afoul of the law, it is much more newsworthy than a similar experience of someone faraway.

For a college or university newspaper, the implication of this news value is clear: what happens on campus has proximity and is therefore newsworthy. Off-campus events are usually considered much less newsworthy—unless they directly affect students.

Consequence is regarded as the long- and short-term significance of an event. The reporter has to look ahead to its implications for the future. The media are often criticized for overlooking stories that have little immediate appeal—but that may change the world in a few years. Perhaps the classic example of this was the obscure assassination in 1914 that triggered World War I. The event was barely covered by many American newspapers, but before the ensuing chain reaction was over, millions of lives were lost. Today, stories about the economy often fall into this category. The media are more likely to cover a president's fall down the White House steps than a 1 percent change in interest rates, but the interest rate change will affect us all infinitely more in the long run.

On a college campus stories about decisions reached by obscure curriculum committees are like this. They profoundly affect the courses every student must take, but they sometimes receive less news coverage than squabbles over trivial expenditures in the student government budget.

Timeliness is what separates journalism from history. Remember that you're writing "news," not "olds." News ages fast. There is a major emphasis on currency in newsreporting—much more than there is in feature, editorial or critical writing. In fact, some press critics believe this "now" emphasis distorts reality. Current events are sometimes reported to the exclusion of long-term *processes*.

Editorialist and historian John Lofton blames the imbalance largely on the two wire services that provide so much of our news. Because of their emphasis on current events, "the image of social and political reality conveyed to the public may be greatly skewed. It is usually shaped by a focus on crisis, drama, and sensation rather than by a study of trends and an evaluation of what is socially important."[3]

Perhaps the key question an editor should ask in deciding how (or even whether) to cover a story is this: will it matter next week? Despite the fact that timeliness is a news value, slow, gradual (and unexciting) processes are also important.

Nevertheless, journalists are sometimes so anxious to make their stories sound timely that they stretch to find a *second-day lead* for yesterday's news. You've probably seen second-day leads like this one:

> Investigators today are continuing to sift through the rubble of yesterday's plane crash in Montana, in which 103 persons died.

The story isn't that investigators are "sifting." It might be more newsworthy if they *weren't* trying to figure out what happened. But because the electronic media had the primary story (about the crash itself) yesterday, both the print and electronic media must come up with an angle that sounds fresh (even if it really isn't) to give the story timeliness today.

Human interest long has been recognized as an important news value. If a story has emotional impact, it may not need any other news values to make the front page. How many heart-warming or humorous stories have you seen lately about dogs, cats and children? Or about the ordinary citizen who risked his life to save a child from drowning in a freezing lake? In a 1979 study the American Society of Newspaper Editors was told that readers "want stories told in terms of people and with human feeling, even compassion."[4]

Human interest can be anything that interests readers. It can be a sexy photograph of someone on the beach, a story about how to make pizza, or a yarn about someone whose house burned down.

Often usefulness is a key aspect of human interest today. The authors of one reporting textbook, Everett Dennis and Arnold Ismach, say today's newspapers are "usepapers" because the audience has changed.[5] They say the content caters to people's selfish interests, focusing on self-help instead of spot news about government. A college paper that follows this philosophy would carry lots of stories about entertainment, lifestyles and housing, part-time employment and just about everything else that is central to student life. Much of this would be called *soft news* rather than *hard news*. Chapter 4 discusses this kind of journalism; such stories are rarely written in the inverted pyramid style.

MacDougall's list of news values—prominence, proximity, consequence, timeliness and human interest—is not necessarily the final word on the subject. Some newswriting textbooks say there is at least one more major news value: conflict.[6] Often the simple existence of a controversy or a confrontation (either physical or philosophical) generates news.

Meanwhile, some media critics feel that the mere fact that textbooks list news values perpetuates the system in which current events are emphasized over subtle developments of enormous long-range importance. Perhaps if we applied these news values, the Rocky Mountains could gradually erode away and become flatlands without the press covering the story. Is something that happens ever-so-slowly newsworthy at any one point in the process? Obviously, these news values should be viewed as guidelines and guidelines only: some of your best stories may not fit neatly into any of them.

Nevertheless, the traditional news values are a starting point as you set out to select the *lead angle* for your news stories. When you look for news, you obviously should watch for things that will significantly affect people's lives, and for events that are local and involve prominent people.

WRITING THE LEAD

Now that we've given you a little background, let's take another look at the elements of a good news story. The lead is certainly the most important part of a news story. It must present the key facts, but it also has to do something much more difficult: it has to interest the reader. If the lead isn't clear and interesting as well as informative, many readers will go on to something else. First impressions count, and the lead is the reader's first impression. It can't be clumsy or confusing.

The modern trend, in fact, is to sacrifice facts for readability in the lead. Many newswriters today would rather have an interesting lead than one that presents all of the key facts. Therefore, the second and third grafs may actually be part of the lead. The first paragraph may be nothing but an introduction to what will follow. There may be several grafs of linkage, or lead-in, before the body of the story. Still, the essence of the story goes in the lead—even if the lead is more than one paragraph long. The body of the story, where the details will be filled in, comes later.

As you write each paragraph of a story, you have to remember that it may be the last graf some of your readers will get to. You're not writing a novel that builds up to a climax and keeps the readers' eyes locked onto the page. In straight newswriting your audience shrinks with every successive paragraph.

To combat this tendency writers sometimes deliberately withhold some key information in the lead. Some stories are even written in "suspended interest" style. But for the most part, journalists simply try to make their leads as interesting as possible, hoping reader interest will carry through to the rest of the story.

To achieve this result journalists have devised a number of different types of leads. Some simply concentrate on the facts, while others attempt to be creative in one way or another. We'll show you some of the most popular kinds of leads here.

"Who" and "What" Leads

A "who" lead emphasizes an important name, usually by making the name the very first words of the lead (the name may be collective as well). You've seen hundreds of "who" leads that are written in this fashion: "President Reagan today announced a major tax cut proposal."

A "what" lead is one in which some *thing* is the key aspect of the story and is mentioned first in the lead. Before writing a "who" or "what" lead, the reporter has to decide which element is really more important. If you lead with a person's name rather than what he or she is doing, you're saying the person is more important than the action. Suppose the lead we just quoted was written this way: "A major plan for cutting taxes was announced by President Reagan." The writer of this lead would be implying that the action (the tax cut) is more newsworthy on this particular occasion than the name of the person making the decision (the president).

Let's take a campus example. Suppose you attend a school called Fallsdale State University, and the president of the United States has announced plans to visit your campus. Which of these leads would better present the news?

> President Reagan will visit Fallsdale
> State next week, the White House has
> confirmed.

> Fallsdale State will host President Rea-
> gan next week, according to the White
> House.

Most experienced editors would agree that in this case the "who" lead would be better. It emphasizes the key fact, which is that the president will be on campus. This is about as prominent a name as you could hope to put in a lead.

But suppose, on the other hand, it was already known that the president would visit one college in your general area, and the big uncertainty was about which one he would select. When his office makes the final decision, wouldn't the "what" lead be better?

Whether a "who" lead or a "what" lead (or perhaps still another kind of lead) is better depends on the circumstances. It's all a matter of which is the most newsworthy angle in the particular situation.

This is a "who" lead from a story that placed in the Hearst Foundation's national newswriting competition:

> Music school Professor Mary Curtis-
> Verna has charged her students thou-
> sands of dollars in recent years for extra
> lessons, in violation of University policy.
>
> Lansing Jones
> University of *Washington Daily*

Can you think of a way to rewrite that lead so it's a "what" lead? Would it be better as a "what" lead? Which would be more important to students on campus, the name of the professor or the nature of the accusation?

Here's another "who" lead, this one an award winner in the Journalism Association of Community Colleges (JACC) competition:

> A half-dozen seasoned politicians took
> a back seat to a black Watts physician and
> a deputy district attorney at a mass anti-
> busing protest in the Pierce stadium
> Wednesday night.
>
> Gerry Brailo and Tom DiSilverio
> Los Angeles Pierce *Roundup*

Most editors would agree that this is not only a good example of a "who" lead, but also a good use of the suspended-interest approach to attract readers. The story went on to name several politicians and to explain that the biggest ovations of all went to the black doctor and the deputy district attorney.

Here's an example of a "what" lead, also an award winner in the Hearst competition:

> A tornado raged through Gainesville moments after daybreak Thursday, causing at least $2 million in destruction and leaving thousands of students and other residents without electricity for hours.
>
> Elizabeth Willson
> University of Florida *Alligator*

Notice that, although this is a "what" lead, it is a *summary* lead in the classic sense: it covers the key elements of the news story.

Other Leads Based on the Five Ws and H

The other Ws and H—when, where, why and how—may also be used as the lead angle. However, there are relatively few circumstances when one of them is really the most important aspect of the story. Some journalism teachers tell their students never to lead with "when" in a straight news story. "Why" or "how" may well be the key element of a story, but it is often difficult to explain "why" or "how" briefly enough that it doesn't hopelessly bog down the lead.

Here is a California Intercollegiate Press Association award winner that is technically a "what" lead, but its most important angle is "where."

> Wind blows almost constantly at Pt. Conception, sweeping across the relatively untouched open pastureland today much as it must have hundreds of years ago, when the area supported the Chumash village of Shishilop.
>
> Tom Bolton
> University of California, Santa Barbara
> *Daily Nexus*

To make it a pure "where" lead, it could be rewritten to say, "At Pt. Conception—where California's coastline abruptly turns north after going almost west for nearly 100 miles—the wind blows almost constantly, sweeping across . . ."

There are times when a "why" lead is appropriate. Award-winning leads of this type are hard to find, but here is how a hypothetical "why" lead might be written: "Because of drastic budget cuts, Fallsdale State has closed fall admissions. This will trim next year's enrollment by at least 1,000 students."

This is a lead from a national Hearst award-winning story. It is a "who" lead, but it emphasizes the "why" angle.

> An ASU chemistry student was critically injured Tuesday when a laboratory experiment exploded in his face, triggering a flash fire that engulfed the room.
>
> Diane Mason
> Arizona State University *State Press*

Whether a lead is technically of the "who," "what," "when," "why," "where" or "how" variety, the purpose and methods are much the same. If it is a straight news story, the lead is intended to interest the reader and to summarize the basic facts.

Specialty Leads

Even in straight newswriting, sometimes a summary lead is not the best approach to a story. In fact, many award-winning stories depart from the traditional approach, possibly because a clever specialty lead stands out. However, cleverness can be overdone, and not every specialty lead will win any awards. Some are utter failures.

One of the more common approaches to lead writing is to use a *direct quote*. This is appropriate *only* if the quote is really newsworthy. Sometimes using a quote for a lead is a lazy way out of a lead-writing dilemma, but not necessarily a good one. Quote leads should be used sparingly.

However, sometimes a quotation lead works well. Here's an example from a national Hearst award-winning story:

> "I think this university is sexist. Anybody can look at the numbers and see that women are still getting the short end of the stick."
>
> Barry Klein
> University of Florida *Alligator*

The story then attributed that quote to the university's highest-ranking female administrator and quoted a black professor who said the university was not doing all it could to recruit black professors. The story was about the school's affirmative action program.

Sometimes a lead can be built around an old saying. This is called an *epigram lead*. Similarly, a lead may be based on a line from a song. If it's well done, the result can be an excellent lead. Here's a JACC award-winning example:

> Diamonds are Linda Shafor's best friend—softball diamonds, that is.
>
> Chris Lopez
> Los Angeles Harbor College *Tides*

Sometimes a *parody* on an old saying also produces an interesting lead, as it did in this Hearst award-winning example:

> What this country needs is a free long-distance telephone call.
>
> Thousands of Americans were thinking that last year, hobbling American Telephone and Telegraph for about $27 million in provable revenue losses, by using a little imagination.
>
> Rodney D. Anderson
> University of Kansas *Daily Kansan*

Another Hearst award-winning lead was based on an old song:

> Way down upon the Suwannee River—where whiskey still flows iced-tea red from fallen cypress trees—battle lines have been drawn.
>
> Bill DiPaolo
> University of Florida *Alligator*

Another kind of specialty lead that is often effective, especially for news features and feature stories, is the *descriptive lead*. The "Pt. Conception" lead reprinted earlier to illustrate the "when" approach is an excellent example of this form.

Here's another one, a Hearst award winner:

> The yellow Volkswagen squealed down Veterans Ave., rebel flag tossing in the Monday morning breeze.
>
> The women in Rawls Hall squealed too—with delight.
>
> But when two car loads of security guards turned to give chase, the "Ooos" turned to "Boos."
>
> Then back to "Ooos" again as the two security cars got tangled with each other at the corner of State Street and DeSoto Ave.
>
> The bad guys were winning—and ladies love outlaws.
>
> "We're getting mooned, not raped!" shouted one Rawls resident.
>
> And they were.
>
> David McCrarey
> Memphis State *Helmsman*

The *direct address lead* is still another specialty lead that shows up from time to time. This one violates a basic rule of straight newswriting, of course, and would not be suitable except for a highly featurized story. Nevertheless, it is a common enough form of lead to justify an example here. This one won a Hearst award for a Virginia Commonwealth University student:

> You sleep peacefully because your car,
> home and family are fully insured. If dis-
> aster strikes, you're covered. A large chunk
> of your paycheck buys that coverage.
>
> Dan Shorter
> Virginia Commonwealth *Reporter*

Since our purpose here is to review the basics of newswriting in a single chapter, there's no way we can catalog all of the different kinds of specialty leads that a creative journalist somewhere or other has concocted. But this sampling will give you the idea. If you can come up with a lead that covers the essence of the news and is colorful, too, you should feel that you've succeeded in the most important part of a newswriter's job.

THE BODY OF THE STORY

Once you have a good lead paragraph (or group of paragraphs), you'll probably find that writing the rest of the story is relatively easy. Some newswriters spend as much time on their leads as they do on the entire body of most of their stories. If the lead really does its job, filling in the details is all that must be done in the body of the story. Once you've organized the facts and made the news judgments needed for lead writing, the rest usually falls into place rather quickly.

Covering All the Angles

There are some important things to remember when you write the body of the story. For one thing, you must follow up all of the angles you allude to in the lead: don't leave the reader hanging. For instance, suppose your lead says, "For only the second time in the college's history, a Fallsdale State student has won a Rhodes Scholarship to attend Oxford University in England."

The body of that story would first identify the student and then describe how he won such an honor. The story would also include quotes: the winning student might talk about his plans, and there might be reactions from college officials. And the story would certainly include biographical information about the new Rhodes Scholar.

However, in writing a story such as this, you must be careful not to overlook what you said in the lead—that this has happened before. It would be easy to get involved in the other important aspects of the story and miss that, but it's essential information. The reader has a right to wonder who the college's one previous Rhodes Scholar was, and perhaps what that person is doing now.

In covering all the diverse angles of a story like this, many beginning news-writers assume they have to cover one angle exhaustively before going on to the next. Actually, it is often better to stick with the inverted pyramid style right on through the story. Present the most important aspects of one subtopic, and then move on to the next, later returning to fill in more details on the first subtopic. It is perfectly acceptable to switch back and forth among related subjects as long as you have transitions to ease the topic-switching. An experienced newswriter weaves all the diverse elements of the story together so skillfully that the reader may not consciously realize the subject has been shifted repeatedly.

Almost every well-written newspaper publishes many stories that follow this format in every issue. In selecting an example of a straight news story, we could have selected from hundreds of award-winning examples. We chose one story that was co-written by members of the editorial staff of the *Observer* at Oxnard College in California (Figure 2.1). It won a 1981 award in the Journalism Association of Community Colleges competition and is especially note-worthy because it accurately reports a complex legal and political dispute, a topic that might prove difficult even for an experienced professional. The story well illustrates the art of weaving varied subtopics into a multifaceted story in a clear and comprehensible way.

Of course, not all news stories deal with subjects that are nearly as complicated as this one. Most of the stories you'll write will probably be far more routine and less challenging. Many of the news stories in most papers are quite short, perhaps running only a few paragraphs. But if you master the art of writing complex, multifaceted stories, the routine ones will be easy.

Interpretive and Investigative Stories

Many news stories go beyond merely reporting the facts in a clear and concise way: they analyze and interpret those facts, attempting to put them in perspective. Still another approach to newswriting has come to be called *investigative reporting*. Both of these approaches deserve some mention here.

Interpreting and analyzing the news is an even older tradition than objective newsreporting. Journalists analyzed and expressed opinions about the news long before they made objectivity a major goal. But as a form of newsreporting, interpretive reporting reemerged after World War I.

How does an interpretive story differ from a noninterpretive one? The difference is subtle, but the interpretive writer spends more time explaining the "how" and "why" of the story. He or she may reach some conclusions about the probable consequences of the facts.

Isn't this just another name for editorializing? Some old-time editors thought it was, but most journalists today see a major distinction between editorializing and interpreting. The two functions obviously overlap, but the interpretive reporter

Figure 2.1   Straight news story written by the
editorial staff of the *Observer,* Oxnard
College, California. Used by permission.

Observer Staff, Oxnard

In their on-going legal battle to oust district superintendent Dr. Raymond E. Loehr from office, Ventura County Community College District trustees have lost the second round

On Monday, a federal court judge refused to overturn a decision he made in July reinstating Loehr.

Loehr was fired in early May on a 3-2 vote by the trustees. He later filed suit against the district asking for reinstatement and $4.2 million in damages against the district and the three trustees—Tom Ely, Dave Bender, and Robert Stone—who supported his ousting.

U.S. District Court Judge Laughlin E. Waters ruled in July that Loehr was not granted his full Constitutional rights of due process, subsequently reinstating Loehr to office.

In Monday's ruling, Waters ruled that there "was no basis to revoke the injunction granted to Dr. Loehr and refused to modify or suspend it," according to Tim Miller, a law clerk for Waters.

Prior to the decision on Monday, district officials stated they did not expect Waters to alter his earlier decision pending the outcome of a suit filed by Loehr.

Officials also stated that the request for a stay was just a necessary legal step in the appeal process

Designated district spokesman Public Information Officer Gerald Olsen stated after Waters' decision Monday that an appeal on Waters' ruling has already been filed in the Ninth U.S. Circuit Court in San Francisco.

Olsen also stated that the attorneys for the district expect to decide "within the next seven to 10 days whether they will also request an emergency stay."

An emergency stay, if granted by a circuit court, would remove Loehr from office once again while the district appeals his reinstatement.

Trustee William Simpson, one of the trustees who voted against Loehr's ousting, said the decision on Monday "wasn't at all surprising," and "is definitely in the best interest of our district."

Simpson, who attended the hearing in Los Angeles, stated that Waters looked irritated at the request to modify his earlier decision and indicated he thought the district was wrong in bringing things back to him."

Loehr said after Monday's decision that he was "obviously pleased with Waters' ruling," and stated that not only did Waters deny the district's request, "but was very explicit in his order that he would not modify the injunction in any way."

Loehr added that Waters stated that "under no circumstances would I be denied pay," and he recognized the fact that "they (the district) put me in a position of defending myself without even knowing what the charges were against me."

"I was not only very happy with the decision, but also with the further amplification of the judge's position," he said.

Waters also said the board was not prohibited from taking further actions against Loehr and gave an "oral clarification" of how the district denied Loehr his rights of due process, according to Olsen.

The trustees, in earlier meetings, have decided that not only will they appeal the decision reinstating Loehr, but they will once again go through the process that led to his original dismissal.

attempts to avoid expressing his or her own opinions about the news. The interpretive reporter may look at the economic trends and then report that most experts agree a recession and high unemployment are imminent, explaining why the various economic indicators point in this direction. But the editorial writer, on the other hand, will express alarm at this trend and urge the federal government to take positive steps to prevent it from happening.

Like the interpretive reporter, the investigative reporter goes a step beyond straight newsreporting. But the investigative reporter's main emphasis is on disciplined *newsgathering*. An investigative reporter may spend months sifting through aging public records in an attempt to establish a pattern of government construction contract awards coinciding with campaign contributions. Perhaps the difference between the typical reporter and the investigative reporter was best described by Paul Williams, author of *Investigative Reporting and Editing*. Asked how investigative reporting is different, he said:

[There is] "no difference" and "a lot of difference." No difference because good reporting assumes an investigative attitude and investigative methods; a lot of difference because investigative reporting in its more recent manifestations has begun to change the definitions of news values. Essentially, the big difference is a gradual shift from the old style of reporting on spectacular single incidents and personal crimes to more original and conscientious reporting on the systematic operations of American society.[7]

Whatever the subtleties of the trends toward interpretive and investigative reporting, both kinds of writing are now well established as legitimate and important forms of newspaper journalism. Both have their place in student as well as professional newspapers. And both impose research or documentation requirements on the reporter that far exceed the newsgathering burden borne by the typical straight newswriter.

WRITING FOR READABILITY

One of the main objectives in newswriting is readability. You want your readers to understand what you have to say.

Several formulas have been developed to compute the readability of writing. These formulas became popular almost half a century ago, as some government and business leaders waged war against the "bureaucratese" that had been (and still is) so common in education, government and business writing. Long-winded, pompous writing seems to be especially appealing to minor government officials, who apparently feel it enhances their prestige and power.

In any case, readability formulas were devised to help combat "bureaucratese." However, they may also help the journalist—or anyone else—who wants to improve the clarity of his or her writing.

Probably the easiest to use of these formulas is the Fog Index devised by Robert Gunning. In his book, *The Technique of Clear Writing*, Gunning explained how writers may obscure their meaning by failing to consider readers' needs and abilities. In essence, Gunning said that big words and long, complex sentences drastically reduce readability.[8] You can use Gunning's formula to check the readability of your writing.

Based on research in the 1940s, Gunning found that the average sentence length in high-quality magazines was about 20 words, while that in popular general interest magazines (such as the *Reader's Digest*) was closer to 15 words. High-quality magazine prose averaged 10 percent difficult words (that is, words longer than three syllables), while about 7 percent of the words in popular magazines were that long.[9]

The Fog Index is based on a combination of sentence length and the number of difficult words used. Here is Gunning's three-step procedure to determine the Fog Index of your own writing.

One: jot down the number of words in successive sentences. If the piece is long, you may wish to take several samples of 100 words, spaced evenly through it. If you do, stop the sentence count with the sentence which ends nearest the 100-word total. Divide the total number of words in the passage by the number of sentences. This gives the average sentence length of the passage.

Two: count the number of words of three syllables or more per 100 words. Don't count the words (1) that are capitalized, (2) that are combinations of short easy words (like "bookkeeper" and "manpower"), [and] (3) that are verb forms made three syllables by adding -ed or -es (like "created" or "trespasses"). This gives you the percentage of hard words in the passage.

Three: to get the Fog Index, total the two factors just counted and multiply by 0.4.[10]

To see how your writing scores on readability, you can compare your Fog Index against Gunning's estimates of reading ability for persons with various levels of education. He said that you're over the danger line in readability if your Fog Index is 13 or higher. That score is above the difficulty level even for literary magazines. For comparison, he found that the *Reader's Digest* scored nine on the Fog Index.

Based on his research, Gunning offered 10 principles of clear writing:

1. Keep sentences short;
2. Prefer the simple to the complex;
3. Prefer the familiar word;
4. Avoid unnecessary words;
5. Put action in your verbs;
6. Write like you talk;
7. Use terms your reader can picture;
8. Tie in with your reader's experience;
9. Make full use of variety;
10. Write to express, not impress.[11]

Almost no journalist would dispute this advice, but Gunning's formula itself has its limitations. For one thing, using Gunning's Fog Index is a little like occasionally taking your temperature, pulse and blood pressure. In everyday situations you want to know your personal norm, but you shouldn't be too alarmed if your score varies from the norm under unusual circumstances. Whether it's an especially complicated story or a health crisis, there are times when your number will go up.

Other questions have been raised about readability formulas such as Gunning's Fog Index, too. Jack Selzer, who teaches business writing at Pennsylvania State University, recently published an article that criticized these formulas on several grounds. Selzer said the formulas are oversimplifications of what makes for good writing; they have been misused. Reading is such an individualized thing that it is difficult to generalize about what really promotes readability. Also, he said adherence to the keep-it-simple rule limits the writer's freedom to develop a good style. The problem, Selzer contends, is that long words and sentences correlate with reading difficulty but do not cause it.[12]

To that, many editors would only grumble about the ability of academicians to obscure an issue. Whether it's correlation or causation, the fact is that short sentences, simple words and readability go together. That's why journalists try so hard to keep their words, sentences and even paragraphs short. The goal is clear communication, not stylistic elegance.

REFERENCES

1. Interview with Russell Baker on the Dick Cavett Show, Public Broadcast Corporation, January 11, 1979.

2. Curtis D. MacDougall, *Interpretative Reporting,* 8th ed. (New York: Macmillan, 1982), pp. 114–120.

3. John Lofton, *The Press and Guardian of the First Amendment* (Columbia, S. C.: University of South Carolina Press, 1980), p. 287.

4. Ruth Clark, ed., *Changing Needs of Changing Readers: A Qualitative Study of the New Social Contract Between Newspaper Editors and Readers,* commissioned by the American Society of Newspaper Editors as part of the Newspaper Readership Project (Yankelovich, Skelly and White, 1979), p. 3.

5. Everette E. Dennis and Arnold H. Ismach, *Reporting Processes and Practices: Newswriting for Today's Readers* (Belmont, Calif.: Wadsworth, 1981), pp. 5–7.

6. Dennis and Ismach, p. 31; and Michael Ryan and James W. Tankard, Jr., *Basic News Reporting* (Palo Alto, Calif.: Mayfield, 1977), p. 109.

7. Paul N. Williams, *Investigative Reporting and Editing* (Englewood Cliffs, N.J.: Prentice-Hall, 1978), p. xi.

8. Robert Gunning, *The Technique of Clear Writing* (New York: McGraw-Hill, 1952), p. 35. Revised 1968. Used by permission.

9. Gunning, *The Technique of Clear Writing,* pp. 34–35.

10. Gunning, *The Technique of Clear Writing,* pp. 36–37.

11. Gunning, *The Technique of Clear Writing,* p. ix.

12. Jack Selzer, "Readability Is a Four-Letter Word," *The Journal of Business Communication* 18, no. 4 (Fall 1981):34.

Reporting the News

Should a college or university newspaper just cover campus news, or should it cover the larger community? This question has been debated for a long time, but for many years most college newspapers concentrated on campus news and left the job of covering off-campus events to professional newspapers. Until the 1960s most college and university newspaper staffs only considered things that happened *physically* nearby to be newsworthy. But during that tumultuous decade, faraway events came to be regarded as newsworthy because of their *psychological* proximity—war and human rights were very much on the minds of students. Ever since then many college newspapers have defined *news* in terms of what is important to students, no matter where it happens.

Some college presidents and deans have resisted this change in the role of the campus press, hoping for a return to the days of keep-the-campus-clean journalism. And they get particularly upset (perhaps with justification) when a college paper ignores campus news in its quest for off-campus stories.

But administrators aren't the only ones who feel this way. Some students also get upset when a story they consider important isn't covered, while an off-campus story they think irrelevant or inappropriate is covered. At the University of California, Irvine, for example, angry students once trashed almost the entire press run of the *New University* because the paper reported a wet T-shirt competition at an off-campus bar. Many students protested the alleged sexism of the event, and they won a short-term curtailment of the paper's funding.[1]

However, college newspapers cover far more important off-campus stories than wet T-shirt contests. Wayne Brasler, who frequently publishes critiques of the student press, says that good off-campus news coverage is a hallmark of the nation's best college papers.[2] Reviewing the 1978 winners of the Pacemaker Award, Brasler found excellent off-campus reporting in all three full-size newspapers that won Pacemakers: the University of Texas *Daily Texan*, the Central Michigan University *Life* and the Los Angeles Valley College *Valley Star*.

Here's what Jim Wojcik, Central Michigan's director of student publications, says about covering campus and off-campus news:

Our primary function, of course, is to serve the university community, with special emphasis on the students, and all the news that will affect them. We also provide them with community news, ranging from city and county commissions to township government, all agencies that have bearing on the students, faculty and staff. And, of course, we localize state and national news that has a bearing on the campus. We try to make our operation as professional as possible so that when students graduate and hit the real world they aren't in for many surprises.[3]

The philosophy at Central Michigan is probably typical for a four-year university newspaper. Student press critic Brasler's review of 1977 Pacemaker winners noted much the same trend, with both the *Daily Texan* and the University of Alabama's *Crimson White* giving thorough coverage of off-campus events.[4] The *Texan,* in particular, was covering news up to the international level, using its editorial staff of 165 salaried persons. The *Crimson White* stayed a little closer to home, covering mainly on-campus, local and state-level news.

On the other hand, Brasler found that the community college Pacemaker winners for 1977 (the Fullerton College *Hornet* in California and the Highline Community College *Thunder Word* in Washington) covered campus news almost exclusively. Both did, however, address national issues in their editorials.

Brasler's findings are not surprising. Most university dailies (and many four-year weeklies) have at least one wire service available, and they often have large enough staffs to assign reporters to off-campus events. Even the largest community college papers rarely have either wire services or many spare reporters to send into the community.

At Los Angeles Valley College, where the *Valley Star* is a five-time Pacemaker winner, journalism professor Eddie Irwin says the paper rarely goes off-campus except for entertainment reviews and board of trustees' meetings.[5] At nearby Los Angeles Pierce College—the home of another large journalism program and Pacemaker-winning newspaper—the paper usually goes off campus only for "the Board of Trustees, some away games and a few interviews of alums," says journalism professor Bob Scheibel. Scheibel and his colleagues emphasize that their paper, *The Roundup,* does go off campus when a story is relevant to the campus. Here is *The Roundup's* policy on off-campus coverage:

> As a rule, items of straight news will be limited to campus activities. After the campus is covered, in the judgment of the editors, then consideration can be given to off-campus events. But the Roundup maintains its right to publish information of off-campus events related to or of interest to The Roundup readership.[6]

One reason many college newspapers follow policies such as this one is simple: there's not even enough space in the paper to cover the campus thoroughly. Spencer Crump, who heads the Journalism Department at Orange Coast College (another large California community college), says limited newspaper space is a major problem on his campus.

Not all community college newspapers subscribe to the philosophy of limited off-campus coverage. At Amarillo (Texas) College, Director of Student Publications Janace Ponder says the paper covers "anything that has consequence for students of Amarillo College."

At four-year colleges off-campus news coverage tends to be much more extensive, often with wire service news. Bill Ward, a Southern Illinois University-Edwardsville professor, has questioned this practice: "Why should page 1 be filled with AP or UPI wire stories with local campus stories buried inside?" Then he answered his own rhetorical question: "The campus newspaper serves its specialized community first. Unfortunately, wire copy is easy to edit, to headline and lay out. Yet, syndicated material never should displace local."[7]

Nevertheless, students are clearly interested in many things beyond the confines of their own campus, and many student newspapers now cover off-campus news routinely. But when it goes off campus, how much impact can a college newspaper have? Researcher Charles Atkin studied the impact of editorial endorsements in the *State News*, the large daily published at Michigan State University. He found that the paper had little effect on its readers' voting patterns in national elections but did influence student voting patterns in a local election.[8] The reason, apparently, was that the readers had access to other media, such as network television, for information about national issues, but not for local ones.

Gene Burd, an urban reporting specialist at the University of Texas, wrote an article in *College Press Review* urging college newspapers to cover news of their cities, states and regions. He noted that there is often a close news-making relationship between the campus and community.[9]

COVERING THE CITY AND REGION

State and local government is a major news source for most college newspapers. All public universities and colleges are affected by what happens in the state legislature; many college papers attempt to cover the legislature, at least via wire service reports. Some campus papers send a staff member to the state capitol when a particularly relevant bill is due for a vote. In some states college papers have jointly covered the legislature.

For public colleges and universities the single most important off-campus news source may be the institution's governing board, usually called the "board of regents," "board of trustees" or "board of curators." These government agencies usually are required by law to meet in public, although most are allowed to exclude visitors (including reporters) when they discuss such matters as hiring and firing top administrators.

For four-year colleges, covering the board often means sending a reporter to a distant city, which may make it prohibitively expensive. However, almost all community colleges have local governing boards that meet on or near the campus.

Unfortunately, at private universities most governing boards may lawfully meet in secret—and do so. That makes covering the board more difficult; the reporter can only interview those who attend the meeting, and hope to cultivate good sources.

City and county governments also take many actions that affect the colleges in their areas. For instance, local governments are almost always involved in the planning for college construction projects, even if the college isn't required to go through the normal building permit process. A reporter for a private college newspaper who attends the right local government meeting may learn things about the school's plans that he or she would never otherwise discover.

Local governments also affect colleges and college students in many other ways. For instance, they regulate zoning and traffic in the areas around the campus. Every student who lives (or parks a car) off campus is affected by what the local government does.

COVERING THE CAMPUS

Whatever else a college or university newspaper covers, its primary responsibility is to cover the campus. That's not easy at a modern college or university with thousands of students, hundreds of faculty members and dozens of academic majors.

A further complicating factor is that colleges and universities today aren't the unified places they once were. It was once the custom for students to "go away to college," which meant living on campus or very nearby. Today fewer than half of all college students are really "away" at college in the sense of living in a residential college atmosphere. The decline in the popularity of dormitories, a building boom in privately owned apartment complexes near colleges and the unparalleled growth of primarily commuter schools have all worked together to make the residential atmosphere an exception to the rule.

This transition has fundamentally changed the experience of going to college for millions of students. A residential college campus tends to have a closely knit atmosphere, with students who are likely to participate in campus activities and know the student leaders. At a primarily commuter institution, on the other hand, most students live, work and maintain social ties somewhere remote from the campus. A college education for them may mean nothing more than sitting in class for 15 hours a week. Commuter students tend to feel little of the traditional sense of belonging. They are by no means "away at college." Student apathy and even alienation are common. This is not to say these problems never occur at residential colleges, but they are certainly more commonplace on commuter campuses.

Obviously, covering the news is a difficult challenge on commuter campuses. But in addition, student editors at commuter colleges have other problems not shared by their counterparts on residential campuses. For instance, recruiting and motivating a staff is a problem. Most of the students work and face other off-campus demands on their time. They simply cannot give the student newspaper the kind of commitment that is common among staff members at residential colleges.

But despite the differences between residential and commuter colleges, the same two basic approaches to campus news coverage are used in both settings.

At both types of colleges, the editors typically use a *beat system,* supplemented by an individual assignment system for major stories. These are the same two approaches used by professional papers in covering the community.

The Beat System

The beat system is based on the idea of breaking up the campus into many coverage units, each small enough for one reporter to handle. This approach has several advantages

For one thing, the reporter has an opportunity to become familiar with the territory and to acquire the background information necessary to write knowledgeably about major issues and problems in his or her area. A beat reporter has time to develop personal relationships with news sources that the one-shot reporter could never match.

Another advantage of the beat system is that it allows the editors to be certain the major areas of the campus are covered systematically. Without this systematic coverage many important stories would be missed.

In fact, assigning reporting students to beats for the campus paper is a common practice. At San Antonio College in Texas, W. B. "Dub" Daugherty and Lynnell Jackson Burkett report that students are assigned to beats in the first week of the beginning reporting lab.[10] On the other hand, at California State University, Los Angeles, students are not given beats until their second course in newswriting, a practice that seems more or less typical in the California State University system.

Also it's much easier to assign each student a beat than to come up with an individual assignment for each one every week. The beat system makes it easy to phase students in reporting classes into staff assignments and allows the new reporters to see their work in print relatively early in a journalism curriculum. This arrangement also enables the course instructor and the editors to share the burden of training new reporters, a job that otherwise could take an inordinate amount of the editors' time.

However, the beat system also has disadvantages. Perhaps the major one is that the system is only as good as the reporter on the beat. If the reporter is good, the beat will be covered well. But if not, it may be weeks or months before the editors even know there's a problem. Some important stories may have been missed by then.

Another problem is that the beat reporter has certain vested rights. If he or she turns out to be mediocre, there's a problem when a really important story comes along. Short of simply removing the beat reporter from the assignment, it's not easy to put someone else on the story.

An additional problem on many campuses is a chronic shortage of reporters to whom beats may be assigned. Even if students are drawn from reporting classes for beats, the list of beats always seems longer than the list of available reporters. Covering a large campus thoroughly takes many people: the beat list in the Los Angeles Pierce College Reporters' Handbook shows about 50 specific beats, ranging from the campus police and the academic senate to the wood shop.[11] Even with some doubling up of beats, that list could be covered only by a big staff.

Despite these problems, the beat system is a proven method of covering a campus—or a city. That's why it is so widely used by both college and professional newspapers.

Typical Beats How are beats established? Typically, the editors sit down and systematically list the major sources of news on campus and then divide them up into areas.

On almost any campus the beats will include all of the academic departments, perhaps combined into areas. One reporter might cover all of the social sciences, another the natural sciences, and so on. In dividing up the academic areas, don't overlook the special programs that may not fall within the normal academic structure. Whether it's a special research institute or the campus farm, it may produce many good stories. Some of the major stories originate in the performing arts areas and in the physical education departments. The entire sports staff is, in a sense, covering one very major beat. But within sports, all of the individual men's and women's sports have to be covered, along with intramurals and recreational activities.

The various administrative offices also should be covered. Most colleges have separate deans or vice-presidents in charge of financial matters, business management and academic affairs. These are all excellent news sources, but don't forget the specialized administrative areas, such as community services and extension programs. Both the campus security or police department and the student affairs administrators are important beats, too.

Some of the more important beats involve student groups. Some college papers assign reporters to all of the major clubs and organizations on campus. If you have fraternities and sororities, both the individual groups and the inter-fraternity council are important news sources. The career- and professionally oriented organizations may also do newsworthy things. And all of the various bureaus and branches of student government must be covered thoroughly. A reporter should certainly be assigned to attend the meetings of the major student boards and commissions, not only because what happens there is newsworthy, but also because such boards invariably include people who can lead reporters to other stories.

On the faculty level the same thing is true. The academic senate and other faculty groups make important decisions, many of which affect students. To the extent that their meetings are open (they're open by law in some states, but not in others), they should be covered.

If your campus is in any way specialized, there may be other beats to cover. If yours is an art or engineering school, or perhaps a church-related college, you will have major beats that might not be found on most campuses. At a religiously oriented college, for instance, the campus body that is in charge of the school's religious life and atmosphere may be one of the most important news sources of all. The list of beat suggestions could go on and on.

Assigning Beats   Once you have a list of beats, how do you assign reporters to them? Sometimes it's done at random, or so it seems. However, many colleges run a first-come, first-served system, with reporters requesting beats. The leftover beats are then assigned to the students who don't volunteer for something else.

This system at least gives students some freedom of choice, but inevitably it results in some of the toughest (and most important) beats going to people who would really rather not have any beat at all—people who would just as soon not be in school. The result, of course, is that some of the major beats may not be covered enthusiastically.

Many colleges use a "best beats to best reporters system." One method of assignment under this system is for the editors to prescreen those available for beat assignments, perhaps with a reporting and writing skills test. Then those who perform best on the test are given the most important beats, with the other beats handed out more or less at random or on a first-come, first-served basis. The "best beats to best reporters" system is used at Palomar College near San Diego, California, according to journalism professor Fred Wilhelm.

Covering the Beats   Once you have beats and beat reporters, what happens then? At Amarillo College, each reporter fills out a one-page *beat report* weekly, indicating with whom he or she spoke and summarizing the major information gained from the interview. The reporter lists any story ideas that emerged from the interview(s) and has the first shot at these assignments.

Former newspaper adviser Susan Vaughn of Indian Valley Colleges in northern California had a full page of beat-reporting instructions in her staff handbook. She credits the ideas to a number of nearby college newspapers, including *The Monitor* at Ohlone College, *La Voz* at De Anza College, *The Pirate's Log* at Modesto College, *El Yanqui* at Monterey Peninsula College, the *Rampage* at Fresno City College, and the *Times* of College of Marin. Here's what the Indian Valley handbook says:

How to Cover a Beat

Once you are assigned a beat, find out all you can about it.

1.   Go to the source of the information suggested, introduce yourself, and tell that person you have his/her beat for the semester and want to know all you can about their functions. Learn who's in his/her office (secretaries, aides, etc.—all possible sources of information).

2.   Get all available information their office puts out. BE SURE TO GET MINUTES AND AGENDAS.

3.   Get a list of all persons and their titles in the offices or on the committees, etc. GET ALL POSSIBLE BACKGROUND INFORMATION.

4.   Find out the best time to talk with the source both BEFORE and AFTER meetings. (Is early morning best, or around 4:30?) This depends upon your schedule and the schedule of your source.

5. If you do not cover the story yourself, be sure that the reporter and photographer who do cover it are well briefed. Refer to morgue clippings for background information.

6. Check out each story you have assigned. If there is something in the story which does not seem plausible—ask the reporter to check it again. If it still does not seem right—*call and check it out yourself.*[12]

Territorial Rights   There are several other things to think about in beat reporting. For one thing, beats often overlap. Any major controversy that arises in a department or program will soon get central administrative attention, and the governing board may even become involved. Obviously, beat reporters can't be too territorial about their assignments. There are times when a reporter has to give way and let someone else take a story that overlaps two or more beats.

Incidentally, that kind of problem is not unique to college campuses. The Watergate scandal, which led to the resignation of Richard Nixon as president of the United States, was first uncovered by Robert Woodward and Carl Bernstein, two police beat reporters for the *Washington Post*. But it quickly became apparent that the story was far more than an ordinary police story, and for a time the reporters on the national political beat thought it should be their story. Woodward and Bernstein won the jurisdictional skirmish and became famous for their coverage of a story that was almost taken away from them.

Like the Watergate story, many campus stories are obtained from other than official sources of information. A good beat reporter gets to know the people who know what's going on—including secretaries and deputies to important people. More than one major story has been broken only because an insider with a guilty conscience chose to talk to a reporter. Such a news source is called a *whistle-blower*.[13]

Whistle-blowers often risk their own careers to speak up about something they feel is wrong. As a result, a reporter may have to promise confidentiality in return for information. This can raise both legal and ethical problems.

Some beats seem dead. There is no question that more news is made in some departments and administrative offices than in others. Still, an imaginative reporter can find some stories in almost any department or organization. For instance, are there any people who have done interesting things? Don't overlook the possibilities for feature stories if there isn't much hard news. Sometimes even the oldest conversation piece of all—the weather—can be turned into an interesting story. For instance, when Erie College North Campus in Buffalo, New York, became an emergency station during a snowstorm, student journalists came up with a colorful weather-related story.[14]

The Individual Assignment System

The beat system is not always the perfect way for a campus newspaper to gather the news. Even papers whose editors are committed to the beat system also make specific assignments outside the system when necessary. Some stories don't fit well into any beat, and on other occasions a beat reporter may miss an important story, thus necessitating an individual assignment.

A number of newspaper advisers have tales to tell about the shortcomings of the beat system. "Most stories result from individual reporter assignments, though some areas are supposed to be checked every week," says Jan Rawson, journalism coordinator at Citrus College in California. Jean Stephens of Sacramento City College agrees: "We sometimes have beats, but they don't work very well with us. Some work out: student government, women's center. Most assignments are individual. The sports page does have beats, and they work there."

Actually, student newspaper staffs find that many news stories come to them. Says Orange Coast College's Spencer Crump; "Most beats produce little news. Most news comes from things people tell staff members or me, either by coming in the office or phoning."

For these reasons, many college and university newspaper editors rely heavily on individual assignments rather than the beat system. Probably the beat system works best where there is a large staff of capable reporters. For staffs that are shorthanded, a rigid beat system is probably not the answer.

INTERVIEWING

In newspaper work, the most common way to get information is to ask someone. Interviews range from very casual informality to starchy formality. Some interviews involve nothing more than a quick telephone call, but others require a reporter to be with the news source for hours—or even days.

Types of Interviews

Each kind of interviewing has advantages and disadvantages. A telephone interview is usually quick and easy to arrange, but it is also easy for an uncomfortable news source to terminate. Another disadvantage is that it provides no opportunity to observe the demeanor of the interviewee. You can't see any of the body-language clues that are so valuable to reporters. If all you want is some noncontroversial facts for a straight news story, a phone call will probably do nicely. But if you want to deal with sensitive issues that may require probing, or if you're doing a feature story, the telephone interview is not the ideal method.

An in-person interview, on the other hand, may be difficult to arrange, and it certainly is less convenient than a telephone call. But once you're there, the interview cannot be cut short so easily if the questioning becomes uncomfortable for the source. And you do have the opportunity to see your news source. If you're alert, you can learn much by merely observing the person's manner. You can tell if he or she is alert, bored, relaxed, nervous or ill at ease.

We should say a little here about press conferences. The press conference has one major advantage over an exclusive in-person interview: there are usually lots of witnesses, and the news source cannot easily claim he or she was misquoted if something that was said proves embarrassing later. However, press conferences are usually about as inconvenient as formal interviews, and no one has an exclusive claim to the story.

Another problem with press conferences is that a reporter rarely has the opportunity to follow up an important question as easily as he or she might in a personal interview. There is just too much competition for the news source's time and attention for intensive follow-up questioning. Moreover, the news source decides who will be called on and can simply ignore reporters who might ask difficult questions. In a competitive newsgathering situation, press conferences have their place, but a personal interview is usually better for the reporter.

Still, the formal interview requires some advanced arranging. To schedule one you will usually be expected to telephone for an appointment. When you call, you'll identify yourself and specify any materials you may need. If you are going to take pictures, you should state that too. Most reporters prefer to conduct an interview at the news source's home base, but sometimes it's necessary to have him or her stop by the newspaper office or to arrange another meeting place.

Preparation

One of the most important aspects of interviewing is your preparation. You should learn all you can about the topic and the interviewee beforehand. If your newspaper has a library or "morgue" of previous stories, check it before the interview. In addition, you may be able to gain useful information by asking staff members and possibly others about the interviewee or topic.

In addition to doing research, you should also formulate a clear plan for the interview. What information do you need? What obstacles do you anticipate, if any? What questions do you plan to ask? Some reporters actually write down a list of questions that they'll ask; others merely think them through beforehand. But in no case should you go into an interview without thoroughly preparing.

Techniques for Interviewing

A number of books have been written about interviewing techniques.[15] One good one is *Creative Interviewing* by Ken Metzler.[16] Metzler says interviews are basically uncomfortable events for everyone involved. He says the reporter can make the situation more pleasant by beginning with informal conversation. And since the news source probably isn't sure what a reporter is after, you should explain your purpose early in the interview.[17]

Metzler also says the reporter's appearance counts in interviewing,[18] although we wish it didn't. There's really no dress code for a reporter conducting an interview, but being dressed in about the same way as the people you'll be interviewing is usually best.

We might add that another important courtesy is being on time. Many of the people you interview are busy executives who may feel they're doing you a favor by granting an interview. Sometimes they'll make you wait in the outer office, but you should never make them wait. If you can't be on time (or, even worse, can't make it at all), call ahead and explain the situation.

In asking questions, you should be specific; vague "tell-me-all-about-it" questions will get you vague, rambling answers. And don't talk too much, Metzler cautions.[19] A reporter can overdefine the questions and end up giving little speeches that leave the source with little to say. A key point is to listen carefully and follow up, keeping the interview on the intended subject.

Sometimes you must ask pointed questions. If so, don't apologize—just ask. Some reporters develop direct and even aggressive interviewing styles to use in such situations. Sometimes the shock produces a moment of candor. However, not everyone is comfortable with the same interviewing style; you'll have to develop techniques that fit with your personality. Some reporters spend more time exchanging small talk about the interviewee's special interests than they spend on the key topics.

Another thing we should emphasize is to be aware of the surroundings. If you're in an office, look around and see what clues might be sitting there in plain view. Are there any unusual plaques, photos or mementos?

Should you take notes or use a tape recorder during an interview?

Obviously, you'll have to write down the spelling of names, numbers, official titles, and other details. In fact, if you don't write down these details, the source will probably not think you're doing your job. Also, you should write down any statement that you expect to use in direct quote. To take notes and keep up with the conversation, you'll probably have to develop some method of shorthand. Most reporters develop their own shorthand abbreviations rather than learning one of the formal systems taught in secretarial schools.

However, there is such a thing as taking too many notes. If you write everything down, you'll certainly slow the pace of the interview, and you may cause the news source to feel inhibited.

A tape recorder tends to make some news sources feel even more inhibited However, it has two major advantages: it helps you get your quotes and facts exactly right, and it gives you some protection against the source later claiming he or she was misquoted. But in addition to its tendency to make people freeze up, tape recorders also have other disadvantages. For one, tape recorders are not always dependable. Both human and mechanical failings can cause them to malfunction. If you count on having the story on tape, you run the risk of having no story at all. Also, the tape recording will slow you down. If you take good notes, you can do the story much more quickly than you could if you had to replay the whole interview again on tape and then take notes.

Most reporters feel that a tape recorder is a useful backup device, but there's no substitute for good, on-the-spot note-taking. Also, under no circumstance should you conceal a tape recorder. For ethical (and sometimes legal) reasons, your news source has a right to know if a tape recorder is running.

COVERING MEETINGS
AND SPEECHES

Journalists also do a lot of newsgathering by covering meetings and speeches. There must be hundreds of newsworthy public meetings and speeches on any college campus each year.

In addition to the governing board, which we discussed earlier, there are numerous other boards with policy-making powers. None have the authority of the board of trustees or regents, of course, but these other student, faculty and administrative boards nonetheless make important decisions.

To cover a meeting well, there are several things you need to do. First, you have to get there early enough to get a good seat so you see and hear everything that is going on. Also, you'll need to get the agenda for the meeting, and, if possible, talk to someone associated with the board to find out what is expected to happen that may not be on the agenda.

One additional thing you'll need to do before the meeting is get the names and titles of the people on the board or commission. Many reporters who are covering a particular board for the first time make a diagram of the meeting table that shows the name of the person who occupies each chair. If you don't have a chance to get all the names before the meeting begins, you might assign a number to each person and find out the names later. That will enable you to take down quotations during the meeting—and then attribute them to the right people.

If you're covering any board or commission for the first time, you'll probably not understand everything that goes on. You'll want to make notes to yourself as the meeting proceeds, so you can remember all of the things you will need to ask about afterward. By all means start developing news sources on the board right away. You may well have to call someone back for additional information as you write your story or stories.

When you write the story, the one thing you should *not* do is write something that sounds like the minutes of the meeting. The minutes are almost always written in chronological order, with no particular emphasis on the important actions taken. The minutes are a formal record of official motions and decisions, often with little explanation of how or why these decisions were reached.

Your meeting story should have a lead that tells your readers what happened that will affect them. In sorting through a 20-item agenda, ask yourself which actions will affect the most people in a significant way.

Sometimes you'll decide there were two or three equally important actions taken at a board or committee meeting. If so, you can write a lead that mentions all of them, or you can write separate stories for each. Reporters often write one main story and several *sidebars* (related but shorter stories) after covering a meeting at which several important things happened. At the end of your main meeting story, it's perfectly acceptable to make a list of the miscellaneous things that happened, giving each one a number, like this:

In other action, the board:

1) . . .
2) . . .
(and so on)

In covering a meeting, accuracy is extremely important. If you aren't sure what happened, or what it means, *ask someone*. Similarly, your quotes must be correct. If you aren't quite sure what someone said (or who said it), don't use the quote.

Much the same thing can be said of speech reporting—accuracy is vital. And covering a speech is often complicated by the fact that there may be a crowd, the sound may be poor, or the speaker may talk faster than you can write.

If you're covering a talk by a public official, it is often possible to get an advance copy of the speech. The official's public relations aide can probably get you a copy if you request it in advance. But even then you have to listen carefully, because public officials often depart from their prepared speeches, and their unplanned, off-the-cuff remarks may be the most newsworthy parts of the whole speech.

Another thing you can do ahead of time is to find out who (if anyone) will be taping the speech. While you should not count on having a tape to fall back on when you cover a speech, if you can arrange to get a copy of the tape (or make your own tape), you have a much better chance of having accurate quotes. But as we said earlier, it takes a lot of extra time—time you may not have before your deadline—to replay the whole tape. It is better to take good notes so you'll only need to replay those portions of the tape that you intend to use for direct quotes.

If a big-time, out-of-town speaker is coming, you may be able to join the official greeting committee at the airport. That may give you a chance to get a short personal interview. If the speaker is local, it may be possible to call the person directly and arrange an interview. An interview after the formal speech has a major advantage: it gives you a chance to get clarification of anything unclear or controversial the speaker may have said. Another reason to arrange a personal interview, of course, is so you can give readers who heard the talk some new information.

When you cover a speech, there are other things to watch besides the speaker. You should also notice the crowd reaction, the number of questions, the crowd size and what sort of entourage the speaker brings.

Writing the speech story is usually not especially difficult if you have good notes. In selecting a lead angle, ask yourself what the speaker said that was new and significant. As in a meeting story, you do *not* write in chronological order unless the speaker dropped a bombshell announcement in the very first sentence. To write a speech story in the inverted pyramid style, you summarize the most important statement in the lead (or quote it if it is both short and colorful). Then you develop the story by presenting the various other things the speaker said—in their order of importance.

There is a rule about quotations: keep them short. Your direct quotes should be no longer than about four typewritten lines. If you wish to quote a longer passage, break it up into a combination of direct quotes, indirect quotes ("he said that . . .") and summary statements (in which you tell what the speaker said in your own words).

Speech reporting is as varied a task as anything in journalism: one assignment may find you in a half-empty class listening to someone talk about a subject that seems trivial, but the next one may give you a chance to interview a mayor, governor or United States senator. It's a kind of newsgathering that varies from excitement to utter boredom.

OTHER NEWSGATHERING METHODS

Interviewing and covering meetings and speeches are important newsgathering methods used by college newspaper reporters, but there are other ways to learn the facts.

In sports and hard news reporting, *observing* an event is an important way to gather information. In fact, any reporter should always be alert for a possible story. Many good stories are written because a reporter happened to notice something unusual and decided to inquire further. You should always watch for anything unusual and keep notes so you won't forget the details of what you've seen.

Public records are another major source of information for journalists. Much information that could be gathered in no other way can be gleaned from records buried in government offices, records that anyone is free to inspect (but almost no one ever does). (Chapter 14 discusses public records.)

Libraries and archives also provide valuable information for journalists who know how to use them. It is amazing to discover just how much information is available on microfilm and in microfiche form. Reference librarians often can provide valuable help for someone looking for information in a library. An excellent guidebook on this subject is *Finding Facts* by William L. Rivers.[20]

Jerome Aumente of Rutgers has described the journalist's data-gathering process this way: "Journalists can approach their information in a number of ways. The most common is the hit-and-run technique of daily reporting—scooping up the bits and pieces under terrible deadline pressures, shaping the fragments so they have balance, style, some grace and a minimum number of cracks showing."[21] Not everyone would agree with this assessment of the process, of course, but it would be hard to dispute the fact that journalists often must gather their information in a rush.

REFERENCES

1. Thomas Fortune, "UC Irvine Paper Survives Battles," *Los Angeles Times*, 8 June, 1979, Part I, p. 30.

2. The Pacemaker Award is presented annually to about five of the best college or university newspapers in the country, as judged by the American Newspaper Publishers Association in cooperation with the Associated College Press. See Wayne Brasler, "1978 Pacemaker Newspaper Awards: What Makes a Pacemaker?" *Scholastic Editor* 58, no.5 (March 1979): 16–23.

3. Brasler, "1978 Pacemaker," p. 21.

4. Wayne Brasler, "1977 Pacemakers: The New Simplicity," *Scholastic Editor* 57, no. 5 (March, 1978): 8–15.

5. This statement was one of the responses to the qualitative survey conducted for this book. The survey was first distributed 21 November 1981, at the Journalism Association of Community Colleges' Southern California Conference at Pasadena City College. Additional copies were distributed by mail that week. The following people submitted their ideas for this chapter: Mike Cornner (Los Angeles Pierce), Spencer Crump (Orange Coast), Jules N. Draznin (Los Angeles Trade Tech), Janyth Fredrickson (Imperial Valley), Tom Kramer (Los Angeles Pierce), Eddie Irwin (Los Angeles Valley), Janace Ponder (Amarillo), Jan Rawson (Citrus), Glen Roberts (San Diego City), Bob Scheibel (Los Angeles Pierce), Jean Stapleton (East Los Angeles), Jean Stephens (Sacramento City), Dee Volz (Ventura), Fred Wilhelm (Palomar) and Roy Wilson (Desert). Also consulted at that conference were Terry Itnyre (Cypress) and Nancy Redmond (Long Beach City).

6. "Policy Specifics," Los Angeles Pierce College *Staff Handbook,* n.d.

7. Bill Ward, "20 Questions Raised While Judging Newspapers," *Scholastic Editor* 57, no. 5 (March 1978): 17.

8. Charles Atkin, "The Role of the Campus Newspaper in the Youth Vote," *College Press Review* 13, no. 4 (Summer 1974): 6–8.

9. Gene Burd, "Urban Affairs Coverage in the College Press: The Possibilities (Part I)," *College Press Review* 13, no. 1 (Autumn 1973): 10–12; and "Urban Affairs Coverage in the College Press: The Problems (Part II)," *College Press Review* 13, no. 2 (Winter 1973): 22–24.

10. W.B. Daugherty and Lynnell Jackson, "Approaches to Basic Reporting," *Junior College Journalist* 1, no. 3 (Spring/Summer 1973): 19.

11. "List of Regular Roundup Beats," Los Angeles Pierce College *Staff Handbook.*

12. Susan H. Vaughn, and journalism staff, "How to Cover a Beat," *Indian Valley Echo Staff Handbook* (Novato, Calif.: College of Arts and Humanities, Indian Valley Colleges, 1977), p. 12. Vaughn credits the ideas in the handbook to other college newspapers in California: the *Monitor,* Ohlone College; *La Voz,* De Anza College; the *Pirate's Log,* Modesto College; *El Yanqui,* Monterey Peninsula College; the *Rampage,* Fresno City College; and the *Times,* College of Marin.

13. Daniel Ellsberg discusses this role in an anthology on whistle-blowing by Charles Peters and Taylor Branch, *Blowing the Whistle* (New York: Praeger Publishers, 1972), pp. 246–75.

14. Richard La Clair, "Snow Job in Buffalo: Weather as News," *Community College Journalist* 5, no. 3 (Spring 1977): 14–15.

15. A good example is Hugh C. Sherwood, *The Journalistic Interview,* rev. ed. (New York: Harper & Row, 1972).

16. Ken Metzler, *Creative Interviewing* (Englewood Cliffs, N.J.: Prentice-Hall, 1977), pp. 3–10.

17. Metzler, *Creative Interviewing,* p. 5.

18. Metzler, *Creative Interviewing,* pp. 6–7.

19. Metzler, *Creative Interviewing,* p. 7.

20. William L. Rivers, *Finding Facts* (Englewood Cliffs, N.J.: Prentice-Hall, 1975).

21. Jerome Aumente, "In-Depth Reporting: A Valuable Perspective," *Nieman Reports* 32, no. 2 (Summer 1978): 15.

Specialized Types of Writing

The best student publications typically have many attributes—creative graphic designs, interesting and technically sound photography, accurate news coverage, timely and intelligent editorial and critical articles, careful copy editing and proofreading, and, above all, just plain good writing.

Chapter 2 introduced (or reintroduced) you to the inverted pyramid style of straight newswriting. That style is basic to newspaper journalism, but most newspapers supplement their straight news coverage with many stories that depart from the traditional news style.

Journalistic writing today encompasses a variety of styles and story types. In addition to straight newswriting, modern college and professional newspapers carry in-depth news analyses, feature articles, editorials, columns, reviews of the arts and many kinds of sports stories.

DEPARTING FROM THE INVERTED PYRAMID STYLE

As Chapter 2 explains, inverted pyramid news stories gradually taper down to the information of least significance. A story that strictly follows the inverted pyramid style can be cut from the bottom, because each paragraph is less important than the preceding one. Such stories do not build to conclusions.

For more than a century, most news stories have been written in this fashion, and the inverted pyramid style may well remain popular for another century. Readers want to know the highlights of a story quickly. They expect the newswriter to get right to the point.

However, some of the most memorable stories that appear in both student and professional newspapers depart from the inverted pyramid style. As important as this style is in journalism, there is also a place for stories that are organized more like a novel, which has a beginning, a middle and an end. Good journalism is sometimes nothing more than good story-telling, but with the story rooted in fact rather than fiction.

Many award-winning feature stories, editorial and critical pieces, and even sports stories follow this pattern rather than fitting within the rigid confines of the inverted pyramid style. In fact, there is a growing trend for journalists to depart from this style even when writing straight news stories. Sometimes complex news stories cannot be explained adequately in the inverted pyramid style.

If the goal is to present a few facts to

busy readers quickly, there is no substitute for the inverted pyramid style. But if the story has other purposes, one of the alternative styles of journalistic writing may be more appropriate.

"I think a rule that has been left out of . . . writing texts is, let the subject matter and its complexity dictate the most uncomplicated way to present it to an uninformed reader," says Donna Dickerson, a journalism professor at the University of South Florida.[1]

THE FEATURE STORY

Many journalists consider the feature story more fun to write than any other kind. The feature story gives one the freedom to say things that could never be said in a straight news story. There is room for emotion in feature writing. Human beings can be depicted as real people, with loves, hates, joys and sorrows. Unfortunately, few journalists have the opportunity to be full-time feature writers. A recent issue of a publication for professional publishers carried 17 help-wanted ads for journalists, and only one of them sought a feature writer.

Nevertheless, most journalists have some opportunities to write feature stories, and campus journalists working for weekly publications probably have more of those opportunities than their professional counterparts. When you're working for a weekly whose deadlines are several days prior to the day of publication, it is difficult to be up-to-date in covering hard news, but you can often produce features that have every bit as much impact on Friday as they did when they were written on Monday. Thus, many stories that might be treated as straight news in professional dailies are handled as features on campus. For instance, when the downtown daily covers the college board of trustees, the story is likely to focus on budgets, tax rates and construction projects. Campus journalists are more apt to write features that tell how those cold facts may affect students.

Precisely what is a feature story? More than 30 years ago, a journalism textbook called it "a human interest yarn emphasizing the emotional aspect of the news."[2] The authors of that book described the news feature as a story rooted in news but existing as more of a counterpoint to news—in effect, the entertainment element within the news. They likened the feature to the salad or dessert portion of a meal, a story lacking the importance, but not the interest, of a news story. They said features were of six kinds: historical, human interest, biographical or personality, travel, explanatory and how-to-do-it, or scientific.[3]

Many journalists today would challenge that definition, calling it much too narrow and restrictive to encompass all of the varied—and significant—kinds of stories that are labeled "features." "New journalists" of the 1960s such as Tom Wolfe taught us that feature stories could go far beyond the traditional definition, borrowing as much from the style and approach of the novelist or poet as from the straight news style.

Another pioneering feature-writing textbook, *Writing and Selling Features* by Helen M. Patterson, said feature writing is an amplification of newswriting, an amplification that a journalist carries out through study, research and interviews. Patterson contended that the information or instructional function of the feature is vital, although she said features must be entertaining too.[4]

Still, some journalists even today disdain feature stories and those who write them. "Soft news," they call feature writing. Some would even agree with one weekly newspaper editor's tongue-in-cheek definition of a feature as "the creative or 'soft-news' aspect of the paper. Uncluttered by such things as facts, statistics or true meaningfulness, most of us love to write features."[5]

Whether they're soft news or hard news, and based on facts or fantasy, features occupy an increasingly important place in print journalism. Many publishers now concede the immediacy of breaking news coverage to the electronic media and go for the depth, color and analysis that broadcasters are forced to bypass in their quest for brevity. Al Hestor, a University of Georgia journalism professor, has predicted drastic changes for the information industry. In a world where the print media increasingly deliver their written material to readers electronically, he predicted that features would be more important than ever.[6] It may not be long until newspapers are delivering hard news to readers via the television screen and publishing features almost entirely in weekly hard-copy editions.

But whatever lies in the future for journalists, it is certain that feature writing is in fashion today, both on campus and in the professional press. At colleges across America student newspaper staffs are encountering more and more new recruits who want to write features—not the disciplined straight news stories that have been the basis of journalism for so long, but creative, colorful features with a beginning, a middle and an ending.

What goes into a good feature story? The late DeWitt Reddick, longtime director of the School of Journalism at the University of Texas at Austin, urged feature writers to be aware of "four basic elements of reader interest."[7] These elements include the ubiquitous idea of human interest, plus oddity, drama and significance.

If this reminds you a little bit of the discussion of news values in Chapter 2, it should. Some of these concepts have long been considered to be key factors in determining the newsworthiness of any story. However, not all of the traditional news values are equally important in feature writing. Timeliness, for instance, is not important in most features. A feature story is often compelling for its quality of human emotion, and this quality is just as strong months later as it was the day after an event occurred.

In their textbook on newswriting, Michael Ryan and James Tankard noted this de-emphasis on timeliness in feature stories. They said that a feature story with an element of timeliness should be called a *news feature*.[8] Actually, the news feature is probably the most common form of feature story, according to another textbook writer, Ronald P. Lovell.[9] Lovell said features fall into five types: news features, sidebar features, short features, people features and investigative features. These types are self-explanatory, except for the sidebar.

What's a *sidebar feature*? It is a colorful story that accompanies a major hard-news story. It may deal with a human interest aspect of the story, and it derives its name from its typical placement adjacent to the main story.

If you ask any ten feature-writing teachers to list the major types of feature stories, you'll probably get ten different lists. As writing teachers, we like to classify features by the author's viewpoint and style. There are, it seems to us, at least five types of feature stories: (1) the profile, (2) the process feature, (3) the how-to feature, (4) the I-was-there feature and (5) the multidimensional profile feature.

The ordinary profile is the easiest kind to write, with the others progressively more difficult. Perhaps new student publications staffers should be given the simpler types for their early assignments.

Profiles

What is usually called a profile is a one-dimensional picture of someone. William Rivers and Shelly Smolkin, authors of *Free-Lancer and Staff Writer,* call this kind of story a *personality sketch* because professional writers often use the word *profile* to describe a long magazine article.[10] Nevertheless, the brief sketches published in student newspapers are often called "profiles," so we'll go along with the popular usage.

An ordinary profile is not usually hard to research or write. In fact, profiles are sometimes written in a hurry, without adequate research: they're often based on a single interview with the subject. That interview may be conducted in the newspaper office, or perhaps at a place where the subject feels more at ease. You often learn more about people if you conduct your interviews on their home turf, the places where they do their newsworthy stuff. Moreover, the bare skeleton of a profile is about all you may have after you've interviewed the subject. It is much better to flesh it out by interviewing other people who know the subject.

Whether you interview people on their turf or yours, the interviewing techniques discussed in Chapter 3 are applicable. The key notion in developing a profile is to set limits on the scope of the story. You're not writing the person's definitive biography, just a brief sketch. You'll probably seek out more information than you'll eventually use and then pare it down when you write the story, which will probably not be longer than two or three typewritten pages. However, be sensitive to what your interviewee does not say. Conspicuous omissions, either in answering direct questions or in presenting a sequence of events, may call for more questioning. Your profile should be brief, but not glaringly incomplete.

Good profiles usually concentrate on one main aspect of the person's life rather than offering a broader but more superficial view. You're not a biographer, at least not yet. Nevertheless, don't overlook the traits the reader will find most interesting. What is the person like? Is he or she enthusiastic or subdued? What does the person look like?

An excellent way to paint a good portrait of the subject is in his or her own words. Include a mixture of direct quotes, indirect quotes and summaries. Intersperse your own observations about the person and, if appropriate, the setting.

In a good profile, the quotes are selected carefully to tell a story. A mere mosaic of quotations isn't usually enough to make a good profile. Fill in the details by summarizing in your own words. To be readable, the direct quotes should be fairly brief.

Asking the right questions often will yield surprising results. It is impossible to overemphasize the importance of learning all you can about your subject before the actual interview.

An interesting example of a profile—a story about a young male prostitute—won a national award in the William Randolph Hearst Foundation journalism competition (Figure 4.1). The author, Richard McDonald of the University of Kentucky, mixed quotes and descriptive passages to portray his subject in rich detail. The story gives the reader a keen insight into the life of a young "hustler."

Not all interview subjects lend themselves to as colorful a story as this one. Nevertheless, interviewing the ordinary and extraordinary people found on every college campus will produce hundreds of interesting personality profiles.

The award-winning profile of the male hustler raises a troubling ethical question: it never discloses the subject's real name. Granted, few stories such as this one could be done if reporters were always obliged to reveal their subjects' identities. However, overzealous journalists sometimes abuse the practice of masking identities.

That point was illustrated in 1981 by a scandal involving the prestigious Pulitzer Prize competition. A young reporter for the *Washington Post* won a Pulitzer for a story about an eight-year-old boy who was given heroin by his mother and her live-in boyfriend. The reporter refused to identify her sources, even to her own editors. It turned out that there was no source: the story was largely fiction, and the humiliated editors of one of the nation's great newspapers had to give back the Pulitzer Prize.

Fortunately, situations such as that one are rare. When a reporter masks a source's identity, his credibility is bound to suffer with some readers; secret-source reporting should be used sparingly. Perhaps the practice is acceptable when a story having social significance could not otherwise be reported. It is not acceptable as a means of gathering "news" that is really only gossip. Nor is it acceptable as a substitute for thorough research.

Process Features

The term *process feature* is a fancy way of describing what some journalists might call a "news feature" or an interpretive news story. A catch-all category, the process feature includes a variety of stories about interesting events or trends. Such a story goes well beyond the basic just-the-facts approach of a straight news story, but it is based on something other than a personality sketch.

Figure 4.1 Feature story from the *Kentucky Kernel,* University of Kentucky. Used by permission of AASDJ–Hearst Foundation Journalism Awards Program.

A HUSTLER

Male prostitute finds that street life can be cold and lonely, but profitable

By Richard McDonald
Kernel Reporter

"Well there ain't no deed that a dude won't do
when he's hustling for a buck or two ..."
(From "Sin City," copyright 1976, Chappell Music, Inc.)

At first glance, there is nothing unusual about the group standing on the corner in the eastern end of downtown Lexington. Marc and his companions look like just another bunch of guys with nothing to do on a weekend evening.

All is not as it seems, though. Marc—like most of his companions—is a hustler—a male prostitute.

Marc (not his real name), a slim, curly-haired 18-year-old, works diligently at his trade. He stares intently into the interiors of many passing cars, looking for the short moment of direct eye contact that may signal the willingness of the man inside to pay him for a brief sexual encounter.

Unlike their female counterparts, most hustlers, including Marc, are subdued in dress and manner. Marc usually leans against the low brick wall on the corner, watching and waiting for a customer to stop. Only then does he move out to the curb. Leaning into the car window, he greets the potential customer only with a short "Hi" or "What's happenin'?"

Marc said he is careful to let the customer—the "John"—do most of the talking. "Especially," he said, "I make sure they mention the cash before I do. That way, the cops can't pick me up for soliciting."

Avoiding the police is almost an obsession with Marc while he's on the block. He dresses inconspicuously in jeans and a pullover shirt; he takes pains to do nothing to draw undue attention to himself. "Lots of times guys will wave at you, but I only wave back if I know them or if I've seen them cruising the block before."

He added, "Even if I've been out with a guy two or three times before, when he picks me up, I always ask him if he's a cop. They," he said referring to the police, "have to tell you."

Marc said he has a relative large number of regular Johns. He estimated that the majority of the men are in their thirties or forties. Many of them are married. "Some of them even tell me about their wives and kids. But they don't tell you too much. Hell, some of these guys down here (other hustlers) would blackmail you if they got half a chance."

According to Marc, some of the men who cruise the block regularly are students. "I've been picked up by a few dudes from UK. This summer, I was even with some 16-year-old kid who just got his driver's license."

While most of his customers are not overt homosexuals, Marc said, "Once in a while a queen will strike out in the bar (a gay bar on the block) and will come out and pick me up."

Marc has been hustling for almost a year and a half. He started last year after dropping out of high school. Somewhat of a problem student, he attended three of Lexington's four public high schools.

"I never could get into the swing of classes and studying," he said. "Plus, the principals didn't like me ... cause I liked to stay high."

He said he found out about hustling from a friend who had done it previously. Marc said his reasons for going on the block were monetary. "Where else could I make this kind of money?"

Hustling isn't his only source of income. Marc also works as a busboy in one of the city's more exclusive restaurants. During the racing meets, he works for the track caterers.

In addition, unlike most female prostitutes, Marc doesn't have to give the lion's share of the proceeds from his tricks to a pimp.

Marc's Johns pay him $15–$65 per trick, depending on the act performed. He refused to say how much he makes on an average night, stating only that, "I make money every time I come out here."

He did say, however, that on a couple of occasions this summer, he made more than $200 in a single night.

Because he still lives at home with his unsuspecting family, most of Marc's tricks are performed in the customers' homes, or when that isn't possible, in the back seats of their cars.

Marc shows a perverse pride in his craft.

"I've been hustling for a year and a half and I'm good at it. I'm not like most of these other guys, I give a dude his money's worth. There are guys who come down here and ask for me by name. They don't do that for anybody else."

Ironically, Marc doesn't consider himself homosexual. "I only make it with another dude when I get paid for it," he said.

Stating that he maintains two sets of friends, a set of gay friends and a set of straight friends, Marc said only one of his straight friends knows he's a hustler. "I'm the kind of guy who has 30 girls calling his house every day; nobody would suspect I do this."

He did admit, however, to enjoying sex with some of his customers. "Hey, I like to feel good; and some of these guys really know how to make you feel good."

Life on the block, though, is not without its dangers. While he has escaped arrest, and has never been asked to do anything he considers sick or distasteful, Marc has had some frightening episodes.

"Once, this guy picked me up and took me to his apartment. As soon as we got there, he started pulling out all kinds of guns. I don't know whether he got off on that, or thought I was going to rob him or something. I just wanted to get my money and leave.

"Another time, some dude took me out to park on some country road. When we finished I got out of the car for something . . . and he pulled off and left me there. I had to walk about 12 miles back downtown that night."

Despite these occurrences, Marc, unlike many of the other hustlers, doesn't carry a knife for protection. "That kind of shit will only get you in more trouble," he said.

What does the future hold for an 18-year-old veteran of the streets? When faced with this question, Marc dropped his mask of hip bravura, his voice becoming soft and pensive

"I don't know, man. It's getting cold, and business has been slow lately. If I could just find a full-time steady job . . . I just don't know . . ."

In the process story, whether it be a "what," a "how" or even a more difficult "why" story, you emphasize the event.

We are not talking about hard news stories as such. News stories typically cover immediate events. Process features may report an ongoing development in the news. A historical feature, which covers a past event in an analytical fashion, is one kind of process feature. The actions and reactions of several people may be the focus of such a story. In general, process features are transactional, which means they pivot on events and circumstances rather than individual choices and actions. There's an old historical saying that asks, "Do men make the events or does the event make the man?" Process features emphasize large-scale events over people. Processes and trends are usually more important than any single individual in this type of story.

Process feature writers should reconsider the "taken for granteds" in their lives. Henry Steele Commager, the renowned historian, explained that outsiders can often write cogent studies of societies other than their own by doing this. They try to explain things the natives take for granted. Commager considers the Frenchman Alexis de Tocqueville's *Democracy in America* to be the best volume ever written about life in the United States, even though it was written 150 years ago. The key to its greatness, Commager says, is that de Tocqueville noticed and wrote about the things Americans took for granted.[11]

A notable example of this sort of feature story once appeared in the San Diego Evening College paper, *Tecolote*. Written by Mary Hardie and Theresa Matheiu, it was entitled, "Alien Army Lays Long Siege to Campus, Defies Defenses." It was about an army of ants on campus. The writers' interest was piqued by a line of ants crossing their path as they left a classroom. Their interviews with a night custodian and his aide, plus their own keen observations and library reading about ants, produced a colorful feature.

Thousands of students had stepped on—or over—the ants, but these two stopped and noticed something everyone else took for granted. The result was an interesting process feature. (See Figure 4.2.)

How-To Features

The how-to feature is just what the name implies: a cookbook approach. Often written in the second-person style, it tells the reader how to do something of interest. Such articles have long been popular in Sunday supplements and magazines, and they sometimes have a place in student publications, too.

However, how-to articles invite mediocrity. For example, beginning writers invariably grind out such articles, often telling readers how to do utterly unimportant things in uninteresting ways. The second-person style can be overused very easily.

To be successful, how-to features must deal with a subject of interest to readers, and the material must be presented in an interesting and clear way. In effect, the writer says to the reader, "First you do this, then do that, and finally do a double this 'n' that." Brevity is often crucial to the success of such stories. An excellent way to decide whether such an article is worth publishing is to test it on several staff members. Do they find it interesting? Do they understand it? Could they follow the directions and achieve the desired result? Would they want to?

College publications once hesitated to publish anything longer than the directions to an out-of-town football stadium in the second-person style, but that taboo is gone. The possibilities for such features today are endless. Modern student editors are willing to publish everything from directions for baking bread and finding summer resort jobs to advice for getting psychological help. Today's emphasis on self-gratification plays into this trend, sometimes in unusual ways.

Often how-to features are written by nonexperts on the subject. Perhaps it's better that way, because the nonexpert is less likely to assume the reader

Figure 4.2   Interpretive news story from *Tecolote*, Evening College, San Diego, California. Used by permission.

ALIEN ARMY LAYS LONG SIEGE TO CAMPUS, DEFIES DEFENSES

By Mary Hardie
and Theresa Matheiu

Signs of an invasion are clearly visible. The most obvious are the trails, stretching along floors and walls, under desks and into drawers, indicating the infiltration of an army of ants here at Mesa campus.

Where are they coming from and why are they here? These are the usual, but also the most pressing questions raised by Mesa students and employees. An investigation into the problem resulted in a reasonable explanation and a suggested plan for solution.

According to Joe Doran, Head Custodian, Second Shift, at Mesa College, a sudden change in weather and food wrappers or soft drink cups not properly disposed of will attract ants immediately.

"They are not confined to one area or building," Doran said. "They are wherever there has been activity."

But he was quick to point out that the least affected place on campus is the student cafeteria.

"There is enough movement through there and trash removal is consistent so the ants don't have a chance to get started. The cafeteria has never had to close due to ant or pest problems."

Doran contends that the classrooms and offices are the worst hit areas. Signs are posted throughout the grounds prohibiting food, drink and smoking in classrooms; however, he said teachers are lax about enforcing this policy.

"Even if food is not permitted in the classroom, it may only take the presence of an empty wrapper or cup in the wastebasket to draw the ants."

Both Doran and Ed Bracken, another Second Shift Custodian, agreed that, in their opinion, the main reason for the constant invasion of ants lies in the location of the Mesa campus itself.

"When they cut off the top of the mesa to build this place they opened up a whole bag of ants," said Bracken.

To control the problem, Mesa employs a pest control agency which, under a maintenance program, services the campus area on a regular basis. But Doran claims this is not enough.

"People should dispose of unwanted food, wrappers, cups, etc. in the proper trash container meant for those items, not in the classroom or office wastebasket. If they would only stop and think what they are doing, the problem could be controlled. It's the source that counts."

Although the ant is a small insect, through wisdom and strength it overcomes all obstacles. Ants are able to lift rocks, build tunnels and form an organized army.

A "terrorizer" in their own way, ants are at every door. Without warning the ants launch their attack. The ant is cunning, sly, and is able, through the use of his antennae, to smell the nearest food. Ants exist because of human carelessness.

Sugar is the main source of attraction for the ant. A simple cup of coke can attract hundreds of these enterprising creatures.

Exterminators have tried to get rid of these pests, but with the student population growth, and the failure to comply with the signs, the ants continue their raids. Custodian Bracken stated, "We keep it down the best we can; if people would keep food cleared and such, we could control the ants better."

knows too much or too little. Also, the nonexpert will have to do his homework, and the result may be much better than it is when someone who thinks he knows the subject tries to wing it without doing any research.

I-Was-There Features

Students who leap into college journalism directly from English classes often crave the freedom to write first-person stories right away. The traditional third-person newswriting style may seem like an impossible straitjacket to such writers. However, the first-person style can easily be overused.

To be credible, a newspaper must strive for objectivity in most of its writing. The first-person story should be the exception, not the rule. The ubiquitous *I* or *we* is very distracting to many readers. The writer (who may or may not be interesting to readers) upstages the event, which is probably what the reader really wants to know about.

Often the best use for an I-was-there feature is as a sidebar to a major news story, a description of an important event by an eyewitness. Several such sidebars may emanate from the same event. Sometimes a reporter who witnessed a major event can report what happened in the first-person style with far more reader impact and color than would be possible in an objective third-person style.

Beyond eyewitness newsreporting, however, there is a place for first-person writing in student publications. If the writer really has a significant and interesting experience to retell, such a story can have far more appeal than a third-person account. For emotional impact, few student-written I-was-there stories can match the one that won first place in the national Hearst competition for Kathleen Conkey of the University of Kansas (Figure 4.3). Conkey visited a skid-row blood donors' center in Kansas City as part of a program to familiarize students with inner-city life. Her story not only richly described her experiences, but also generated a mood of suspense. Few readers would put the *Daily Kansan* down after reading the first few paragraphs of this story.

However, not all first-person stories are based on experiences as memorable as this one. Karen Tiffany of Los Angeles Pierce College won a first-place award at a Journalism Association of Community Colleges on-the-spot writing contest with a first-person story in which she became a hotel elevator—for the sake of getting a good story. The result was an anthropomorphic effort, a story written the way an elevator would tell it if it could (Figure 4.4). Pet magazines often tell freelancers to avoid this hackneyed approach, but this one was original enough to sweep the competition. Note the writer's brisk use of dialog and sparing use of the first person. And Tiffany held to her theme. "I hate conventions" reverberates throughout the story.

Multidimensional Profiles

Of the five basic kinds of feature stories discussed here, the multidimensional story is probably the most challenging. Magazine writers may simply call such

LIVING FOR MOMENT
WAY OF INNER CITY LIFE

By Kathleen Conkey
Staff Reporter

Saturday morning I awoke with $10 on my mind. That was what the Plasma Donor Center on 20th and Main paid for a pint of plasma. I had been nearly broke since Thursday and I wanted the feel of money in my pocket again. Ten dollars isn't a lot of money, but it filled my head with visions of a good, full meal.

That full meal would be my first since Thursday night, when I left Lawrence with seven other KU people to go on an Urban Plunge, a program sponsored by KU-Y to introduce students to life in inner Kansas City, Mo.

Tracy Spellman, KU-Y coordinator, and I arrived at the plasma center shortly after it opened at 7:30 a.m. On the streets outside, men were out with their small brown bags of oblivion.

We walked into the center and found about 40 men in line. Apparently, when people have no place to sleep they rise early.

All the men were wearing the street uniform—soiled pants, several coats and dull-looking eyes. We went to the window and signed in. The woman told us we would have to wait four to six hours because we were new. She directed us through a door to give a urine specimen. Past the door we saw 28 identical simulated leather lounging chairs, each with a pole attached on which hung a clipboard and a plastic bag containing a clear liquid.

Back in the checkup room, a woman in white—none of the workers has medical identifications—wrapped a rubber tie around my arm and searched for a blood vessel.

"This one will do," she said and pointed to a vein in my right arm.

She did the same to Spellman but couldn't find a big enough vein.

"I don't think this girl should donate," the woman said.

Spellman objected.

"Look, I'm not going to lie to you. Those needles are big," the worker said and showed us the filling of a ball point pen to illustrate the needle's size.

"And," she added, "you'll have it in your arm for at least two hours."

Spellman decided not to donate. She said she would come back to check on me later. A woman behind a desk took two pieces of ID from me—a donor must be at least 18—and told me to wait.

I sat down and watched two young men argue with a worker who refused to let them donate. They said they had last given blood in Las Vegas a week ago, but the woman thought their needle marks were only a day old. If she was right, the men were desperate for money because taking less than 48 hours to recover from giving plasma can be dangerous. The men finally gave up.

Of the people there, only five of us were new donors. Most of the others sell their blood regularly. A donor can sell twice in a seven-day period. The management encourages people to return often. A sign in the waiting room said, "Donate 25 times straight in a row and receive $25 extra on the 25th donation."

I was called and told to stand on a scale. They asked a series of questions about my health. One question was "Do you eat well?" I asked the woman if most of the men here could say they ate well.

"Well enough for them, I guess," she said.

I sat down. It was 8:30 a.m. The man next to me introduced himself as Robert. He told me he worked as a janitor at the Kansas City Art Institute and has lived in a mission at 11th and Main since he came to Kansas City a year ago. He has been selling blood twice a week for a year.

"I'm here every Wednesday and Saturday," he said, "So you be sure and come on those days and we'll talk. I'm saving money to go to California. I like to travel. I was in Georgia before I came here. Before that I was in Illinois. I had a girlfriend there. She was a runaway, needed a place to live, so we started living together. But somebody told her mama I was a black guy. She was white, you know, and her mama came all the way to Illinois to get her daughter away from me. You go out with black guys, Kathy?"

"I have before," I said.

They called my name again. This time they pricked my finger twice to get blood samples. Then they sent me to another room where they took two Polaroid pictures of me for identification, took my temperature and my blood pressure. They sent me back to wait with Robert.

The man on the other side of me said he had just hopped a freight from Maine and was on his way to Nebraska. He had been in Kansas City 16 hours and was selling his blood for meal money.

The doctor came out and called my name. I followed her to her office. She must have been 70 years old and seemed very tired. When she learned I was a college student, she said, "People who come here are a little different from what you're used to associating with, huh?"

She hit my knees with a rubber hammer, asked a few questions and explained the plasma donating process.

The donator pumps out one pint of blood. That pint is taken to a centrifuge, which separates the plasma from the red blood cells. The red blood cells are then pumped back into the bloodstream along with a saline solution to thin the mixture. The centrifuged material is refrigerated and when they pump the blood back into the bloodstream, it feels like ice running through the veins. Then the entire process is repeated.

"When the worker brings the red blood cells back to you," the doctor said, "they will check to make sure the cells are yours. You must check too. Look at the bag and make sure your name and number are right. If they put someone else's cells into

your body, it could be fatal. This is your responsibility."

I went back to the outer room and was issued two plasma bags and a chart to keep track of my donations. As I went back to the room with the chairs, I heard a woman out front saying, "No way, Sam. You're too drunk to give blood today."

My plasma bags were taken from me and I was told to sit in chair 18. I sat down to find Robert sitting right across from me. He smiled and waved with the arm that wasn't connected to the huge needle.

There were five workers getting blood from the people to the centrifuge as fast as possible. They knew the names of all the regulars and joked with them about their drinking habits.

The men were in good moods. The subject of conversation was unchanging: what and how much each man was going to drink when he got his $10. White Port seemed to be the favorite. They talked about their favorite streets and spots to go when drinking. Robert said he always went to the hotel across the street and got a room with a TV for a night.

"I don't walk the streets when I'm drunk," he said. "You know, you end up falling over and getting a busted lip. I like to take my rum and Coke and be alone with the TV."

The man who had hopped a freight from Maine told me that he had once worked in a hotel. I asked whether he was a bellboy.

"Hell no. I wouldn't do that. It's degrading, " he said.

"How is selling your blood any better?" I asked.

"Well, it's mine isn't it?" he said. "It's mine to sell. When you're a bellboy, you take tips, other people's scraps."

Across the room, Robert was falling asleep. A sign prohibits sleeping and eating while donating so I called him to wake him up.

"Hey, baby," he said. "When we get done, we're going to go get drunk, OK? Over at the Red Carpet?"

They had taken my first pint of blood, and I was waiting for my bag to return from the centrifuge. I began to feel lightheaded. I couldn't focus my eyes or hold up my head. I thought I was going to pass out. I took deep breaths and remained still. It passed.

"Sure, Robert, " I answered. "We'll go get a drink. But can we eat somewhere first?"

I had never drunk in the middle of the day before. But, drinking with the people I had been spending so much time with seemed an appropriate way to end my stay in Kansas City.

It was almost noon when they finally pulled the needle from my arm. Robert waited for me. We signed for our money and were given a small envelope containing two $5 bills. Before we left, a woman painted our thumbs with fluorescent paint so that we couldn't sell blood at a different center within the next 48 hours. Robert and I headed for a diner across the street.

We had roast turkey and gravy with mashed potatoes and a Coke for $2.20. It was nice not to worry about the money. We finished eating and went next door to the Red Carpet Bar. I ordered the first of three screwdrivers, all of them with too much vodka. Robert ordered a beer. He was saving up for his heavy drinking later that night.

"Let's not drink here, Kathy," he said. "Let's go buy some rum and Coke and go to my hotel room."

I had begun to be so much a part of the inner-city life that I actually considered going to Robert's room. I had to remind myself that I wasn't trapped in the city. I could leave anytime and go home to Lawrence, my books and my friends.

But, if I really lived that kind of life, if I couldn't escape it just by getting in a car and leaving, I would not have had the will to resist Robert's offer. Just like the men who spend their last dollar on booze, the moment is all one can live for in the inner city.

I was relieved to see Spellman come into the Red Carpet after my third drink. She had been searching for me and some-one at the blood center told her I might be here. She sat down with us. Because she smiled at a man standing at the bar, he ordered her a drink. At the end of the bar an old woman sat slouched over, her head almost touching the bar.

The man who had bought Spellman a drink swaggered to our table. He was dressed like a pimp, and when he spoke, his voice was like honey.

"Allow me to introduce myself," he said. "I am Candy. That's right ladies, the Candystick, God's gift to poor women. Maker of babies and finder of the womb."

Robert rolled his eyes. I laughed. I was beginning to feel drunk and I was glad. Just looking at Spellman made me happy because I knew I was finally going home. It didn't worry me that Robert and Candy were trying to pick us up because in minutes we would be driving away.

Spellman had gone to Wayne Minor, a government low-rent housing project, that morning. She started to tell me how depressing it was. But I didn't want to listen. I couldn't feel pity anymore. I didn't even feel guilty that I was getting out and others were trapped. I just wanted out.

Spellman and I got up to leave. It was 1:30 p.m. Robert tried to convince me to stay by whispering softly in my ear. I didn't hear him. Spellman and I got into the car and drove to the church. We gathered our things and left.

On the way out of the city, I kept my eyes closed. I didn't want to see it again. I slept all the way home.

When I got home at 3 p.m., I stripped off my dirty clothes and got into the shower. I leaned against the wall and let the water batter my body for a long time. I wanted to feel clean and warm. I didn't want to think. After the shower, I went to my bookshelves and thought how nice it would be to use my brain for pleasure, rather than survival.

I picked up a book I had been wanting to read and laid back on my soft, safe bed and began to read "Alice in Wonderland."

Figure 4.4   Feature story by Karen Tiffany of
Los Angeles Pierce College, Los Angeles,
California. Used by permission.

FREESTYLE CONTEST

By Karen Tiffany
Los Angeles Pierce College

"Push four, Henry."

"Yes, dear."

Whrrrrr.

It's going to be another *long* weekend. I don't know why they do this to me. I hate conventions.

Up and down. Up and down. I realize it's my job but honestly, how much do I have to put up with?

Open.

Oh my God. All of those people are going to try and fit in here? Haven't they read my sign that tells about my weight capacity? *He* must weigh at *least* 260 pounds.

Close.

Whrrrrr.

Somebody needs a shower. It must be the fat guy. I hear they sweat more than the average person. I can see why.

Open.

It must be dinner time. Great, I'll just take a breather. Oh my aching cables. Shooby dooby do. What goes up, must come down. Spinning wheels, got to go 'round. Talkin'. . . .

Oh, oh. Where'd that kid come from? Better yet, where are his parents? I hate little kids. They love to see my buttons light up. They must think that if they push all of my buttons that I'll forget where I'm going. Ha, ha, kid. No way.

He's in. Damn it. Why isn't he out playing on the freeway where he belongs? There he goes pushing my buttons. Oh no, not the phone! Once they start playing with that there's no stopping them. Oh good. I never thought I'd be glad to have people board me. Now he'll have to leave me alone.

Dinner must be over. Now it's really rush hour. Everybody is drinking and looking for parties. I wouldn't mind a couple of shots myself—30 weight or maybe multi-grade. Just enough to loosen up the old cables.

Open.

These guys don't look too bad. They don't seem *too* rowdy.

"Let's make a beer run."

No wonder they seem all right. They haven't even started yet. "OK, but let's go up to my room so I can get some bucks."

"Kirk to Enterprise."

"Enterprise."

"Scotty, beam us up."

Kirk presses number ten and I beam him and his crew up.

Whrrrrr.

I deposit the crew of the Enterprise in exchange for a couple shady looking characters. This could prove to be interesting.

Open.

Here's a cute young thing. Let's see if they make any moves.

Character #1 pulls out a bottle of whiskey, takes a swig and offers the bottle to the girl.

Real class.

Looking repulsed by his offer, she declines and moves closer to my doors.

Character #2 decides to try the "indirect" approach.

"Hey babe, how about the three of us having a little party up in our room?"

Open.

"How about *buzzing off*, turkey?"

Close.

"Oh well, she looked like a real drag anyway."

Open.

Boy, am I beat. It's 3 a.m. and these crazy journalists are still partying. Another day and a half of this. I can't take it. I hate conventions.

a story a "profile," but it bears little resemblance to the one-source profiles we described earlier.

As in simple profiles, a person is depicted, but here the story is based on far more extensive work. Several other sources of information will supplement one or more in-depth interviews with the subject of the article. In fact, some of the best material may come from the subject's friends and associates. In *Scholastic Editor,* Mary C. Rothgreb urged campus journalists to gather "anecdotes about the person from friends, co-workers and colleagues. If these are pertinent and add to the article, they should be included in the piece to shed light on the person's personality."[12]

Such multidimensional research can lead to a powerful feature story. Professional journalists sometimes write stories that offer excellent ideas for campus stories, and such is the case with "Love Story: the Ballad of Elmer Reeves," written by *Los Angeles Times* copy editor Dick Rorabeck.

Rorabeck crafted a bittersweet tale by discovering the history of a 103-year-old love poem scribbled in an old school book he found in a used-book store. Rorabeck identified both the author of the poem, Elmer Reeves, and the girl who inspired the poem, one Ida May Ryan. Now Elmer and Ida May had been dead for years, but Rorabeck interviewed old people who knew Elmer in his hometown of Waverly, Iowa. He also explored the files of the town's newspaper from the date the poem was written. With careful research, he reconstructed Elmer's life and wrote a beautiful story with multiple transitions from 1877 to 1980 and back again.

You may not stumble onto another poem by someone like Elmer Reeves, but students have written in your college's library books—and elsewhere around campus—for years. Check back in the files of the newspaper, ask around at the alumni office or perhaps look through old yearbooks. Perhaps there are stories just as touching as Elmer's in your school's past. If the story is thoroughly researched and written with care, a 20-year-old romance might be just as interesting as Elmer's 100-year-old tale.

There are hundreds of good multidimensional feature ideas on every college campus. Don't overlook the obvious and familiar things and people when you're looking for a subject. Are there interesting programs or even buildings on your campus? What about alumni with interesting stories to tell?

OPINION WRITING

Opinion writing is the oldest form of journalism in America. Modern newspapers evolved from the political and religious tracts, broadsheets and periodicals of colonial and revolutionary times. By comparison, the concept of objective newsreporting is relatively new, not having developed until the nineteenth century. But by 1900 most major newspapers had separated their opinion and news functions. Although opinions often creep onto the news pages, journalists today try hard to keep the the two functions separate. It is often said that no journalist is completely objective, no matter how committed to the ideal of objectivity he or she may be. We all approach a story with subjective values and prejudices that inevitably creep into our writing.

Nevertheless, most American newspapers strive to separate news from opinion. And as the opinion function developed, three different kinds of opinion articles emerged: (1) the staff-written editorial; (2) the critical review of the arts; and (3) the column or letter to the editor in which an individual on or off the staff expresses his or her own personal views.

Student publications have usually followed the example set by the professionals, not only maintaining a separation between the news and opinion functions, but also offering all three kinds of opinion writing common in the daily press. Of course there have been times when the student press in America has gone far beyond the bounds of what is considered acceptable in most commercial newspapers, openly mixing the news and opinion functions. Perhaps the most notable example of this occurred during the late 1960s. In that period, some student newspapers abandoned any pretext of objectivity; their news stories became essays advocating social change. Their kind of journalism was highly readable—and socially significant—but it was also a marked departure from the prevailing practice of separating the news and opinion functions. And their credibility suffered as a result.

Most student newspapers have now returned to the more customary approach of separating news from opinion wherever possible, and of clearly labeling their opinion pieces as such. Editorials, columns and critical reviews are all important aspects of the total package that is the modern student newspaper.

Editorials

The editorial is the voice of the publication. Typically written in the first person plural style ("We believe that . . ."), it represents a consensus of the top editors' opinions. On most large student newspapers, as on professional dailies, an editorial board discusses possible editorial topics and positions. The debate at such sessions may be intense; but ultimately a majority opinion emerges, and the group may develop a rough outline for an editorial. One person drafts the editorial, which may then be reviewed by other members of the editorial board. Since the editorial that is eventually published represents a combination of several persons' views, it usually carries no by-line.

Some college papers follow a policy of requiring unanimity in editorial board decisions. If the members cannot reach a consensus, pro and con columns may appear instead of a staff-written editorial.

Because an editorial represents the official position of the staff, editorials in student newspapers often arouse the ire of school officials. Countless attempts to censor the student press have resulted from editorials that offended an administrator—or that an administrator feared would offend an important constituency. Administrators sometimes think that they, and not the student editors, are the real publishers of student newspapers and thus have the right to dictate editorial policy. However, the nation's courts have not usually viewed administrators as the publishers of student newspapers, a point the chapter on freedom of the student press explains more fully. To the consternation of school officials, student editors sometimes take vigorous editorial stands, even on off-campus issues. If the First Amendment is to be taken seriously, that is the editor's right.

However, another aspect of student editorializing sometimes troubles professional editorial writers: student editors often exercise this right without formal training in editorial writing. The National Conference of Editorial Writers, a professional organization of newspaper editorial writers, conducted a survey and learned that the number of colleges requiring an editorial writing course as part of a journalism major has been cut in half since 1960. Summarizing the study, the NCEW observed:

Clearly, editorial writing no longer is considered a basic course. Rather, it is a "frill" course and one not too popular with either students or faculty. The widespread feeling is that because it is unlikely that journalism school graduates will write editorials for some time, it is better to drill them in the fundamentals of reporting and other courses.[13]

The brief discussion of editorial writing offered here is no substitute for a full course on the subject, but for those who will write editorials without taking such a course, we can only provide an overview of the task.

First, a good editorial is based on hard facts. Anyone can vent his or her prejudices, but thorough research undergirds good editorials. According to another survey conducted by the National Conference of Editorial Writers, professionals base their editorials on current news stories, reviews of previous stories in newspaper "morgues" or libraries, or discussions with reporters, plus library research in books and magazines.[14] Editorials express opinions, but those opinions are based on documented facts, not uninformed prejudices. For instance, no campus newspaper should editorially criticize an administrator or student leader for making a particular decision until the decision-maker has been invited to explain why he or she made it.

Once the topic has been thoroughly researched, the next step is to write the editorial. At that point, the job is to organize the facts and marshal convincing arguments to make your point. In its structure, an editorial resembles an essay more than it resembles an inverted pyramid news story. An editorial has an introduction that should interest the reader and set forth the issue to be discussed. Next, the body of the editorial presents the arguments for the writer's point of view, with a rebuttal of popular opposing arguments. An editorial that ignores important opposing arguments has little chance to achieve its desired result—which is to persuade. Finally, mustering all of the eloquence possible, the writer reaches a conclusion, wrapping up the entire presentation. Often the editorial calls for specific action, although sometimes good editorials merely weigh the alternatives without urging action.

One succinct set of guidelines for editorial writing appeared in *Communication: Journalism Education Today*. It offered a six-point list of suggestions for editorial writers:

1. Keep your editorials factual. Although there is a tendency to get emotional, you must always stick to the facts and not ramble or babble.

2. Do not leave any facts out. All editorials must have the key facts, and while you are getting emotional or humorous, there is a good possibility that you are going to overlook some facts. Check, check and double check.

3. Don't get caught in a rut. Find new ways to say old things. Spice up your editorials and get some variety in them. Don't distort your information, but at the same time use your imagination.

4. Don't sit down at your typewriter and try to write an editorial when you are angry. In many instances your arguments will not be logical and your frame of mind will creep into your editorial. Often you will fail to achieve your objectives if you write when you are angry.

5. Be objective and fair. Don't exclude any side of the argument, and be certain to seek out views of individuals who oppose the subject of the editorial.

6. Learn to be a patient editorial writer. You can't expect to write two or three editorials and have all your friends claim you are the best editorial writer in the school. Also, if you are fighting for a "cause," then you must remember that you must keep hammering away at the issue. It might take a series of editorials to accomplish your objective.[15]

Another excellent bit of advice came from DeWitt Reddick, who said editorial writers should ask three questions before they start to write: (1) What can be accomplished through this editorial? (2) Where does this subject most vibrantly touch the lives of most readers? and (3) What *new* facts can be offered that will interest readers?[16]

All of this advice may be a little idealistic. What often happens in many college newsrooms is that it's deadline night—and probably late that night. An editorial is needed, and nobody has any good ideas for a subject. Something gets dashed off in a rush, with possibly mediocre results. All of the old admonitions about planning ahead are relevant here.

Perhaps not every editorial can be a brilliant appeal for social change. Nor should it be. Many editorials rightly deal with mundane subjects. Not all editorials even attempt to persuade. There is a place for an editorial that praises someone or simply notes the humor or irony of a situation. But student publications should not default in their editorial function. An editorial page has a legitimate place in a student newspaper, and it should have some editorials on it.

Sometimes the occasion demands a strong editorial, and sometimes editorial writers both on and off campus respond to the challenge effectively. A few years ago the editors of the *Northern Star* at Northern Illinois University decided they had to demand the resignation of their university president. They responded with an editorial that not only calmly and rationally set forth their reasons for this strong stand, but also won first place nationally in the Hearst Foundation competition for campus editorial writers. (See Figure 4.5.)

Figure 4.5   Editorial by editors of the
Northern Star, Northern Illinois University.
Used by permission of AASDJ–Hearst
Foundation Journalism Awards Program.

IT'S TIME FOR NELSON TO GO

Even a mighty ship can flounder and eventually sink with an inadequate captain at the wheel. It is with this in mind that we seriously question Richard Nelson's continuing tenure as president of this university.

Nelson generally is regarded as a warm and generous person. But how does that make him an effective leader of the state's second-largest public university? Nelson's seven years at the helm have been pockmarked with inadequacies and aberrations. They no longer can be tolerated.

This university is growing stronger every day. Many of its departments and programs have been recognized as state and national leaders in their fields. This university needs strong, aggressive leadership, not an administration hobbled by problems and handicaps.

We have at this university a man who is under indictment for a felony crime. This does NOT, of course, mean he is guilty. It does mean, though, that his name is linked with doubt, guilt and suspicion in the minds of many taxpayers, state officials and NIU employees. This clouds the relationship these people have with the chief of the number two Illinois public university. Do we want this?

We have at this university a president that makes a habit of forgetting things. University administrators say work piles up on Nelson's desk and never gets done. Example: Nelson hasn't even appointed members yet for a committee charged with examining the student fee structure and making recommendations for change—recommendations that are due by the end of this month. As one administrator puts it, "He never seems to attend to detail. He just lets things go." There is no such thing as a "minor" detail in a multi-million dollar operation. Is this the kind of president we need?

We have at this university a president who is less aggressive than other Regency presidents in his dealings with Regents, Illinois Board of Higher Education members and state officials. He does not aggressively seek support for NIU from other-than-state financial and social institutions. It seems to us that the president of a university sometimes has to bare his teeth and go for the throat, so to speak, to bring honor, prestige and money to a university. Nelson has not done this, nor is he likely to.

We have at this university a president whose Huskie Booster Club officers resigned en masse because, they said, of a lack of communication between Nelson and the boosters. The officers of that club are DeKalb's political, financial, and social heavyweights—realtors, insurance men, bankers, retailers. Do we want a president who alienates them?

We have at this university a president who cannot understand why NIU has so much bad Chicago press. Perhaps he doesn't realize that his subordinates' hanging up on, swearing at, and acting abusive toward Chicago reporters makes for bad public relations. Last year's controversy with the University Health Service, during which NIU officials banned photographers from some parts of the health service building and during which officials swore at and hung up on reporters, demonstrates NIU's consistently poor public relations. Poor public relations tactics mean poor press coverage. Which is why the Chicago metropolitan area sees NIU as crisis-laden.

We have at this university a president who pulls janitors—whose salaries are paid by students—away from their dormitory duties to clean his house because his housekeeper quit. And he apparently believes these are the kinds of "benefits" to which he is entitled. Is this the type of president we want?

We have at this university a president who likes upholding the closing of university meetings that even the author of the Illinois Open Meetings Act, a former state legislator, says should remain open. Nelson's pretense is that those meetings aren't under the jurisdiction of the act. These closings allow secrecy to creep into the administering of this university, something a good president should not allow to happen.

In short, we have at this university a president who seems to have an extraordinary amount of difficulty administering this institution. We don't think Nelson is up to the job.

This is a mighty institution. It has great potential. It seems to us there are many more-qualified persons who would jump at the chance to become president of a great midwestern university at a $40,000-plus a year salary. We should be able to do better.

We think it's time for our president to resign.

Critical Reviews

Critical reviewing has been a growth area for college newspapers. Reviews of the arts were once rare in many college papers, but almost all college papers publish them now. Many campus publications carry separate entertainment pages (or even entire sections) with numerous reviews of motion pictures, record albums and live performances. It has become routine for artists' publicists to include campus papers on their mailing lists for freebies—including passes to concerts, free record albums and tickets for motion picture previews.

Structurally, critical reviews are often freewheeling. Likewise, the language may be picturesque: reviewers are liberated from almost all of the restraints with which straight newswriters must live.

However, a good review is more than a collection of judgments—it should at least explain why the reviewer finds a particular artistic endeavor good or bad. Still, reviewers are free to be subjective. All the reviewer really must do is write in a style that encourages readership. The review should have an interesting introduction, and it should certainly have an eloquent conclusion. In between, the reviewer should base his conclusions on sound observations and reasoning rather than petty biases. To the extent that the reviewer begins with a point of view, he or she should inform the reader of that fact.

Ethically, campus reviews of the arts raise several issues. One, of course, is the question of how much space should be devoted to off-campus activities at the expense of campus news. On the one hand, it can be argued that reviewing professional artists should be left to professional reviewers, freeing student newspapers to devote their limited space to campus news. But on the other hand, critical reviews are sometimes among the best-read items in a campus newspaper. And students may be far more interested in the latest trends in music or the cinema than they are in the machinations of the sometimes inane politicians who congregate in student governments.

Another ethical issue involves the qualifications of both the reviewer and the artist being reviewed. Campus reviewers are often walk-in volunteers, not regular staff members with several journalism courses behind them. Such reviewers may be eminently qualified by their interest in the art form and their skill as writers—or they may lack both these attributes. One of the more difficult tasks that faces a campus editor is identifying competent reviewers and finding tactful ways to dismiss incompetent ones.

Likewise, questions are often raised about the standards campus reviewers demand of performers who may also be students. When campus reviewers say bad things about a big-time rock star, no one is likely to be hurt unfairly. However, when student reviewers demand professional competence of student performers, they are being unfair.

Textbook author Curtis MacDougall offered three basic suggestions for beginning reviewers: (1) describe the event or subject objectively, (2) explain the artist's intention and (3) pass expert judgment on the success of the artist in achieving his or her intention.[17] That last point should be a warning to students reviewing the work of other students: caution, if not gentleness, should be in order. Are you better qualified to be a reviewer than the students on stage are as performers?

It is often said that there is a difference between a review of the arts and criticism of the arts. A critic is expected to be an expert on his subject and may pass a harsh, but sophisticated, kind of judgment. A reviewer, on the other hand, will limit his comments to something much more restrained. Perhaps reviewing has more of a place than criticism in the campus press.

Beginning reviewers should think about a few practical considerations. For one, it is not usually a good idea to give away the whole story line of a play, motion picture, or book. Also, identify the people and artistic works you cite. Your readers may not be as familiar as you are with other artists and their works. Flaunting your wide familiarity with a particular field of artistic endeavor may not impress as many readers as it confuses.

Nevertheless, the critical function has a place in student newspapers. The campus publication that is lucky enough to have a well-informed and conscientious reviewer should give the reviewer's work the prominent display it deserves.

Columns and Opinion Pieces

Three of the West Coast's most popular columnists got together not so long ago at the University of California's San Diego campus. They were Herb Caen of the *San Francisco Chronicle*, Neil Morgan of the *San Diego Evening Tribune* (who later became *Tribune* editor) and Jack Smith of the *Los Angeles Times*. They agreed that two kinds of columns exist: the *items* column and the *thematic* column. Caen and Morgan, who write items columns, agreed that the thematic kind, which Smith writes, is more difficult to write.

Columns take many forms. Some thematic columns are nothing less than editorials that didn't win majority support on a newspaper's editorial board. Others are much more personalized opinion pieces. And some have no persuasive intent at all but are merely personal views on some topic. Jack Smith has attracted a very wide following by writing warm but rarely polemic personal columns. Item columns, of course, are rarely either political or persuasive; their writers are trying to entertain and nothing more.

Campus newspapers have little trouble finding people willing to write columns, but identifying good columnists may be another matter. Volunteers will often show up wanting to write columns on their favorite subjects, which may or may not be of general interest. The editor's job is to select columnists who are talented (and interesting) writers and can meet a deadline. But more important, their subject matter must have ongoing reader appeal. Some writers can generate one or two great columns, but quickly run out of new material.

Recognizing these problems, many campus papers open their editorial (or op-ed) pages to occasional contributors as well as regular columnists. Sometimes any student (or faculty member) is invited to contribute an occasional column or opinion piece, while regular columnist status is denied to all but the most gifted writers who may happen along. Some campus papers even face regulations that require all opinion pieces to be signed—editorials included.

Obviously, student newspaper columns and opinion pieces vary tremendously in style, scope and purpose. The same spot on the op-ed page may carry a self-righteous essay in one issue and a completely frivolous piece in the next. For the uniqueness of its perspective, few student-written columns can match one entitled "Welfare Machine: Girls without fathers become mothers without husbands," a column written by a Temple University journalism student (Figure 4.6). It appeared in the *Philadelphia Bulletin*.

The author, Patricia Geary, was a "welfare mother" with five children, and her column explained the forces that tend to lock people into the welfare system from one generation to the next. The column won an award in the Hearst Foundation competition.

In a totally different vein, Mark Barnhill of Los Angeles Pierce College won first prize in a Journalism Association of Community Colleges opinion-writing competition with a first-person account of his first community college district Board of Trustees meeting. He compared the district's elected governing board with his campus' student government and concluded that neither body really had a clear view of its responsibilities. (See Figure 4.7.)

Like a feature story, a column may entertain as well as inform, and like an editorial, a column may express opinions. Regular publication is what distinguishes a column from a randomly published feature or opinion piece. Yet the grind of regular publication quickly tempts some collegiate columnists to take a vacation.

Among the features of student newspapers that attract the most reader interest—and are surely the most fun to write—are the columns. Any good student newspaper will strive to offer a variety of interesting and stimulating columns, covering a wide range of subjects and viewpoints.

SPORTS WRITING

Because the authors of this book both started as sports writers, it wasn't easy for us to leave this topic for last. Sports writing may be relatively easy to learn, but it is hard to do well. Sports writing is sometimes a training ground for other

Figure 4.6   From a column written by
a Temple University student for the
Philadelphia Bulletin. Used by permission of
AASDJ–Hearst Foundation Journalism Awards
Program.

WELFARE MACHINE

Girls without fathers become mothers without husbands

Patricia Geary

Welfare mothers are called lazy because they do not want to work, neglectful because they have more than their share of teen-age problems as single parents, and stupid because they got saddled with a lot of kids whose fathers leave them.

About the few cases of fraud, taxpayers have reason to complain. But the majority of welfare mothers are trapped in situations by the need to survive. And it's helpful to see how they got that way.

All but 2,600 of the 81,650 welfare recipients in Philadelphia as of November 1977 were classified as living in single-headed households; the majority were women raising their children.

Ironically the state itself helps perpetuate the welfare cycle. It's easier to obtain assistance as a single parent. Because of this, possible short-term recipients become long-term recipients; in turn, this sets a pattern based on the theory that "mothers make mothers."

The intensive interview and red tape that a couple experiences when applying for temporary assistance causes many mothers to apply as separated wives. Although the family receives less income by not including the father, the quarterly interviews with the caseworker and the pressure applied by the caseworker to take any menial job are avoided. Not only does a single woman have only two interviews a year, she is not pressured to obtain employment because of her mother role. It appears beneficial to the needy family; however, the deception is disastrous.

As a result of this smaller than necessary income, the family is more deprived. It is true that some males in this situation do find jobs and their wives continue to receive grants; they are men who have found desirable employment, and their families are the short-term recipients who commit fraud to save for some otherwise unobtainable purchase or until they are thrown off welfare.

But in the majority of cases families separate and the mother and the children become long-term recipients. It happens like this: The tightness of money in the household causes the wife to apply pressure, that her husband intentionally avoided in the beginning, to find any menial job. Conflicts evolve. The wife challenges the man's ability to provide for the family because she is in the position to provide for it through her welfare check. Why should she cook him her food or give him her money for cigarets?

Love does not take priority under these circumstances; survival comes first.

Subsequently, this new family composition sets a pattern. Most young welfare mothers are daughters of welfare mothers. Many mothers live together and in some households there are three generations of children. When the father leaves, the responsibilities of two parents are left to one, the mother. And obviously, she is unable to handle crises the way two parents can.

One result is teen-age pregnancies. Poor fatherless teen-agers are not the only ones having sex, but they account for the majority of young pregnancies. After the first careless pregnancy, these girls are rewarded with a bigger income and the state gets another recipient who heads a single-parent household.

The children of this second generation of young mothers have even less chance to avoid the welfare cycle. Young mothers become aware that independence of a sort can be obtained without a husband or a career. A pattern is established. The third generation of teen-age daughters has little or no knowledge of a two-parent household, and they learn how to survive solely on welfare.

The number of welfare dependents, and of births to unwed teen-agers, is alarming. Oddly, the major cause is wel-fare policy, and the state, which sets this policy, needs to look more closely at its role in creating welfare recipients.

(Patricia Geary, a journalism student at Temple University, has five children and has lived in public housing for ten years.)

---

kinds of journalism. Students may become sports writers because of their interest in sports rather than because of any interest in writing; the interest in writing develops later.

Game Stories and Features

Collegiate sports writing falls into two main categories. First, there is the traditional story about an athletic event—a specialized kind of news story noted for its color and, unfortunately, clichés. These stories may either precede or follow the athletic event, but college papers often emphasize pregame stories for reasons we'll explain shortly.

The other major type of sports writing is the sports feature, which is really not very different from other feature stories—except for its subject matter. Profiles about sports celebrities are a staple item in most campus newspapers, and they're researched and written in much the same manner as other profile stories. The same is true of process features about developments or issues in college athletics. Most campus newspapers carry stories about the annual budget squabbles between athletic departments and campus administrators, to cite just one ongoing topic for news features in the sports field.

A good example of a sports feature is an award-winning story by a University of Arizona student, Andy Van De Voorde. He wrote a profile about a collector who had 22,000 baseball trading cards (Figure 4.8). The collector, a statistician in the university's information office, made his living working with sports, but the story still provided an interesting relief for readers accustomed to seeing features only about players and coaches on the sports pages.

In covering the hard news of sports events, weekly campus newspapers are at a decided disadvantage. Most readers will know the outcome of important games long before the campus paper hits the stands. Student newspapers are perennially scooped by broadcasters and commercial dailies when it comes to play-by-play coverage of football and basketball games. About all the campus paper can hope to do in such a case is find a fresh angle on the game story or perhaps cover it in greater depth than did the commercial press. Perhaps most important, many college weeklies emphasize pregame stories over game wrap-up stories because this is one place where they can be just as timely as anybody else.

Figure 4.7   Opinion piece by Mark Barnhill
of Los Angeles Pierce College, Los Angeles
California. Used by permission.

OPINION OTHER THAN EDITORIAL

First Place: Mark Barnhill
Los Angeles Pierce College

Each semester at Pierce as I have become increasingly acquainted with the workings of the ASB, I have often marveled at what I perceived to be its unique methods.

Nonetheless I've looked upon the ASB as a relatively harmless diversion; a place where students could learn about political organization and its practical application.

It was no big deal to me if sometimes the ASB got so caught up on political mechanics and parliamentary procedure that issues became clouded and obtuse.

I was never worried because I realized it was all a part of the learning process—surely there were cooler heads at the District administrative level to oversee and evaluate these student decisions.

But that was before I attended my first Board of Trustees meeting.

Before I came to realize that if the ASB can be compared to a circus, then it is small-time compared to the three-ring bigtop they run downtown.

What I saw that day both surprised and worried me.

I saw someone speak in front of the Board and, after using the five-minute limit imposed on speakers, request an additional short period to finish her presentation.

"Just two more paragraphs," she assured the Board.

What followed was a heated debate on her request. The debate centered basically on whether to give her a time extension, and whether giving the time would set a precedent for other speakers.

Finally, after all the discussion, they agreed to allow her the extension, with the agreement that it would be an isolated incident, setting no precedent.

It took just seconds for her to finish her speech, but the ending seemed disjointed—the speech had been bisected by a debate that was as long as her entire presentation.

And I thought that the ASB was hung up on mechanics and procedure.

That day I also saw a proposal in front of the Board which, from the tone of the discussion, seemed destined to be voted down.

At that point the chancellor, a nonvoting member of the Board but apparently a proponent of that proposal, withdrew it before a vote could be taken.

When the debate continued, and it looked as if the proposal might pass, he decided to resubmit it. It passed.

Finally, I saw a board member leave the room during a lengthy debate and, returning after at least a half-hour absence, cast a vote on that issue.

I realize that there are times when one might be compelled to leave the room. There are even speaker boxes in other rooms that broadcast what's being said in the meeting.

But if a person has to leave the room, can he devote his full attention to that broadcast of the debate on an issue? If not, is he qualified to vote fairly on that issue?

I used to believe that the ASB was too caught up in procedure and mechanics to accurately perceive the importance of every aspect of every issue.

Now I also believe that the District sometimes gets so caught up in administrative mechanics that it loses sight of its primary goal—education.

Without some type of order and administration that goal cannot be adequately served, but with too much its importance may easily be overshadowed and minimized.

Figure 4.8   Sports feature by University of Arizona student Andy Van De Voorde. Used by permission.

For UA senior

BASEBALL IN CUT OF THE CARDS

One day in 1963, 8-year-old Gary Johnson walked into a small Circle K in Douglas and threw a few pennies on the counter to pay for his first pack of Topps baseball cards.

Once he worked his way past the two rock-hard slabs of famous stale bubble gum, Johnson must have seen something he liked. Sixteen years later that lone pack has grown into a monstrous 22,000-card collection that takes up a big space in Johnson's living room and in his life.

Johnson, a University senior, works on (what else?) Arizona baseball statistics for the University's Sports Information Services when he's not adding to the stacks of baseball legends and no-names kept behind his couch. The sprawling collection already rivals the Library of Congress in its thoroughness, but Johnson said he has no intentions of stopping now.

"I don't plan to give it up," he said. "When I started getting older, it was embarrassing to go into a store and buy them, so now I just order the whole set from the company."

It may seem a little unusual for a grown, married man to devote himself to a passion most kids give up about the time they give up Bazooka bubble gum. But from the looks of things, Johnson isn't the only baseball card fanatic around.

"A couple of summers ago I didn't have much to do so I took out a newspaper ad for cards," he said. "I got about 25 calls the next week from all sorts of people—doctors, lawyers, real-estate men and all kinds of professionals."

Johnson has a lot of company in his field, but his 22,000-piece assemblage has topped all comers so far, making him the apparent granddaddy of area collectors.

"There may be guys with more than I have, but if there are I haven't met them yet," he said.

Johnson said a few of the cards have special meaning to him. "I've always been a Yankee fan," he said. "There's one with Yogi Berra and Mickey Mantle both on it."

Countless generations of baseball cards have been distributed across America and Johnson said some of them don't fit into the normal mold. "Some of the cards are pretty strange," Johnson said.

"For instance, some of them show pitchers posing with a bat. One of them even shows (Arizona baseball coach and former Cleveland Indian infielder) Jerry Kindall with a glove."

Johnson said that several Jerry Kindall cards are still floating around and he has put his hands on as many as he could find. "They're all signed now," he said.

Johnson has two reproductions of an extremely rare Honus Wagner card, the original of which he said is worth $1,500. On the other side of the coin, he admits to having several cards bearing the easily forgettable visage of "Marvelous Marv" Throneberry, formerly of the New York Mets.

Baseball die-hards remember Throneberry as the man who forever engraved his name in baseball lore on the day he hit his first major league home run. After sending the ball over the fence, Throneberry jubilantly loped around the bases. But the victory celebration at home plate was interrupted when the opposing third baseman told the umpire Throneberry hadn't touched third. "Don't worry about it," replied the ump. "He didn't touch first or second either."

Marvelous Marv aside, Johnson's collection probably still doesn't greatly impress Annie Johnson. But Johnson said his wife is gradually becoming accustomed to his time-consuming hobby.

"She gives me a funny look whenever I decide to spend money on a new set," he said. "But she knows she'll have to get used to it. She knows I want to make my life in baseball."

Johnson's work with baseball stats at Arizona has convinced him to pursue a career in public relations with a major league club. If he is hired by the big leagues, Johnson said, "the job won't even seem like a job."

Baseball cards can do that to you.

Andy Van De Voorde
University of Arizona

A college sports staff may even have advantages over the professional competition in researching pregame stories. The campus sports writers, sports publicists and perhaps even the coaches at rival schools may be willing to tell a student reporter things they'd never tell someone from a big-time daily paper or television network. When you do a pregame story, don't just talk to your own coaches and consider the research complete: contact the other side too.

In their effort to offer their readers something original, some campus papers concentrate on the sports that attract less community interest, such as intercollegiate wrestling, swimming, golf and rowing. Excelling in sports feature writing is especially important for campus weeklies that must compete with commercial dailies in their sports coverage.

Still, campus papers, and particularly campus dailies, can do an excellent job of covering the hard news of sports events, even in competition with the wire services, big-city dailies and network television. The 1980 California Intercollegiate Press Association sports writing competition produced several examples of outstanding game coverage by student sports writers. The top award in the CIPA competition went to Mike Ventre, sports editor of the University of Southern California *Daily Trojan* for a story about the Rose Bowl game (Figure 4.9). The runner-up story in that competition was a report on another nationally publicized late-season football game.

Ventre dared to call USC's 17–16 win over Ohio State "one of the best football games ever," an accolade that it may be your prerogative to write if you happen to cover a university that plays big-time football. Still, Ventre's story represents much that is good in sports writing. His story was a game wrap-up, but it also included quotes obtained from postgame interviews and concentrated on second-day angles to interest readers who had already seen the game on television.

The Challenges of Sports Writing

Good sports writing doesn't come easily for most journalists. A good sports writer, first of all, must find original ways to say things that have been said thousands of times before. In no other kind of writing is there a greater temptation to fall into the habit of using old clichés. The first time a sports writer called a close game a "cliffhanger," it was clever. The tenth time, it wasn't so innovative. By now, hundreds of "cliffhangers" have been played in all major sports. Your challenge is to find a new way to tell your readers about the next close game you cover.

Figure 4.9   Sports story by Mike Ventre,
sports editor of the *Daily Trojan,* University of
Southern California. Used by permission.

USC WINS ROSES
THE GREAT WHITE WAY

By Mike Ventre
Sports Editor

As Rose Bowls go, this one was a hybrid. It had two exceptional quarterbacks, one a senior giving a curtain call, one a sophomore on a collision course with John Heisman's legacy. It had the best football player in the country (by decree of John Robinson and a mass of experts selected by New York's Downtown Athletic Club). It had dramatic excitement, laughs and tears, thrills and spills. It had one loser and one winner.

USC beat Ohio State in the Rose Bowl Tuesday, 17–16, in what had to be one of the best football games ever. It was not without flaws. Both the Trojans and Buckeyes made costly errors that disqualifies the game from most coaching manuals. But both teams seemed to sacrifice cautious precision for the uncertain rewards of risk-taking. The 1980 Rose Bowl was one continuous riverboat ride, with a surprise ending that would have warmed O. Henry's heart.

The hero, undoubtedly, was Heisman Trophy winner Charles White. White rambled for a Rose Bowl-record 247 yards on a Rose Bowl-record 39 carries. The senior tailback did it with power, speed and basic football smarts. It would be fitting to call it a phenomenal one-man show that did in the Buckeyes on the first day of the 80s but that was not the case, nor is it ever for USC.

The credit should be sliced into equal parts for the offensive line, senior quarterback Paul McDonald, fullback Marcus Allen, a stubborn Trojan defense and, for providing challenging competition, an equally stubborn Ohio State team, who made it quite clear that the Big Ten's collective New Year's resolution to dispel any inferiority myth is no empty promise.

Art Schlichter had a lot to do with the Buckeyes' newfound savvy. The sophomore quarterback connected on 11 of 21 passes for 297 yards and one stunning touchdown, a 67-yard moonshot to split end Gary Williams at the end of the first half that jerked the high horse right out from under USC.

The Buckeye defense also proved to be big time, even when their personnel was less-than-gargantuan. "Their defense was great, especially inside the 20," said a haggard but happy John Robinson in the post-game interview room. "I don't know how many times we got inside the 20 and couldn't get in. One thing that disappointed me was that they got the very big play on us, where going in we felt we could contain that."

In addition to Williams' touchdown strike, he also snared a third-down pass from Schlichter in the first quarter for 53 yards to the USC two, setting up a USC clinic in goal-line defense. In three straight punches from the 2, Ohio State netted only 1. On fourth and goal at the one, Schlichter tried to scamper to the right where USC middle linebacker Dennis Johnson greeted him with a pair of open arms that closed the goal-line route.

"We take a lot of pride in our defense, especially in goal line," said Johnson, "because we play with reckless abandon. Nobody scores on us."

That may be true from only a few yards away Dennis, but tell that to Vlade Janakievski. The OSU placekicker hit three field goals, the last a 24 yarder that put the Buckeyes up by six.

USC then drove to the OSU 24-yard line but again failed to score when McDonald threw to Dan Garcia on fourth down and four and it fell incomplete.

The Buckeyes now needed to hold onto the ball with 7:00 remaining and either sustain a time-consuming drive to wither away USC'S chances or bring Janakievski for more footwork. The USC defense made sure neither would happen.

Schlichter moved his team to the USC 47, but was abruptly halted when on third down and four, linebacker Chip Banks, on perhaps the unheralded "key" play of the game, powered past the Ohio State lineman and nailed Schlichter for a nine-yard loss, forcing a punt.

"I just came hard," Banks said later. "It was third down and I knew I had to buckle down. I was by my man before he even got out of a three-point stance."

USC got the ball on their own 17 with 5:21 left, and it was as if at that precise moment some nervous stage hand ran into the dressing room and yelled, "Charles, you're on," although most of the USC offensive unit insists nothing was or needed to be said.

Paul McDonald—"We've all been in that situation before. I don't think anything had to be said. We knew what we had to do: get a drive together and score."

Chris Foote—"There wasn't really much said. There was just kind of a feeling in the huddle. And we just said. "OK, let's get down to business and let's do it."

Brad Budde—"We just kind of glared at each other. Words were there without being spoken."

Anthony Munoz—"Playing for four years we've been in that situation before. We just knew we had to take it in."

On first down, White stampeded through the middle for 32 yards, spinning off a tackler and immediately renewing thousands of broken hopes. On second down, more of the same, this time for 28 yards. It wasn't the O.K. Corral, but it was a showdown.

White took a breather as his understudy, Michael Hayes, ran for seven yards to the OSU 16. Then Allen got the first down with a five-yard run.

White then reentered the game, confidently gesturing to the 105,526 fans in attendance in a scene comparable to Babe Ruth's famous 'called shot.' In four plays from the 11-yard line, White carried the ball closer and closer until one topsy-turvy leap over a heap of scarlet and gray brought USC the Roses.

"This was a great football game," Robinson said. "You can't underestimate that. There were mistakes, coaches make mistakes, but damn it, this was a great football game, and I don't know what they charged to get into this place but it was worth it."

"They most certainly are great competitors, as are the Buckeyes," said a subdued Ohio State coach Earle Bruce. "We just didn't mix it up enough to put enough points on the board. Sixteen points is not enough to beat Southern Cal."

It was billed as a thriller, and it didn't disappoint. White has the Heisman. And for sheer drama from a singler player, he deserved an Oscar, with honorable mention going to Ohio State for setting the stage.

Similarly, it isn't clever any more to call basketball players "roundballers" or baseball players "diamondmen" or "horsehiders." If you must use synonyms or epithets, try to find new ones. Not only is it trite to call football players "gridders," but it's confusing to some readers. In fact, even if it isn't trite, jargon should be avoided. Every use of a sports term (without defining it) and every use of a cliché reduces the quality of your sports writing.

Another characteristic of good sports writing is a good command of the rules of grammar and syntax. The rules of English are as important on the sports pages as they are anywhere else in a newspaper. One particular grammatical problem seems to plague sports writers everywhere: failing to understand that a collective noun is singular. For example, there is only one Ohio State University. You're not supposed to say, "Ohio State defeated *their* archrivals, the University of Michigan." It may sound awkward, but Ohio State is an *it*. However, the Ohio State Buckeyes (the team name) are a *they*. If you say, "The Buckeyes defeated *their* archrivals," you are correct. While *Ohio State* and *team* are collective nouns and therefore singular, a term such as *Buckeyes* is not—it's plural.

In addition to being original and grammatically sound, sports writing should be, as the authors of one textbook suggested, "vigorous, virile, [and] audacious."[18] The writing should be succinct and clear, and it should convey a feel for the action of the event.

Sports writers have a freedom to editorialize that is unheard of on the news side, but that, too, has its limits. One of the major criticisms of both campus and community newspaper sports writing is the tendency of the writers to be "homers." A homer is a writer who is a cheerleader for the home team. At their worst, homers use the first-person plural in describing the good guys (the home team): "our football team" or "We clobbered State, 97–61." Sports writers may be free to editorialize to an extent that would be unacceptable on the news pages, but the readers have a right to expect some objectivity in the reporting. The coach who demands that the student press be "loyal" and promote the home team is asking the writers to violate the ethics of their field.

At the opposite extreme from the homer is the sports writer who expects the campus teams to be professional. Most college athletes are not and never will be professionals—they're amateurs. Stories, and particularly sports columns, sometimes can do great injustices by being hypercritical. Like the reviewer writing about a campus drama production, the sports commentator reviewing student athletes' performances should not forget that the athlete (like the reviewer himself) is not yet a professional.

Perhaps even worse are inexperienced campus sports analysts who offer their readers superficial and sophomoric treatises about professional sports. Their expertise may be glaringly thin, and it is hard to see what contribution the paper has made to its readers by publishing their work. Some student-written stories about professional sports are truly insightful and worth reading, but at other times it's hard not to feel the space should have been devoted to campus athletics instead. If you don't cover your college's sports program thoroughly, who will?

In recent years, campus sports staffs have faced a new challenge, one created by federal laws requiring equal expenditures for men's and women's sports. Intercollegiate women's sports are growing rapidly in both stature and audience appeal. Still, the attendance at most women's sports events doesn't begin to match attendance at men's games.

The dilemma for campus newspapers, then, is whether to cover men's and women's sports equally or to reflect the disparity in reader interest suggested by the higher attendance and give men's sports top billing. But is there really more interest in men's sports than in women's because of discriminatory media coverage, or does the discriminatory coverage merely reflect reader preferences? On some campuses, women's groups have demanded greater coverage of women's sports news. In response to lobbying by female coaches for more coverage, a community college newspaper adviser once replied, "They may have Title IX, but we have the First Amendment!"

Whatever the answers to the philosophical questions about covering women's sports, the fact is that women's sports events are becoming increasingly important campus news, and many student newspapers across America are treating them accordingly.

Another major change that recent years have brought to campus sports sections is the trend toward more coverage of recreational and health activities. As Americans by the millions have turned off their television sets and gone outside to jog, hike, ride bicycles, swim or play golf, sports writers have responded with sports feature coverage of these activities. Only a small minority of all Americans can take part in big-time competitive sports events, but almost everyone can engage in personal athletic activities, and the media have increasingly recognized the new trend.

However, school officials have sometimes resisted efforts by student newspaper staffs to cover topics other than traditional intercollegiate athletics. For example, Glen Roberts, adviser to the San Diego City College *City Times,* was nearly fired for allowing his staff to drop the sports page and replace it with a recreation page. The staff had surveyed readers and found little interest in a sports page but much interest in participatory recreation activities.

Nevertheless, college officials ordered Roberts to reinstate the sports page after coaches complained. Then they tried to fire him for what they called "insubordination" when he refused to overrule his staff. His job was saved eventually after months of controversy, but only because the governing board followed a state hearing officer's recommendation that Roberts not be fired. At this writing, the *City Times* still has no traditional sports page, although the recreation page usually includes coverage of intercollegiate athletics.

As American interests in sports and recreation change, sports writers must keep up with their readers' new interests. Sports coverage that is limited to wrap-up stories about last week's games and advance stories on upcoming games may not be in tune with the rapidly changing times. Sports pages that carry features on important issues in sports—and offer game coverage that is colorful and creative—are much more likely to capture and hold readers.

REFERENCES

1. Correspondence from Donna Dickerson to the publisher, February 1982.

2. Roland E. Wolsely and Laurence R. Campbell, *Exploring Journalism,* 2nd ed. (New York: Prentice-Hall, 1949), p. 451

3. Wolsely and Campbell, *Exploring Journalism,* p. 451.

4. Helen M. Patterson, *Writing and Selling Feature Articles* (Englewood Cliffs, N.J.: Prentice-Hall, 1956), p. 8.

5. Jim Alvord, "Presenting," *California Publisher* 59, no. 11 (August 1980): 16.

6. Al Hestor, "The Media and the User: A New Relationship," in *Newspapers and the Future* (Athens, Ga.: Henry W. Grady School of Journalism and Mass Communication, University of Georgia, 1980), pp. 1–11.

7. Dewitt C. Reddick, *Modern Feature Writing* (New York: Harper and Brothers, 1949), pp. 24–35.

8. Michael Ryan and James W. Tankard, Jr., *Basic News Reporting* (Palo Alto, Calif.: Mayfield, 1977), pp. 16–17.

9. Ronald P. Lovell, *The Newspaper: An Introduction to Newswriting and Reporting* (Belmont, Calif.: Wadsworth, 1980), p. 339.

10. William Rivers and Shelly Smolkin, *Free-lancer and Staff Writer*, 3rd ed. (Belmont, Calif.: Wadsworth, 1981), pp. 90–96, 208.

11. "A Conversation with Henry Steele Commager," *Bill Moyers' Journal* (Public Broadcast System, 1979).

12. Mary C. Rothgreb, "How to Put Personality in Those Features," *Scholastic Editor* 56, no. 6 (April–May 1979): 7.

13. Le Roy Smith, "Editorial Writing Takes a Back Seat," *Masthead* 31, no. 2 (Summer 1979): 28.

14. G. Cleveland Wilhoit and Dan G. Drew, "Profile of the North American Editorial Writer, 1971–1979," *Masthead* 31, no. 4 (Winter 1979–1980): 11.

15. E. Joseph Broussard, "Writing Editorials," *Communication: Journalism Education Today* 12, no. 3 (Spring 1979): 16. Used by permission.

16. Dewitt C. Reddick, *The Mass Media and the School Newspaper* (Belmont, Calif.: Wadsworth, 1976), p. 224.

17. Curtis D. MacDougall, *Interpretative Reporting* (New York: Macmillan, 1977), pp. 554–555.

18. Julian Harriss, Kelly Leiter and Stanley Johnson, *The Complete Reporter*, 3rd ed. (New York: Macmillan, 1977), p. 392.

Consistency in Style

The term *style* has a special meaning in newspapering. To a poet or a novelist, style means the way one writes: the choice of words, sentence structure and the like. A talented writer might be said to have a good style. But to a journalist, style also means consistency in the details of writing.

Suppose there's a building on your campus named the Zorchmeister Memorial Student Union or Zorchmeister Union for short. Do you capitalize all the words? Or could you write "Zorchmeister union," or just "student union" without capitalizing? What if you just say "the union"? Or is it "The Union"?

When you announce a campus club meeting, you have several style problems to resolve. For instance, would you say "Ski Club"? Or is it "Ski club"? Suppose the Ski Club is going to meet at three o'clock Wednesday, January 23. Do you say "3 p.m."? Or maybe "3:00 p.m."? Or is it "3 P.M."? Or perhaps "3:00 PM"? If your paper is published Friday, January 18, how do you give the date of the Ski Club meeting? Is it "next Wednesday"? Or do you say "January 23" or maybe "Jan. 23"? Or would you just say "Wednesday"?

These are the sorts of questions a style guide answers. A style guide tells you when to capitalize important words and when to make them lowercase. It tells you when to abbreviate familiar terms and when to write them out in full. It specifies how to use numerals for various purposes, such as sports stories and lists. And a style guide tells you how to handle people's names and titles, to cite just a few of the things covered by a good style guide.

Some people think these kinds of questions are trivial. But if a newspaper is inconsistent about the little details, will the reader believe what it says about the big things? More than one reader survey has shown that petty inconsistencies seriously damage a paper's credibility. That's why the nation's major newspapers all follow style guides. Many big papers have their own special style guides, but virtually all are heavily influenced by the *Associated Press Stylebook* or the *United Press International Stylebook*. These two guidebooks, which answer thousands of questions, are almost identical (a necessity because many newspapers use stories from both AP and UPI and the style of all stories must be consistent). However, they are reference works: no one would attempt to memorize everything in either one of them. A wire service stylebook, like a dictionary, should be within easy reach of every reporter's desk.

You may have been introduced to one

or both of these stylebooks in your first newswriting class. So why are we discussing style again here?

The AP and UPI stylebooks are great if you want to find out how to spell *Kuwait,* or whether to use the abbreviation AFL-CIO or spell out the name of the organization. But they won't give you much help if you need to find out if the campus "Little Theater" is spelled *theater* or *theatre.* AP style is *theater,* but many colleges use the British spelling (*theatre*) instead, perhaps because the Theatre Department prefers that spelling. Nor will the *AP Stylebook* tell you when to abbreviate "Associated Students" to "AS" or when to abbreviate the name of a well-known nearby university. These are purely local matters, and many of them are of little general concern to professional newspapers. However, a campus newspaper may well use the term *Associated Students* or some equivalent in nearly every issue, so it has to have a style that specifies when the term is abbreviated.

To handle these kinds of problems, a campus newspaper needs its own style guide. In the interest of consistency, the AP or UPI style should be your starting point, but it's only a starting point. You will need to develop your own supplemental style guide if you don't already have one. If you do have one, you may wish to check it against the AP or UPI stylebook to see if it is as consistent as possible. Also, you might compare your style guide with the college catalog. It makes little sense to refer to the "Campus Theater" if the catalog consistently calls the place the "College Theatre."

"A foolish consistency is the hobgoblin of little minds," Ralph Waldo Emerson (the nineteenth-century American social commentator) once wrote. Perhaps he was right when it comes to moral issues, but it isn't very professional to be inconsistent about little things like spelling, capitalization and abbreviations.

Newspaper style guides are never completely consistent, and perhaps they shouldn't be. Every style has exceptions. The ideal style, however, should be logical and reasonable, and it should not flout the rules of English grammar. Even more importantly, it shouldn't invite mistakes. If by instinct or previous training most writers tend to say something in a certain way, perhaps that's the way it should be said. If a staff is going to learn the basic rules of style and follow them, those rules should be as easy to learn as possible. With that in mind, we offer some suggestions for a campus style guide.

PRACTICAL SUGGESTIONS FOR A STYLE GUIDE

Capitalization

Your style guide should tell the writers when to capitalize the names of campus buildings. It might even list the correct names of all the major buildings (along with acceptable short forms of the names). A typical campus style may specify that the full names of campus buildings are capitalized (they are, after all, proper nouns), while lowercase is used for informal and shortened names. To return to our earlier example, if you have a Zorchmeister Memorial Student Union, you may want to capitalize the full name, but use lowercase if you just say "student union." If the building is called "Student Union" and nothing more, you may wish to capitalize that name. Obviously, the major buildings have long names on some campuses, names rooted in local history. On other campuses the names tend to be short and unpretentious. Your style should be appropriate for your campus.

Another major question will be how to treat academic subjects and academic departments. Many campus stylebooks specify that general subjects are not capitalized unless they are proper nouns (as are languages and the names of countries: "French" or "Russian studies," for instance). However, the official name of an academic unit (for example, Journalism Department) is also a proper noun and probably should be capitalized even if the word *journalism* (standing alone) is not.

The names of campus organizations present another question. Typically, a style guide will specify that *Ski Club,* for instance, should be capitalized. A related problem is deciding what to do about the official entities on campus. If the academic vice-president writes a memo, he's sure to capitalize "Office of the Vice-President for Academic Affairs." You may not want to let him get away with that sort of pomposity, at least not in your newspaper. You may prefer a style that sometimes makes the title lowercase (the question of how you handle the title when it accompanies a name is discussed later).

Your campus probably has a board of trustees or board of regents—or perhaps the system to which it belongs has a governing board. You'll need a style that specifies when to capitalize the name of that body.

Racial designations present another capitalization problem: when do you capitalize *black, white* or *Latino?* The *AP Stylebook* offers some guidance on this point under the heading "Nationalities and Races," but it doesn't specify what reference to use in connection with all of the specific ethnic groups you may have on campus. If there's a substantial population of Latin descent, for example, you may need to adopt a style on this point. The term *Chicano* was once more widely accepted than it is today; terms such as *Hispanic* or *Latino* may be more appropriate and would probably be capitalized at all times.

Titles

Titles also pose problems. Most newspapers capitalize official titles when they precede a person's name, but not when they stand alone or follow the name.

When referring to the college president, you may wish to follow this rule: capitalize when you say "college President William Smith," but use lowercase when you say "Dr. William Smith, college president."

Many college papers follow the rule that unofficial and occupational titles, unlike official ones, are lowercase even when they appear before a name. For instance, if someone is identified as "coach William Smith" or "lawyer Mary Smith," that title would not be capitalized under many newspapers' styles. Likewise, if you refer to an athlete as "left fielder William Smith," for example, that title would not be capitalized. In fact, some newspapers have strict rules against placing descriptive titles (such as "lawyer" or "left fielder") before names, mainly because some grammarians object to the practice.

What about campus officials with doctor's degrees? Some campus newspapers make it a policy to use the title "Dr." *once* in the story. It is used on first reference, along with the full name, unless the title precedes the name. Then you might make it your style to say "college President William Smith" on first reference, and then "Dr. Smith" on second reference, calling the man just "Smith" thereafter.

Courtesy titles such as "Mr." and "Ms." have been controversial lately. An increasing number of campus newspapers are adopting the same policy as that followed by many professional papers: only the dead and perhaps heads of state get them. High-school newspapers usually refer to teachers and administrators by their courtesy titles out of respect, but college papers often do not. When you interview the college president in his or her office, it is usually not appropriate to address him or her by last name alone, but when you write a story about the interview, that is exactly how you'll most likely refer to him or her.

For instance, if the president's name is John Smith, you'll probably call him "Dr. Smith" or "Mr. Smith" during the interview. Your story, however, will only say "John Smith, college president" or "President John Smith" on the first reference. After that you'll probably just say "Smith."

Journalists once had a double standard about courtesy titles: men didn't get them but women did. But as a result of the feminist movement's drive for sexual equality, an increasing number of newspapers now treat men and women alike. Whereas once a woman named Smith would have been called either "Miss Smith" or "Mrs. Smith" on subsequent references in a story, today more and more newspapers are calling her "Smith," just as they would if she were male. Some newspapers have one rule on this point for their news and sports sections, with another for the "family" or "view" section (the section that was once called the "women's section" or "society"). At this writing the AP/UPI style still requires courtesy titles for women, but not for men. Meanwhile, some major newspapers (such as the *New York Times*) use courtesy titles for both men and women. Courtesy titles may be a controversial issue on your campus, and whatever style you adopt could provoke debate.

Abbreviations

One of the major local style issues a campus paper must resolve is what to do about abbreviating familiar place and organization names.

There is a widely recognized general rule about abbreviations: if the name itself is a proper noun, it is abbreviated in capital letters without periods unless it is a geographic or political entity (such as U.S.A. or N.J.). Lowercase abbreviations usually take periods to prevent reader confusion.

However, there is no general rule about which names may be abbreviated. A good rule for a campus newspaper is to abbreviate the names of places and organizations on first reference only when the vast majority of readers are thoroughly familiar with the abbreviation. If the students generally understand that "AS" means "Associated Students," then there is little need to spell the words out, even on first reference. Similarly, if a major university such as Ohio State, Massachusetts Institute of Technology, or University of California at Los Angeles is nearby, it may be superfluous to say anything except "OSU," "MIT" or "UCLA."

There are pitfalls in using an abbreviation such as "OSU," however. "OSU" can mean "Oklahoma State University," "Oregon State University" or "Ohio State University," for instance. Make sure your readers really know which one you're referring to before you permit an abbreviation such as "OSU" on first reference in a story.

Some campus papers follow a style of spelling out most proper nouns on first reference, but with the abbreviation in parentheses, like this: "Ohio State University (OSU) will have military recruiters on campus Thursday."

The names of local organizations are often abbreviated in campus papers, at least on second reference. Some papers refer to their boards of trustees as "BOT" on second reference; others believe it is less confusing to simply say "the board" or "the trustees" after saying "Board of Trustees" the first time.

Every campus newspaper needs a style for references to rooms in campus buildings, too. If a meeting will be held in room 214 of the Zorchmeister Memorial Student Union, the style might be anything from "Z-214" to "SU-214" or "union 214," depending on local practice. It may be wise to follow the style used in the schedule of classes to avoid confusion.

Numerals

The basic newspaper style for numerals is to use Arabic numerals for two-digit and longer numbers (10 and above), while spelling out one through nine. Most newspapers recognize a variety of exceptions for addresses, lists, sports scores and the like.

You may wish to follow the AP style on this point, or to adopt a more specific local rule on such matters as "3-unit course" (or is it "three-unit course"?).

A SAMPLE STYLE GUIDE

Having outlined some of the major style questions a campus newspaper staff needs to address, we conclude this chapter with a sample style guide developed by a college newspaper. This particular one has evolved over two decades at California State University, Fullerton. Some of its topical references are purely local and would not be applicable on other campuses, but it provides a good example of how one campus daily met its need for a consistent style.

This style guide may be adapted to the needs of other college publications by revising the specific references to buildings, titles, departments and so forth.

In addition to the material included in this sample style guide, many college papers' stylebooks also feature lists of basic facts about the campus to assist writers. An organizational chart showing the correct names and titles of administrators is helpful to new reporters. Of course, the college catalog may well be the most important single reference work (and style guide) available for a campus news staff; perhaps the stylebook should remind reporters to consult the college catalog for correct spellings of officials' names.

DAILY TITAN STYLE GUIDE

California State University, Fullerton

All copy prepared for publication in the Daily Titan must follow the general style rules found in the *AP Stylebook*. This guide provides a few specific rules on matters not covered by the *AP Stylebook*, particularly style questions specific to this campus. Where AP style and Daily Titan style differ, follow this style guide.

I. Capitalization

A. Academic subjects: capitalize languages, department names, titles of specific courses (for example, English, History Department, World Communications Systems), but not general subjects (biology, history), except for languages (always proper nouns).

B. Emphases or sequences of a department are always lowercase (for example, public relations sequence, news-editorial sequence), except for those that are separate degree programs, such as Oral History (a specific degree earned in the History Department).

C. Capitalize the complete names of campus buildings and departments, as well as schools and divisions of the university: Langsdorf Hall, but administration building. Humanities Building, Performing Arts Center, Science Building, Visual Arts Center, Arena Theatre, but say "campus police headquarters." Note that "Library" is the full name of the Cal State Fullerton Library building. Capitalize *Quad* when referring to the central area between the Library and Science building.

D. All campus groups, organizations and clubs are capitalized (for example, Students for a Democratic Society, Art Club, Sigma Alpha Epsilon, Pep Squad, Pep Band, and so forth). *Campus police* is lowercase (campus police).

When referring to a campus police officer use "security officer" (lowercase) on first reference.

E. Titles: long titles should be put *after* the name and in lowercase. As a general rule, titles of three or more words are put after the name. Academic titles generally fall into five levels: instructor, assistant professor, associate professor, professor (that is, full professor) and lecturer. The term *professor* should not be applied to persons holding the rank of instructor or lecturer. Note also that to identify a person as "professor of communications," for instance, designates that person as a full professor and should only be applied to persons holding this highest academic rank. Check all titles in the back of the current catalog. See also Section V dealing with names.

F. Never capitalize *spring, summer, fall* or *winter* unless it is part of a title (for example, Spring, 1981, but not spring semester). Use capitals when the season is immediately followed by the year.

G. Racial designations by color such as *black* and *white* are not capitalized. *Chicano* is capitalized. The term *Negro* is not to be used unless an individual requests it. Racial designations are always capitalized when appearing within titles or organizations. Avoid racial distinctions unless clearly relevant to a story.

H. When referring to a student (for example, communications student), the term is not capitalized.

II. Abbreviations

A. All branches of the University of California may be designated as "UC" followed by the name of the campus on first reference and then abbreviated (UC Irvine, UC Riverside, then UCI, UCR). Exception: the abbreviation UCLA is acceptable on first reference.

B. In the California State University and Colleges system, refer to the campuses as follows: Cal State Fullerton, then CSUF; Cal State Long Beach, then CSULB; but say "Cal Poly Pomona" on subsequent references as well as first reference. Note also that four of the campuses have neither "Cal State" nor "Cal Poly" in their names (San Jose State, San Diego State, San Francisco State, and Humboldt State).

C. The abbreviation USC (the University of Southern California) may be used on first reference.

D. When referring to the state university system, "California State University and Colleges" may be used on first reference. On second reference use "state university system" instead of "CSUC" wherever possible to avoid reader confusion.

E. *The Associated Students, Inc.,* must be spelled out on first reference if used as a noun. If an adjective (as in "AS president"), it may be abbreviated without periods. On subsequent references, it is abbreviated except in direct quotes.

F. To indicate specific rooms use this style: H-213 for room 213 of the Humanities Building. Also use "multipurpose room A and B," not capitalized.

G. When you abbreviate *California* (as with a city name), say "Calif.," not "CA."

H. Full-time equivalent units should be spelled out and explained on first reference. "FTE" is okay thereafter.

I. Refer to the Cal State Fullerton newspaper as the Daily Titan (no italics) or the paper, but not "the Titan."

J. Avoid using abbreviations for organizations or groups not known to the general student body. As a general rule, spell out names on first reference and avoid using an acronym even on later references whenever it might cause confusion.

III. Punctuation

A. Apostrophe in years is omitted: 1960s, not '60s.

B. To show possessive in names ending in *s* simply add an apostrophe: Andy Williams' music.

C. The possessive of *Titans* (as used in sports) is *Titans'*.

D. It's *redshirted* (one word), not *red-shirted*.

E. Lists of three or more names are handled as follows: "Scholarship winners include Bob Brown, Jose Cruz and Susan Smith" (no comma before *and*). However, if the list includes titles, punctuate it thus: "Officers are Bob Brown, president; Jose Cruz, vice-president; and Susan Smith, secretary-treasurer."

IV. Numerals

A. Spell out numbers below 10 and use Arabic numbers for 10 and above. For dates, times, percentages, measurements and heights use Arabic numbers at all times. Check AP style before submitting any story containing frequent references to numbers.

B. For dates, times, ages, heights and game scores use styles suggested in the *AP Stylebook*. However, note that the Daily Titan policy is to refer to events that have occurred or will occur within seven days of the date of publication by the day alone, while using only the date (that is, month and day) for events further into the past or future.

C. To list a phone extension, use the word *extension* (spelled out): extension 218.

V. Names

A. Always refer to a person by full name and title on first reference. Do not use the middle initial except when a person requests it. Acceptable when requested: the first initial and a middle name, such as Dr. L. Donald Shields, university president. On second reference, use the last name or some secondary identification.

B. Refer to AP style for use of "Dr." with a name as a title. There is a distinction between a medical doctor and other holders of doctoral degrees. In the Daily Titan, use the title "Dr." only once when referring to persons holding academic (that is, nonmedical) degrees. On subsequent references use last names alone.

C. Never use Mr., Mrs., Miss, or Ms. as a courtesy title with a name. Refer to a woman as you would a man, using her last name alone on second reference.

D. In general, do not use a first name alone in a story.

E. Avoid sexist references, such as "If anyone is interested, he may . . ." or "If a student is fined, he . . ." Also avoid using "One may pay . . ." Instead, say "Students may pay . . ." Use a plural noun so the appropriate pronoun is *they* wherever possible.

F. Use "representative" or "spokesperson," not "spokesman." Do not use "chairman" for academic department heads. Instead say "Communications Department chair," for instance.

VI. Specific Usages

A. Movies, books, plays, songs, and so forth, follow AP style and are set off by quotation marks, not italics. Periodicals such as newspapers and magazines are not even set off by quotation marks.

B. Use American spellings instead of British ones unless the British usage is part of an official title as it is in Cal State Fullerton's Theatre Department.

C. Use the date (for example, Jan. 13) for events more than a week from the day of publication, but use only the day (for example, Thursday) and not the date for events within a week of publication.

VII. Spelling

The following words are often misspelled or may be spelled more than one way. Here is the spelling we use:

adviser
all-American
bureaucracy
bylaws (one word, not capitalized, no hyphen)
employee (not *employe*)
goodbye
grammar
judgment
percent (one word)

principle (a rule or concept)
principal (someone or something of importance)
professor
weird (e before i; note that i comes first in wield)

Please check anything not covered here in the AP Stylebook.

The Copy Desk Function

When a reporter writes a story and submits it to the editor, much work still must be done before the story can be published. It must be copy edited and possibly even rewritten. In addition, crucial decisions must be made about which stories are important enough to justify prominent placement on the front page and which should be relegated to a small spot on an inside page. (This function is called *news play* or *news judgment*.) Finally, a suitable headline must be written.

These functions are just as important as the writing process itself, and some of them may take more time than the reporter spent writing the story in the first place.

The copy desk is the last line of defense against major errors—errors that could cause the newspaper embarrassment or possibly even lead to a lawsuit. The copy desk is where awkward sentences, misspelled words and factual errors ranging from the trivial to the monumental are supposed to be caught. It is where the gaps in stories are filled in: sometimes a reporter may be too close to his or her subject to realize that the story leaves important questions unanswered. Finally, the copy desk has the last shot at anything that might cause a legal problem.

The copy desk is often where the headlines are written, although college newspapers may assign that responsibility to page editors. Sometimes the news judgments are made at the copy desk, although the responsibility for that function also varies from one newspaper to another. Often an editorial board composed of the major editors makes these decisions. On still other newspaper staffs, news decisions may be made by the editor in chief or managing editor.

COPY EDITING

Copy editing is one of the most vital jobs in a newsroom. Most of the nation's leading dailies recognize this fact by paying copy editors salaries at least as high as those paid to experienced reporters—and often higher. Many reporters are *promoted* to the copy desk—and the move is indeed considered a promotion on many newspapers. Granted, some journalists would rather be in the field than be confined to a desk job as copy editors are, but others look forward to and relish a copy editor's responsibilities. Editing copy—and doing it quickly but thoroughly—is a high calling.

A good copy editor looks for many different potential problems as he or she reads a reporter's story. First of all, of course, the copy editor is looking for factual errors.

Some errors are obvious; others are so inconspicuous they may slip by all but the most alert editors. Copy editors must constantly check the facts against standard reference books ranging from the local telephone directory to a major encyclopedia. In addition, copy editors try to be alert for internal contradictions in a story. Do the facts given in the first paragraph agree with the facts given later?

Moreover, the copy editor has to watch for gaps in the facts. Is the whole story here? Is there other information that might improve a story? If the editor decides more facts are needed, the reporter must be informed that additional investigation will be necessary before the story can be published.

In addition to fact-checking, a copy editor must be concerned with the legal implications of a story. Is there anything that might expose the newspaper to the risk of a lawsuit? If so, is the risk worth taking in the interest of reporting the news? That may be a difficult decision, but it is a decision copy editors often must make, sometimes in consultation with the newspaper's lawyer.

While a copy editor is watching for factual and legal problems, he or she is also looking for all sorts of mechanical and writing problems. Is the story clear? Is there any way to say it better? Does the story take ten words to say something that could be explained in five? Does the story flow well, or is it choppy and confusing? Is the story readable, or does it have a high *Fog Index* (discussed in Chapter 2)?

Finally, the copy editor must catch the little errors that can cause big problems if they occur often. Are there any spelling or grammatical mistakes? Are there any style errors?

Let's take a closer look at each of these kinds of problems.

Getting the Facts Right

No newspaper can maintain its credibility for long if it contains many factual errors. Fact-checking is one of the most important parts of copy editing, but it isn't an easy task. To show you why, we'll present a story that might have a problem.

In the interest of fairness, throughout this chapter we use hypothetical examples instead of examples taken from real college newspapers. Our hypothetical school is called Fallsdale State University, and it has an enrollment of 12,000. The campus paper is published three days a week. See if you can tell what major problem, if any, this story might have:

> Five Fallsdale students have won scholarships from the Irving G. Melville Foundation.
>
> The foundation, headquartered in New York, awards scholarships to more than 1,000 students each year on college campuses all over America.

The awards, announced today, are based on financial need and academic achievement. Each student will receive a $500 grant that may be used for any purpose.

The winners from Fallsdale are Roxanne Farber, a senior journalism major; John Lopez, a junior P.E. major; Traci Miklos, a senior majoring in history; Gil Miller, a freshman whose major is undecided; Paul Scott, a junior computer science major; and Heidi Smith, a senior business major.

Do you see anything wrong with this story, from a factual standpoint? Do you really have enough information to say for sure that there is or isn't a factual error?

If you're an alert copy reader, you know exactly what the problem is. The story says there are five scholarship winners, but the list includes six names. Which is correct?

How do you deal with this sort of problem? Do you just change the lead so it says there are six local winners? That may be the right thing to do, but suppose the lead was correct and the person who wrote the story inadvertently included the name of one scholarship winner from another school. A story such as this almost certainly originated as a press release from the foundation, and it would not be difficult for the person who did the rewrite to include an extra name by accident.

We'll say more about rewriting press releases later, but the first step in checking the facts in a story like this one is to go back to the original release. The reporter who rewrites a press release should turn in the original release along with the story precisely because the editors may need to check something in the release itself.

If the release has the same error as the reporter's story, then the foundation will have to be contacted before the story can be published. Professionally written press releases almost always include the name and phone number of someone to contact for more information, and that person should be called if the error was in the original release. The public relations person who wrote it will probably waste no time in getting you the correct information.

However, if a story with a major factual error was based on a staff member's original reporting, the first step is to contact the staff member. He or she, in turn, may have to get back to the news source and that may take time. The story may have to be delayed for an issue, but it's better to have it right later than to publish an incorrect story now. There's probably no reason this particular story could not be held for later publication. If the story simply must be published right away, one solution is to write around the error, eliminating the specific statement about how many students won scholarships. Another possibility is to consult a student directory, which might reveal whether all six of these people are in fact students on campus.

Reading Critically

When you edit copy, you may come across many potential factual errors, not all of them involving direct contradictions. But you can spot other factual errors if you learn to read stories critically. Here's another example:

> The board of trustees last night approved a $27.2 million 1983–84 budget for Fallsdale State University.
>
> The new budget, up 5 percent from the current year, earmarks $1.5 million to build the new gymnasium. Also, faculty salaries will be up by $2.1 million.
>
> In voting to grant the professors' pay hike, the trustees expressed regret that there had been no increase for two consecutive years.
>
> "I wish we could've given our faculty a bigger salary increase to make up for last year, but the money just wasn't there," said board Chairman Paul Joselyn.

Do you see the problem in this story? It shouldn't take a math major to spot several discrepancies.

The problem, of course, is that the budget couldn't possibly be up just 5 percent with all the new spending listed in the second paragraph—unless drastic cuts were made elsewhere in the budget. And if that were the case, it would be a very newsworthy angle, something that should clearly be reported before the marginally newsworthy quote from the board chairman.

Whenever you see a number or a percentage such as this, you should double-check it. If a story says the budget totals $27.2 million and is up 5 percent from last year, it's not hard to calculate last year's budget. If it says there was a 5 percent increase, divide this year's budget ($27.2 million) by 1.05 and you'll have last year's budget, which turns out to be $25.9 million. Then if you subtract last year's budget from the new budget, you will have the actual dollar increase, which is $1.3 million in this case. Then you can see that the claimed new spending far exceeds this amount.

Once you know there's a discrepancy, you will need to do some additional fact-checking. Probably the president's office, or perhaps a vice-president for finance, will have the correct figures. If yours is a public institution, the budget is almost certainly a matter of public record; you have a right to see it. Even at a private college, the administration would have every reason to want the correct numbers and percentages published rather than contradictory ones.

This sample story also raises some other factual questions. Read the story again, and see if you can spot any other major gaps in the reporting. To write a more complete story, what other information would you need? Think about it for a minute.

If you decided you would like to know why the board chairman is apologizing for what appears to be a monstrous faculty salary increase, you're certainly onto one angle that needs further investigating. Assuming that half of the university's total budget is for faculty salaries—and even that is probably guessing on the high side—that would mean about $13.5 million is budgeted for salaries. Let's see how that checks out. A $2.1 million increase would mean about $11.4 million was spent on faculty salaries last year. Now, let's find out what percentage salary increase this is. Dividing $2.1 million by $11.4 million, we see that this represents a whopping 18 percent faculty salary increase. Even if the university spent two-thirds of last year's total budget on faculty salaries (which is unlikely), the pay increase would still be about 12 percent.

In this age of tight budgets, such a pay increase would be a bonanza for almost any faculty. The board chairman certainly wouldn't be apologizing for such a large pay raise—except maybe to the taxpayers.

There's also another obvious problem in the story. It says $1.5 million is budgeted to build a gymnasium. Is that supposed to be the total cost of the gymnasium? At today's prices, that sum would barely pay for the planning and site preparation for a college gymnasium. Maybe the story is correct because most of the funding is coming from some other source, but if that is the case the story shouldn't flatly say the $1.5 million is "to build the new gymnasium." That sentence certainly warrants further checking.

In general, a good copy editor looks at the facts, questioning everything a story says. Could it possibly be wrong? Does it seem implausible?

Beware Superlatives

In addition to numbers, there are other potential problem areas involving the facts. Check out this story:

> For the first time in Fallsdale State's 107-year history, a student will graduate with a perfect 4.0 grade average.
>
> John O'Connell, an electrical engineering major, is the valedictorian of the 1984 June graduating class, and will receive summa cum laude honors at next Friday's ceremony.
>
> O'Connell, who plans to enter graduate school at Stanford University next fall, is. . . .

That's a nice little story. Wouldn't it be wonderful to have an academic record like that? He's going to graduate school, but he could probably earn a lot of money if he decided to go into private industry instead. He might make a good subject for a feature, eh?

If you said yes in response to those questions, you're undoubtedly right on all counts. But if your journalistic sense of skepticism didn't get the better of you, you may not be looking at the facts critically enough. There's probably no reason to doubt that O'Connell really is graduating with a 4.0 (straight A) average and going on to grad school. These facts are easy enough to verify. What is questionable is that no other student in 107 years has ever maintained a 4.0 grade average.

Whenever you see a superlative like this, you should be suspicious. When a story says something or someone is the best, the worst, the first, the last or the only one of its kind, be careful. The odds very often are against such a superlative being true, and it should certainly be double-checked. Does anyone who's around now really know the grade records of every student who attended the school 50 or 100 years ago? Has someone really gone back through every student's transcript to check the accuracy of that statement? Most colleges have a student graduating with a straight-A average at least every few years.

It might be safe to say O'Connell is the first student in recent years to graduate with a 4.0 average, but to be certain he's really the first in history would require extensive research. If the registrar's office has the documentation, that's terrific. Go ahead and say it. But if the story is merely based on someone's hunch, you should be wary.

Facts, names, numbers, percentages, titles and superlatives invite errors. As a copy editor, you should be suspicious enough to question everything and believe nothing until you know there's documentation. A copy editor has to be a professional skeptic. Every engineering student learns Murphy's Law: if anything can go wrong, it will. Every journalism student should learn a corollary to that: if a fact looks wrong, it may be wrong, but if it couldn't possibly be wrong, it's probably wrong. That's why you always check the facts.

Legal Pitfalls

An even more serious problem than the threat of publishing an embarrassing factual error is the danger of publishing something that may produce a lawsuit. Probably more lawsuits have resulted from slipups on the copy desk than from all of the deliberate personal attacks ever printed in American newspapers.

The primary legal danger that the copy desk has to watch for is libel. (Chapter 13 discusses the law of libel in detail, and it should be read in conjunction with this section.) Briefly, a newspaper risks a libel suit whenever it publishes a story that is defamatory (that is, it may hurt someone's reputation), unless one of the libel *defenses* exists. These defenses include *truth* and *privilege* (which applies to accurate reporting of certain kinds of public records and public meetings). Also, expressions of *opinion* that are clearly labeled as such are given broad protection under the U.S. Constitution and, in most states, under a libel defense known as *fair comment*. The media have some extra leeway in covering the activities of public figures, but no editor should count on getting away with publishing a defamatory story just because it's about a celebrity or politician.

Because of the way libel law is written, a heavy burden rests on the copy desk of every newspaper: the copy editors have to be certain that every story that might hurt anyone's reputation falls within one of the libel defenses. And if you quote a statement made by a news source, it's not enough to prove that you quoted the source accurately. Rather, the newspaper is usually responsible for the substantive truth of the statement itself. If the statement is libelous, both the person who said it and the newspaper that reported it may be sued.

Let's talk about some specific situations that may be dangerous.

Any story that might damage someone's reputation should put the copy reader on guard. Be particularly careful with stories involving any hint of crime, unethical behavior, incompetence, low moral standards, involvement with unsavory people or membership in unpopular organizations.

When you have this kind of story, be careful about the *identification*. Incorrect or imprecise identifications have produced numerous lawsuits—lawsuits that could have been avoided if the copy desk had been more alert. The *Washington Post* once lost a libel suit for reporting that a lawyer named Harry Kennedy was accused of a serious crime. That was completely true, but there were two lawyers in town named Harry Kennedy, and the one charged with the crime liked to use his middle initials, identifying himself as "Harry P. L. Kennedy." The other Harry Kennedy didn't normally use his middle initial. The problem was that the *Post* just said "Harry Kennedy" in the story, even though referring to Harry P. L. Kennedy.[1] As a result, the other Harry Kennedy sued for libel and won.

The *Los Angeles Times* once had a similar problem. There were two medical doctors in southern California with similar names: R. Allen Behrendt and Ralph A. Behrend. Not only did they have the same initials and almost identical last names, but they had also worked at the same hospital in the small town of Banning, California. Dr. Behrend was arrested for alleged theft and use of narcotics, and the *Times* spelled his name *Behrendt*. For putting a *t* at the end of the doctor's name, the *Times* faced a big lawsuit—from the real Dr. Behrendt.[2]

In these cases and dozens of others like them, an alert copy editor could have prevented a lawsuit. Whenever a story might be libelous, be as specific as possible in identifying the person: use the full name, address and occupation. And then recheck the spelling of the name. If your identifications aren't specific enough, you may libel innocent people with the guilty.

Even if the identification is accurate, crime stories can be dangerous. If the story is based on an accurate report of a public record (such as charges being filed against someone in an official court proceeding), there is little danger. But if there's a police investigation and someone has been questioned by police without being charged with a crime, the story is loaded with potential for libel. Never say someone is suspected or accused of a crime until formal charges have been filed. Even then, be sure to use qualifiers such as *accused* or *alleged*, although they provide only partial protection.

Courts have often considered the use of a qualifier such as *alleged* as a mitigating factor in deciding libel cases—and it's certainly better to include the qualifiers than to leave them out—but more than one libel judgment has been won by an "alleged murderer" who was later exonerated. Another thing to remember about qualifiers is that they may not fit in the headline. Numerous libel suits have resulted from stories that were perfectly safe—but with headlines that weren't so safe.

Newspapers publish stories that could cause libel suits every day and get away with it. But hundreds of libel suits are filed every year against newspapers, including student newspapers. When dealing with a story that reflects badly on someone's reputation, you have to be very precise in reporting the facts.

Editing for Mechanics

Once you've checked a story for factual accuracy, gaps in the facts and potential libel, the major task is editing for *writing quality*. In so doing, you're looking for two things: good writing and adherence to the rules of spelling, style and grammar. We'll discuss mechanical problems first.

In this chapter, we cannot cover everything you'll find in a good book on English composition,[3] but there are a few mechanical errors that seem to be so commonplace they deserve special mention here.

One chronic problem involves *comma splices* and *run-on sentences*. Here's an example:

John Smith has trouble with grammar he failed English 100.

This is a run-on sentence. It is really two sentences, each with its own subject and predicate. However, the two simply run together without any punctuation to separate them. Now, suppose we add a comma:

John Smith has trouble with grammar, he failed English 100.

This is called a comma splice. There are still two separate sentences, and a comma is not an appropriate way of linking them. Here's one proper way to link the two:

John Smith has trouble with grammar; he failed English 100.

Although a comma cannot ordinarily be used to link two complete sentences, a semicolon will do the job. So will a colon (:) or a dash (—). There are also other ways to solve the problem. One is to *subordinate* one sentence to the other, making it a dependent clause. Here's an example:

Because John Smith has trouble with grammar, he failed English 100.

If we add a word to transform one of the two sentences into a dependent clause, the result is a grammatically correct sentence. Another way to solve the problem is to add a *conjunction* between the two sentences to link them.

John Smith has trouble with grammar, and he failed English 100.

A conjunction corrects the problem, but there is something you should consider about conjunctions: there aren't very many legitimate ones. Suppose you had this sentence:

John Smith has trouble with grammar, however he passed English 100 by studying hard.

To make the sentence make sense, we had to change the meaning, but does the use of *however* as a linking word bother you? It should. As it is used here, *however* is *not* a conjunction. There are circumstances under which *however* can be a conjunction, but this isn't one of those circumstances. If you link two complete sentences with *however,* what you have is grammatically incorrect. *However* is not equivalent to the word *but. But* is a conjunction and could be used as a linking word in our sample sentence. Other conjunctions that could be used to link two sentences in this fashion include *and, for, or, nor, yet* and *so.*

However may be used as a connective adverb to provide a transition between two separate sentences. Here's how our sample sentences should be punctuated to use *however* correctly:

John Smith has trouble with grammar. However, he passed English 100 by studying hard.

Good transitions are important to good writing; this use of *however* is not only correct but also recommended. Other transitional words that could be used in the same way include *nevertheless, furthermore, moreover, therefore* and *thus.* Any of these words may appear at the beginning of a sentence, often followed by a comma. They may also be used in the middle of the sentence, as in this example:

He passed English 100, however, by studying hard.

Another major problem area in grammar is the use and misuse of possessives. Suppose you find this in a story:

. . . at several university's in the area.

We see this sort of usage often in student newspapers, but it's not correct. In that phrase, a *plural* word (that is, *universities*) is needed, not a possessive. However, sometimes a possessive is needed, as in this example:

. . . at the university's new downtown campus.

That one is correct, but what about this?

. . . at the universities' new downtown campus.

This example is correct only if two or more universities are jointly operating a new downtown campus. Let's summarize the basic rules on possessives:

1. If a word is singular, add 's to make it possessive unless the word already ends in s. If the word ends in s, you normally add only the apostrophe (') after the s to make it possessive.

2. If a word is plural, you usually just put an apostrophe on the end to make it possessive (*universities* is plural; *universities'* is plural and possessive).

3. Never put an apostrophe next to an s at the end of a word if it's not possessive or a contraction. However, notice that *it's* always means *it is*. If you want to use the possessive form of the pronoun *it*, the correct form is *its* with no apostrophe. For instance, you would say, "It's time to go home." On the other hand, you would say, "This car is ahead of its time." If you can't replace *it's* with *it is*, the apostrophe doesn't belong there.

Another troubling grammatical problem for journalists is putting commas in the right place in *appositives*. Here is an example of an appositive with commas where they belong:

John Smith, president of the Ad Club, resigned today.

Because journalists are taught to identify everyone they name in their stories, appositives appear in news copy very frequently. And often there's only one comma when there should be either two commas or no commas. *Never use just one comma in an identification unless it's at the end of a sentence.* It is correct to say "John Smith, Ad Club president, announced . . ." It is also correct to say "Ad Club President John Smith announced . . ." But what about this one?

President of the Ad Club, John Smith resigned today.

This example is incorrect. You cannot use just one comma here. That title is too long to precede the name anyway, but if you must use it before the name, do it this way:

The president of the Ad Club, John Smith, resigned today.

You must have two commas in this appositive use. *It is not correct to place a title before a name and set it off with only one comma unless the name is at the end of a sentence.* Moreover, it is incorrect to use any commas in a title before the name unless the title and not the name is the subject of the sentence. It is incorrect to say, "President of the Ad Club, John Smith, resigned today." To make "president of the Ad Club" the subject rather than the modifier, you need an article in front of it: "*The* president of the Ad Club, John Smith, resigned today."

To summarize, unless you begin the title with *a, an* or *the,* you cannot use any commas in a title that precedes a name. If you do begin with one of these words, you *must* have *two* commas (one on each side of the name) unless the name is at the end of a sentence and is followed by a period. If the title comes after the name, you always use two commas to set off the title—again except at the end of a sentence.

Using Adjectives and Adverbs

Knowing when to use adverbs and adjectives (and when to avoid them) is also important for a copy editor. They have a place in newswriting, but just barely. They're more at home in features and opinion pieces, but even there they can be overused. It is tempting to use a phrase such as this: "Some 500 students waited in a long registration line." *Long* is superfluous: few 500-person lines are short. The adverb *some* is vague, but perhaps necessary: does anyone know exactly how many students were there? *About* might be a better word.

Adjectives can add color and strength to a sentence, but they can also clutter it up. If an adjective does not add important new information, don't use it.

Likewise, adverbs can be misused. They tend to look like afterthoughts; writers sometimes add them to attributions when they aren't needed. To say "he shouted forcefully" or "she said cheerfully" is often unnecessary. If the verb itself is a strong one, the adverb adds little new information.

Using Verbs

Another basic rule of journalistic writing is to choose verbs carefully. Verbs carry connotations that you may or may not want. To say "he claimed" is quite different from saying "he pointed out." *Claimed* implies that the writer doubts the statement, while *pointed out* suggests that the writer believes it. These verbs should be used only when you intend those connotations.

There's nothing wrong with using *said* repeatedly in a story. Verbs such as *contended, announced, declared, asked* or *argued* may also be used—but sparingly.

In general, the active voice is preferable to the passive in journalism. It's usually better to say "Smith won the election" than "The election was won by Smith." However, there is an exception: in a lead you may want to emphasize the "what" angle over the "who" angle, and it may be necessary to use the passive voice to do that.

Using Parentheses, Colons, Semicolons and Dashes

Another device that can enhance your writing is the use of parentheses, colons (:), semicolons (;) and dashes (—). If you want to present two closely related thoughts in one sentence, you may use one of these devices. You could say, "Adjectives may be used—or misused—in newswriting." Or you could say, "Adjectives may be used (or misused) in newswriting." Dashes tend to emphasize the phrase or sentence inside them, while parentheses de-emphasize what's inside.

Semicolons may be used to append a thought at the end of a sentence. The second thought should also be a complete sentence. This quotation is correctly punctuated: "Correct punctuation makes writing easier to read; it tells readers where to pause."

The colon may be used to precede appositives, summaries, lists, quotations and explanations. In this text we sometimes use a colon before quotations and examples.

Spelling Errors

Turning to other copy editing problems, we have a suggestion: never try to read copy unless both a dictionary and your style guide are within reach. Spelling errors are painfully obvious to some readers. Many of your readers may not realize it if you libel someone or get a major fact confused, but a spelling error sits there on the page, advertising the mediocrity of the copy reading.

Another journalistic corollary to Murphy's Law is this one: the likelihood of a word being misspelled is directly proportional to the type size in which it appears. When copy editing and proofreading, it's a good idea to check the headlines *first*.

Editing for Writing Quality

Often the most time-consuming job on the copy desk is not editing, but rewriting. It is a copy editor's job to catch not only factual, legal and mechanical problems, but also to make the writing as clear and concise as possible. In a newspaper, space is valuable. So is the reader's time. Don't waste time and space by using ten words to say something that can be said more clearly in five or six words. Your goal is to *communicate*, not to impress anyone with your vocabulary. Don't use a big word if a little one conveys the same meaning.

Chapter 2 discussed readability formulas. It is important to remember what we said there. In newswriting, avoid long sentences whenever possible. And particularly avoid a whole series of long sentences.

But quality writing consists of more than just little words and short sentences. The writing must also *flow*. That means the writing must move through the subject without abrupt lurches and jumps. Even in straight newswriting, transitions are necessary to carry you from one subject to the next. Figure 2.1 (p. 17) shows a multifaceted news story that flows well despite the many elements that had to be woven together into a single unit.

The Problem of Editorializing

A copy editor has to consider several other potential problems in each story. For instance, he or she must watch for improper instances of editorializing.

Most newspapers now give their writers considerable freedom to draw conclusions, but excessive editorializing still occurs.

It is generally considered acceptable for a newswriter to present the facts and then explain to the reader what the facts may mean. But expressing *value judgments* is another matter. It is, for instance, one thing to report that a college budget deficit will probably lead to a tuition increase. But it's another matter to say that the prospect is alarming or outrageous. If a news source says it, it's fine to quote the source as expressing outrage. However, a reporter isn't supposed to express such opinions on his or her own authority. That prerogative is reserved for the editorial writer.

A copy editor should be on the lookout for editorializing in news stories. The reporter may be too close to the story to see the editorializing as a problem, but it may be a problem for readers who expect objectivity in the campus paper.

The concept of objectivity also includes balance. One of the questions a copy editor has to ask about each story is whether it is fair to all sides of an issue. If the story involves an issue on which opinion is divided, are all points of view included? Does the story give roughly equal space to each competing viewpoint? If not, is it possible to have someone seek out those whose views are not included?

Moreover, fairness includes *positional balance*. It is not enough to give the same number of column inches to each side. Fairness also requires that you give each side equal prominence: you should avoid burying one side by presenting all of the arguments for the other side first.

Attribution Problems

Another thing the copy reader has to watch for is *attribution*. Are the quotations and other expressions of opinion all attributed to their sources? All of the quotes should have attribution, although it is not always mandatory to use the source's name. As Chapter 14 explains, sometimes a reporter may properly promise confidentiality to a news source. But even then, the story needs attribution, even if it's something like this:

> Tuition will be increased $25 per unit next fall, according to a source in the administration who asked not to be identified.

A story about a tuition increase is clearly newsworthy in a college newspaper; the story certainly should be published as soon as it can be documented adequately, even though an official announcement may be months away. At some point, attribution to an unnamed source may be the only way out. This is obviously a difficult ethical dilemma.

The Problem of Blue-Penciling

As we conclude this discussion of copy editing, we should mention another ethical dilemma faced by copy readers. How much should one student rewrite another's story?

There's no question that having your copy rewritten is a learning experience. Many of us have benefited tremendously from an editor's blue-penciling. But there comes a time when the rewriting may be purely preferential. Sometimes there is more than one good way to say something; if a reporter's story is clear, concise, factually accurate and mechanically correct, it may not be wise to make extensive revisions. Even if you would personally prefer to say it in different words, perhaps you should refrain from wholesale rewriting if the story is sound as submitted.

We're not saying a story that is incomplete, incorrect or unclear should go through untouched. The whole point of copy reading is to improve the writing whenever possible. But there comes a time to give a writer some creative freedom—and the satisfaction of seeing his or her *own* words in print.

REWRITING PRESS RELEASES

One of the things that journalists often must do is edit (or rewrite) press releases. A great many of the stories that appear in newspapers—some estimates run as high as 75 percent—begin as press releases. There's no question but that press releases are important sources of information for the news media.

However, a journalist who is asked to edit a press release should bear in mind that the public relations practitioner who wrote it probably has a different purpose than does the newspaper. The PR practitioner is an employee or agent of an organization: his or her job is to secure favorable publicity for that organization, not to offer a balanced presentation covering all possible angles on a given issue.

This doesn't mean there is anything inherently dishonest about press releases or the practice of public relations. To the contrary, the Public Relations Society of America has a tough code of ethics, and most PR practitioners try hard to adhere to the ethical standards of their profession.

Nevertheless, a PR practitioner is not obligated to cover all of the angles to a story that a journalist might consider newsworthy. Press releases vary widely in their scope and purposes as well as in their quality.

Some press releases merely announce an event that is clearly newsworthy. The local symphony association may have an upcoming concert series that it wishes to publicize, for instance. The release will announce the times, dates and programs for the concerts, and a newspaper would normally have no reason to doubt the completeness or accuracy of the press release. Editing a release such as this might involve nothing more than making it conform to the newspaper's style and perhaps cutting it to fit into the space available.

However, some newspapers completely rewrite all news releases, even well-written ones from local civic organizations. The reason: the release may have been sent to other media as well, and the only way to be sure that exactly the same story doesn't appear in another paper is to rewrite. Occasionally a release is sent as an *exclusive* or *special* to one newspaper. That means no other medium received that release, and it may be published without fear of its appearing elsewhere.

Aside from news releases that announce public events, press releases fall into several categories. Some are intended to promote a cause—and the cause may be very much in the public interest. Releases about fund-raising drives for local civic organizations fall into this category. Like announcements of local events, these releases are often suitable for publication with little editing except for style and length.

Newspapers also receive many releases from organizations that may or may not be committed to public service but that have a newsworthy local angle. A local resident may have won an award or accepted a new position in a company. On a college campus such releases may announce that a student has received a scholarship or perhaps secured an internship with a company. While these news releases may be newsworthy, they tend to require rewriting. Many organizations send out releases with local names in their leads but with the remainder of the story amounting to free advertising for the group or company's goals or products. It is not unusual to find a release with a newsworthy lead about a local person—followed by two pages of pure advertising.

Even worse than these is the news release that completely lacks news. Many corporations and institutions send out hundreds of releases a year, often to mailing lists of thousands of media ranging from campus newspapers to the national television networks. The releases may be purely commercial in nature, or they may be intended to help build a good public image for the organization. On the other hand, the release may be from a politician who is trying to secure free publicity by declaring his or her opposition to every national vice ever invented.

The entertainment industry—motion picture producers, recording companies and the like—tend to blanket student newspapers with "news" releases. The release is likely to be one long editorial puffing the movie or artist. It seems doubtful that a campus paper is really serving its students by publishing such releases very often. Publishing a staff-written review is one thing, but running a Hollywood publicist's handout is quite another.

On page 94 is a hypothetical corporate news release with a newsworthy angle, followed by a rewrite appropriate for a college newspaper.

Although Bayshore Minisystems and the people named in the story are fictitious, hundreds of stories like this one arrive in newspaper offices every year. Because there is a local angle, a campus newspaper might publish a rewritten and much shorter version, such as the story that follows the news release.

News from:
Bayshore Minisystems, Inc.
10101 Silicon Valley Blvd.
Siliconvale, Calif. 90000

For further information call:
Mike Megabyte
(408) 999–9999

Fallsdale Student Wins Scholarship

William J. Reesin, a junior computer science major at Fallsdale State University, has been awarded a $5,000 scholarship by Bayshore Minisystems, Inc.

Reesin, who will graduate next June, will serve as an intern at Bayshore this summer. He will assist in the preparation of new programs for Bayshore's line of small business computers, which offer price and performance features unparalleled in the minicomputer mainframe industry.

Bayshore, which last year grossed $772 million, is a leading manufacturer of both minicomputer mainframes and peripherals such as high-resolution user-oriented video terminals.

The company, formed only five years ago, surged to the top in its field on the initiative and creativity of Charles J. Roos and Martin Marvinsen, the company's founders.

Today Bayshore mainframes provide dependable service in 44 countries on five continents in applications such as inventory control, payroll, accounts payable, accounts receivable and word processing.

> William J. Reesin, a junior computer science major, has won a $5,000 scholarship from a computer firm.
>
> Reesin, who will graduate next June, will be a programmer for Bayshore Minisystems, Inc., this summer.
>
> (Find out more about Reesin himself or end the story at this point).

Some college newspapers—especially at large universities—probably wouldn't run such a story in any form. But from the viewpoint of the corporate PR person, it can't hurt to give it a try. If it runs, the company gets a lot of free publicity among college students who might soon be prospective employees or customers. If the release ends up in the editor's trash, all that's lost is a postage stamp.

In sum, press releases often provide valuable information to college newspapers. Perhaps the release can't be published as submitted, but at least it may provide an idea that could lead to a good story later. On the other hand, some news releases are clearly newsworthy and can be published almost as submitted.

NEWS JUDGMENTS

It is difficult to talk about copy editing without discussing a related topic—news values. In this chapter, we've already suggested that a story about an impending tuition increase or the college budget would be newsworthy to most college and university newspapers. And we've said that a local angle may make a press release newsworthy.

An important part of editing is deciding which stories to play prominently, and which ones to bury on inside pages. Those decisions should be based on a knowledge of both news values in general and the campus in particular. Some stories may be far more newsworthy (or controversial) on one campus than on another.

For example, a story about a distinguished designer coming to speak about careers in art and design might not make a very big splash at a large university that attracts hundreds of distinguished visitors every semester. But at a small art school, it could be the lead story in the campus paper.

Or consider this example. When a photographer for *Playboy* magazine made the rounds of the Southwest (athletic) Conference to shoot a photo series on "Women of the Southwest Conference," there was little reaction at most of the campuses he visited. Predictably, at most of the universities about the only reaction to the news story about the event was from women who wanted to be photographed—and from a few of the curious who wanted to see it happen. But at Baylor University, a conservative church-related school, the result was a furor that led to a mass firing of the student newspaper's editors. This controversy is discussed in Chapter 12.

An issue that produces nothing but yawns on one campus may bring a major crisis at another. At any college or university, a good guideline for news judgments is that whatever affects the lives or beliefs of many students is newsworthy. In the late 1960s, the hottest issue on many campuses was the Vietnam War. Students faced the very real threat of the military draft, and even those who didn't face the draft themselves tended to oppose the war on moral grounds. Not surprisingly, campus newspapers in those days were filled with news coverage and editorial commentary about the burning issues of war and peace. In comparison, when the Soviet Union got involved in a similarly unpleasant guerrilla war in Afghanistan, there was little reaction on American college campuses and little news or editorial treatment in the campus press.

Any subject that is close to home—physically or philosophically—is more likely to be newsworthy than would be obscure or faraway matters. However, we sometimes question the lavish coverage some college papers give to the minute details of student government activities. On many college and university campuses, fewer than 10 percent of the eligible students vote in campus elections in spite of all the news coverage. And if you take a survey in a class, only a minority of the students are likely to know the names of more than one or two of their elected leaders. This isn't true at small, residential colleges, but if you attend a large commuter institution, look around and see if we aren't describing the situation at your campus.

Despite that, campus newspapers sometimes devote hundreds of column inches to a debate about how a few thousand dollars out of a million-dollar student government budget are going to be spent. A controversy over giving the Forensics Club $800 to attend a regional competition may be covered week after week, although it affects only a handful of students.

If so few students even vote in student body elections, wouldn't it be better news judgment to determine what really does interest the students and devote more space to those issues? Now we're not saying you shouldn't cover student government. It is newsworthy, of course. Indeed, inadequate reporting of student government may contribute to voter apathy on some campuses. We just wonder if student politics—as opposed to student activities—aren't given too much news play on some campuses.

But whatever may be the predominant issues and concerns on your campus, good news judgment means covering the stories that are vital and significant to your readers.

HEADLINES

Writing headlines is an art and a skill. It probably requires more word precision than any other kind of journalistic writing. The lead may have to capture the essence of a story in 25 or 30 words, but the headline has to do the same thing in as few as three or four.

DeWitt Reddick, former dean of the School of Communication at the University of Texas at Austin, said headlines have four basic functions:

1. They show the relative importance of stories by their size and placement.
2. They reveal the essence of the story.
3. They attract readers to stories.
4. They enhance page design.[4]

Rules for Writing Headlines

Over the years, a few rules about headlines have become widely accepted. The most important rule is that the headline must agree with the story and should focus on the *lead angle* in the story. If you find yourself writing a headline about something that isn't mentioned until the fifth paragraph of an inverted pyramid news story, that means one of two things: you're off the mark in your choice of material for the headline or the story has a buried lead (that is, the most important news is not in the lead). Normally, the lead of the story and the headline should focus on the same thing.

Another important rule is that headlines are usually written in the present tense even when the event occurred in the past:

**College president names
two new vice-presidents**

Obviously, the new vice-presidents have already been named, but the headline makes it sound as if it's happening right now. Newspapers try to achieve a sense of timeliness, and writing present-tense headlines is one of the ways it is done.

Some newspapers use past-tense headlines to report events that have already occurred, but they are in the minority.

However, when the story is about an event that has not yet happened, the present tense is usually abandoned and the headline makes it clear the event is in the future:

College president will announce new appointments by next week

Alternatively, the headline might be worded this way:

College president to announce new appointments by next week

When the event hasn't happened yet, it is customary to say it "will" happen or (is) "to" happen.

Another of the rules of headline writing has to do with the verbs *is* and *are*. They are often omitted from the headline when they are auxiliary or helping verbs. You would say:

Dean to speak at convocation

You would probably not say:

Dean is to speak at convocation

This brings us to a third basic headline rule: you omit the articles (*a, an* and *the*). You would not say:

The dean to speak at the convocation

Also, the word *and* is normally omitted and replaced by a comma, as in this headline:

Dean, president pledge to cooperate with staff

However, if the headline has two thoughts, each with its own *subject and verb*, the *and* is replaced by a semicolon, as in this headline:

President announces retirement; board praises his 'dedication'

The semicolon is used only if the two thoughts each have a subject and verb. For a compound subject or compound object, you use a comma instead:

President announces retirement, anticipates 'lots of fishing trips'

There are several other headline rules you should know about. For one thing, single rather than double quotation marks are normally used in headlines. Most (but not all) newspapers follow this rule.

Another rule is to avoid obscure abbreviations and unfamiliar names. Because you have so little room to maneuver when you're writing a headline, it is tempting to write in a kind of shorthand that readers may or may not understand. You may refer to people by last name only in a headline, but only if the name is thoroughly familiar to readers. Generally understood abbreviations may be used, following the same style on capitalization and periods as you would in body copy. If you're writing headlines for a college newspaper in Illinois, your readers will probably understand what you mean if you say "NIU" (all caps, no periods) in a headline when you mean "Northern Illinois University." But if you aren't sure your readers will understand what "NIU" means, don't say it.

Many newspapers follow a rule that forbids dividing *word units* between two lines of a headline. That means you would not put an adjective on one line and the noun it modifies on the next. You would try to avoid using a headline like this one:

Chemists win major award for research

The word-unit rule also forbids ending a line with a preposition, but that aspect of the rule is frequently violated, especially in one-column headlines. Sometimes headline writers find it very difficult to say anything without using a preposition at the end of a line.

Another rule you may encounter is a ban on *passive* verbs in headlines. There is general agreement that headlines with strong, active-voice verbs do a better job of attracting readers than do headlines with passive verbs. Some newspapers go so far as to forbid any use of passive verbs in headlines, at least on their news and sports pages. Whether it's a firm rule or just a recommendation, a headline such as this one should be avoided:

Research award received by chemistry department

In spite of its faults, the earlier version of the chemistry award headline is better than this one because it has an active-voice verb.

Capitalization in headlines is a controversial issue. There are two basic philosophies about it. Some newspapers take the view that a headline is really a title and should be treated in much the same way as the title of a book or magazine article. That means capitalizing all of the major words in the headline, as shown here:

**Dean, President Pledge
To Cooperate with Staff**

Some newspapers go so far as to capitalize every word in the headline, even little words such as *for* and *in*. A style in which at least the major words are capitalized is called an *up style*.

On the other hand, an increasing number of newspapers take the view that the headline is really nothing more than an introduction to the story and that it should be treated as if it were a sentence in the story. Under that philosophy, it makes little sense to capitalize anything except the first word of the headline and any proper nouns or adjectives. This approach is called a *down style*, and down style headlines look like this one:

**Trustees propose merger
of science departments**

Several terms are used to describe special kinds of headlines. A *banner* is a headline that runs all the way across a newspaper page, usually in type nearly an inch high. (Headline sizes are specified in *points*, a term discussed in Chapter 10.) Except when the story is exceptionally important, most papers limit a banner headline to one line.

When a smaller headline appears below the main headline, the smaller headline is called a *deck*. Some newspapers use no secondary headlines at all today. In bygone times newspapers would use five or six decks below the main headline, each discussing a different aspect of the story. Decks are still commonly found in newspapers that use traditional makeup. Sometimes the term *deck* is used to describe *any* headline: a one-line headline may be called a *one-deck* headline.

The term *kicker* usually refers to a small headline appearing above and slightly to the left of the main headline. Sometimes a kicker is centered and may not be smaller than the main headline, but it's always above it. Kickers are underlined in some newspapers, but not in others. When there is a kicker, the main headline is usually indented about the width of two characters. Here is an example of a kicker, with its main headline:

USC, UCLA affected

NCAA announces probation
for two big universities

Note that the kicker is a separate thought that amplifies the main headline. It is *not* normally an integral part of the main headline. Most newspapers follow the policy that the main headline has to make sense even without the kicker.

Except when the headline appears below a kicker, it is usually set *flush left,* which means each line of the headline begins at the left margin rather than being centered. However, the right margin of the headline may be uneven.

Some newspapers now center their headlines, especially one-line headlines inside boxes.

A headline has to fit, but usually not exactly. It is considered acceptable if the headline falls a little short of the entire width of the column—again except in the case of banner headlines. Since headlines do have to fit within a narrow space, their wording has to be juggled to achieve the best possible fit—and the length of a headline often has to be estimated before it is set in type. That brings us to that nemesis of headline writers: counting headlines.

Headline Counting

Headline counting is nothing more than a way to estimate whether a headline will fit in a given column width before typesetting it. Each typeface and size has a *count* of a certain number of *units* per column. For instance, the count for a one-inch-high banner headline on a full-size newspaper page often comes to about 35 units. That means the headline writer must come up with a headline that counts out to 35 units or at least comes very close to that. Because the counts vary with the size and style of headlines used, there is no one set of headline counts that will work everywhere. There should be a headline count chart for your typefaces mounted on the wall in your newsroom.

In counting headlines, most lowercase letters are worth one unit each. However, the two fattest letters (*m* and *w*) count one and one-half units each, while the four skinniest lowercase letters (the letters that spell the word *lift*) almost always count only one-half unit apiece. But there are a few typestyles in which *f* and *t* count as a full unit. In many type families the lowercase letters *j* and *r* also count as just one-half unit.

Most capital letters count one and one-half units each, but in many typefaces a capital *I* counts one unit, and the capitals *M* and *W* count two units each. The spaces between words are sometimes counted as one-half and at other times as one full unit, depending on how much the particular newspaper chooses to squeeze words together. Numerals usually count as one unit, while most punctuation marks count as one-half unit.

If you try counting headlines by adding these half and whole units, you're apt to find it tedious and frustrating, at least at first. Some people can tally up all the halves and one-and-one-halves without difficulty, but others have to do it slowly. Some people put marks below the line for each full unit and marks above the line for half units. Here's an illustration of how a banner headline would be counted using this method:

Half units: 1   1   1   1 1 1 1 1 111   111 11   11111

Michigan beats OSU, takes Big Ten title

Full units: 11 11 111 111 1 111   1111 1 1 111   1

Using the counting method just described, this headline has a total of thirty-four and one-half units. There are twenty-four full units (marked below the headline) and twenty-one half units (marked above the headline). If the spaces between words were counted as full units instead of half units, the headline would have thirty-seven and one-half units, and it would not fit if the correct count is thirty-five. In general, the headline can be a little under the full count, but not over it.

There are several alternate ways to count headlines. One, suggested by Roy Wilson, journalism professor at California's College of the Desert, uses dashes for half units and vertical lines for full units. To some editors, that seems less confusing that the use of marks above and below the line. Another method is to count each word separately and write down the total. Then the totals for all of the words are summed. This makes it easier to substitute words when the first headline doesn't fit.

Because counting headlines by any of these methods is time-consuming, some newspapers tell their headline writers simply to assume that every letter, number, punctuation mark and space is worth one unit. On the average, that system usually yields numbers not far from the correct ones. And it has the big advantage that it allows the headline to be counted on an ordinary typewriter. If you set your left margin at zero and then just type the words you want, you can immediately see the count on the typewriter. Some daily newspapers have used this method successfully for years.

However, technology is now rescuing journalists from all of the drudgery of counting headlines. Some video display terminals (now used at most professional daily newspapers) are capable of precisely counting headlines as the writer enters the words. Thus, the VDT tells the writer immediately if the headline will fit. But if you don't have VDTs yet, you will have to count your headlines manually for the time being.

Once you've mastered the technique of counting headlines, the challenge of headline writing is to think of *synonyms*. Decide what you want to say in the headline, and then look for words to substitute if the original words don't fit.

Headline writing is admittedly something of an art: some people find it to be easy; others don't. There are really no limits on the creativity that is possible in headline writing. Some headlines use puns or alliteration (several words starting with the same letter in the alphabet). Others simply summarize the news in a clear, no-nonsense way. Sports editors probably write more than their share of "cute" headlines, and most readers seem to accept that tendency philosophically, if not enthusiastically.

On the other hand, editorial page headlines tend toward the somber. Although the normal rule is that a headline should have a verb—and preferably a strong action verb—many newspapers use no verbs at all in the headlines for staff-written editorials. These headlines are really titles and nothing more.

Headline writing for the news pages should probably fall somewhere between the deadly serious mood of the editorial page and the sometimes frivolous mood of the sports page. But regardless of which part of the paper you are writing for, headline writing can be a challenge, and a lot of journalists think it's fun, too.

REFERENCES

1. *Washington Post* v. *Kennedy*, 3 F.2d 207 (1924).

2. *Behrendt* v. *Times-Mirror Corp.*, 30 C.A.2d 77 (1939).

3. See Jane Walpole's, *A Writer's Guide: Easy Ground Rules For Successful Written English* (Englewood Cliffs, N.J.: Prentice-Hall, 1980), pp. 22–29.

4. DeWitt C. Reddick, *The Mass Media and the School Newspaper* (Belmont, Calif.: Wadsworth, 1976), pp. 295–304.

Recruiting and Organizing a Staff

I n essence, there are two ways to run a college newspaper: a few editors can do all of the work themselves, or they can recruit and motivate other people to help with the job.

If the goal is to produce a first-rate publication without the key staff members devoting their whole lives to the job, then good recruiting and organizational methods are vital. A well-organized staff should be able to produce an eight-page weekly tabloid, for instance, without anyone (even the top editor) spending more than perhaps eight or ten hours a week on the job. It takes more time to produce a campus daily, of course, and that makes it even more important for the top editors to recruit a good staff and delegate responsibility to that staff.

Putting out the campus newspaper is *not* a full-time job—at least it shouldn't be. Everyone on the staff has other responsibilities. The secret of keeping the size of the job within bounds is for everyone to know his or her responsibilities and to do the job efficiently.

Of course, a campus newsroom tends to become something of a clubhouse; when that happens, many staff members are there far more than they really need to be, just because it is a warm and friendly place. That's good, but it also creates a dilemma.

It is important for staff members to feel welcome in the newsroom—even if they're not on assignment at that particular moment. However, it's hard to work efficiently with a group of your friends standing around your desk being sociable. The newsroom should be a clubhouse but not too much of a clubhouse.

A related problem is the all-night production and pasteup sessions that occur on some campuses. Some staffs almost seem to enjoy holding these all-night gatherings to put the paper to bed. Perhaps these sessions have a unifying effect on a staff, but the hard fact is that something else inevitably suffers. We have listened sympathetically as students explained away missed assignments and tests by saying, "We were up all night putting out the paper." Unfortunately, faculty members in other departments are less sympathetic, and even journalism professors have a right to expect students to fulfill their academic obligations too.

To be successful and stay sane, student editors have to find ways to recruit big enough staffs—and organize them well enough—to get the paper out without anybody staying up all night, failing classes or losing an off-campus job. Other things besides the newspaper are important, even to dedicated campus journalists.

RECRUITING ON AND OFF CAMPUS

A lot of people think only athletic coaches go out and recruit, but recruiting goes on in other fields—including journalism. Like coaches, newspaper advisers often play a central role in this process, assisted by students and perhaps alumni. Some advisers see it as the key to the success of their programs.

"The most important foundation of any program [is] R-E-C-R-U-I-T-I-N-G," says Steve Ames, adviser of the Pepperdine University *Graphic*, a Pacemaker Award winner.[1]

Actually, recruiting is a two-step process. First, you have to get good journalism students to choose your college. And second, you have to get them onto the news staff—and keep them there. At many large universities, student newspaper editors and faculty advisers can only watch helplessly as hundreds of talented journalism students pass through the revolving door, serving their required time (if any) on the paper and then moving on.

In fact, faculty members at state universities disagree about the recruiting process. Joseph E. Spevak, a former adviser to the San Diego State University *Daily Aztec*, says recruiting for the newspaper staff doesn't really occur at the university level. Rather, universities recruit for the total journalism program, he says.[2]

That's more true on some campuses than on others. Rick Pullen, head of the news-editorial sequence at California State University, Fullerton, emphasizes the importance of recruiting specifically for the student newspaper. "We actively recruit high school and community college students for the *Daily Titan* staff, and we give the best ones scholarships," he says.[3]

In any case, recruiting takes many forms. A student newspaper with a winning tradition often gets new recruits just because of its reputation. The presence of good journalism students and a good newspaper on a campus attracts more good journalism students.

But there are other ways to recruit, too. Even when the recruiting is for the journalism program as a whole rather than just for the newspaper, the newspaper surely benefits.

Recruiting Methods

Many journalism departments conduct high-school press days, send out the college paper to high-school newspaper staffs and offer scholarships to attract students. Some also send out representatives—often students as well as faculty—to recruit new students.

Perhaps typical of the recruiting methods at many colleges are those used at San Jose City College. Journalism instructor Art Carey points out that his program faces difficult recruiting problems: his campus "is housed in an aging physical plant and must compete for students with five more attractive and more modern community colleges and with a large state university only three miles away. Recruiting is necessary to stay alive."[4]

Carey uses ten recruiting methods, including these:

High-school journalism days

Audiovisual shows of the newspaper operation

Brochures

Working with counselors

On-campus person-to-person promotion

Editor exchanges with high-school newspapers

An awards program for staff members

Offering a "home-away-from-home" atmosphere[5]

Carey says counselors are his most productive sources of new staff members. He invites the counselors on his own campus to see the program and keeps them supplied with brochures to give to prospective students. And he maintains regular contact with high-school counselors.[6]

A brochure is another common recruiting device. Many colleges and universities have them for their journalism programs, and an increasing number also have brochures designed to recruit specifically for the newspaper. A typical brochure may be nothing more than one 8½-by-11-inch sheet, printed on both sides and folded twice. It can be typeset and perhaps even printed on campus at minimal cost.

Some departments go far beyond this, however. They publish magazines intended to promote their programs and display the best work of the students. Many of these publications are both impressive departmental showpieces and top recruiting tools. Some, like the excellent magazine published at Ryerson Polytechnical Institute in Toronto, Ontario, are distributed nationally or, in this case, internationally.

Another approach is to produce a newspaper-style promotional publication. San Antonio (Texas) College produces an eight-page tabloid departmental newspaper, *Dateline: SAC*. It is edited by former student newspaper staffers.[7]

Audiovisual shows illustrating the program and its facilities are also a proven recruiting tool. Sometimes staff photographers do still photos for a slide show with taped sound. The college's instructional media center will sometimes provide technical assistance on such a project. At other colleges, broadcasting or cinema students have done full productions on videotape or 16-mm film to display the program.

Once you have such a film, tape or slide show, what do you do with it? Sometimes faculty members or student editors take the AV material on recruiting trips and arrange showings at various institutions they visit.

Off-campus recruiting trips are a proven way to attract new students. Some colleges recruit only within a limited area, while others may cover an entire state or region. Community colleges often have attendance boundaries that limit the territory. Of course, like their colleagues in athletics, journalism teachers and student editors sometimes "raid" the territory of other institutions. But unlike athletes, student journalists risk few sanctions when they move to a new address to become eligible to attend their chosen college.

Some colleges are lucky enough to have special recruitment opportunities. California State University, Fresno, is in that position. Because Fresno is near the center of California, the annual conference of California's Journalism Association of Community Colleges is held there. That brings more than 500 of the state's best community college journalists from about 60 colleges to Fresno State's backyard. Arthur Margosian, a journalism professor and former dean at Fresno State, often strolls around the JACC conference, talking to students informally. However, other four-year faculty members who don't live nearby also make the annual trek to JACC, at least in part for recruiting purposes. And Margosian also makes personal visits to community colleges as much as 200 miles away.[8]

The same thing happens all over the country. Many journalism professors and student editors attend high-school and community college conferences for recruiting purposes. Some serve as panelists or competition judges, further increasing their visibility. And some set up information tables in a hotel lobby or registration area.

In general, anything that makes people aware of your program helps in recruiting, says Clifford M. Brock, author of an article on recruiting for community college journalism programs.[9]

Press Days

Perhaps the single most visible recruiting device for many colleges is a high-school or community college journalism day. Many colleges and universities have them, and some consider them to be an excellent means of attracting students. Other colleges, however, have found them to be less than a resounding success.

Typical press days use competition as the major attraction. Many include both mail-in and on-the-spot contests. In a mail-in contest, previously published materials such as news and feature stories, photographs and often entire newspapers are judged, with awards given to the winners in each category.

In an on-the-spot contest, on the other hand, all entrants do a story, photograph, page layout or ad design under deadline pressure during the press day itself. Again, the entries are judged and the winners recognized, often during an awards ceremony at the end of the press day. Such an awards ceremony is usually an emotional event, with enthusiastic cheering for the winners. It makes a good finale to a day-long program that may have included panel discussions and big-name speakers as well as the competition. Some four-year universities have separate competitions for high-school and community college students.

Some press days are steeped in tradition, having been conducted annually for many years. The University of Southern California, for instance, has held an annual press day since the 1920s. A special issue of the *Daily Trojan* is published, with front-page coverage of the awards program.

At many colleges a press day is tied in with a scholarship program. The top student award winners may be offered scholarships on the spot or invited back to compete for scholarships.

However, despite all the drama and excitement of a well-run press day, not everyone finds them productive. Some institutions, such as El Camino College near Los Angeles, have discontinued long-established press days. At El Camino, W. A. Kamrath, adviser to the El Camino *Warwhoop* (another winner of the Pacemaker Award), had more and more doubts over the 25 years he conducted an annual press day. "Finally, I did a survey in a Journalism 1 (newswriting) class, and there wasn't anyone there who had attended the press day. Press day wasn't bringing us students, so we discontinued it," Kamrath explained.[10]

Perhaps a press day is a more effective recruiting tool for a four-year university with a big scholarship budget than it is for a community college with no tuition charges—and few scholarships to offer. Certainly press days are productive recruiting tools for some colleges, but other institutions with large, successful journalism programs don't have press days. There are obviously other ways to recruit, often by simple word-of-mouth advertising.

KEEPING A STAFF

The second half of the recruiting problem for a student newspaper staff is keeping good staff members once they're on campus. This is a chronic problem at state universities, which may have hundreds of journalism majors but only a handful of people on the student newspaper staff.

On some campuses the problem is further complicated by the presence of two or more student newspapers. Often one paper is a laboratory publication in the journalism department, while the other is semi-independent or operates with student government sponsorship. Some journalism departments have rules designed to discourage their students from serving on the "other" paper. Others, of course, accept the competition as a healthy situation that forces both papers to do a better job.

Both community colleges and four-year schools that offer academic credit for work on the newspaper usually impose strict limits on the number of semesters a student may serve for credit. This policy may force motivated and capable students out prematurely, although the rule has a legitimate purpose: to assure that students get a broad liberal education and do not concentrate too much in any one field.

On some campuses offering a journalism or communication major, students are not required to serve on the newspaper staff at all. While a good argument can be made for this policy, its effect is to make on-campus recruiting much more difficult.

In the face of these kinds of problems, how do you recruit? One good way is to recruit in the journalism classes, if there are any. Most faculty members will allow—or may actually do—in-class recruiting.

Some years ago, an interesting variation was used at Nicholls State University in Thibodeaux, Louisiana. Alfred N. Delahaye, then adviser to the *Nicholls Worth*, would meet with the staff each semester after the dean's list was announced. They would select from this list students they wanted to actively recruit, and they would personally seek them out. So effective was the result, Delahaye recalled, that "at one time there was a myth you had to have a 3.5 average to be on the staff."[11]

Scholarships

Probably the most effective of all methods to recruit and keep staff members is to award scholarships—but make them contingent on the recipient's serving on the staff. That is the standard procedure with most athletic scholarships: if you quit the team, you lose the scholarship. Some colleges attach the same restriction to journalism scholarships.

For instance, some institutions have built award-winning traditions under such a system. Students must work a specified number of hours per week on one of the publication staffs to earn their scholarships. As a result, good journalism students often begin working on the publications as freshmen and remain on the staff right through their senior year. Editors (and faculty advisers) on campuses where the best students are gone after a semester or two often dream of a system like this.

The scholarship-for-staff-work system does, of course, raise questions. First, the students are tied to the program: because few can afford the tuition, they must either serve on the staff or drop out of school. Some people would question such a system on philosophical grounds. Also, the system wouldn't work at public institutions whose tuition is so minimal that scholarships are not a strong inducement. Further, many journalism and communication departments are primarily concerned about the overall program rather than the newspaper. In a department with this philosophy, it would be inappropriate to require students to work on the newspaper staff, the campus radio station or anywhere else in order to retain their scholarships.

Creating a Pleasant Work Environment

Perhaps the best recruiting device for college newspaper staffs that do not award large scholarships is to make the work and the atmosphere as pleasant as possible. That means two things: (1) you need to do what you can to build the morale; and (2) you have to be well-enough organized that the workload isn't excessive. (Much of the rest of this chapter is about staff organization; we'll discuss building morale here.)

Several things can be done to make the news staff an organization students want to belong to. Of course, working for the newspaper in and of itself is an inducement, since it offers students a creative outlet, a chance to gain recognition and opportunities to meet well-known people (among other advantages).

Many college newspapers seek to build staff morale and cohesiveness through social functions. In addition to off-campus staff parties, some staffs have retreats. This means securing a facility in a resort area and going away for the weekend. Bob Scheibel and Tom Kramer of Los Angeles Pierce, for instance, own homes in the High Sierras and regularly host staff gatherings there, in a setting dramatically different from the campus' metropolitan environment. Wil Sims of Modesto (California) College does much the same thing, but on a larger scale: he has arranged retreats where newspapers staffs from several nearby colleges can get together, sometimes in places like Yosemite National Park.[12]

The atmosphere in the staff room (or rooms) is important for staff morale. We said earlier that a staff room can be so much of a clubhouse that no one can work efficiently, but the room also has to be an inviting and friendly place. There should be desk space for everyone, and perhaps a small conference area with sofas (as well as amenities such as a small refrigerator and coffee pots), thus providing a more informal place for staff members to talk without distracting those with deadlines to meet.

If possible, the key leaders should have individual offices off the staff room, but if these offices are too private, the problem of editor-staff isolation may develop. The copy desk should have plenty of reference books and magazines. If there's no money to pay for them, check into getting used books and magazines that would otherwise be discarded by the library.

One key point: it is very important that other classes not be scheduled in the newspaper staff room(s). If other classes are scheduled there, it will be very frustrating for both the staff and the instructor of the class. For the staff it means all production may have to stop just when a deadline is imminent. For the instructor it means constant interruptions that may make orderly teaching impossible. There's no way you can shut down the student newspaper for an hour or two: the phones inevitably will ring, and people will come in. We've tried to teach classes in newspaper staff rooms and concluded it can't be done.

Money and Academic Credit

Two of the primary inducements for student newspaper staff members are, of course, money and academic credit. However, both have their limitations. Many student newspaper staffs are salaried, but the pay rarely approaches the minimum wage, given the long hours student journalists often spend on the job. The pay is almost always in the form of a fixed stipend; it is rarely an hourly salary, except for typesetting and pasteup employees. More will be said shortly about staff salaries. Academic credit is also a valuable reward, but the newspaper production course usually cannot be repeated more than two or three semesters for credit. On some campuses, it can be taken only once for credit. After that, those who choose to remain on the staff are volunteers.

An awards program is another good way to attract and motivate a staff. Most college newspaper staffs have end-of-the-semester awards dinners, with special recognition for those who have excelled in writing, advertising, photography, editing and general service to the publication. Also, many newspaper staff rooms have conspicuous and well-filled trophy cases that display the evidence of a winning tradition. If your newspaper has been an award winner, the evidence should be where everyone can see it.

To a great extent, a winning tradition perpetuates itself. When you win, make sure that fact is publicized, both on campus and around your service area.

ORGANIZING A STAFF

Norman Isaacs, who has been the chairman of the National News Council, headed a 1970 special study of student newspapers on eight campuses in the University of California system. Only two of these eight universities had journalism programs, and one of those programs has since been disbanded. Thus, the student newspapers were (and still are) semi-independent extracurricular activities.

In its follow-up guidelines, the Isaacs commission said:

The worst shortcomings and offenses found among the newspapers on the various campuses, in the commission's eyes, generally result from simple ineptitude and inexperience—sometimes from exhaustion.

For these reasons the Commission recommends journalism seminars for staffs, stipends and other attractions sufficient to assure adequate manpower, and a paid adviser for each newspaper.[13]

These recommendations were never fully implemented in the University of California system, but they are nonetheless good advice for any college that wants a quality student newspaper.

Unfortunately, doing those things would cost money that often isn't available. Still, within your campus' own financial limits, there are things you can do to improve your organization.

Editor Selection

The key person on a student newspaper staff is the editor in chief: this person must be the primary motivator and leader, even if he or she shares decision-making authority with an editorial board.

Editors are selected in many ways. At some colleges they are chosen by the faculty adviser or even by the college administration. At the other end of the spectrum, some are elected. Often some kind of student-faculty publications board makes the decision.

The editor-selection process is a touchy matter, of course. The editor has to satisfy a lot of people. Administrators want someone who won't turn the school upside down—or do anything short of that to challenge the system. Administrative censorship is a major problem for some student newspapers. On the other hand, most professors may not mind if the student newspaper does a little muckraking, and some may even enjoy it; but if the paper has problems with grammar, spelling or factual accuracy, the editor and the faculty adviser will both hear about it.

Students make a number of demands on an editor, some of them mutually exclusive. Every student organization wants favorable publicity, and many would like editorial support as well. The staff itself, of course, wants an editor who will be a good leader.

Few editors can please all of the different groups. Obviously, whoever selects the editor will have some leverage with the paper. Perhaps of all the selection methods, the one least likely to produce a qualified candidate is a general student body election—which perhaps says something about democracy. It takes time for someone to learn not only the craft of journalism but also how the newspaper itself operates. Perhaps some people really are born with leadership skills, journalistic ability or even both. But an editor needs more than those two qualities, and the lack of these other attributes may not be evident during an election campaign. Nevertheless, a number of colleges and universities elect editors, often after a board prescreens candidates for basic qualifications.

When the editor of the *Daily Bruin* at the University of California, Los Angeles (UCLA), was first chosen by student body vote, some 60 hours of hearings were required to sort out alleged improprieties in the process.[14] The process was apparently ironed out, but UCLA later switched to a system in which a communications board made the selection.

Many other large universities have boards that select the editors. Here is how Stanley L. Soffin of Michigan State describes the process at the *State News:*

The editor is selected by the State News Board of Directors in the Spring to start summer term. Editor applicants must submit [a] lengthy application and statement of goals and be interviewed by staff and board members.

Desk editors are selected by the editor. Students interested in trying out for desk editor are trained by that editor and then sit in on a tryout basis and have an informal interview with the editor.

Reporters are usually hired starting as interns. Students interested in internships apply and finalists are tested and interviewed. Exceptional students are sometimes hired on directly as reporters.[15]

While other universities with independent or semi-independent newspapers often follow similar editor-selection procedures, when the newspaper is a teaching tool in the journalism department, the journalism faculty is likely to play a major role in the process. California State University, Fresno, provides a good example of both of these systems operating simultaneously. A campus publications board governs *The Daily Collegian* and chooses its editor. But the editor of *Insight,* the lab paper in the journalism department, is selected by consensus of the journalism faculty, says journalism professor Margosian.[16]

The contrast at Fresno goes beyond editor selection. The *Daily Collegian* staff is paid expenses but not a straight salary. *Insight* staff members, on the other hand, receive three semester units of academic credit for working about ten hours a week. The *Collegian* has no faculty adviser; *Insight* does, and various professors take turns in the position. *Insight* is a full-size paper that emphasizes depth reporting on major issues, many of them off-campus. *The Daily Collegian* is a tabloid paper that emphasizes campus news.

Who staffs the independent daily if there's a journalism department newspaper? "Our students," says Margosian, "whom the faculty urge to get the daily experience."[17] Several students have been editor of both newspapers—but not simultaneously.

In the Fresno-type situation there are fairly clear lines of authority. The journalism department is responsible for what goes into *Insight* but has no say over the *Daily Collegian.* Since the journalism professors have no authority over the *Collegian's* content, they are not held accountable for it by the administration.

On some campuses the arrangement isn't that tidy. At San Diego State, for instance, journalism professor Spevak says that for many years his department had "responsibility, but not authority."[18] That is a common dilemma for faculty advisers at both two- and four-year public colleges. The student staff may have complete editorial freedom under the First Amendment, but the administration still holds the faculty adviser accountable for what goes into the paper. As many advisers will tell you, this can be an untenable position. The legal dilemma it can create is discussed in Chapter 12.

At many community colleges and smaller four-year colleges, the editor is more likely to be appointed by the faculty adviser or a faculty committee. Perhaps typical is the arrangement at San Diego City College, as described by newspaper adviser Glen Roberts. "Normally, we have an editor-in-chief and page editors. I pick the editor-in-chief. The editor and I decide together the page editors," Roberts says.[19]

If the adviser has the power to appoint—and remove—editors, the chain of command works much differently than it does if the editor is elected or appointed by an outside board. The problem of removing an editor from office is discussed later.

The Editorial Board

Most college newspapers operate with editorial decision-making authority divided between the editor in chief and an *editorial board* composed of perhaps five of the top editors. If management functions are shared by a managing editor, an executive editor or other senior editors, they also serve on the board. On some campuses, so do page editors, copy and makeup editors and perhaps other staff leaders.

The responsibilities of editorial boards are almost as varied as their composition. Usually, though, the board has the final say over the paper's positions taken in editorials (see Chapter 4). Board members may engage in vigorous debate, and perhaps vote, in the process of settling on an official position for the paper. The majority of the board usually has the final say, even if the editor in chief disagrees.

The other major responsibility of many editorial boards is to decide questions of news judgment. Often the board will meet briefly before each edition to decide which stories are important enough for page one and which will go inside. The board may even decide which will be the lead story if the front page has a traditional design with a clearly defined lead story.

Aside from these things, an editorial board may have various other management or mediation responsibilities. It might be called upon to determine which of two disputing editors will have jurisdiction over a story that overlaps their respective areas of responsibility. The board might also decide which special section gets open pages and which will be stuck with ad-heavy pages. Other major decisions such as changes in the publication schedule or the number of pages to be published may also be within the board's domain.

Obviously, the board can be a powerful force on some news staffs, usurping many of the traditional prerogatives of an editor in chief. Some colleges even have a required class in the curriculum for editorial board members. On other campuses, though, the board may be only a figurehead body with few powers. Some editorial boards almost never even meet. This, we think, is not good. There should be a balance between group decision making by the board and individual leadership by the editor.

Dividing the Workload

Below the editor in chief, there are two common staff arrangements among college newspapers. Some are organized much like professional dailies, with the responsibility divided by editorial functions. At others the responsibility is divided by pages or sections.

Not surprisingly, large campus dailies with near-professional staffs and a steady stream of deadlines often choose the professional system. Under this arrangement, copy for many different pages flows to copy editors, who run a copy desk operation with several assistants. These people may write headlines as well as read copy. Often a separate team does the page layouts, but that, too, is sometimes a copy desk responsibility. However, different people may make the story assignments.

Even with this system, there is usually a separate staff to handle the specialized areas such as sports, entertainment and, possibly, feature pages. Sometimes the senior editors are responsible for the editorial and opinion pages.

This system often includes rotating *day editors* who are responsible for overall production once a week. These day editors will be responsible for everything that happens beyond the copy desk, including page dummying and the pasteup operation. On a paper large enough to have this type of staff organization, the editors are not likely to do their own pasteups on a daily basis: several paid production employees will do that job. However, day editors (or some of the senior editors if there are no day editors) will normally be on hand during the pasteup process. (Pasteup is described in Chapter 11.)

The page-editor system is much more common among smaller dailies and weeklies. That system gives each page editor the primary responsibility for his or her page or pages. The specialization here is by content rather than by the nature of the editorial function to be performed.

Although the titles may vary, one person is the news or city editor and is responsible for page one and other hard news pages. An opinion editor or editorial editor handles the editorial page, and the sports editor handles intercollegiate athletics, intramurals and recreation. Sometimes there are separate editors for entertainment and features, or the two may be combined.

The key feature of the page-editor system is that each editor is in charge of everything that has to do with his or her page: story assignments, copy reading, page makeup and usually pasteup. This system gives each editor some experience at all of the different tasks an editor must perform, and it clearly works well. However, it is probably more efficient (in terms of the time required to do a given job well) to divide the editorial tasks by function, with one editor specializing in each.

Actually, many college papers use a combination of the two systems. Although they have page editors, some papers also have a central copy desk that reads copy for all pages of the paper. At the other end of the spectrum, even the largest dailies still have people who are really page editors (although they aren't called that) to handle specialized fields such as sports and entertainment.

In some cases, the division of labor varies from one semester to the next, depending on the skills and interests of the people available. Whatever system you adopt, the most important thing is to make sure the people chosen for each job know what their duties are—and are capable of doing them. If each person has a well-defined set of responsibilities and carries them out, the paper will run smoothly.

COMPENSATION FOR COLLEGE JOURNALISTS

Some student newspaper staff members are volunteers, but as we said earlier, most are compensated in some way—typically in money, academic credit or scholarship assistance. Of course, even without formal compensation, there are rewards in college journalism, but there has been a growing recognition lately that the staff deserves payment in something more tangible than by-lines. More and more colleges are deciding that payment should be in dollars.

However, few college editors can live on their newspaper salaries. Most could earn more money if they worked the same number of hours at a fast-food restaurant.

One study by Guido Stempel III, an Ohio University journalism professor, found that half of the 40 four-year institutions he studied paid their editors in chief at least as much as the tuition.[20] That was in 1969, however, and salaries for top editors may not have kept pace with inflation.

Even at Michigan State, where the *State News* has a daily circulation of 40,000, the top editor was earning only $135 a week in 1981. That's a fraction of what a professional editor on a paper that size would have been making. Reporters' salaries varied from $40 to $55 a week, depending on experience.[21]

These salaries aren't even close to the salary of the janitor who cleans the building, but they are quite high compared to editors' salaries at many campus newspapers. The compensation varies considerably from college to college.

Here's a description of the pay and staffing arrangement of the Northern Arizona University *Lumberjack,* a twice-weekly laboratory paper that has won the Rocky Mountain Collegiate Press Association's "outstanding newspaper" award. The information was provided by Ray Newton, chairman of the Journalism Department there.

We have paid student staff writers (eight) and three editors to cover the major campus beats. We then use students in the JLS 201-Intermediate Reporting class to cover other beats. Hence, any given semester we have about 40 student reporters who generate at least one and possibly two stories a week for use in the newspaper. These stories are evaluated and edited by faculty who teach the course. They then are routed to the student editor, who makes the decision whether to or not to use the stories. We use AP copy only when necessary. The primary use is for editing and reporting classes.[22]

At community colleges the top editors are often compensated, but not always in direct salaries. At Amarillo College the top editor receives a performance scholarship worth $1,100 per year, while other editors earn scholarships of $600 to $800 a year. Outstanding high-school journalists are recruited with $350 scholarships.

In a study of 463 two-year colleges, only one-third provided cash awards even to the top editors, but another third (34 percent) provided scholarships, tuition payments or grants, leaving only one-third of all community college editors with no compensation other than academic credit.[23]

However, most community colleges charge minimal tuition, and in California there is no tuition fee at all. Thus, even without a salary or scholarship, a community college editor may be better off financially than many of his or her four-year colleagues.

We've been discussing salaries for reporters and editors up to this point. The compensation for advertising staffs is another matter. At both community and four-year colleges, ad salespeople are almost always paid. They earn commissions of 10 to 20 percent on all ads they sell.

PERSONNEL PROBLEMS

Like other organizations, student newspapers sometimes have personnel problems. What happens when a staff member is not doing his or her job, for
whatever reason?

When the problem is with a reporter or subordinate editor, most editors in
chief have the authority to make a reassignment or even a dismissal if less
drastic measures fail. However, when the editor in chief is the problem, the
situation may be much more difficult. Even if the problem is nothing more
controversial than chronic nonperformance of duties or poor leadership, a firing
may be difficult and controversial, and a lengthy procedure may be required.

Moreover, when the "problem" is that the editor is exercising his or her
First Amendment right to speak out on a controversial issue, any firing or disciplinary action may violate the U.S. Constitution, at least if it happens at a
public institution. This issue is discussed in Chapter 12.

On campuses where a publications board selects editors, this board usually
retains the exclusive power to remove editors, too. The result is that the only
people aware of the problem (the other editors and the faculty adviser) may
have no power to do anything about it when the editor in chief isn't doing his
or her job. At best, they can file a formal complaint and seek a hearing before
the board. The editor's term may be over before any formal action can be taken.

Even on campuses where a faculty adviser has the authority to remove an
editor, it is a difficult decision. Editors are human beings, with all of the problems and distractions that everyone else must face. In our 30 years combined
experience teaching college journalism, we've seen a variety of unique and
troubling staff personnel and morale problems. We've seen editors survive and
even excel while working full-time and carrying a full academic load (simultaneously). But we've also seen editors fail all of their classes to get out the
paper, and we've seen editors neglect the paper to stay afloat academically.
We've known editors who excelled on the job while facing difficult personal
problems. We once saw a 20-year-old female editor do a terrific job amidst an
incredible domestic crisis: her mother and father were having violent fights,
and the mother eventually shot the father during one of them. Through it all,
the editor did her job—and remained calm and cheerful (on the surface, at
least).

Unfortunately, editors have been known to fail miserably in the face of far
less traumatic outside pressures. We've seen talented editors fall madly in love
and completely neglect their editorial duties. In one instance, a gifted editor
left his wife and had an affair with a staff member—who left her husband in
the process. Neither of them considered the paper much of a priority, and the
editor was eventually fired in midsemester, amidst a staff morale crisis.

Now it's certainly not unusual for two staff members to become romanti-
cally involved without any of those repercussions. Sometimes everyone goes
on doing his or her job, and almost no one else even knows about it. But at
other times, love affairs—like financial troubles, family crises and health problems—can render good staff member temporarily incompetent.

Unpleasant as it may be, there are times when tough personnel decisions are just as necessary in college journalism as in any other organizational setting. Such decisions should never be made unilaterally on the basis of personal dislikes, and they should never be made without giving the person adequate warning and time to improve; but in the end these difficult decisions are sometimes necessary.

REFERENCES

1. Steve Ames, letter to authors, 10 December 1981.

2. Telephone conversation with Joseph E. Spevak, 30 December 1981.

3. Interview with Rick D. Pullen, 18 January 1982.

4. Art Carey, "Ten Ways to Get (and Keep) Journalism Students," *Community College Journalist* 8, no. 3 (Spring 1980): 13–15.

5. Carey, "Ten Ways to Get (and Keep) Journalism Students," p. 15.

6. Carey, "Ten Ways to Get (and Keep) Journalism Students," p. 15.

7. "On the Other Hand, Look at It This Way," *Community College Journalist* 8, no. 3 (Spring 1980): 26.

8. Telephone conversation with Arthur Margosian, 30 December 1981.

9. Clifford M. Brock "Increase Visibility," *Community College Journalist* 8, no. 3 (Spring 1980): 24–26.

10. Interview with W. A. Kamrath, 14 April 1981.

11. Telephone conversation with Alfred N. Delahaye, 31 December 1981.

12. Wil Sims, "Retreat, Hell," *Community College Journalist* 6, no. 3 (Spring 1978): 4–6.

13. Report on the Special Commission on the Student Press to the President of the University of California, *The Student Newspaper* (Washington, D.C.: American Council on Education, 1970), p. 51.

14. "College Press Review," *NCCPA Review* 12 (May 1956): 7.

15. Stanley L. Soffin, letter to authors, 8 November 1981.

16. Telephone conversation with Margosian.

17. Telephone conversation with Margosian.

18. Telephone conversation with Spevak.

19. Telephone conversation with Glen Roberts, 5 November 1981.

20. Guido H. Stempel III, "Pay of College Editors up Slightly This Year," *College Press Review* 8, no. 4 (Winter/Spring 1969): 12.

21. Soffin, letter to authors.

22. Ray Newton, letter to authors, 3 November 1981.

23. Joe Mirando, "(Re)Search for Success in Student Publications," *Community College Journalist* 8, no. 1 (Fall 1979): 23–24.

Advertising and Fiscal Solvency

More than ever before, advertising pays the bills for college and university newspapers. In this era of tight government budgets, student newspapers all over the country are seeing their traditional sources of financial support erode away, forcing them to survive almost entirely on advertising revenue.

Of course, a number of major university newspapers have been self-sufficient on ad revenue for years, and some of them have million-dollar budgets. But today more and more small- and medium-size college newspapers are also relying mostly on advertising to pay the printer, the post office and the editors' salaries, if any. The taxpayers' dollars just aren't there any more.

For example, in 1978 California voters passed a state constitutional amendment that cut property taxes in half and that led to a budget crisis for state and local government agencies, including the colleges and universities. Within the first year after the tax-cutting vote, the average community college newspaper in the state sustained a 14 percent budget cut, according to one survey.[1] In the years since, even greater cuts have occurred as college officials have scrutinized every "nonessential" expenditure in their effort to balance their budgets.

Student body fees have also failed to keep up with inflation, and many campus newspapers have seen that source of revenue shrink rapidly, too. At colleges where the student fee once covered half or two-thirds of the newspaper budget, it may cover 10 to 20 percent of operating costs today.

There was a time when many college newspapers regarded advertising as a nice sideline, something you carried as a service to students and to make the paper look professional. Now a strong advertising base is absolutely essential for most college newspapers: without advertising there would be no newspaper.

Fortunately, this increasing dependency on advertising has coincided with an increasing recognition by advertisers that the college market is important. Not only do college students have money to spend while they're in school, but they are also potential lifelong customers. "A lot of advertisers feel that, if they win college students over now, they'll have loyal customers for 50 years," says Dave Parker, the professional business manager of the *Daily Titan* at Cal State Fullerton.[2]

In fact, the mere presence of full-time professionals like Parker shows just how important advertising has become to college newspapers. While students remain in control of the editorial side of most college newspapers, dozens of papers now have professional advertising and management people.

Because advertising is so vital to college newspapers today, you should know a little about it, even if your primary interests are in other areas.

ADVERTISING: AN OVERVIEW

Advertising, like so many other fields, has its own vocabulary. To talk about advertising, you need to know a little of it. Generally, newspaper advertising falls into three broad categories: *legal, classified* and *display*.

Types of Advertising

Legal advertising consists of notices about public agency budgets, calls for bids on public buildings, fictitious business name notices and court filings. Typically, legal ads are buried in columns of gray type that hardly anybody reads. Few college papers carry them: the law usually requires them to be placed in legally adjudicated general circulation newspapers.

Classified advertising consists of mostly small ads in fine print, divided up by subject matter. Most college newspapers carry this kind of advertising, and it is a good source of revenue for some. But others view classified ads as a service and publish them at little or no cost to students. At Northern Arizona University, for instance, students and faculty may place classified ads free of charge, except under a few headings such as "personals." The NAU *Lumberjack* even lets local businesses place free classified ads to list jobs and rental housing for students.[3]

The big revenue producer for college newspapers is display advertising. *Display* is a catch-all term describing almost everything except classified and legal ads. It gets its name from the fact that it usually consists of large display types and artwork. Display ads are intended to be seen; they are designed for visual and emotional impact.

One hybrid kind of advertising is called *classified display*. These ads appear in the classified section but look like display ads, with large typefaces and art. Not all college papers accept this kind of advertising.

Generally, newspaper display advertising is of two types: *retail* and *national*. Like professional papers, college papers have separate rate structures for national advertising—which is handled by large advertising agencies—and for local retail advertising, which the paper usually handles with its own sales and copy-writing people. Although it is called "retail," local display advertising doesn't always come from retail businesses. We'll say more about national and retail advertising rates shortly.

Advertisements can also be categorized another way: by their type of con-tent or purpose. In addition to advertising designed to sell a product or service, there is *image* or *institutional* advertising, *political advertising* and the *house ad*.

Image or institutional advertising is typically placed by large corporations that want to build public awareness of their policies or general product line. Some advertisers place such ads to argue for causes they believe in. Mobil Oil Corporation, for example, has engaged in extensive advertising campaigns to present its views on such matters as energy. Most ads intended to sell an idea rather than a product or service fall into this category.

Political advertising is just what the name implies: advertising intended to win voter support for a candidate or ballot proposition. Most college newspapers are willing to accept political advertising, although some require payment in advance. Apparently some political candidates overspend their campaign budgets in their zeal to get elected and then consider college papers to be last in line as the bills start to pile up.

Advertising Rates

As we said earlier, advertising rates are based on a two-tiered system, with different rate schedules for retail and national advertising. Table 8.1 shows the ad rates charged by four representative college newspapers: a community college weekly, a four-year twice-weekly paper and two university dailies.

The local retail rates are quoted by the *column inch,* a space one column wide and one inch deep. However, the rate is often based on a narrower column width than is normally used today on the news pages. At one time newspaper column widths were generally standardized, but in recent years editors have tried innovative designs with wide columns and extensive use of white space. Meanwhile, the column widths for advertising often remained unchanged or were actually made narrower so more columns of advertising could be fitted on a page. This allowed newspapers to generate more ad revenue per page

Table 8.1 Examples of College Newspaper Advertising Rates for 1981

Institution (newspaper, frequency)	Enrollment	Open rate per inch	Lowest rate per inch	National rate per line
Fullerton College (*Hornet,* weekly)	20,000*	$3.30	$2.75	$.37†
Northern Arizona U. (*Lumberjack,* twice per week)	13,000	4.15	2.95	.32
U. of Tennessee (*Daily Beacon,* daily)	30,000	4.50	3.95	.52
Michigan State U. (*State News,* daily)	40,000	5.70	4.20	.46

* Enrollment data are based on advertising rate card statements. It includes part-time as well as full-time students.

† Since there are 14 *agate lines* per inch, a rate of $.37 per line is equivalent to $5.18 per column inch. However, the net after agency discounts and commissions is much lower.

without officially raising the ad rates. It's a little like the classic tactic of candy merchandisers, who have repeatedly reduced the size of their product while maintaining or raising the price.

The proliferation of odd shapes and sizes of newspaper columns became a major problem for national advertisers in the 1970s, and it led some of them to abandon newspapers for other media. In response to that problem, the major newspapers agreed on what are called *standard advertising units,* or SAUs. They are specific ad sizes that all participating newspapers will accept. A number of college papers now accept SAU ads.

Retail rates vary with the amount of space an advertiser is willing to buy. The *open rate* is the rate charged a customer who buys only a little display advertising. A customer who signs a contract to buy advertising regularly gets a *volume discount.* As Table 8.1 shows, most college papers charge considerably less per column inch if an advertiser qualifies for a volume discount.

National advertising rates are quoted by a different unit of measurement, the *agate line.* It is an arbitrary unit of measurement based on the size of a very small type that is seldom used today. Nevertheless, it remains the standard. The term *advertising lineage* (pronounced *line-age* with a long *i*) is used by newspapers to describe the amount of advertising they have published: a newspaper that carries a lot of advertising is said to have a high *ad lineage.* Because there are 14 agate lines per inch, it is not difficult to convert the national ad rate to column inches—you just multiply it by 14. Table 8.1 shows that the *Daily Beacon* at the University of Tennessee charges $.52 per line for national advertising, so the rate figures out to $7.28 per column inch. That is much higher than the local advertising rate.

Advertising Representatives

National ad rates are higher than local rates because there are so many middlemen between the advertiser and the publisher. First of all, virtually all national advertising accounts are handled by big agencies such as the J. Walter Thompson Company or McCann-Erickson. These agencies provide extensive (and valuable) creative and research services for the advertiser, and in return they get a commission, usually 15 percent of the gross billing.

It would be impractical for individual college newspapers to solicit advertising directly from all of the advertising agencies, so they rely on national advertising representatives to deal with the agencies on their behalf. These representatives procure national advertising for many, college papers at once and collect a fee (or "discount") for their services. Several firms provide this kind of service, with CASS (Communications and Advertising Services to Students) currently the largest.

Most college papers feel it's worthwhile to have a national advertising representative, because the national "reps" not only do all of the selling but also handle many administrative details of the liaison between college newspapers and the big ad agencies.

The discounts and commissions sound complicated, but the end result is that college papers usually net about 60 to 65 percent of their quoted national advertising rates. Thus, the net income from a column inch of national advertising is only a little higher than the net from a column inch of local advertising.

There is, of course, also a commission on local advertising. Ad salespeople receive a commission of 10 to 20 percent as compensation for their efforts. Many college students have worked their way through school by selling local retail advertising.

Setting Rates

How are advertising rates determined?

In newspaper advertising the key factor in setting ad rates is *circulation*. The advertiser is concerned about something called *cost per thousand* (sometimes called *CPM*). Therefore, the higher the circulation, the higher the rate can be.

Among professional papers there is an extremely close relationship between circulation and ad rates. A paper whose CPM is even slightly higher than a competitor's is likely to lose a lot of advertising.

However, among college papers the CPM seems to fluctuate wildly. For instance, the Fullerton College *Hornet* charges an open rate of only $3.30 per column inch, while the Northern Arizona *Lumberjack,* with both a smaller circulation and a smaller campus enrollment, charges $4.15.

From an advertiser's viewpoint, undocumented circulation or student enrollment claims can be a problem. Years ago professional papers organized an auditing organization to verify circulation claims. The organization, called the Audit Bureau of Circulations, serves many newspapers and magazines, verifying their circulation. Obviously, it was created to prevent unscrupulous publishers from deceiving advertisers. Many papers proudly display the ABC seal to signify that their circulation is verified by an independent audit.

Unfortunately, few college papers participate in the ABC auditing program, for a variety of reasons. Thus, the advertiser often must take the campus paper's word for its circulation. Student enrollment is somewhat easier to verify independently, but even enrollment figures can be a bit difficult to pin down.

Some colleges quote large enrollments that include many part-time students, while others report a full-time equivalent enrollment, a lower figure. Those who base enrollment figures on the total number of warm bodies on campus argue that each of these people is a potential customer, regardless of academic status.

That may be true, but what about part-time students who come to the campus only one night per week? Suppose they're on campus early in the week, and the paper is a weekly that is published later in the week. Are they likely to see it?

These kinds of problems trouble advertisers in deciding which college newspapers are the best advertising bargains. But there are other variables, too.

Advertisers are concerned about *demographics*. Demographics describe the socioeconomic traits of people, including such factors as income and educational levels. Advertisers want to reach not just sheer numbers of people, but the right people: potential customers. Obviously, it's better to reach 5,000 students with a lot of discretionary money to spend than to reach 10,000 who are starving.

Colleges vary considerably in demographics. At some community colleges, the great majority of the students are adults who have full-time jobs and, hence, substantially more income than most full-time students. Some community college newspapers emphasize that demographic trait of their student bodies to sell more ads.

On the other hand, at major universities a disproportionate number of students tend to come from well-to-do families. Those students may purchase more than their share of luxury items. For example, the *State News* at Michigan State says that 86 percent of its readers own stereo equipment.[4]

In short, the scramble for advertising dollars leads some college newspapers to talk about their students' own income levels, while others emphasize the fact that the students' parents are prosperous. Ad selling is a battle of statistics among professional newspapers, and college newspapers play the numbers game too.

There are, of course, still other factors, such as the prestige of the institution. Some major universities get far more advertising volume than might be justified by the circulation and demographic statistics alone. When advertisers decide which college newspapers they want their ads in, they tend to think of big-name schools. Schools that excel at sports such as football often find that one of the indirect rewards is extra advertising dollars for the school newspaper.

The disparity in advertising revenue among nearby schools with similar enrollments can be substantial. For example, as of 1980 the UCLA *Daily Bruin* was bringing in about $800,000 a year in net advertising revenue, with a student enrollment of about 28,000.[5] But across the Los Angeles basin at California State University, Fullerton, an enrollment of 22,000 translated into only about $200,000 in ad revenue for the same year. And at Fullerton College, a 20,000-student community college only three miles from Cal State, the *Hornet* had only about $40,000 in ad revenue. But even that total is unusual for a community college. A 1980 survey by Florence Reynolds of Ohlone College in Fremont, California, showed the *Hornet's* budget and ad revenue to be among the state's highest.[6] In fact, the *Hornet,* like many college newspapers today, is virtually self-sufficient on ad revenue.

Fullerton College places an emphasis on advertising. Larry Taylor, the faculty adviser of the Pacemaker-winning *Hornet,* is one of the few community college newspaper advisers whose professional background is in advertising rather than editorial journalism.[7] The *Hornet* also has a comparatively large ad sales staff according to Reynolds' survey, which is summarized in Table 8.2.

A frustration faced by some student newspapers is that they actually *make money* on their advertising—but they don't get the money. For some years the

Table 8.2 California Survey of Student Newspaper Costs

College	Rank*	Budget	Staff size Editorial	Staff size Advertising	Total staff†
Orange Coast	2	$36,000	30	6	38
Pierce	4	30,000	25	12	38
Fullerton	13	30,000	15	4	27
Sacramento	14	21,300	15	2	21
Harbor	36	20,000	14	–	22
De Anza	27	18,000	16	3	33
East L.A.	20	16,000	20	1	23
San Jose	45	13,000	12	1	18
Shasta	47	12,000	25	3	34
West Valley	21	10,000	14	2	18
Los Medanos	80	9,500	20	–	22
Laney	41	9,500	–	–	25
Skyline	65	9,000	9	–	11
Sequoias	44	9,000	13	2	20
Hartnell	69	9,000	8	2	14
Santa Ana	38	8,000	15	1	23
Merced	55	8,000	6	–	8
Citrus	51	7,656	7	–	12
Contra Costa	56	7,500	18	1	20
Ohlone	70	7,200	12	3	26
Oxnard	84	6,500	13	2	17
Modesto	49	5,750	7	–	11
West Hills	91	5,500	10	–	22
Desert	79	5,000	8	1	13
Cosumnes River	75	5,000	–	–	20
Solano	59	3,000	20	–	20

SOURCE: (Compiled by Florence Reynolds, Ohlone College Newspaper Adviser. An expanded version of this data appeared as "JACC Statewide Survey of Student Newspapers, Spring, 1980," *JACC Newsletter,* 29 September 1980, p. 15.)

* The colleges are ranked according to the number of full-time students attending prior to 4:30 P.M. The ranks are based on 1978 attendance data for 106 colleges.

† The numbers of photographers, artists and graphics students on newspaper staffs are not given under separate columns but are included under "total staff."

Los Angeles Pierce College *Roundup,* for example, generated more ad revenue than its total operating budget, but college officials reallocated the profits to other things. That arrangement was finally ended in 1981, and the *Roundup* is now allowed to keep its ad revenue.

One surprising fact revealed by Reynolds' study of California community colleges is the wide discrepancy in newspaper budgets among colleges with similar enrollments. Pierce and Fullerton College have relatively large budgets, and they produce award-winning newspapers. But they also produce advertising revenue to match. That suggests that some other community college newspaper staffs might be able to generate more advertising revenue than they do now and perhaps use the money to expand their papers.

DEALING WITH ADVERTISERS AND AGENCIES

Given the importance of advertising sales to a college newspaper today, there are some practicalities about advertising to consider. For instance, one of the first steps in building an effective sales program is to develop an attractive *rate card*.

Rate Cards

Every college newspaper should have a rate card, which is a brochure setting forth all of the different ad rates that are available. The card also presents some of the demographic and circulation information that might persuade advertisers to choose the paper as an advertising medium. A good rate card is loaded with statistics to back up its claims about its readership. (Sample rate cards from Fullerton College, Northern Arizona University and the University of Tennessee, Knoxville, are shown in Figures 8.1, 8.2 and 8.3.)

Some college papers supplement their rate cards with other promotional materials. Fullerton College, for instance, provides a market description piece, printed on good 8½-by-11-inch paper stock. Headed "It Pays to Advertise in the Hornet," it presents both national and local data to support that claim. It points to a national survey showing that college papers enjoy much higher readership among college students than do professional papers.

The University of Tennessee, Knoxville, gives prospective advertisers an attractive folder with separate insert sheets printed on quality paper. The inserts tell the advertiser why the *Daily Beacon* is a good advertising buy, what products and services students and faculty buy, how to design a good ad and why a newspaper is a better bet for an advertiser than radio or television.[8]

These brochures make an impressive case for college newspaper advertising; if your paper doesn't have something like them, it might be wise to consider preparing something similar.

Ad Verification and Collections

Most advertisers expect to receive *tear sheets* (or *checking copies*) of their ad before they will pay. In fact, both local advertisers and agencies have been known to refuse to pay if their checking copies do not arrive in the agreed-to numbers.[9] College newspapers have to be sure that someone systematically provides these copies to advertisers.

A related problem is that it takes time to get checking copies to advertisers or agencies, and it takes the advertiser or agency more time to verify that the ad was published as requested. All of this delays payment. It is common for an ad to be published in one academic year or semester, with payment not forthcoming until the next, thus complicating the bookkeeping process.

In fact, bookkeeping and collecting delinquent accounts can be a major headache for college newspaper staffs, which is one reason so many colleges

Figure 8.1   Ad rate card for the *Hornet,*
Fullerton College California. Used by
permission.

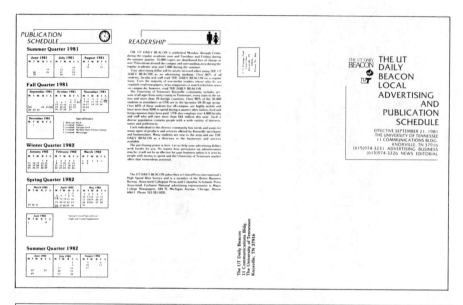

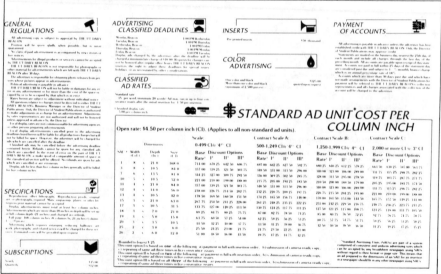

Figure 8.2   Ad rate card for the *Daily
Beacon,* University of Tennessee, Knoxville.
Used by permission.

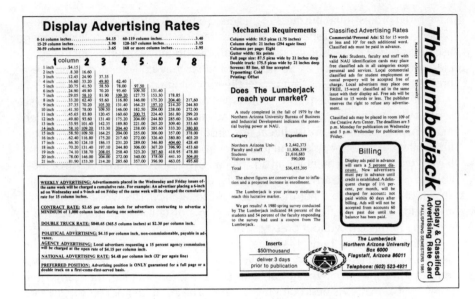

Figure 8.3 Ad rate card for the *Lumberjack,*
Northern Arizona University, Flagstaff. Used
by permission.

have hired professional business managers. Some advertisers don't take college papers very seriously, especially at bill-collection time. Many college papers use professional collection agencies to work delinquent accounts, but the agencies often keep as much as 50 percent of what they collect. Bad debts are a problem for all businesses, but especially for college newspapers.

The bad-debt problem with some types of advertising has proven to be so serious that many college papers require advance payment. As we said earlier, many papers require it for political ads. Ironically, some student newspapers find that the hardest people of all to collect from are *students*. As a result, some papers require prepayment for all ads placed by their own students. Also, most college papers require advance payment for any advertisement that comes from an out-of-town source other than a recognized agency. The worst offenders of all are ads emanating from a post office box in a distant state. Such ads should never be published without prepayment.

If the advertising budget is large, another problem is keeping track of the debts. Some college newspapers have gone to computerized accounting systems to solve that problem. At Cal State Fullerton, for instance, the *Daily Titan* purchased a small-business computer system. The computer not only takes care of the bookkeeping but also serves as a word processor to generate personal-looking form letters to prospective advertisers (and to deadbeats who haven't paid up).

The *Daily Titan* system consists of a Northstar Horizon II mainframe computer and a Televideo display terminal, which together cost about $3,500. Word processing and accounting software cost another $1,000. The *Titan* has access to a high-speed letter-quality computer printer in the Communications Department. Had it been necessary to buy a printer, that would have cost another $2,500.

Several other brands of computers, including Apple, Radio Shack and Xerox, offer similar performance capabilities in the same price range. Given the convenience it offers, such a system is worth considering if you have substantial advertising revenue. A student newspaper is, after all, a small business, and the solutions to management problems that work for other small businesses will also work in a newspaper business office.

Dealing with Merchants

Larry Taylor, adviser to the Fullerton College *Hornet,* has several suggestions for students just getting started in advertising sales. For one thing, Taylor says, ads including a coupon for students to clip and return to the merchant can be a problem. College students may enthusiastically clip a coupon that offers two pizzas for the price of one at a local restaurant, but coupons offering 10 or 20 percent discounts in clothing stores rarely get much action. Students may learn of the store from the ad and later shop there, but not many will take the coupon with them, Taylor says. Since the merchant uses the coupons to judge the effectiveness of the ad, a coupon ad can be disastrous for the college paper if only a few students show up with coupons.

Coupons can cause other problems for the unwary. For instance, if two coupons end up back to back (that is, on opposite sides of the same sheet), neither advertiser will be very happy.

Another point is that many merchants want a particular *placement* for their advertising, but there are many reasons why it may be impossible to keep a promise that an ad will appear in a certain place. A student advertising salesperson should be very careful not to make such a promise.

While magazines sell ads on the basis of a specific placement (such as the back cover) and charge a premium price for it, the practice can lead to many misunderstandings for college newspapers.

Perhaps a good policy on ad position is the one that appears in the University of Tennessee *Daily Beacon* rate card. It says, "Position will be given gladly when possible, but is never guaranteed."

Specific Products and Advertising Acceptability

One of the most controversial aspects of college newspaper advertising is the *content* of some ads. Most college papers these days accept ads for beer and wine, tobacco products and women's health care clinics that offer abortions. However, these kinds of advertising are forbidden on some campuses, either by administrative fiat or the paper's own policy.

At tax-supported universities, such advertising restrictions raise First Amendment problems. But aside from the First Amendment issue, the newspaper staff even at a tax-supported institution has a right to refuse what it deems to be unacceptable advertising. Most college papers regard their ad columns as something of an open forum, and they welcome unpopular political views along with popular ones. However, policies on this vary with the character of the institution.

Newspapers at community colleges and church-related four-year colleges are more likely to face administrative restrictions on their advertising content than are newspapers at state universities. In the case of community colleges this is ironic, because the average age of the students is typically *higher* at community colleges than at the big universities.

In recent years beer marketers have launched ambitious advertising campaigns in college papers. Many college papers get one-third to one-half of their national advertising revenue from the various brands of beer. And the tobacco companies may not be far behind.

"We expect to see a real boom in tobacco advertising in the next few years," says Cal State Fullerton business manager Parker. "The tobacco companies can't advertise on radio and television, and they see what the beer companies are doing in college newspapers."

On some campuses accepting these ads may become a hotly debated issue. On one hand, some students, faculty members and administrators will argue that cigarette smoking is a health hazard that should not be encouraged in a college newspaper. But an increasing number of college newspaper advertising managers reply that the tobacco ad dollars will only go to other media if the money-starved college press doesn't accept these ads.

And therein is the dilemma that the media face everywhere in a free society: advertising is vital to pay the bills, but advertising at times promotes causes or products of which some readers disapprove.

CIRCULATION

Since advertising revenue is so closely tied to circulation, this chapter is the appropriate place to touch briefly on the problems of college newspaper circulation.

Circulation is considered a routine chore by many staffs, but newspaper circulation problems are almost never addressed in a journalism major. Only five institutions in the United States offer full-fledged courses in circulation management.[10]

Some staffs solve their circulation problems with a red wagon—literally. The papers may be distributed to newsstands in hallways, foyers and along well-traveled walkways by a student with a wagon in tow. The "circulation manager" may be a friend of a friend of a staff member, or even the editor may end up doing the job.

The Tennessee *Daily Beacon* rate card says there are 85 free distribution points on campus. At Michigan State, the *State News* has a professional circulation manager who directs student drivers. These drivers distribute papers to every campus building, and papers are also delivered to the state capitol in nearby Lansing.

Amarillo College in Texas also pays a circulation manager to deliver papers by foot and car at its three campuses. A few college newspapers, such as the *Trade Winds* at Los Angeles Trade Technical College, have each staff member deliver papers to some of the campus distribution sites. At Imperial Valley College in southeastern California, there are only five distribution points on campus, but the paper is also distributed to local high schools.

Most college newspapers also have a mail subscription list that includes advertisers, other college newspapers, some alumni, local high schools, professional mass media and a few miscellaneous subscribers. Sometimes college clerical help can be obtained for the mailing, but not always. Many colleges have computerized mailing lists, and most have bulk mail permits to keep the costs as reasonable as possible.

An efficient circulation system is important to success of a college paper; if students, faculty and other readers can't find the paper, its influence will be sharply curtailed. In the quest for advertising revenue and solid editorial product, the problems of circulation should not be overlooked.

REFERENCES

1. Tom Pasqua, "In the Wake of Proposition 13: Journalism May Be an Endangered Program," *Community College Journalist* 7, no. 2 (Winter 1979): 4–6.

2. Interview with Dave Parker, 18 January 1982.

3. Ray Newton, letter to authors, 3 November 1981.

4. Stanley L. Soffin, letter to authors, 8 November 1981.

5. Donald M. Ferrell, "UCLA Minority Newspapers Face Financial Trouble," *Journalism Educator* 36, no. 3 (October 1981): 27–28.

5. Florence Reynolds, "JACC Statewide Survey of Student Newspaper Costs," *JACC Newsletter*, 29 September 1980, pp. 15–16.

7. All information relating to the Fullerton *Hornet* was supplied by Larry Taylor, letter to the authors, 16 November 1981, and personal conversation, 21 November 1981.

8. The University of Tennessee *Daily Beacon* information was supplied by the advertising staff, 10 December 1981.

9. Warren Mack, "Read Ad Contracts in Detail or You May Not Get Paid," *Community College Journalist* 4, no. 2 (Winter 1976): 4–5.

10. Ronald T. Farrar, "Circulation Management Project Shows Promise," *Journalism Educator* 36, no. 3 (October 1981): 44.

Creative (and Not-So-Creative) Photojournalism

Probably the first thing most readers notice about your newspaper is the photography. If it's creative and technically sound, their first impression will be a good one. If it isn't, they will think less of the paper—no matter how good the writing, news coverage and design may be.

This chapter is about photography, but it isn't about basic photographic techniques. We'll assume you—or your photographers—know how to use a camera, expose film and perform basic photo lab tasks such as developing film and making enlargements. Of necessity, we're leaving those subjects to other textbooks. But one thing we can do is offer some suggestions to improve your photography, based on our experience as judges in newspaper award competitions. By illustrating student photojournalism at its best—and at its worst—perhaps we can help you upgrade your product. First, we'll show you some classic photographic errors, errors you will probably recognize even if you aren't a photographer. Then we'll present examples of the kind of student photography that wins national awards and offer some suggestions for photo editing techniques that will complement your photography.

CLASSIC TECHNICAL ERRORS

No matter how good the photography classes may be, there are some fundamental technical errors that show up all too often in student newspapers. If you can avoid these problems, you'll be well on your way toward establishing reader confidence in your photography. Most of the photos that appear in the first half of this chapter were deliberately composed, developed or printed poorly; we'd like to thank the staff of the *Daily Titan* at California State University, Fullerton, for helping us demonstrate what not to do in photography.

The Indoor Snowstorm

Sometimes an otherwise good photograph has little white spots and wiggly lines all over it. It may look almost as if the picture got caught in a snowstorm—even if the picture was taken indoors. Figure 9.1 illustrates this problem.

The snowstorm was created in a darkroom. The person who printed the picture didn't clean the negative carefully. We'll skip the lectures about cleanliness being a

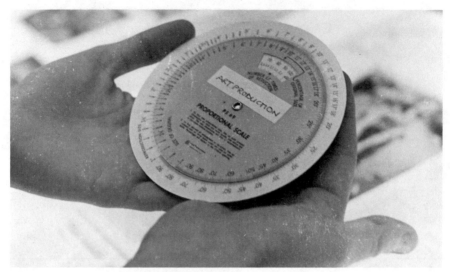

Figure 9.1   This photo is the result of a dusty negative. To see what this proportion scaling wheel is supposed to look like, check Figure 9.23, which is a similar print, but made from a negative cleaned carefully with a camel-hair brush.

virtue. It really doesn't matter whether your darkroom is a cluttered mess or something straight out of a photo textbook. What does matter is cleaning every negative with a good camel-hair brush before you make a print. And you should look at your prints carefully *under normal room light, not just under a safelight,* before you declare the job finished and dump the chemicals. If a print has snow on it when it wasn't snowing, clean the negative again and make another print. If no amount of brushing will help, you may have water marks or dust that settled on the negative while it was wet. If so, rewash the negative and soak it in a wetting agent such as Kodak Photo-Flo before drying it.

The Shaky Shutterbug

Remember what your camera's instruction manual said about holding the camera steady? Well, the photographer who came up with the photo in Figure 9.2 forgot. Even at relatively fast shutter speeds (such as 1/125 of a second), you can give a picture a fuzzy effect by moving the camera when you press the shutter.

Don't confuse this problem with either incorrect focusing or *soft* focusing. If you want a soft, portrait-like effect, you can get a special lens for that. In photojournalism, you probably won't want that effect very often, but when you do there is a way to achieve it without making everything blurry. Likewise, there's a place for pictures in which the background is deliberately out of focus.

Figure 9.2   The blurred image in this photo
is the result of camera motion. The solution:
hold the camera steady, using a tripod if
necessary.

Photographers often use a large lens opening to reduce the depth of field—so
that only the subject is in sharp focus. That, too, is fine.

However, if you were using a normal lens and everything in the picture
came out fuzzy (including both the foreground and distant objects), the problem
was most likely camera motion. There are times when you'll want to *pan* with
your camera—when you are following a fast-moving object with the camera
and want everything else in the picture to be blurred. Properly done, that can

produce a dramatic feeling of motion. But normally, you want your subject to be sharp and clear—not fuzzy.

To avoid the fuzziness problem, hold the camera steady—bracing it against a fixed object, if necessary—and gently squeeze the shutter. A faster shutter speed will help, but you should be able to get sharp pictures without a tripod at speeds of $\frac{1}{60}$ of a second or even slower. If you can't do that, you need to work on developing a steady hand with your camera. When you brace the camera against a wall, the hood of a car or some other stationary object, be careful not to let it block the lens.

Only the Shadow Knows

Strobes are wonderful gadgets. They make it possible to get news photos at times and places where you'd only get blank film if you tried to use available light. But they have their limitations. For example, if you're too close to your subject, the strobe may make your subject look like a ghost—pale white, with no facial detail (see Figure 9.3).

One solution is to use a smaller aperture (lens opening), and perhaps back away from your subject a little. If you're in a room with a low, light-colored ceiling, you can bounce the flash off the ceiling. That eliminates the harshness of direct strobe lighting. The lighting will be more diffused and there won't be many deep shadows (see Figure 9.4).

When using a strobe, you should always *bracket* exposures. No matter how "automatic" your strobe may be, try several shots, using both a smaller and larger aperture than the one recommended by your light meter or the film instructions.

There's also another thing to remember about strobe photography: if the strobe is a significant distance from the lens, you may get distracting shadows. If you can lift the strobe off its normal mount and hold it *above* the lens, the shadow will usually fall harmlessly behind and below your subject. Unfortunately, many strobes are designed to mount directly on a *hot foot* on your camera, without a *sync* cable: the hot foot is what triggers the strobe at the correct instant. If you expect to shoot news photos often, look into obtaining an accessory cable so you have the freedom to remove the strobe and vary the effect of the lighting.

Another solution to the shadow problem is to move your subject into the middle of a room, away from any wall or other surface on which a shadow might fall. Unless you have a well-lighted room, of course, the result will be a nearly black background—and that may not be desirable either.

The Textured Look

As a special effect, a textured look can be striking. A textured screen can give an otherwise ordinary picture a dramatic appearance. But ordinary graininess is another matter.

More often than not, a grainy news photo will distract your readers far more

Figure 9.3   This photo shows what happens when the strobe is too close to the subject. All of the facial detail is gone, and the result is a ghost-like appearance.

Figure 9.4   This photo was taken in exactly the same place as the one in Figure 9.3, but with the strobe light bounced off the ceiling.

than it will impress them (see Figure 9.5). In newspaper photojournalism the typical picture should be sharp and clear—the grain should not be evident to the casual viewer. If your pictures are consistently grainy, consider using a fine-grain developer. Or perhaps you're leaving the film in the developer a little too long. The graininess increases drastically if the film is left in some developers only one or two minutes too long. That's particularly true if the developer is warmer than the recommended 68 degrees Fahrenheit. And if you're "pushing" a film such as Tri-X for a higher than normal ASA rating, the grain problem will be more severe.

Of course, graininess is inevitable with extreme enlargements. If you're using a 35-mm camera, Tri-X film and a developer such as Kodak D-76, you may be pushing your luck in the graininess department if you print anything larger than 8 by 10. A film such as Panatomic-X and a fine-grain developer will help, but at the expense of film speed.

BASIC ERRORS IN COMPOSITION

A newspaper photo can be technically flawless and still be a terrible picture. Otherwise well edited college newspapers sometimes commit basic errors in photo composition, some of them so obvious you'd think they wouldn't happen.

Figure 9.5   This photo has a grain problem.
Sometimes a grainy picture can achieve a
dramatic effect, but more often it distracts
readers, who usually expect newspaper
pictures to be clear and sharp.

For years, there have been jokes about trees and telephone poles growing out
of people's heads, but pictures that violate the cardinal rules of good composition still show up all too often.

Like the basic technical flaws, these errors in composition are painfully
evident once you know what you're looking for. A few examples (Figures 9.6–
9.11) will make the problems quite apparent.

Figure 9.6   The camera angle is crucial to good photography. To see why shooting upward isn't usually recommended in portrait photography, compare this with the photos in Figures 9.3 and 9.4.

Figure 9.7   Award photos are clichés in phototojournalism. This photo could be improved by having the people stand closer together and do something other than hold the plaque. Other problems: the background is crowded and the plaque creates an unwanted reflection. Any smooth surface is a potential mirror for a strobe.

Figure 9.8   The background in this photo looks too cluttered.

Figure 9.9   This photo was taken in almost the same place as Figure 9.8, but the photographer moved closer to the subject and opened the lens several f-stops to reduce the depth of field.

THE PRINCIPLES OF COMPOSITION

Perhaps a review of the basic principles of photo composition would be helpful at this point. In photography, the term *composition* refers to the way the elements of the picture (line, tone, mass, contrast and color) are organized. Some combinations of photographic content are more aesthetically pleasing than others. A good photojournalist knows this and uses the elements of the picture to communicate a message without distracting the viewer.

In almost all cases a news photo should have a *center of interest,* a focal point. This is the thing the viewer notices first; make it the essence of your photojournalistic message. Nothing else in the photograph should distract the viewer from the focal point.

That means the background should not be distracting. As we said earlier, the background should not be cluttered. Nor should it have trees, wires, utility poles or shadows that distract the reader from the main subject of the picture. You can reduce the likelihood that the background will be distracting by having it out of focus, with the subject in sharp focus. Or you can use contrast to

Figure 9.10 Whether the object growing out of the head is a tree or a lamp post, pictures like this continue to show up in newspapers.

Figure 9.11 It's called line-em-up-and-shoot-em, and it ranks second only to ribbon-cutting and award presentation photos in its lack of creativity. So how do you pose a group of people to avoid these clichés? One suggestion: look at record album covers!

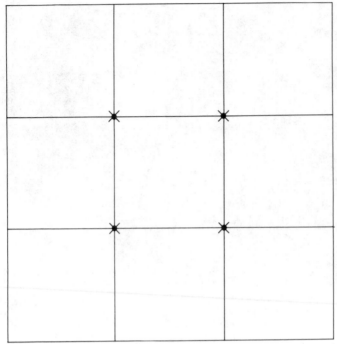

Figure 9.12   The rule of thirds is used to divide a photograph both vertically and horizontally. Any of the four points where these lines converge is a good place for the center of interest.

accentuate your subject: a brightly lighted subject against a dark background—or a dark subject silhouetted against a light background—can be effective, although these techniques should not be overused in photojournalism.

The focal point should itself be comprehensible to the viewer. That is why it's usually not good to cram eight people into a photo that will be published two columns wide if the goal is for the people to be recognizable. And that is why the subject should normally be in sharp focus and adequately lighted. Although dark silhouettes make striking photographs—and certainly have a place in photojournalism—most news photos are intended to communicate information to the reader. The reader usually wants to know what a newsworthy person looks like under normal lighting, not with special effects. There is a place for art photography in newspapers, too, but normally a newspaper photograph should *communicate*.

Another thing you should consider in setting up a picture is the *rule of thirds*. In essence, the rule of thirds says you should think of a photograph as being divided into thirds, both vertically and horizontally. As Figures 9.12 and 9.13 illustrate, the four points where the three-way dividing lines in the photo meet are good areas for the focal point in a photo. In general, it is *not* a good

Figure 9.13 This photo shows an application of the rule of thirds. It is rarely desirable to place the center of visual interest exactly in the middle of a photograph.

idea to place the focal point of a picture in dead center. Nor is it a good idea to have the foreground and background (the sky, for instance) each occupy exactly half the photograph. It is usually better to have two-thirds foreground and one-third background in such a photo.

When you place the subject near one of the three-way dividing lines in a photograph, it is usually best to have the subject looking into the picture, not out of it. Likewise, if there is motion, the motion should be into the picture, not out of it.

As you set up a picture, try a variety of *camera angles*. Sometimes it's best to stand directly in front of your subject, but more often stepping a little to one side gives a better feeling of depth. Creative photographers move around, looking for the angle that gives the best possible perspective. Some editors tell photographers to shoot an *overview* that gives the big picture and then to move in close to capture the detail.

In photographing people, the angle can be very important. Shooting from eye level is often best; if you shoot from very far above or below eye level, you will distort the proportions of the person's features—something you probably don't want to do in most news photos of people. Nevertheless, experiment with different perspectives, too. If you refer back to Figure 9.6, you'll see an example of an inappropriate camera angle.

Using wide-angle and telephoto lenses effectively also produces many award-winning photos. Sometimes a talented photographer envisions a creative way to portray something ordinary from an unusual perspective. The photographer who has interchangeable lenses—but almost always uses the normal lens—misses many opportunities for good photography.

Sometimes the key to a great photo is its emotional impact. Perhaps it captures a poignant moment in time, a moment when someone shows his feelings in a graphic way. Many of the best news photos ever taken are great because of the human emotion they reveal.

At other times good photography is a matter of freezing the action at the precise moment when the drama is highest. Great sports photos often combine high drama and emotional impact. If you capture the facial expressions of victorious (or defeated) athletes, you may come up with outstanding photos—but you must be in the right place at the right instant.

To summarize, try to shoot from a variety of angles. Get close to the subject to achieve good detail, and try shooting from farther away to present an overview. Remember to be aware of the background: it should be unobtrusive. The focal point should be in sharp focus and properly lighted, and usually it should be positioned by the rule of thirds, with the action moving into the picture, not out of it.

A GALLERY OF WINNERS

Up to now, we've been presenting mostly examples of bad photojournalism—pictures that have basic flaws of composition or technique.

The photos in Figures 9.14 through 9.22 are national award winners. Each photo is from the portfolio of a student who placed in the national photojournalism championships, sponsored by the AASDJ-Hearst Foundation Journalism Awards Program. Open to students attending any nationally accredited school or department of journalism and mass communications, the program annually awards more than $100,000 in scholarships to outstanding student journalists.

Many of these photos are memorable not because of anything inherently magical about the subject matter, but because the photographer took something very ordinary and put it in an out-of-the-ordinary perspective. The skilled photojournalist captures reality in a special way.

These photos may give you ideas for many picture possibilities on and near your own campus.

Figure 9.14   David Griffin of Ohio University
won the 1977 Hearst National
Photojournalism Championships with this
photo. Used by permission of AASDJ–Hearst
Foundation Journalism Awards Program.

Figure 9.15   Dennis Tennant of West Virginia
University took this ordinary scene and made
it unusual by moving in as close as his lens
would allow and by silhouetting one ant
against the sun. Used by permission of
AASDJ–Hearst Foundation Journalism Awards
Program.

Figure 9.16   This photo won a national
fourth place award for Dale Atkins of
Michigan State University. Used by
permission of AASDJ–Hearst Foundation
Journalism Awards Program.

Figure 9.17   College photojournalists have
fewer opportunities to cover such spot news
events as fires and floods than do their
professional counterparts, but Dan J. Dry of
Ohio University won first place in the 1976
Hearst Photojournalism Championships with
this photo. Used by permission of AASDJ–
Hearst Foundation Journalism Awards
Program.

Figure 9.18   The judges selected this photo of John Spenkelink, a convicted murderer who was about to be executed, as the best single photo entered in the 1979 Hearst National Photojournalism Championships. The photographer: Bill Wax of the University of Florida. Used by permission of AASDJ–Hearst Foundation Journalism Awards Program.

PHOTO EDITING

So far, we've shown you some outstanding student photojournalism and some examples of the basic mistakes to avoid. But taking good pictures is only part of the job in photojournalism. The other half is the photo editor's job.

Good picture editing brings out the best in a good photograph and can reduce the visual impact of the flaws in a mediocre picture.

However, it isn't always obvious whether a given photograph is excellent, mediocre or not even suitable for publication. In selecting photos for publication, an editor should consider the following:

1.   Is the photo technically sound? Does it violate any of the principles of good photography? If so, look for something else to run if possible.

2.   Is the photo aesthetically pleasing? Does it adhere to the principles of good photo composition? And does it have visual impact?

3.   Does the photo communicate, and does it communicate the message you want it to communicate? In photojournalism, you're usually looking for

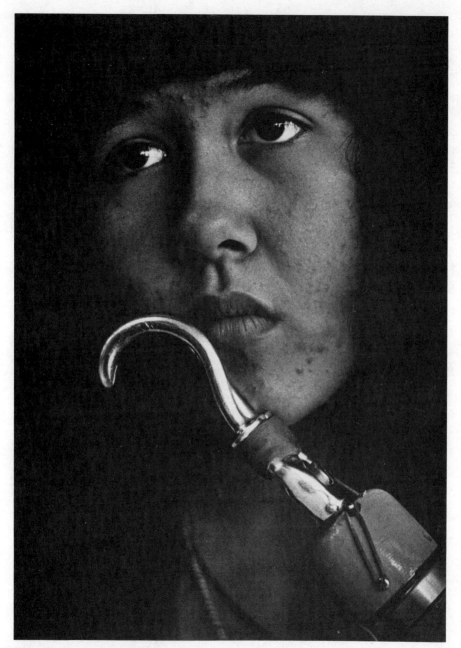

Figure 9.19.   Few pictures have the
emotional calibre of this portrait by
Michael Yada of the University of Southern
California, who won first place in the
1980 Photojournalism championships.
Used by permission of AASDJ—Hearst
Foundation Journalism Awards Program.

Figure 9.20 This football photo by Greg
Greer of the University of Missouri has a new
element: these athletes are deaf and use sign
language to call their plays. Used by
permission of AASDJ–Hearst Foundation
Journalism Awards Program.

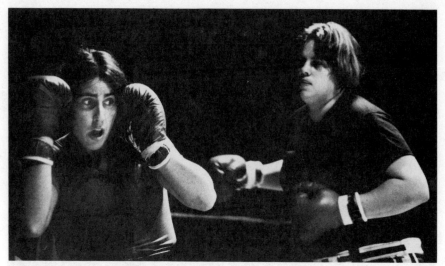

Figure 9.21   Two female boxers produced
this national award winner for Steven Zerby
of the University of Minnesota in 1981. Used
by permission of AASDJ–Hearst Foundation
Journalism Awards Program.

more than just a pretty picture: you need pictures that are newsworthy. This is not to say you shouldn't run pictures now and then just because they're photographically appealing, but you should normally run newsworthy photos in preference to those that aren't so newsworthy. However, there's nothing wrong with running a *floater* (a photo that doesn't accompany a story). But if the photo is intended to illustrate a story, does it do the job?

4. Will the photo enhance the attractiveness of the page on which it will appear? A photo is just one element in the design of a page; does it fit with everything else?

Once the decision is made to run a given photo, the next problem is deciding how to play it. Today, the rule of thumb is almost always this: if it's a good photo, run it big. Find a way to crop it so that it enhances the overall page design, and go with it.

In determining how to crop a photograph, many editors use paper or cardboard masks to experiment with various possibilities. The goal is to accentuate the subject and to crop out extraneous material. Newspaper space is valuable, and you don't want to waste it. Is there open space (or even worse, clutter) that doesn't add anything to the picture? If so, can it be cropped out without doing violence to the focal point of the picture? The classic advice here is to *crop tightly.*

Figure 9.22 Contrasting angles produced a
striking photograph for Sandy Felsenthal of
Memphis State University, first place winner
in the 1981 Hearst Photojournalism
Championships. Used by permission of
AASDJ–Hearst Foundation Journalism Awards
Program.

In addition, you should use your cropping masks to experiment with various shapes. A square photograph is rarely the ideal. Don't be afraid of cropping a photo so it will be extremely wide—or deep—if the subject matter is suited for that treatment. Almost all of the best-designed newspapers today run large photographs when the quality justifies doing so, and they freely deviate from the old, nearly square format. If the picture is a good one, don't cram it into a one- or two-column space. Almost everything except a mug shot is a candidate for better play than that. A dramatic photograph can be ruined if it's poorly cropped or crammed into too small a space. When you have an outstanding photo, give it the space it needs and crop it to accentuate its drama.

But what if you have a mediocre picture that simply must be published? Perhaps the photo can be reshot. Most of the people you photograph on college campuses are still around later. If the photo is of a breaking news event and cannot be reshot, is there a way to crop it to minimize the defects? Can the flaws be cropped out? If you absolutely must run a bad picture, and no amount of cropping will save it, perhaps it's time to consider thinking *small*. Run the picture where it will be as inconspicuous as possible.

Photo Scaling

Obviously, photos must often be enlarged and reduced to fit into fixed column widths. But when one is enlarged or reduced to a certain width, how deep will it be?

There are several simple ways to *size* photographs. Perhaps the easiest is with a *proportion scale,* often called a *sizing wheel.* (Art and drafting supply stores often sell them.) A sizing wheel, as the name implies, is round, and it has two dials (see Figure 9.23). To use the wheel, you line up the *original width* on the inside dial, and the *new width* on the outer dial. Then without moving the two scales in relation to each other, you locate the original depth on the inside dial. The new depth will be directly opposite the original depth, but on the outer dial. Many proportion scales will also tell you the percentage of enlargement or reduction necessary for the picture to fit in the intended space. If you have your photographs screened and sized by a print shop, you may be required to specify the percentage of enlargement or reduction necessary.

If your print shop does your photo screening for you, incidentally, you'll probably also need to know about *windows.* If screened negatives are to be *stripped in* to your newspaper page negatives, you will need to put dull black (or red) pieces of construction paper in the places where there are to be photos and other screened artwork. These black windows will produce clear areas on the page negative, allowing the shop to place the screened negatives of your photos on the page without actually cutting a hole in the page negative. Figure 9.24 shows a window in place on a pasteup board.

The other alternative, a process used by an increasing number of student newspapers as a cost-saving measure, is to make screened prints of your photographs in your own darkroom and deliver the pages completely camera-ready,

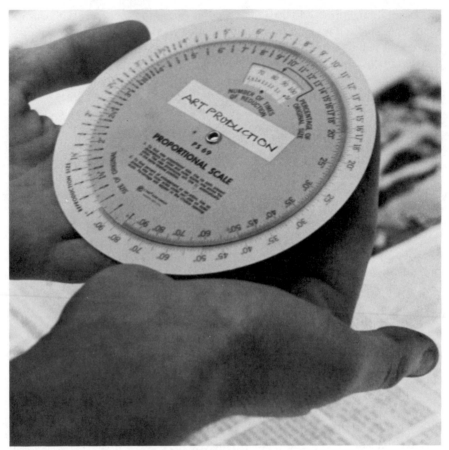

Figure 9.23 This photo shows a proportion scale, or sizing wheel. It enables an editor to quickly determine how deep a photo will be when enlarged or reduced to fit in a given column width.

with the photos in place. This allows the entire page to be photographed once, saving both the cost of additional process camera shots to screen your photos and the labor costs of stripping in the halftones. Graphic arts suppliers can provide the screens and vacuum boxes required to prescreen photographs.

But perhaps we're getting a bit technical. What we've been talking about is very familiar to some college newspaper staffs, but it may sound like gobbledygook to others. Maybe you just send the printer pages and photographs, and don't really care what happens after that. All you want to do is figure out

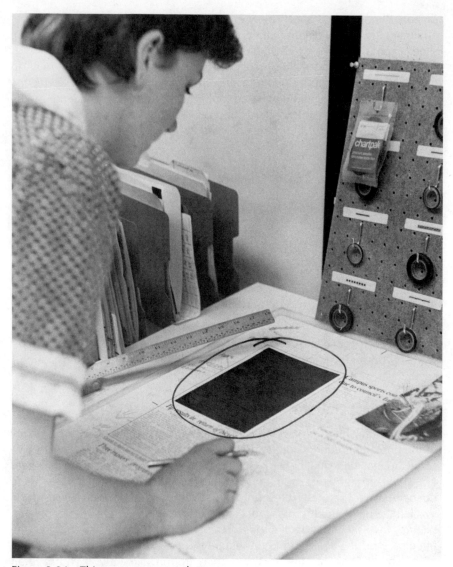

Figure 9.24 This newspaper page has a window (circled) into which a halftone (photograph) will be stripped when the print shop prepares the full-size page negative prior to offset printing. Because it is black, the window area will be unexposed on the negative.

how deep the pictures will be after they're enlarged or reduced, and you don't want to get within ten feet of a proportion scale.

Fair enough. There are two other ways to estimate the depth of a photograph after enlargement or reduction. One way is the *diagonal line* method. Draw a diagonal line across a sheet of paper the same size and shape as the picture, and mark the new width on that line. Then measure down to the bottom of the sheet. From that point, you will have the new depth (see Figure 9.25).

If you don't mind a little math, there's another quick and easy way to determine the new depth of a photo after enlargement or reduction. Divide the new width by the original width and multiply the result (the dividend) by the original depth. Here's an example. Suppose you have an 8-by-10 photograph, and you want to run it 2 columns wide (let's call that 4 inches). This is the formula you would use:

$$\frac{\text{new width}}{\text{original width}} \times \text{original depth} = \text{new depth}$$

Now let's plug in the numbers:

  original width = 8
  original depth = 10
  new width = 4

Thus:

$$\frac{4}{8} \times 10 = 5$$

Therefore, the new depth is 5 inches. You'll have to allow that much space on your dummy for the photo (and don't forget to allow extra room for the caption).

Other Considerations

In photo editing there are several other things to keep in mind besides the quality of the photo and dummying the right amount of space for it. You have to give some thought to the matter of placing the photo in a suitable place on the page.

There are some rules about photo placement. Sometimes you may want to deliberately violate these rules, but at least you should know the rules exist.

First, a photograph should not "look off the page." If there are people in a picture, they should be facing toward the center of the page, not out into the margins. And if a story and photo happen to be positioned side by side, the photo should look into the story, not away from it. Similarly, if you have an action photo, the action should appear to be moving into the page, not off into the margin.

Sometimes it is possible to *flop* a picture to make it look onto the page rather than off the page. Many editors today vehemently object to flopping pictures for any reason, because it distorts reality. But if you must do it, place the negative in the enlarger upside down and make the new print. However, be careful when you flop a picture: everything will be reversed, including lettering. If a person in a photo has any distinguishing marks on either side of his or her face, the photo should not be flopped. Also, be careful about flopping photos of musicians and athletes: you might make a southpaw of a well-known right-handed quarterback or you might make a violinist look ridiculous.

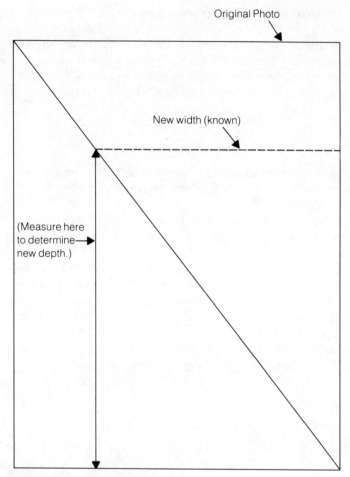

Original Photo

New width (known)

(Measure here
to determine→
new depth.)

Figure 9.25 The diagonal line method of
photo scaling.

Another rule is that a picture should not be placed on the fold if the newspaper is normally folded in half. This rule isn't usually observed on tabloid newspapers, but if yours is a full-size paper, you may want to consider it. The reasoning behind the rule, of course, is that many people have the paper folded when they read it, and they see only half of the picture at any one time. However, many of the best-designed newspapers today ignore this rule. Their editors believe the visual impact of a large photo running nearly the length of the page outweighs the disadvantages of having the picture run across the fold.

A third rule that some newspapers follow is to avoid placing editorial artwork—including photographs—too close to any advertising. One good reason for using photographs in the first place is to break up the gray appearance of the page. To put the editorial art near the display advertising—which usually has both artwork and large type, with ample white space—is a waste of the photograph.

Another consideration: most newspapers still strive to *balance* the left and right sides of their pages (see Chapter 10). This means a large photo on one side should be balanced on the other side by a strong graphic element (for example, another photo, a large headline or perhaps a boxed story).

CONCLUSION

Creative photography is one of the hallmarks of any first-rate college newspaper. Even if you consistently offer your readers brilliant reporting and modern design, they'll look at the pictures first.

If your photography is uncreative or technically slipshod, it will create a strong negative impression among your readers. No amount of editorial excellence will overcome the damage bad photography can do.

Good photography has to be a priority. It may not be your only priority, but the quest for memorable pictures should be a major goal when you produce every issue. If you take pride in any part of your product, don't tolerate mediocrity in the editorial art you publish. And when you have good photography, feel free to flaunt it: if a photo is really good enough to publish, it's good enough to display prominently. "Decide what you think a photo is worth and then run it one column larger," says one experienced college newspaper adviser.

Contemporary Design and Typography

Once you have stories, advertisements, photographs and perhaps other kinds of art, the next problem is deciding how to place all of this material on your newspaper's pages. You probably have a tight deadline, and you must quickly make some decisions about page layout.

Professional newspapers are often designed in just this way—by someone in a rush to meet a deadline. But, designers say, it shouldn't be like that. For years, graphics specialists have objected to editors' tendencies to make up their pages on the spot instead of designing them in advance. The result, they say, is often a thrown-together look. Body type, headlines, art work and ads may be indiscriminately tossed in wherever they fit, without much thought to the larger problem of designing an aesthetically pleasing product.

"The 1,750 daily newspapers and about 8,000 weeklies in the United States are divided between two basic formats: awkward and less awkward, with only a minority in the latter group," say Arthur Turnbull and Russell Baird, the authors of a well-known textbook on graphic design.[1]

Over the long history of the American newspaper, that observation usually has been true. Editors traditionally have felt that their editorial content was far more impor-

tant than the design. Moreover, many editors believed that any attempt to create an overall design for a newspaper would violate the principles of newspapering: the makeup should be determined by the day's news, and not vice versa. As a result, newspapers were often a sea of gray type, arranged in long vertical columns with no attention to the visual needs or preferences of readers.

Fortunately, that attitude has rapidly changed in recent years. Because of competition from the electronic media, covering late-breaking news seems less important than it once was, and many newspapers are moving toward a "magazine concept," attempting to analyze and explain the news instead of merely reporting facts. That has led many editors to change their thinking about newspaper design, too. Most editors today realize the importance of giving the readers an attractive package, one designed for its visual appeal.

Perhaps even more important, there has been a technological revolution in the newspaper business. No longer are newspapers set in lead type, with all of the mechanical limitations that system imposed. With today's photo-offset printing methods and *cold type* pasteup process, the newspaper designer has almost total freedom to vary the appearance of the product. Because the newspaper is reproduced photographically, the designer is free to arrange the headlines, body type and art work almost any way he or she chooses.

The result of all this has been a dramatic change in the appearance of American newspapers. Whereas most newspapers once had eight narrow columns of type, divided with column rules, most newspapers today use fewer and wider columns, with white space replacing the old column rules. Moreover, offset printing yields much better quality photo reproduction than the old letterpress method, and newspaper designers have responded to the new opportunity by publishing much larger pictures. The dominant element on many newspaper pages today is a striking photograph, not a gigantic headline. It's been said more than once that old-time editors did their screaming with black headlines, while modern editors use photography for the same purpose.

There have been other big changes in newspaper design, too. Once it was fashionable to cram as many stories as possible on the front page. It hasn't been that long since makeup editors knew they could expect an angry phone call from the publisher if the front-page story count fell below 12. The front page was a sort of headline service, telling the reader the highlights—but little else—of many stories.

Today, of course, that function is performed by radio and television newscasts. People look to their newspapers to fill in the details that could not be reported in the limited time available on radio or television. They expect the front page to present a few major stories in depth rather than have a little bit to say about everything that has happened in the last 24 hours.

This one fact has profoundly changed newspaper design. No longer do most newspapers have cluttered front pages with many headlines screaming for attention. The front page is now a much more orderly place, with only a few stories neatly arranged, often in a *modular* fashion (that is, with each story and any related artwork placed together in a rectangular module or unit).

Modular makeup is so fundamentally different from the traditional approach that many of the old terms and concepts found in editing textbooks are no longer applicable. Makeup editors used to think in terms of *brace* and *focus* makeup, with the reader supposedly being led from the upper right-hand corner to the lower corners of the page, with perhaps a brief detour to the upper left-hand corner. The corners had to be *anchored* with stories or photographs.

Page makeup is a different world today. Terms such as *focus, brace* and *anchoring the corners* have been replaced by phrases like *center of visual impact.*[2] The goal is to attract the reader's eyes to the dominant element on the page first, and from there to other modular elements of the page. In fact, the operative term today in newspaper editing is *design* rather than *makeup,* since most newspapers now have policies that describe how the paper is to look from day to day. No longer is the paper "designed" on an ad hoc basis ten minutes before the deadline.

This trend is apparent everywhere in American journalism. Even the papers whose appearance has been traditionally the most conservative have made notable changes in their design in recent years. In the late 1970s even the stately *New York Times* switched to a six-column format for its traditional hard-news pages. The *Times* abandoned its conservative makeup policies altogether for special sections such as sports.

But of all American newspapers, among the most innovative have been the nation's college and university newspapers. Long before their downtown counterparts discovered modular makeup, many campus papers developed distinctive modular formats that used wider columns of type, horizontal layouts and plenty of white space.

To illustrate the principles of typography and page design, this chapter uses award-winning college newspapers for its examples: each sample page was taken from a newspaper that has won the coveted Pacemaker Award of the American Newspaper Publishers Association, an award that goes to about ten of the nation's best college newspapers each year. There are many other very well designed college newspapers, but the papers displayed here are among the leaders in design.

AN INTRODUCTION TO TYPOGRAPHY

A good starting point for any presentation on newspaper design is to discuss type. No other single element has more effect on the look of a newspaper than the selection of typefaces.

Although there are thousands of different typefaces, they fall into several categories. Type styles fall into broad *families* bearing names such as Bodoni, Futura, Tempo, Helvetica, Garamond and Baskerville. And within each of these families a variety of *type styles* is available, including both bold and lighter versions of the same type.

Typefaces are classified in several ways. First, we describe types as either *serif* types or *sans serif* types, depending on whether the letters are embellished with little appendages called serifs. Figure 10.1 is a sample of a popular serif typeface known as Bodoni. For comparison, Figure 10.2 is a sample of Futura, a widely used sans serif typeface. Like most other sans serif faces, Futura is noted for its clean, straight lines. Compare the capital *I* in the two typefaces. The little decorations at the top and bottom of the Bodoni *I* are the serifs.

Of the two styles, the serif type is the older. At one time virtually all newspapers used serif types for everything, but in the last half century a great many papers have abandoned serif headline types, although most still use serif styles for *body type* (that is, the text matter). Readability studies have yielded some conflicting results, but the general consensus is that text matter is more readable if a serif type style is used. This may be true only because most readers are accustomed to serif rather than sans serif body type.

Of the serif type styles, Bodoni is not among the oldest. In fact, among serif typefaces Bodoni is classified as "modern." It was designed about 1788, considerably later than the serif typefaces that are classified as "old style" and

abcdefghijklmnopqrstuvwxyz
ABCDEFGHIJKLMNOPQRSTUVWXYZ
1234567890 (&.,:;!?"""'"-*$¢%/)

Figure 10.1 This is a sample of Bodoni, a
modern serif typeface.

"transitional."[3] Figure 10.3 shows a sample of Garamond, an old-style typeface that was designed about 1615, and Baskerville, a transitional typeface designed in 1757. To modern readers, these typefaces may all seem so similar that they are hard to tell apart, but at one time graphic artists made a great point of analyzing their distinguishing features. The so-called modern typefaces such as Bodoni are unique primarily in that the thickness of the lines forming the letters often varies from one side of a character to the other and in that the serifs are squared off (as opposed to the more rounded look of the serifs in earlier types).

Besides the serif versus sans serif distinction, types are classified in other ways. An *italic* type is one in which the characters lean to the right. Either a serif or sans serif type may be *italicized,* as shown in the examples of Bodoni and Futura italic in Figure 10.4. In newspaper makeup, italic types are sometimes interspersed with nonitalic (sometimes called *roman*) type of the same family to provide typographic variety. However, some newspapers use italic types sparingly if at all, feeling they are inappropriate for news pages.

A type may also be classified as *bold, condensed* or *extended.* As the name suggests, a bold type uses thicker lines than is normal for other styles in the same type family, producing a blacker appearance. On the other hand, a light version of the same type will have thinner than normal lines. A condensed style may or may not have thinner lines, but the letters are narrower and less round, which means more characters will fit into a given amount of space. Figure 10.5 shows a sample of four styles, all falling within one family: Caslon, Caslon italic, Caslon bold and Caslon bold condensed.

With so many different typefaces to choose from, how do newspapers select their typography? Like so many decisions involving aesthetic considerations, it's a matter of taste. Most newspapers today use sans serif headline types such

abcdefghijklmnopqrstuvwxyz
ABCDEFGHIJKLMNOPQRSTUVWXYZ
1234567890 (&.,:;!?'''''-*$¢%/)

Figure 10.2 This is Futura, a popular sans
serif type.

abcdefghijklmnopqrstuvwxyz
ABCDEFGHIJKLMNOPQRSTUVWXYZ
1234567890 (&.,:;!?'"""-*$¢%/£)

abcdefghijklmnopqrstuvwxyz
ABCDEFGHIJKLMNOPQRSTUVWXYZ
1234567890 (&.,:;!?'"""-*$¢%/)

Figure 10.3   Here is a sample of Garamond,
an old-style serif type (above), and Baskerville,
a transitional typeface.

as Futura, or one of the newer sans serif designs such as Helvetica or Univers. Some newspapers use sans serif types for their news pages but retain the serif type such as Bodoni for the editorial and feature sections. On the other hand, some newspapers that still use serif headlines for their news pages have switched to bold sans serif styles for their sports pages. Take a close look at the daily newspapers in your area. Which type styles do they use? Does the type selection differ from one section of the paper to the next?

Perhaps the most important single consideration about type selection is continuity. A newspaper may use entirely different families of type on its news

abcdefghijklmnopqrstuvwxyz
ABCDEFGHIJKLMNOPQRSTUVWXYZ
1234567890(&.,:;!?'"""-$¢%/£)*

abcdefghijklmnopqrstuvwxyz
ABCDEFGHIJKLMNOPQRSTUVWXYZ
1234567890 (&.,:;!?'""·$¢%/£)*

Figure 10.4   Many type families include an
italic type. Here is Bodoni bold italic (above)
and Futura italic.

abcdefghijklmnopqrstuvwxyz
ABCDEFGHIJKLMNOPQRSTUVWXYZ
1234567890(&.,:;!?'""''-[]*$¢%/£)

abcdefghijklmnopqrstuvwxyz
ABCDEFGHIJKLMNOPQRSTUVWXYZ
1234567890 (&.,:;!?'""''-$¢%/£)*

abcdefghijklmnopqrstuvwxyz
ABCDEFGHIJKLMNOPQRSTUVWXYZ
1234567890 &.,:;!?'""''-$¢

abcctdefghijklmnopqrsstttuvwxyz
ABCDEFGHIJKLMNOPQRSTUVWXYZ
1234567890 (&.,:;!?'""''-$¢%/£)

Figure 10.5   For comparison, here are four
type styles from the Caslon family: Caslon,
Caslon italic, Caslon bold and Caslon bold
condensed.

and editorial pages, but on a given page, a choice should be consistent. No
more than one or two families of type should be used for headlines on any
page, although condensed, extended, light, bold and italic versions of the same
type may be used interchangeably.

Measuring Types and Pages

As you learn about newspaper design, you'll need to learn a couple of new
units of measurement. The size of a typeface is expressed in *points,* while many
measurements in the graphic arts, including the width of newspaper columns,
are in *picas.*

Points and picas?

Basically, it's not hard to learn these units of measurement: there are about
6 picas to an inch and 72 points to an inch. If someone says a newspaper

column is 15 picas wide, that means the column is about 2½ inches wide. We keep saying "about" because a pica is just a little less than ⅙ of an inch. To be more exact, 108 picas are equal to 17 and ¹⁵⁄₁₆ inches, not precisely 18 inches. Still, the difference is so slight that journalists commonly say there are 6 picas to an inch, and for all practical purposes, they're right.

Now, let's talk about points. A point is ¹⁄₁₂ of a pica, so there are 12 points to a pica and, thus, about 72 points per inch. You need to know this because type sizes are specified in points. If you work for a newspaper very long, you'll hear a lot about 72-point type (that is, letters about an inch tall), 36-point type (half-inch letters), and 9- or 10-point type (the size of the body type in most newspapers).

However, these things are never quite as simple as they might be, and a 72-point type isn't really 1 inch tall. In fact, it isn't even 72 points tall. When type sizes were first established, the sizes were based on the overall size of a *slug* of metal type, which had little shoulders above and below the character itself. The slug was a foundation on which the character rested. A 72-point type slug was an inch from top to bottom, but the characters were smaller than that. Even though we almost never use metal type these days, the vernacular has not changed. A 72-point type has characters with a height of less than 1 inch.

In fact, a 72-point type is even smaller than you might expect, because the 72-point designation includes the height of what are called *ascenders* and *descenders*. An ascender is the portion of a lowercase letter that rises above the average height of other lowercase letters, such as the straight line of an *h* or *b*. A descender is the portion of some lowercase letters that drops below the bottom line of other letters, such as the tail on a *y* or *q*. Figure 10.6 shows descenders and ascenders.

Why does all of this matter? It matters because you'll need to know how big a 72-point capital letter is, and it's nowhere near an inch tall. In most typefaces, a 72-point capital letter is about ¾ of an inch high. In some styles, however, a 72-point capital may be as little as ⅝ of an inch high.

If you work for any newspaper for long, you'll probably have to decide when to specify a 72-point type for a headline and when to specify something much smaller, such as 24- or 30-point type. Unfortunately, you can't really think in terms of inches when you make these decisions. However, it won't take you long to get a "feel" for various type sizes. After a semester or so, most editors can look at a page and immediately tell what point size every headline is.

In dealing with types you need to know one more concept: *leading* (pronounced *ledding*). In the days of hot metal type it was customary to place thin strips of metal between the lines of type to create a more open look. It was found that body type was much more readable if the lines weren't crammed close together. The process of spreading the lines apart came to be called *leading* because strips of lead were used to separate the lines.

Although the hot metal process is no longer used, the concept of separating the lines of type is still commonly called leading. To promote readability, it is customary to add 1 or 2 points of extra space between lines. If you're using a

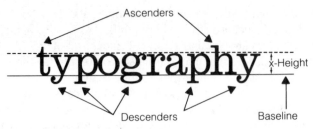

Figure 10.6   The ascenders rise above the "x-height" of the lowercase letters, while the descenders drop below the base line.

9-point body type, you will probably want to specify at least a 10-point line spacing, or 1-point leading. Figure 10.7 shows the same paragraph set in 9-point type, with no extra leading (that is, 9-point with 9-point line spacing, often called *9 on 9*), and with 1- and 3-point leading (10- and 12-point line spacing, or just "9 on 10" or "9 on 12").

So far, we've talked about type families and explained a little about serif and sans serif types, and about italic, bold and condensed styles. We've also defined points, picas and leading. While this is not a definitive summary of the principles of typography it is enough to prepare you for the discussion of newspaper design.

DESIGNING A COLLEGE PAPER

Once you understand the basic tools that are used in newspaper design, you're ready to think about designing or redesigning your college paper. Or perhaps you just want to know the advantages and disadvantages of the design you already have.

The first step is to think about basic styles and objectives. Do you want your newspaper to reflect a conservative tone? Or should it feel modern and light in tone? Do you want something a little sensational or perhaps more restrained in its presentation?

Most award-winning college papers today offer some of each of those qualities. The best-designed papers are very readable. They feature modular page designs that leave the reader with little doubt about which picture or illustration goes with which story. In such papers, you'll find a low story count on page one, perhaps only two or three stories if it's a tabloid (or half-size) paper and only a few more if it's full-size. Also, you'll find large photographs and frequent uses of nonphotographic art to explain and illustrate the stories. Many stories and their associated art may appear in boxes, with liberal use of white space.

Headlines? You'll find good college papers using a variety of typefaces, including both sans serif and clean, modern-looking serif families. Your deci-

Although the hot metal process is no longer used, the concept of separating the lines of type is still commonly called leading. To promote readability, it is customary to add 1 or 2 points of extra space between lines. If you're using a 9-point body type, you will probably want to specify at least a 10-point line spacing, or 1-point leading. Figure 10.7 shows the same paragraph set in 9-point type, with no extra leading (that is, 9-point with 9-point line spacing, often called 9 on 9), and with 1- and 3-point leading (10- and 12-point line spacing, or just "9 on 10" or "9 on 12").

Although the hot metal process is no longer used, the concept of separating the lines of type is still commonly called leading. To promote readability, it is customary to add 1 or 2 points of extra space between lines. If you're using a 9-point body type, you will probably want to specify at least a 10-point line spacing, or 1-point leading. Figure 10.7 shows the same paragraph set in 9-point type, with no extra leading (that is, 9-point with 9-point line spacing, often called 9 on 9), and with 1- and 3-point leading (10- and 12-point line spacing, or just "9 on 10" or "9 on 12").

Although the hot metal process is no longer used, the concept of separating the lines of type is still commonly called leading. To promote readability, it is customary to add 1 or 2 points of extra space between lines. If you're using a 9-point body type, you will probably want to specify at least a 10-point line spacing, or 1-point leading. Figure 10.7 shows the same paragraph set in 9-point type, with no extra leading (that is, 9-point with 9-point line spacing, often called 9 on 9), and with 1- and 3-point leading (10- and 12-point line spacing, or just "9 on 10" or "9 on 12").

Figure 10.7   These three paragraphs are set in the same typeface and the same size, but with no leading (top), 1 point of leading (center) and 3 points of leading (bottom).

sion here is likely to be dictated by personal preference—and by the practical matter of what happens to be available for your particular typesetting equipment.

Tabloid or Full-Size?

As you make preliminary design decisions, one of the most important is whether to produce a tabloid or full-size newspaper. There are pros and cons for each format.

Probably the main advantage of the full-size format is that it is the standard in the American newspaper industry. A full-size college paper looks more the way most readers probably think a "real" newspaper should look. Also, makeup experience on a full-size paper is more directly applicable in the professional world. If yours is a laboratory newspaper and staff members often go on to work with professional papers, this may be an important consideration.

There are also some financial considerations. Some advertisers will want to buy a full page or maybe a half page, regardless of the size of the page. Since you most likely sell ads by the column inch and not by the page, you can sell such an advertiser twice as much space if you have a full-size newspaper. Also, some print shops charge less than twice as much per page to print a full-size paper, which means you get more space for your printing dollar (because a full-size paper is usually twice as big as a tabloid).

On the other hand, there are advantages to the tabloid format. For one thing, a tabloid newspaper is unquestionably easier for the reader to handle than a full-size paper. Also, most designers consider the tabloid format less unwieldy than the full-size format: it's easier to design clean, attractive pages for the tabloid paper. Another advantage is that, with the smaller pages, it's much more feasible to devote an entire page (or even a two-page spread) to a single topic. You can probably have more special sections if you use the tabloid format, since you have twice as many pages to work with. Also, you have more flexibility in going to magazine format if your paper is a tabloid. You probably wouldn't think of making an entire full-size front page into a magazine-style cover, with only a photograph and perhaps a table of contents, but that's exactly what some tabloid college papers do.

Another advantage to the tabloid format is that, because the paper can be made smaller without embarrassment, a smaller staff can produce it. It's considered acceptable to produce a four-page tabloid paper, but not a two-page full-size paper (even though the two are really the same size). To put it another way, many readers think an eight-page tabloid feels more substantial than a four-page standard, even though the two have the same amount of space.

Because of the strong arguments that can be made on both sides in the tabloid versus full-size debate, some college newspapers switch back and forth now and then. That may cause havoc for the college library, which probably would like all of the bound volumes to be the same size, but perhaps it's inevitable. The *Daily Titan* at California State University, Fullerton, for instance, has switched from tabloid to full-size or vice versa no fewer than five times since it went daily in 1968, and has won makeup awards in both formats. Some colleges produce a full-size student newspaper during the regular year but drop down to a tabloid format for the summer editions. Figure 10.8 shows the *Summer Graphic* from Pepperdine University in Malibu, California. The *Graphic*, a Pacemaker Award winner in 1977 and 1981, is normally standard size, but the summer edition is a striking magazine-style tabloid.

Developing a Design Style

Chapter 5 presented an example of a student newspaper style guide that covered such purely editorial matters as capitalization, abbreviations and uses of numerals. When you develop a basic design for your newspaper, you should also have a *design style guide*.

The design style should specify the families of headlines and the size and style of body type used for various purposes. It should be specific on such

the **summer graphic**

Jackson replaces Beck as campus life director
Page 3

Intramurals sponsors backpacking trip to Havasupai Falls
Page 6 and 7

Malibu residents gather at popular marketplace
Page 9

Men's tennis team captures WCAC championship and earns invitation to NCAA playoffs
Page 10

Battle X airs Friday night, students react
Page 11

Figure 10.8   The *Summer Graphic* from Pepperdine University is a tabloid newspaper with a magazine-style front page. During the regular year the paper is full-size and uses modular newspaper makeup. Used by permission.

matters as the amount of leading, normal column widths, and whether the text is to be justified or unjustified. The term *justified* means having an even right-hand margin. *Unjustified* type is ragged or uneven on the right margin. At one time virtually all newspapers were justified, but today an increasing number are switching to the ragged-right look.

That move is by no means noncontroversial. Mario Garcia, author of a respected book on newspaper design, has this to say about the ragged-right effect:

Justified columns work best for the front page. There is a certain informality about unjustified columns that should not be present for every item carried on a typical front page. . . . One story or feature set in ragged right may create variety and help the page visually; an entire page so set may tend to look disorganized.[4]

Whether your type is to be entirely justified, entirely ragged right or a little of each, the design style should specify the newspaper's policy on this point.

The design style should also specify the policy on headlines. For instance, how large are your *banner headlines* (that is, headlines that run all the way across the page)? Many newspapers specify 60- or 72-point type for banners. And what about two-line, three-column headlines? Are they limited to 36- or 42-point type, or may they be made larger if the story justifies it?

Another consideration is whether to use *kickers,* which are overlines that appear above the main headline and are usually underlined. If so, is the main headline indented underneath the kicker? That is the usual practice.

What about the main headlines? The style guide should indicate whether they are always *flush left* (that is, even with the left margin) or whether they may also be centered. And what about headlines inside boxes? Are they centered or flush left? Also, when may the headline appear other than above the story? Within a box, a headline is sometimes positioned to the left of the story or even below it.

The style guide should also lay down ground rules for the little points on which consistency matters. How will by-lines be handled? Are they all caps? Are they centered or flush left? And what typeface and size is used for by-lines? Similarly, the rules on photo captions (or *cutlines*) should be specified. The style guide should set forth the type style and size for captions along with the rules for writing them. Do you want captions to begin with three or four words in all caps? If so, are those words to be something of a headline, followed by a dash, or are they just the first words of the opening sentence?

Another question a design style guide should address is *jumps.* When are stories to be continued on an inside page? There is general agreement that many readers will not bother to follow a jump: perhaps fewer than 50 percent of those who read the first part of a story will turn to an inside page to read the rest. On the other hand, many stories simply cannot be given adequate treatment on page one, so jumps may be inevitable. But if you jump stories, what is the policy on inside-page headlines for them? And what about *continued* lines? How will they be treated?

Perhaps most important of all, the design style should specify the basic look of the paper. Will it be modular or more traditional? What special sections will be published, and how often? What about the headline schedule? Which families and styles will be used in each section? All of the general policies that determine the look of the paper should be addressed in a design style guide.

Examples of College Newspaper Design

Obviously, designing or redesigning a college newspaper is a major undertaking. Figure 10.9 is a feature story that appeared in the Pepperdine University *Graphic* in 1980, describing how one staff approached the job of redesigning a paper that had already won numerous awards for its design, including an ANPA Pacemaker. (Shortly after the redesign, the paper won another Pacemaker.)

Figure 10.10 shows three front pages from the Pepperdine *Graphic:* one before the redesign effort, one immediately afterward and one a year later, when the staff switched to a sans serif headline schedule. Note that the new headline schedule includes some very condensed styles. Some designers would question that change, arguing that the condensed styles are not really modern. Moreover, some also question the extensive use of ragged-right body type; the earlier design with its sans serif headlines and justified text would be more "modern," in their view.

Newspaper design is obviously a very subjective thing. What really matters is whether a given design is pleasing to the staff—and to the readers the paper must serve. If the design also happens to win awards—as both the "before" and "after" designs here did—so much the better.

To illustrate the variety of designs adopted by award-winning student newspapers, we'll offer some additional examples. If the Pepperdine *Graphic* does innovative things some designers would question—and gets away with it—the University of Kansas *Daily Kansan,* another 1981 Pacemaker winner, offers modern modular makeup that is close to the mainstream of contemporary design thinking. Figure 10.11 shows the *Kansan,* with its clean but conservative five-column modular format, serif headlines and justified text. The *Kansan* obviously emphasizes its content, and the front-page design is intended to display the news effectively.

In comparison to the Pepperdine *Graphic* or the *Daily Kansan,* the Fort Hays (Kansas) State University *Leader* (also a Pacemaker winner), shown in Figure 10.12, is more traditional. Its front page is not entirely modular, but it lavishly displays its excellent photography. Its six-column format is more typical of professional papers today. Note the use of a special column of smaller news items on the left side of the page, another feature found in many professional newspapers.

Two of the community college Pacemaker winners, the San Antonio College (Texas) *Ranger* and the Los Angeles Pierce College *Roundup,* are shown in

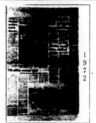

focus

sept. 25, 1980 B7

The Graphic has undergone considerable design changes since 1937 when George Pepperdine College first opened and *the graphic* printed its first issue ever on the Los Angeles campus.

New *graphic* layout format creates 'radical' change

"Lord knows we've got to change"
—Carlos Santana

by Rich Taylor
guest writer

Whether or not the present *graphic* staff took a cue from the above lyrics isn't known for sure, but one thing is guaranteed— *the graphic* has a new look.

If you're a Pepperdine old-timer and have glanced through the preceding pages, you've undoubtedly noticed the change. If you're an incoming freshman or a transfer student at Seaver College, welcome to *the graphic's* "new" look.

When Pepperdine University came to Malibu in 1972, *the graphic* donned a new look and midway through the '70s it changed its design again. Now, as we begin a new decade, *the graphic* is making a third design change since its inception at Malibu. It promises to be the best change yet.

"Of all the changes I've seen after going through all the old archives and back issues, this is the most dramatic, radical change to come about in layout design," said Dr. Steve Ames, adviser of *the graphic*.

It has often been said that to be successful you must change. Two local papers, the *Santa Monica Evening Outlook* and *Los Angeles Times*, have recently changed design and layout format, but have continued to strive for continuity. This is what *the graphic* is hoping to achieve.

The Graphic's facelift was not the result of an overnight decision, nor was it a one-man operation. Journalism students in past years thought design revamping would increase readership and speed up production of the paper.

John Hauser, presently editor-in-chief of *the graphic*, and Lisa Vanco, who was appointed to the newly-created position of design coordinator, decided to tackle the problem and add some spice, flavor and attractiveness to the paper.

After meetings with Ames, Hauser and Vanco subscribed to four major newspapers across the country which they felt were leading the way in layout and design. The papers were the *St. Petersburg Times* in Florida, *The Morning Call* in Allentown, Penn., *The Telegraph-Herald* in Dubuque, Iowa and the *San Angelo Standard-Times* in Texas.

The *St. Petersburg Times* is one of the foremost advocates of contemporary design for newspapers while *The Morning Call* presents a very attractive face to its readers. Executive policy at both publications encourages attention to design.

The *Telegraph-Herald* has been a leader in giving newspapers their new look and the *San Angelo Standard-Times* increased its circulation considerably after changing to a more lively, contemporary design.

While receiving these papers all summer, student publications were formulating ideas for its own new look. Finally, after hours of debating, conclusions were drawn by Hauser and Vanco; with Ames in agreement, the change took place.

As for subscribing to the papers Vanco said, "We followed most of the ideas which we had from the start. A lot of them came from *The Morning Call.* Before, new people were dissatisfied with *the graphic's* look because it didn't induce them to read it. With the new design and ideas we got from other papers we hope more people will want to read the paper."

Newspapers were not the only source for suggestions in design and format. Several books were used as references, namely: "Publication Design" by Roy Nelson; "Modern Newspaper Design" by Edmund Arnold and "The Graphics of Communication" by Turnbull and Baird.

Most of the books agreed that the impact of television, magazines, and new technology has brought about, for many contemporary North American newspapers, a new approach to the packaging of their product. Essentially, this approach states that newspapers must give more attention to their appearance, and make a strong commitment to accepting the changes involved.

In this, *the graphic* is following suit.

Actually, emphasis on design is beginning to make an impact across the country. At an American Press Institute Seminar on Newspaper Design, four guidelines were thrust upon major newspapers: make newspapers more visably attractive while building a consistent design theme throughout; do not let the design overwhelm the message (content); create graphics and design elements that are not just colorful and frilly but convey information to the reader; design with simplicity and restraint. The graphic is planning to use these ideas, while emphasizing that the most important change is a design which helps the reader.

"I'm delighted Lisa and John have tackled a thorny problem and spent many hours of summer analyzing the four major newspapers," said Ames, "and in a most professional way selected ideas in those newspapers which will give *the graphic* a most unusual but identifiable look.

"When I came to Pepperdine in the fall of 1978 the layout they were using had been used for two years. One thing I found most objectionable about quadrant form is that news was almost second to art. Our new form emphasizes both," said Ames.

"I had wanted to make a change when I came, but I also felt, students should be a part of that change because it is a student newspaper."

A few of the major changes are:
—A modular functional look rather than strictly modular.
—Ragged right type rather than justified.
—High priority on news content.
—New headline type.
—Stories and pictures arranged in groups with hairline boxes sometimes around them.
—Bold lead-ins on stories and bold blurbs.
—Increased width in columns.

As is the case in most instances of change, all people involved are enthusiastic. "I'm very excited about the new style," said Hauser.

"We're just adding to what has always been a well-designed paper. This is also a perfect time to make a change because we have a very young staff. If they learn the new style now they'll know it even better when they're juniors and seniors."

Hauser adds that a few changes will be made in content. "We want to have more interpretive-type articles and improve the general quality of all articles through a five-step proofreading process. As for entertainment, we want to concentrate more on the on-campus events and only include outside entertainment if there is room. In sports, we plan to cover the other teams in the conference more than in the past."

Vanco envisions things running smoother and feels the new style will allow for more creativity. "If something is done that we don't like, we're open to change," she said.

Ames is planning to keep tabs on the new style also. He will have a weekly accuracy check on content through news sources. This will give them a chance to respond positively or negatively. He will also edit a "graphic in review" monthly which will be distributed to faculty, administration and those on mailing lists. The review will critique *the graphic's* efforts for the month.

It's quite evident that Carlos Santana has enjoyed success by integrating new styles into his already-popular music while maintaining continuity throughout the years.

As for *the graphic*—well, they're changing too.

EDITOR'S NOTE: Rich Taylor served as editor-in-chief of *the graphic* during the winter trimester of 1979. Readers are encouraged to express their opinions concerning the new design by submitting letters to the editor.

Figure 10.9 Feature story from the Pepperdine *Graphic*. Used by permission.

Figures 10.13 and 10.14. The *Ranger* uses bold typography and dramatic photography to achieve a striking front-page look. The *Ranger* also freely changes column widths on the front page, providing typographic variety.

The *Roundup* illustrates another innovation about which not all designers— or editors—would agree. Its nameplate is sometimes vertical and sometimes horizontal. Either way, the paper has a clean and modern design, but some designers would contend that the vertical nameplate is distracting and creates unnecessary problems for the editors who design the rest of the page.[5] In fact, even the faculty advisers of the *Roundup* disagree about the vertical name-

174   **Chapter Ten**

Tuition up $16 a unit; flat-rate next

by SUSAN STEELMAN
editor-in-chief

Tuition and room and board rates were announced Friday for the 1980-81 academic year in an open letter from Dr. Howard White, university president.

The tuition rate for Seaver College was set at $159 per unit, $16 above the current $143, and room and board will rise to $1,200 from $1,085.

Included in the letter from White was an announcement that a flat-rate system of tuition will be implemented beginning in fall 1981.

"Flat-rate is the only logical way to go here," said Dr. John Nicks, vice president for academic affairs. University officials have discussed a flat-rate system for three years, but the program was not implemented sooner because there were several areas that needed to be cleared on, according to Phil Garr, Student Government Association (SGA) president.

The 11.2 percent increase in tuition and the 9 percent room and board increase are both below the 13 percent national inflation rate. According to Nicks, the university is planning to make up the difference by extending fund-raising activities.

Nicks said university operating costs for the 1978-79 academic year were $38 million and approximately two-thirds of that money came from tuition dollars. The remainder was made up by $7.3 million in gifts and $4 million in financial aid.

"We are increasing our focus on endowments," Nicks said. He explained that endowments are gifts of money a university receives that it doesn't spend directly. "It is something like a savings account. You spend the interest but not the principal," he said.

Along with increasing the focus on endowments, the university also plans

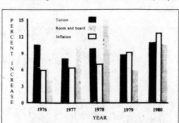

SEAVER COLLEGE EXPENSES VS. INFLATION, 1976-80

to increase financial aid in accordance with the tuition increase. Israel Rodriguez, director of financial aid, said, "We consider each financial aid package individually to determine each student's financial need."

Rodriguez said that in the past Seaver has compensated for tuition increases, adding that this is the time for students to look for other sources of income outside the university.

"We retain 80 percent of our students, which is above the national average of 55 percent," Rodriguez said. "Obviously Pepperdine is doing something right and that includes financial aid."

According to Nicks, the only people affected by the flat-rate conversion will be the current freshmen and sophomores. The administration believes that the number of part-time students will be reduced by the flat-rate system, which would alleviate some of the university's overcrowding problems.

The administration is still reviewing the flat-rate system and has not released any specific guidelines. Garr believes the students need a better definition of flat-rate and is hoping a representative from the administration

will speak at a convocation assembly about the plan.

The flat-rate system was proposed to SGA last fall, Garr said, and met a positive reaction. Garr also said that several questions were asked by SGA members about various aspects of the plan.

Garr said the three major concerns were:
1. There needed to be an adjustment period from unit tuition to flat-rate tuition.
2. Athletes would have a hard time taking 16 units per trimester because of busy sports schedules.
3. Students needing fewer units because of graduation would stil have to pay for 16 units.

When Nicks returned to SGA he had adequate answers for all these concerns, according to Garr, including:
1. There will be an 18-month preparation period.
2. In most cases, scholarships will make up for the extra units for athletes. And, students do not have to take a full load; they just have to pay for it.
3. Students have time to plan in advance so they will not have a smaller amount of units their final trimester.

---

the graphic

seaver college of pepperdine university—malibu, calif. vol. 8 no. 13 jan. 24, 1980

New committee to handle complaints against media

by CURTISS OLSEN
managing editor

For the first time, Seaver College communication students will be offered an alternative board of appeal.

The board, called the media committee, will arbitrate written complaints lodged by students against media outlets, personnel or advisers.

According to Dr. Stewart Hudson, Communication Division chairman, "the committee is modeled after committees of this kind all over the country. Good schools that mature develop these kinds of committees."

Hudson stressed that the committee could be used only when a student problem had gone through the channels of editors and advisers.

"It became obvious that we needed a committee of this sort when we had that episode with the Graphic editors," said Dr. Ron Whittaker, director of broadcasting, in reference to last January when five student editors were fired from their positions.

Whittaker was called, along with several other members of the Communication Division, to help develop the initial guidelines the group would follow.

Those guidelines, according to Dr.

Norman Hughes, academic dean, "are general with the exception of the section on membership. That section is very specific as to who will qualify for service on the committee."

The official document, drawn up by department leaders, calls for the committee to consist of seven voting and two non-voting members representing various segments of the Seaver community.

The first step the guidelines state is for a non-communication division representative to be appointed by Dr. Howard White, university president, to serve as chairman on a yearly basis.

Half of the six remaining members will consist of three students including the Student Government Association (SGA) president, a general student representative elected by the SGA from its ranks and an upper-division broadcasting or journalism major selected by fellow majors.

Although generally in favor of the new committee, involved faculty members offered different perspectives on its purpose and effect.

Whittaker pointed out that the new committee would spread the burden of decisions. "Decisions on important issues should be diffused and not laid

on one person's desk," he said.

Dr. Steve Ames, director of student publications, alluded to student benefits resulting from the formation of the committee. "I believe it will give students an avenue by which they may express themselves if they disagree with a decision made by a media adviser," he said.

The first task scheduled for the new committee will be to approve specific guidelines submitted by the media departments in the division.

Nick DeBonis, coordinator of radio, is in favor of the definition of adviser-student roles.

"It benefits students because it eliminates ambiguity as to what is expected of them," DeBonis said. "It also benefits me as an adviser because it gives me a directional foundation which eliminates arbitrary decision-making."

DeBonis had his reservations, however. "I don't want this committee to overstep the purpose it was created for, which is to serve as an advisory panel. The panel should always be a passive entity, acting only when advice is sought from it.

"We've all agreed to abide by what the committee decides," said DeBonis.

Photo by Joe Logan

"Wild and crazy" comedian Steve Martin (right) visited Raleigh Runnels Memorial Pool Thursday to film a portion of his upcoming TV special.

Comic

> "I am 100 percent opposed to any pullout, for any reason. We make the sacrifice, we pay our own way, we're not connected to the government. It's not their life dream that's being tampered with."
> —shot putter Al Feuerbach

Two athletes fear boycott

Olympic politics reach all the way to Pepperdine

by LARRY ISRAELSON
news editor

As the turbulence in the Middle East continues, two Seaver College Olympic hopefuls have joined the ranks of those forced to realize their dreams of international glory may be tampered with in a big way.

With President Carter's reaffirmation last night that the United States will boycott the Moscow Olympics if Soviet troops remain in Afghanistan, uncertainty has moved in to share top billing with sweat in the training efforts of water polo player Terry Schroeder, sailor Glen Uslan, and every other standout amateur athlete in the country.

And, none of the athletes is too happy about the situation.

"It seems like a bad dream," said Schroeder, "but I can't really worry about it. I've just got to

keep training and hope things work out."

Schroeder, who started practicing with his Olympic teammates last weekend, said Uslan, a top contender to represent the U.S. in the Olympic 470 class, both agreed that the games should not be used as a political tool.

"Everyone says that politics and athletics shouldn't be combined, I think we should go to the games regardless," said Uslan.

"It's not the right thing to do," Schroeder said. "It's gonna get Russia mad and might even lead to more serious things. The Olympic movement is going to die off, too. Probably no communist countries will come to Los Angeles in 1984."

Schroeder and Uslan also feel, however, that it would be better to support a boycott than break

up U.S. team unity.

"From what I've heard it looks like the whole team would boycott," said Uslan. "Ninety percent of the Olympic team belongs to the NCAA (National Collegiate Athletic Association) and they say boycott. You really can't send a contingent for the U.S. with only 10 percent of your team."

"We don't need fighting within our own country," Uslan also said. "Nobody wants to be the only American in Russia."

Schroeder was concerned with another alternative to snubbing the Soviets: "I'd much rather boycott than go to war."

The timing of an official decision also worried Uslan.

"I just hope (Carter) doesn't do it at the last

minute," he said. "At least that would make a lot less of a disappointment."

Schroeder, on the other hand, said, "I don't think (timing) will matter. At this time, what's the difference between training six more months or one more month?"

Another point that bothered Uslan was possible repercussions of U.S. criticism of the Soviets.

"If we do go, I wonder if we're really safe," he said. "You can't help but remember things that happened in 1972."

Arab terrorists shocked the world that year when they kidnapped a group of Israeli athletes at the Munich games. The hostages and captors were all eventually killed.

Both athletes expressed fear at having their preparation lead to almost nothing.

"It means a lot to me," said Schroeder, who sat out the 1979 NCAA season to prepare for the games. "It's something I've worked for a long time."

"I'd be extremely disappointed to have been training this hard for the last three years and then have it taken away from me," Uslan said. "But, I'm not the only one in this situation."

---

the graphic

seaver college of pepperdine university—malibu, calif. vol. 9 feb. 5, 1981

inside

city   pgs. 2-3
focus   pg. 4
  USF road trip—pg. 4
arts   pg. 5
  'Cuckoo' cast—pg. 5
sports   pgs. 6-7
  Waves begin stand—pg.6
perspective   pg. 8

seaver students follow Wave basketball team to san francisco last weekend
see SF trip pg 4

SLC restores Sig Eps charter after appeal

by Gail Weston
associate perspective editor

A recent review by the Student Life Committee (SLC) has resulted in the return of the Sigma Epsilon (SE) fraternity's charter.

The charter had been suspended in October of 1980 because of "the use of alcohol at fraternity-related parties." SE, along with the still unchartered Phi Zeta Chi fraternity, was charged with distributing beer at a social function held at the Malibu West Yacht Club.

To regain its charter, the fraternity was required to make two appeals, none before Jan. 19, to the Inter-Greek Council (IGC) and the SLC. However, since IGC could not muster a quorum for the vote, the fraternity went directly to the SLC, who voted unanimously to return the charter.

"Our presentation (which had to be both oral and written) was very honest," Kevin Kirby, SE president, said. "We admitted that no matter how hard we try a certain amount of drinking will go on among members of a fraternity. But, we will still try."

Kirby said he had an "agreement" with the university. "That gray area between fraternity and a gathering of friends is where trouble arises," he said. "We have agreed to talk with the administration about activities that might be questionable before they occur."

Kirby thinks the relationship between SE and the administration is a good one. "We feel closer to the school now. Both of us
see **Sig Eps** pg. 3

International setting

photography by Joe Luper

Pepperdine's John Murphy goes up to block hit from Kenji Toriba of the Japanese collegiate all-star team in Firestone Fieldhouse Tuesday. Waves lost in three games.

White denies faculty power to question his decision

by John Selindh, editor-in-chief
and Dwayne Moring, associate news editor

Dr. Howard White, university president, said that part of a resolution passed by the Seaver College Faculty Organization Friday questioning recent Pepperdine administrative changes, was in "error."

The resolution, introduced by Dr. Kenneth Perrin, chairman of the natural science division, was passed by a 36 to 12 vote at the organization's regularly scheduled meeting.

The resolution asked that decisions leading to the resignation of Dr. John Nicks as vice president of academic affairs and the appointment of Dr. Herbert Luft, currently director of the Year in Europe (YIE) program, to the position of executive vice president, be reconsidered.

"I think the resolution is in error in believing that I don't have the right to appoint an executive vice president," White said. "I believe that I do have that right. Therefore I do not believe that it is appropriate to say a unilateral action was wrong."

White also said, "I felt it was a good resolution in expressing confidence in Dr. Nicks, and I can understand why the people would want to do that because he is a wonderful person."

In its concluding statement, the resolution read; "For any university to run effectively, it is imperative that there be a feeling of cooperation and mutual good between the administration and faculty. The recent unilateral
see **White** pg. 2

SGA expresses support of Pepperdine's objectives

by Gordon Greene
staff writer

In a resolution prepared by Rod Gaudin, student government association (SGA) president, on behalf of the president's advisory cabinet, the SGA expressed its support of the spiritual emphasis and Christian goals of Pepperdine University.

The resolution, which passed Tuesday night, stemmed from an SGA cabinet "Goals and Objectives" seminar held two weeks ago. It states, "Be it resolved, that the Student Government Association, while not always agreeing with the way in which

George Pepperdine's goals are implemented, supports in general the goals and direction of Pepperdine University as a Christian institution, and Be it resolved, that the SGA believes that the goals and direction of Pepperdine's Christian emphasis should continue to be such that it is designed to incorporate all students regardless of their particular Christian denomination or faith with which they are affiliated."

Gaudin, reporting on the cabinet seminar said, "There was not a real consensus on how
see **SGA** pg. 2

Luft responds to doubts

by Rick Cupp
staff writer

In the wake of the controversy about the resignation of Dr. John Nicks, vice president of academic affairs, Dr. Herbert Luft has denied that he will be a "yes man" for Dr. Howard White, university president.

Luft's appointment to the position, effective April 1, has been criticized by some faculty members who doubt his competence.

Nicks' office assumed many of the duties of the executive vice presidency, a post left unfilled since White became president in 1978.

It is felt by some faculty members that Luft, a close friend of White's, will not be sympathetic to the faculty's needs and that Nicks was asked to

❝I'm not going to be a person everyone will recognize as a man who cannot say yes or no without speaking with White—otherwise I wouldn't be easing his load. ❞

Herbert Luft

resign because he was willing to stand up to White in support of the faculty.

Luft declined comment on the resignation of Nicks, but emphasized he personally did not wish to be viewed as a destructive force by faculty members.

"I intend to be an intergrative

force," Luft said. He said he plans to use cooperation to act as a go-between for faculty and administration leaders and White.

Luft, presently the resident director of the Year-in-Europe program (YIE) in Heidelberg, Germany, will be second in actual control of the university below only White.

Luft, 38, who received his bachelors and masters degrees from Pepperdine and his doctorate from USC, was a student in the classes of several professors still teaching here.

Luft said he had anticipated that some people would link his relationship with White, who has known Luft since 1963 and who performed his wedding ceremony, but said their friendship
see **Luft** pg. 2

L.A. campus tempted by more prospective buyers

Administrative building of L.A. campus located at the corner of 97th and Vermont.

by Gary Fakhoury
associate arts editor

Pepperdine University has received numerous offers to purchase either part or all of its Los Angeles campus from various prospective buyers. But there are "presently no acceptable offers," according to Mike O'Neal, vice president for finance and legal council.

"The university has been receiving offers for several years now, but at the moment, there are some offers which are close to being acceptable, and the university is still deciding," O'Neal said.

According to O'Neal, the university has yet to decide whether its best interest would include selling all or part of the 35-acre campus, 55 percent of which is developed.

Once the lawn of a private estate, the L.A. campus served as the sole undergraduate campus from the time George Pep-

perdine founded the school in 1937 to 1972 when all of the baccalaureate and some of the master's programs began being directed from the Seaver College campus.

In the spring of 1980, many of the L.A. campus administrative offices, such as Finance and Registration, were moved to the Malibu campus in an attempt to consolidate those offices.

The palm-covered campus is located on the corner of 97th and Vermont streets, less than 15 minutes from downtown L.A. presidents who served during the 35 years on the L.A. campus were Drs. Batzell Baxter, Hugh Tiner, M. Norvel Young and William Banowsky.

The L.A. facility includes the Graduate School of Business and Management, the Graduate School of Education and the Graduate School of Professional Studies, which is being phased out this year. The facility now includes 31 buildings, a library which houses 150,000 volumes, a bookstore, warehouse, classrooms and offices.

Figure 10.10b   The *Graphic* has a new design featuring ragged-right body type and serif headlines. Used by permission.

Further sanctions considered on undergrad law library use

by Jim Benson

Seaver College students, prohibited from using the Pepperdine School of Law Library until finals end there Dec. 18, may soon face new sanctions on the use of the facility because of disruptive behavior by some undergraduates.

Ron Phillips, dean of the School of Law, said he has received "a number of reports in the last few weeks of groups of students coming together, getting very noisy, sneaking food and drinks into the library and causing just general disruption."

In addition, Phillips said, there has been a problem with undergraduates "going into law review offices, other student offices, even taking over the faculty lounge when no one else is in there."

School of Law administrators are seeking a solution to these problems (which Phillips said the library staff cannot control), but no decisions have yet been made.

The law library will remain off limits to Seaver students "at least" through the final examination period, Phillips said, indicating a decision between now and then could prolong the period.

The ban applies to students from other law schools (who Phillips said had also been disruptive) and the general public as well as undergraduates here.

While use of the law library is limited to School of Law students, Phillips said that "if an undergraduate had a specific work project that required access to the materials, then I would suggest that he or she talk to the librarian and see whether or not an exception can be granted. It would be up to the library staff to make that determination."

Nancy Kitchen, the director of the law library, said she works with instructors at Seaver to make certain all projects involving student use of the facility are completed before the library is closed to undergraduates during finals.

The Graphic

Nov. 30, 1981   Seaver College, Pepperdine University—Malibu, Calif.   Vol. 10, No. 10

Resolution to allocate lighting funds passes

Unanimous vote for track illumination

by Rick Cupp

A resolution to allocate $15,000 to $20,000 for night-time lighting of the track was passed unanimously Tuesday by the Student Government Association (SGA).

The lights are expected to prevent possible injury and guard against potential aggressors. The university would fund this addition.

"First we have to get an OK from the maintenance department. If they OK it, it will go before the space committee," Rick Rowland, chairman of the athletic committee, said.

The lights are needed, Rowland said, because "there have been a lot of accidents, and some people are scared to go down there (the track area), some go in groups."

The lights were not only wanted by students, but also by Malibu residents who are members of the Crest Club (which uses Pepperdine facilities).

There was wide support of the resolution within SGA. "I think this resolution should pass because it's dangerous down there at night," Liz Whatley, chairman of the publicity committee, said.

Bob Smith, SGA president, thinks there is no "difference of opinion on whether or not there's a need for the lighting."

"There never have been lights on the track and there is a real concern by students," Rowland said.

The resolution specifies that "low lights" will be used on the track to prevent community complaints and cut the cost of a highly elevated lighting system.

Rowland emphasized that "high lights" are out of the question because "the community would never approve of that."

He said the brightness of high lights are disturbing to nearby residents, and that "there are enough complaints from the community just about lighting The Phillips Theme Tower."

The Theme Tower is only lit during the holiday season, he said, because the community is more tolerant of the light around Christmas time.

Rowland said lighting for night-time baseball games will never be allowed for the same reason of disturbing the community.

After the meeting Smith discussed plans for a possible Foreign Student Affairs Committee, which would have the dual purpose of meeting "the distinctive needs and wants" of foreign students by giving them more of a voice in student government.

The possibility of such a committee is being researched by SGA members John Rauschkolb, Cyrus Sartippour and two other students they have selected to assist them.

Smith said, "One of our main goals has been to get more foreign students involved on campus on a representative basis."

He said the research was needed because "Anytime we form a committee it's a major move. In this particular instance we felt we should do more extensive research on the subject.

"People have pretty much formed opinions of how they feel about it," Smith said, predicting that the plan will be discussed heavily when brought up for a vote. "The issue goes far beyond foreign students." He declined to elaborate on the issue until the plan comes up for a vote.

In other action, SGA unanimously voted to allocate $160 to purchase 600 "mind games" to give to students as a part of "survival kits" during finals week. The motion to appropriate the funds was initiated by Bob White, leader of the Foods Advisory Committee.

Also passed was a motion introduced by Smith to spend $275 on a faculty-student basketball game on Feb. 6.

SGA will split the cost of the game with SAGA. Smith said, "We shouldn't expect any return from this," because there will probably be no admission charge.

Victor Anger (54) and UCLA's Kenny Fields (54) and Michael Sanders struggle for a rebound during Saturday's game at UCLA. (For the game story, see the basketball insert.)   *photography by Kathy Strong*

Inside

Graphic poll
Results of readership survey revealed.

A4

Scientific art
Seaver student's biological illustrations on display in gallery.

A5

Pacesetter
Co-captain praised as team asset.

A6

Index

Warner approves TV-3 cable extension plan

University's consent needed before implementation

by Rick Cupp

A plan which would extend Seaver College's TV-3 television programming to 10,000 potential viewers has been approved by Warner Cable of Malibu, Dr. Ron Whittaker, coordinator of television and film for the campus, said.

If the university administration, presently studying the plan, gives its approval, TV-3 will be aired to "undoubtedly the most desirable audience of any cable system in the country," Whittaker said.

"The Malibu community represents some of the most influential people in film and television industries, including the major media decision makers," he said. "There are some people trying to enter broadcasting who would give their left arm for an opportunity to enter their living rooms."

Whittaker figures the expansion will draw many more talented broadcasting students to Seaver because of the exposure they would receive. He said that although there are approximately 180 broadcasting majors at Seaver College, "only a small core" are dedicated and reliable.

The university would also benefit, he said, by having its activities seen by the Malibu audience.

Because Los Angeles TV stations do not deal with the events and concerns of Malibu to any real extent, Whittaker said, an expanded TV-3 would be the only source of television news and information designed to serve the needs of the Malibu community.

Before TV-3 will be allowed to use the cable system, however, it must agree to meet the minimum technical and program content standards required by Warner.

Most of these requirements are a statement of the laws governing cablecasting already existing.

To meet the needs of the Malibu community, a "Malibu News and Information Service" was selected, and is to be responsible for gathering news, information and announcements of interest to the community.

> 66 We will have to stretch our technical resources to the limit, and maybe a bit beyond, to try to meet the higher standards required of telecasting. 99
> *Dr. Ron Whittaker*

The information is planned to be broadcast on an electronically generated 16-page graphics service. Residents of Malibu will be able to send in announcements for broadcast, and Whittaker hopes they will "greatly increase the value and interest in the TV-3 programming" throughout Malibu.

Along with the five-hour-a-night information service, TV-3 will broadcast four regular programs: "Newswatch-3," "Inside the Waves," "Wednesday" and "After Class."

There will also be color telecasts of major sporting events from Firestone Fieldhouse and a wide range of university events of special interest, including dramatic and musical productions from Smothers Theatre.

If the expanded broadcasting is approved, all programming to Malibu would initially be by videotape delay. But after about one year it will probably be possible to broadcast live.

Whittaker said live broadcasts would be "very important for our nightly 30-minute TV newscasts and for play-by-play coverage of sporting events."

In the past, TV-3 has operated basically as an instructional facility rather than as a broadcast production facility.

Whittaker said the station was not initially intended for outside broadcast because of inhibiting costs. He said the technical equipment needed for cable broadcasting to Malibu is much more sophisticated than that presently needed.

"We will have to stretch our technical resources to the limit, and maybe a bit beyond, to try to meet the higher technical standards required of telecasting," he said.

Whittaker is generally optimistic about TV-3's possible programming extension. "All in all, the new television service would be of great benefit to school-community relations and it would also provide a valuable function for both the university and the Malibu community," he said.

Figure 10.10c   The design revised yet again to a sans serif headline schedule with extensive use of condensed typefaces. Used by permission.

The University Daily

KANSAN

University of Kansas
Lawrence, Kansas

Monday, November 30, 1981
Vol. 92, No. 67 USPS 650-640

Allen takes leave during investigation

Richard Allen

By United Press International

WASHINGTON—Richard Allen, saying he feels he has "done nothing wrong," took administrative leave as President Reagan's national security adviser yesterday so he could speak out about the $1,000 "thank-you" payment he received from a Japanese magazine.

"I certainly exercised bad judgment in not immediately taking it (the envelope containing the money) to the acting counsel to the president and writing a memo about it," Allen said in an interview on NBC's "Meet the Press."

THAT ACTION "was always in my mind," Allen said, and "I had no other intention."

But the incident occurred on Jan. 21, the first day of the new administration, and in the press of appointments and duties, Allen said, the money was placed in a safe and he "simply forgot."

Allen said he intercepted the envelope as it was being forced into Mrs. Reagan's hand after a brief photo session with Japanese journalists.

The money was presented by journalists working for the magazine Shufu no Tomo (Housewife's Friend) as a "thank you" to Mrs. Reagan, the Japanese said in Tokyo.

Allen said he gave the envelope to his secretary, who placed it in the office safe, and forgot it.

"It was a case of forgetfulness, no matter how hard that is to accept," he said.

Shortly thereafter Allen moved to his new office and not only did not have the key to the old office but never had the combination to the safe.

Allen said he talked to Reagan Saturday about his intention to step down until the investigation was completed, and "he indicated he agreed with the decision and understood the basis on which I made it."

Larry Speakes, deputy White House press secretary, said the president "hasn't passed judgment in any way" on the case.

"Dick made a request and the president honored it," he said.

SPEAKES SAID Allen's deputy, Adm. James (Bud) Nance, former aircraft carrier skipper and retired staff member of the Joint Chiefs of Staff, had been asked to "assume Allen's duties."

Edwin Meese, top presidential counselor, said Allen's action was his own idea, and "since he felt constrained to defend himself (in public) it was a good thing to go on administrative leave."

Meese said that Allen talked to him and to the president Saturday, and apparently thought about it overnight, then, "he talked to me today and he felt it was the right thing to do and he decided to do it."

"There's no reason whatever why I cannot resume my duties and perform at the same level as before once the investigation is concluded," Allen said.

"I expect to resume," he said. "Certainly, I would like to go back."

Allen said that no one had asked him about the money, and "I did not know how the investigation began in September."

Asked to whom he attributes some "anonymous and quite damaging quotes" from the Justice Department and White House, he said he did not know, but was "appalled by the sensationalism and innuendoes" that have been printed in the course of the case.

"I don't know if anyone was interested in promoting such confusion," he said. "I certainly feel I have done nothing wrong, and that is one reason I am here, to answer all questions."

Check finds some extinguishers empty

By MICHAEL ROBINSON
Staff Reporter

A KU housing department check of fire extinguishers at Jayhawker Towers Apartments, prompted by charges from Towers residents that some extinguishers did not work, has turned up several inoperative extinguishers, a housing official said yesterday.

J.J. Wilson, director of housing, said that a department equipment check, begun last Monday, had turned up "five or six" extinguishers that needed recharging.

Towers residents charged last week that some of the extinguishers in the apartments did not work during a Nov. 22 fire that caused $50,000 damage to Tower B.

Firefighters rescued six students from the apartment building.

Wilson said that the extinguishers were checked last July, and a state fire marshal's review of the equipment in September, including a check on the alarm system, did not turn up any problems.

"They were all checked recently, but there was some question about usage," Wilson said, referring to the residents' charges.

He said that housing officials were still in the process of checking the Towers, and would check all University housing.

"We're asking the residents also to turn in equipment if it's been discharged," he said. "They know better than we do if they've been discharged for any reason."

The empty extinguishers have been replaced with full ones from a pool of extinguishers and are now being recharged, Wilson said.

He estimated that there were about 500 extinguishers in University-owned housing. The buildings that will be checked are the residence halls, the scholarship halls and Stouffer Place Apartments, as well as the Towers.

The Jayhawker Towers fire is being investigated as an arson, as is a Nov. 6 fire at Naismith Hall, a privately owned residence hall.

The Naismith Hall fire caused $90,000 in damage.

Besides the ineffectiveness of some of the fire extinguishers, there were other complaints about fire safety at the Towers.

Several residents said that smoke had reached the sixth floor of Tower B before the fire alarms went off.

One resident said that he was crawling beneath the smoke in the sixth floor hallway when the alarms went off.

In the Towers' alarm system, one alarm is in each apartment and fewer than four smoke detectors are in each hallway.

Fire officials said that both fires began in the building elevators. So far, police have no suspects in either case.

Wilson said that housing checks should be completed by the end of December.

Special to the Kansan

Workers use a crane to lift the "Salina Piece" from a truck that transported the gift to West Campus.

von Ende's duties include rugby and trouble-shooting

By LISA MASSOTH
Staff Reporter

Richard von Ende, executive secretary of the University, paced back and forth in a black and white striped rugby shirt, navy shorts, white knee socks and cleats.

Rather unusual attire for a University administrator, his dress was a sure target for barbs.

"I never knew you had such cute knees," said a co-worker on her way out the door.

He was waiting for a secretary to run off the agenda for the governor's budget hearing, but his mind was a mile away, on the field at 23rd and Iowa streets. His cleats thumped on the carpeted floor of the chancellor's complex.

Finally, he snatched the papers from the secretary and strode out the door carrying his street clothes and cowboy boots.

A DAY'S WORK OF administrating was done and it was time for his twice-a-week release—rugby. Von Ende is a member of the KU Rugby Football Club.

He walks toward the field roughly rotating his arms to warm them up. He waits for just the right moment, then jogs onto the field, hurtles his body, head first, against the pack of his teammates and shoves like a bull.

Bill Boyle, rugby team captain, said von Ende had fit in with the young team very well.

"We don't think of him as the executive secretary of the University," Boyle said.

The rugby team begins its "Death Run," jogging, sprinting, hopping on one foot, then the other, then both. Von Ende, 39, lags a little behind some of the younger men. Around the third corner, the executive secretary slows to a walk, then stops and throws up his lunch.

"I knew I shouldn't have eaten that ham salad sandwich," he said, walking to the middle of the field. As the team approaches, he jogs out and rejoins the pack, jogging, hopping and sprinting.

VON ENDE LOVES to play rugby, especially when it rains.

"It slows everyone down to my speed," he said.

Von Ende's speed is usually slow. He is a quiet and reserved person, who calls himself "a country boy from Abilene, Texas."

Monday Morning

Richard von Ende

He speaks so softly, even when giving presentations at meetings, that it is often difficult to hear him. Whole sentences can be lost if someone shuffles papers too loudly.

Maybe this mannerism developed during his years of quiet conversations to discuss a sensitive legislative issue or an administrative concern.

Although he talks softly, it's his job to talk a lot.

He says he is shy with people he doesn't know, but there don't seem to be many people who don't know him. He chats with alumni at football games, making sure they are all in the seats they want. He talks with legislators over lunch at the Topeka Club. He talks with Chancellor Gene A. Budig and other administrators to iron out problems. And he talks with University of Kansas Medical Center personnel to solve disputes.

ONE OF VON ENDE'S most important duties is that of trouble-shooter for the chancellor. He has to dive in headfirst and deal with people in difficult situations, enabling the chancellor to remain above as an authority figure.

"I have to take a lot of shit," he said. "It

See Von Ende page 5

Sculpture gets new location; original site to be restored

By STEVE ROBRAHN
Staff Reporter

After months of being trampled in controversy, the park area at 16th and Indiana streets will return to its normal grassy state.

A concrete base that had been built for the abstract sculpture "Salina Piece" will be removed, Thomas Anderson, director of facilities operations, said yesterday.

"The triangle will be restored to its original contour," he said. "And it will be grassy again."

Anderson revealed plans for the park area after the sculpture stubbornly resisted a moving crew Friday as it was taken to a new home on West Campus.

THE FIRST TIME that the crane used by the crew tried to lift the 40-ton black sculpture Friday morning, it shifted evasively, tipping the crane off balance, Anderson said.

The sculpture was quickly lowered back to the ground until it was finally loaded onto a heavy-duty moving trailer.

Anderson said he had been put in charge of moving the "Salina Piece" last week after KU officials annoinced that the grassy area at 16th and Indiana streets was not appropriate for a sculpture of that magnitude.

Roy Holwick, president of Holwick Heavy Moving Co. of Topeka, told Anderson that he had been surprised at how heavy the sculpture really was, Anderson said.

"He had to go right to the maximum on what the crane could do," Anderson said. "We knew how much it weighed, but when it was checked against a chart inside the cab of the crane, it really surprised him."

THE SCULPTURE was not damaged during the move, he said.

Lawrence and KU police cleared a path to move the sculpute through traffic, Anderson said. Traffic was blocked at 19th and Naismith streets and 19th and Iowa streets while the sculpture was being moved.

"After we got it on the trailer, the move went just like clockwork," he said. "The University police had everything in place and the caravan rolled to West Campus without stopping."

The crane unloaded the sculpture near the facilities operations storage yard just west of Iowa Street where it will remain until a structural engineering study is completed, Anderson said.

The move took a little more than five hours.

The University of Kansas accepted a recommendation of three faculty engineers to engage an outside consulting engineering firm to inspect the sculpture's safety.

KU administrators asked that the faculty engineers examine the sculpture on Oct. 23, after the "Salina Piece" fell following an Oct. 9 attempt to raise the sculpture to its normal 45-degree angle.

During the time that it rested in the grassy triangle area, vandals repeatedly defaced the sculpture and a group of alumni threatened to begin an advertising campaign opposing it.

Because the sculpture was originally designed for private use and will now be displayed on public property, the University wanted to make sure it was safe, Robert Cobb, executive vice chancellor, said last week.

"The University will locate a suitable West Campus site for the 'Salina Piece'," Cobb said.

THE UNIVERSITY was committed to the timely installation of the sculpture in a manner befitting it, the sculptor's creativity and the donor's generosity, he said.

Cobb said that by erecting the piece as quickly as possible, he hoped to reassure all future donors of art work to the University that the "Salina Piece" received the care that it deserved.

The exact site on West Campus has not been determined yet, he said.

John M. Simpson, KU alumnus and former state senator, donated the "Salina Piece" to the University last spring when he moved from his home near Salina to the Kansas City area.

K.C. concert sold out

Fans rush to request Stones tickets

By JOE REBEIN
Staff Reporter

Students huddled around radios, raptly listening to the announcement.

A declaration of war, the death of a national leader?

No, just the unexpected announcement last week that rock group the Rolling Stones would come to Kansas City, Mo., in December for two concerts.

The Rolling Stones had not planned to stop in Kansas City, but were persuaded by rock promoters during their St. Louis concert to make a detour in their schedule to come to Kansas City.

News of the concert, which came about noon last Tuesday just before Thanksgiving break, sparked a flurry of note-taking as students scribbled on notebooks, newspapers or anything handy to get the instructions on how to send for tickets.

Rona Brinck, Kansas City, Mo., sophomore, said there was almost "mass panic" at Templin Hall when the concert announcement was made.

"I was working in the cafeteria when I heard," she said. "Everybody was running around trying to find pencils and paper to get the ticket information."

THE CONCERT, scheduled for Dec. 14 and 15 in Kemper Arena, sold out in less than 24 hours, with more than 30,000 tickets snapped up, according to officials at Contemporary Productions, the St. Louis firm that is promoting the concert with Kemper Arena.

Because it was a first-come, first-serve basis, there was almost a riot as students hustled to the local post offices to mail their orders.

"All of the sudden, around noon on Tuesday, there was a tremendous rush of people," Cheryl Farmer, secretary at the Lawrence Post Office, 645 Vermont St., said last week.

"People were calling in all afternoon asking about the concert. All I could say was, 'Who are the Rolling Stones?' "

Farmer said more than $8,000 in money orders was sold Tuesday afternoon and that more than 500 people got their orders in.

"Some students drove to post offices in Kansas City and mailed their orders there to save a little time," she said.

NOT ALL OF THE students who wanted to go to the concert got their ticket requests in on time.

"By the time I got the $17 scrapped together, the concert had sold out," said Dave Holmberg, Overbrook sophomore. "I am not surprised it sold out so quickly. It's not every day that the Rolling Stones come to this area."

David Hoffman, Lawrence senior, said that at first, he had thought the announcement about the concert was false.

"When a friend called and told me about the concert, I figured it was just a hoax," Hoffman said.

Hoffman, who traveled to Boulder, Colo., earlier this month to see the Rolling Stones, said he sent in his money anyway.

"I wasn't upset that the Stones came to this area after I had traveled to Colorado," he said. "But I think that the price per ticket was outrageously expensive.

"But for the Rolling Stones, I am willing to sacrifice."

RAIN

Weather

Today will be rainy with intermittent showers and a high in the lower 40's, according to the National Weather Service in Topeka.

Winds will be from the northeast at 10 to 20 mph.

Tomorrow will be cooler under partly cloudy skies with a chance of continued showers.

10.11 A page from the *Daily Kansan* (University of Kansas) showing modular format. Used by permission.

Friday morning
March 6, 1981
Fort Hays State University

the university Leader

Volume 73
Number 43
Hays, Kan. 67601

What's News

News

Tiger basketball fans will get a chance to show their support for the team during a pep rally at 11 a.m. tomorrow at the Mall. The Tigers will travel to Kansas City, Mo. for the NAIA national championships.

Although the Tigers will be in action at Kemper Arena in Kansas City, Mo., President Gerald Tomanek has announced that classes will still be in session Monday.

The University Leader will not publish a newspaper Friday, due to spring break. However, Tuesday's paper will be published as usual.

The Allocations Committee met Wednesday to hear some of the last budget requests. An emergency allocation was approved. *See page 1.*

Money

President Reagan proposes changes in the National Guaranteed Student Loans. *See page 2.*

Forum

A Streetcar Named Desire is reviewed. Also, a columnist discusses evolution. *See page 4.*

Fine Arts

The Good Doctor will be presented Wednesday in Felten-Start Theatre by Commedia. *See page 5.*

Suds & Flicks has become a popular event — a different story from last year. *See page 5.*

Sports

The Tiger basketball team is on its way to the NAIA national championships. The first game will be at 9 p.m. Monday in Kansas City, Mo.

The Tiger gymnastics team received third place in national competition for team scores last night in Gross Memorial Coliseum. Seven gymnasts qualified for individual competition tonight. *See page 7.*

SGA, ASK sponsor postcard campaign

by Kenton Kersting
Staff Reporter

The wheel that squeaks loudest gets oiled.

This, in part, is the principle behind a Student Government Association postcard campaign. The cards are to be sent to state senators and representatives by Fort Hays State students who wish to express concerns regarding education in Kansas.

Mark Tallman, FHS campus director of Associated Students of Kansas, is heading the program on behalf of ASK and SGA.

SGA purchased several hundred prepaid postcards and recruited the assistance of various campus groups and organizations to distribute the cards to students.

Students are to write about educational concerns — faculty and student salaries, tuition hikes and other issues to members of the Legislature from students' districts.

The philosophy behind the campaign is to make sure that students voices are heard and their needs expressed before the Legislature makes changes in the education budget, Tallman said.

Two purposes of the drive are to make sure that those who really need financial aid do not lose their funding and that cuts at the federal level are distributed equally, Tallman said.

"We hope to show the people in Topeka that students do take time to learn about issues and communicate their positions," Tallman said. "Also, if students do this, it will help make them aware of what the issues are and hopefully develop an interest in them."

The goal is to distribute 300 cards. So far 200-250 cards have been sent or are ready to be sent, Tallman said.

Tallman said Joe Bloss, student senator at large, has played a significant role in the campaign.

Plans are to send letters to all campus organizations asking them to distribute postcards at their meetings and participate in a letter writing campaign on the national level.

"To my knowledge, this is the first time that anything this extensive has been done at FHS," Tallman said. He said that, as far as he knows, no other Kansas school is executing a plan this extensive.

Will the squeaky wheel get oiled?

"Results may not come this year," Tallman said, "but, someday, there will be a payoff."

Celebration!

Mark Wilson, Columbus, Ohio senior, is shown with arms raised high following the traditional championship net cutting ceremonies after the Tigers defeated Washburn, 66-62.

Transfer students face adjustment difficulties

by Lisa Quakenbush
Staff Reporter

Each semester, Fort Hays State opens its doors to welcome new students to campus.

Yet, not all of these new faces are freshmen; some are transfer students from community colleges found in many areas of the country.

Although most students fit into the crowd, some have problems adjusting to the FHS atmosphere, Dorothy Knoll, associate dean of students, said.

Knoll said that although transfer students have attended college for one for two years, they still feel new and are often insecure.

"Many transfer students have attended a community college that was possibly in their hometown or not far away. They have friends there, and the friends don't always move to a new school with them," Knoll said.

"Freshmen often live in the residence halls. Many times, the transfer student will choose to live off campus. In a hall, there are always friends around. This isn't true in an apartment or house," Knoll said. "This is a major reason for their insecurity. They feel a sense of isolation and perhaps don't know who to turn to."

Transfer students do not always have the advantage in making new friends at college, either, Knoll said.

"After being in school for two years, most kids are already in with a group of friends — a nucleus they don't want to break," Knoll said. "So it makes it hard for transfer students to break through those barriers."

Knoll said not all transfer students have these problems, but many come to her to discuss them.

Another problem that seems to plague transfer students is a dropping grade point average.

"Most find classes in colleges harder than in community colleges," she said. "Students find their GPA is dropping, and they never get it back up to what it once was."

Knoll said one possibility for GPA drops could be that transfer students have already completed their general requirements from former colleges, so they jump right into their major classes.

Many students may not have finished college if it were not for community colleges, she said.

"Without that community college in a hometown, the students may not have even begun post-secondary education. If it wasn't for community colleges, many students would not get here," Knoll said.

Not all transfer students feel this way about coming to college, Knoll said. When they do, however, "I'm glad I can try to help them work it out," she said.

Business conference to feature various exhibits

The key speaker at the Fourth Annual Business Education Conference tomorrow will be Scott Peterson, business education instructor at Columbia Heights High School, Columbia Heights, Minn.

The conference is scheduled to begin at 9 a.m. in the Black and Gold Room of the Memorial Union.

"Peterson is an authority in the area of accounting, which is the topic on which he will speak," Dr. Wally Guyot, chairman of the department of business education, said. "He is an active speaker on the subject and has authored several practice materials dealing with accounting.

"Peterson was also recently honored by the Minnesota Certified Public Accountant's Association for having taught 45 of the CPAs currently practicing in the state of Minnesota," Guyot said.

The conference is sponsored by the Fort Hays State department of business and in part by the Pi Omega Pi business honorary.

Approximately 275 invitations have been sent to area business education instructors in vocational and high schools, community colleges and FHS' sister universities.

"We don't expect them all to attend," Guyot said. "About 60-70 of the schools, maybe, will attend."

The business department is encouraging business students to attend, Guyot said, especially those who plan to be teachers.

Various exhibitors will also be featured at the conference, Guyot said. "We'll have a couple of publishing companies and some business cooperations, including Northwestern Business Systems from Hays," he said. "These companies will be explaining their machines and how they work; there will be no actual selling at the conference."

Committee reviews budget requests, handbook

by Jane Heiman
Assistant Copy Editor

At the Student Government Association Allocations Committee meeting Wednesday night, SGA and Associated Students of Kansas budget requests of $30,000 and $3,590 respectively, were reviewed, as well as the SGA student handbook budget. An emergency allocation was also approved and a request was heard from Kappa Iota Delta Sigma.

The SGA and ASK budgets were reviewed because the proposals were brought up before the committee in last week's meeting without a quorum, and no decision could be made.

"I think this is a fair, lean budget request," Jim Anderson, SGA president, said.

Two increases were mentioned in the request concerning salaries and telephone expenses.

Anderson said that every Board of Regents school agreed to a 40-cents-per-student payment to ASK. This is an increase of 15 cents over this year's membership dues.

Allocation requests for the student handbook were presented next.

Last year, the handbook received supplemental allocations from the committee in the spring.

The Office of Student Affairs pays minimum wage for 300 hours work in putting the handbook together.

The number of copies of the book will be increased to approximately 6,000 next year, Anderson said.

The Office of Student Affairs uses the books during summer freshman and transfer enrollment, Dave Brown, handbook production coordinator, said. The office wants extra copies to distribute to campus visitors.

"I feel the book is used widely," Anderson said. "I think the freshmen were really impressed by the book and felt it's really helpful."

Bob Wilson, student body vice president, questioned upperclassmen's use of the book.

"I think the handbook is used by upperclassmen," Brown said. "They especially use the building hours, calendar and other information that is printed only in the handbook," Brown said.

Anderson said the book would basically be the same. "There will be some updating, of course, and four more pages will be added," he said.

The additional pages were added because of suggestions for improvements and for additional coverage on housing, Brown said.

An emergency supplemental allocations request from the Special Events Committee was brought before the committee by Wilson.

When the Yugoslavian Folk Dancers perform in Gross Memorial Coliseum, additional equipment will be needed. Approximately $500-$700 will be needed to rent extra sound equipment from Salina.

Kevin Faulkner, business senator, mentioned the sound system SGA considered buying earlier in the year.

The system would have covered the presentation, except for a few microphones which could be borrowed or rented, Brown said. However, the system would not have been here in time for this event, he said.

KIDS then presented its budget of $10,000 to the committee. KIDS is a newly formed group whose main purpose is to organize Pooh Corners, a campus "nurtury" center. The center will be located in Rarick Hall.

Denise Link, Great Bend junior, presented KIDS' budget request to the committee.

The center will provide day and evening care for children. Pooh Corners has the capacity to keep 20 children at a time. Priority for center use will go to full and part-time students, and then to staff, faculty and community members.

A payment scale has been based on what the group is capable of paying. Students will pay $1.07 per hour without the budget request and 53 cents per hour if the request is met, Michael Currier, assistant professor of education and Pooh Corners director, said. Staff members will pay 50 percent more than students, and faculty will pay twice as much as students.

Currier said that a day care center in Hays costs $300 per month for two children. He estimated that the savings to students, if the committee would approve the request, would be $721 per semester — more than tuition costs.

It was estimated that one out of 40 students would be able to use this service.

Senate grants emergency aid for band trip, sound system

by Luella Terry
Staff Reporter

Student Senate addressed several issues of emergency business last night, including the athletic band's trip to the National Association of Intercollegiate Athletics basketball tournament in Kansas City, Mo. and rental of a sound system for Saturday's Yugoslavian ballet performance in Gross Memorial Coliseum.

After considerable debate, senate agreed to allocate $1,200 to the pep band for travel expenses to Monday's game. If the Tigers are successful, $1,800 more will be needed to cover lodging expenses and should the winning streak continue, $1,000 more would be in order for additional lodging expenses. A total of $4,000 was requested and granted, with the agreement that any remaining money would be returned to the fund.

Kevin Falkner, business senator, said the pep band plans to have a money-raising campaign some time in the future to make up for some of the trip's expenses. Faulkner suggested that due to school patriotism.

See 'Senate debates' page 2

10.12 A page from the *University Leader* (Fort Hays State University) showing six-column format. Used by permission.

plate.[6] But whether the nameplate runs across the top or down the side, the *Roundup* is a consistent award winner in competition among California's 100-plus community colleges. Faculty advisers at some rival colleges think the *Roundup* could run its nameplate upside down at the bottom of page one and still win awards.

Some Makeup Principles

Before you actually sit down to place stories and art on a page, you'll need to consider the principles of page makeup. As we noted earlier, many ideas that were once taught as makeup principles are no longer quite so widely followed. American newspapers are rapidly evolving in design, and one era's guiding principles may be the anachronisms of the next. Nevertheless, there are some guidelines you should know about.

Mario Garcia emphasizes the importance of what he calls the *center of visual impact* on a page.[7] In traditional makeup, editors often assumed that the reader looked first at the upper right-hand corner of the page. Therefore, the most important story was usually placed there—and still is on many professional dailies that follow traditional makeup principles. In the traditional view, the purpose of makeup was to guide the reader to the most important story first and from there around the page to the less important stories. The problem with that, as it turns out, is that the reader is more likely to look first at the center of visual impact, which isn't necessarily the upper right-hand corner.

Most college papers have abandoned the strict adherence to the rule of placing the most important story in the upper right-hand corner. Instead, the main story goes in the center of visual impact, which is often near the center of the page. The center of visual impact may be a large headline or perhaps a striking illustration. Whatever it is, it's the thing the reader's eyes naturally fall upon first.

Thus, in designing a page, it is often best to choose the center of visual impact and go from there. The center of visual impact can be in various places, including the top of the page or the center. It can even be the bottom of the page. Wherever it is, there should be a focal point. A page should not have two competing centers of interest: one should be dominant, says Garcia. Once the reader has looked at the center of visual impact, his or her eyes should be guided naturally to other items on the page.

When designing pages today you will most likely work with modular units. These units may consist of art, stories or a combination of the two. The units are usually rectangular rather than square, both for practical and aesthetic reasons. As a practical matter, few content blocks lend themselves naturally to the square shape. And as a matter of aesthetics, the square is not the ideal shape. Modular blocks may be vertical, horizontal or a few of each.

There has been a marked trend toward *horizontal makeup* in recent years. Readership studies have shown that a shallow but wide story will be more widely read than a deep, narrow one. A long column of type seems forbidding to many readers. If you're going to run a story that is 12 column inches long

THE RANGER

San Antonio College
Dec. 4, 1981
San Antonio, Texas
Vol. 56, No. 121

Campus celebrates holiday

A concert Saturday night featuring music students will open campus Christmas celebrations. The music department will present the Christmas choir concert at 7:30 p.m. Saturday in the auditorium of McAllister Fine Arts Center.

The program will begin with the College Chorale directed by Theron Kirk, music chairman, performing traditional English carols. A Christmas cantata with small orchestra accompaniment will feature solos by Irene Liden, music professor, and Wayne Ellison, freshman music major.

The Early Music Ensemble will accompany the Madrigal Singers during the second half of the performance. Music Professor Peter Kline and the Brass Ensemble will play traditional carols in the foyer of the fine arts center before the concert.

In another Christmas event featuring music students, the College Band will perform at noon Dec. 11 in El Alamo Room of Loftin Student Center.

Kirk will direct the band through a selection of contemporary, pop and traditional Christmas songs ranging from "Silent Night" to "Jingle Bell Rock."

Other campus Christmas events include activities at student religious centers and two Las Possadas celebrations.

Caroling, gift-making, hayrides, worship services and ski trips compose a holiday collage of activities as student centers celebrate Christmas and greet the new year.

The Methodist Student Center is sponsoring an Alternative Christmas Fair from 1 p.m. to 4 p.m. Tuesday-Friday at the center, 102 Belknap Place.

"We will show students how to make attractive, personalized and inexpensive Christmas gifts," Dr. David Semrad, center director, said.

He said students will learn to make gifts of macrame, string art and decoupage.

"In addition we will teach candlemaking, how to make wind chimes and candlestick holders—and perhaps jewelry," Semrad said.

There will be a nominal charge for materials, which can be as little as 25 cents. Some donated materials are free, he added.

(See **Organizations, Page 7A**)

The Tower of Americas brightens downtown.

Tourists and natives alike enjoy the holiday decorations along the river walk.

Photos by Theresia Brosch

Students petition for early permits

Nearly 1,500 students signed a petition sponsored by the Data Processing Management Association requesting early time permits for currently enrolled students.

Early time permits will enable students to obtain the classes needed to graduate, Al Stehling, chairman of data processing, said.

"Quite a few students were unable to register for classes they needed to graduate. Some students may be frustrated and not return to school.

"I am frustrated that we're not available to provide the facilities and instructors that are required to meet the demands of the community," Stehling said.

Three hundred students were turned away from classes this semester due to inadequate space, he said.

"I'd say we turned away 300 students this fall and I'd say, we'll predict, we'll turn away 500 to 600 students in the spring with duplicated head count." Stehling said. Duplicated head count is the same student trying to register for different classes, he explained.

"Somebody needs to look into this and go ahead and start doing something to resolve them (the problems of inadequate facilities).

"I think some decisions being made are not being made with the student in mind," he added.

Marie Coultress, DPMA public relations person, and Becky Moody, DPMA member, presented the petition to Dean Truett L. Chance.

Chance replied with a memorandum which stated, "We understand your problems and appreciate your concern. We likewise solicite your understanding of our need to establish and maintain a system to serve as near as may be the needs and interests of all our students."

Signatures totaled 1,426 on the petition which went to the dean.

Sixty more signatures for the petition have since been received, which brings the total to 1,486. They will be given to Chance this week. Jesse Gonzales, DPMA president, said.

Enrollment continues

More than 4,700 students had picked up spring time permits Monday and Tuesday, the first two days they were issued.

Pat Terrell, associate registrar, said the number of permits issued for the first two days this year does not equal the number issued for the first two days of last year's spring semester.

"For the day division permits issued, we had a total of 3,300 last year. This year we have issued 3,213, which is only 87 less. For evening division permits issued, we had a total of 1,794 last year. This year we had only 1,497, which is 297 less," he said.

Although the figures are not complete, Terrell thinks total number of permits issued this year will equal last year's total.

Those students who have missed their alphabetical pick-up day can obtain a permit beginning Monday.

Day permits will be available from 8 a.m. to 3:30 p.m. Monday-Friday in Room 200 of Fletcher Administration Center.

Evening permits will be available from 5 p.m. to 8 p.m. Monday-Thursday in Room 115 of Fletcher Administration Center.

Both day and evening permits will be issued from 8 a.m. to 11 a.m. Jan. 9.

Samelson: desire to share

By Michael Cary
Staff Writer

Dr. William Samelson

A desire to share knowledge with others inspired Dr. William Samelson to enter the teaching profession.

Samelson, foreign languages department chairman, is one of two nominees for the Piper Professor award for teaching excellence at the college level in Texas.

"If I did anything I would teach. I am naturally inclined to teach. I am motivated to share my knowledge with others.

"Whatever you know in life there is always someone with which to share that knowledge. If you are inclined to share, you are a teacher," Samelson said.

The nominee defined teaching excellence. "When you can see that you have elevated a person to a level of knowledge the person did not possess at the time you started, that is excellence in teaching.

"When you have given a person the tools to go on and better himself or herself, that is teaching excellence."

Samelson works hard at maintaining teaching excellence. "That is why I study constantly. I am still studying. Many things have changed since I have studied formally.

"To be effective in my profession I must keep up with innovations. If you want to be creative you have to keep up with it," he said.

Samelson is pleased to be a nominee for the Piper award. "I am thrilled, it's a great honor that my peers have recognized my merit. It's a great feeling to get recognition from your own people. I would say it's equal to the award itself," he said.

January will mark the professor's 26th year at this college. When Samelson came here, there were two instructors in the foreign languages department.

"Between two of us, we taught Spanish, French, German and Latin. I have instituted nine more languages. Now we have 21 instructors and we teach 13 languages," he said.

Born in Poland in 1928, Samelson came to America in 1948 after receiving a B.S. degree in medicine from the University of Heidelberg, Germany.

Samelson received a B.A. in languages and linguistics in 1950 from Case Western Reserve University in Cleveland, an M.A. in languages and literature in 1953 from Kent State University, a Fellowship in comparative literature and linguistics in 1954 from the University of Illinois, and Ph.D. in literature and linguistics in 1960 from the University of Texas at Austin.

On May 26, 1954, he became a U.S. citizen.

In 1968, the Texas Legislature honored him by proclaiming him an Honorary Citizen of Texas and Admiral of the Texas Navy.

In 1970, he was invited by the federal government of Germany to be their guest in honor for his accomplishments in letters and philosophy.

Since 1970, Samelson has concentrated on teaching and writing in the field of English as a Second Language

Pugh places students first

By Kim Aho
Staff Writer

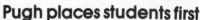

Connianne Pugh

These types of stray animals occupy Connianne Pugh's spare time. Her organizational skills are utilized here during the day and for a menagerie in the evening.

Pugh is one of two Piper Professor nominees. The Minnie Stevens Piper Foundation grants 10 awards annually to Texas college faculty for $2,500 each for "superior teaching at the college level."

"I love stray animals. We pick up almost anything," the business technology professor said Monday in an interview.

Pugh's philosophy of teaching revolves around the student.

"It all centers around the student. Putting the student first and the content second," she said.

Credit for nomination for the Piper Professor award is given to Pugh's associates.

"I have a great faculty behind me. We all work together and have pretty much the same philosphy," the Indiana University graduate said.

"It's really an honor. I think that's the biggest part of it, being nominated and supported by your peers," Pugh said.

Maintaining a positive attitude while refining clerical skills are what Pugh accentuates in her classes.

"I think developing their skills and attitudes is so important in business, a positive attitude towards whom they work for and their work environment," she added.

The career of teaching was chosen by Pugh because of a professor who taught her on the undergraduate level at Indiana Central University.

"I was most influenced by one woman I worked for in the office. She had been honored several times. I learned her ways of organization, of lesson plans and procedures for class activity.

"I try a new approach every semester," she added. Pugh has won the Teacher of the Year award for the Alamo District XX with the Texas Business Education Association for the 1980-81 school year.

Pugh has worked as a legal secretary, office secretary and public relations person in Indianapolis. She left the Incarnate Word College faculty for her position here when her subject, shorthand, was dropped.

Collating information makes qualified office personnel, she said.

"Their ability to put it all together by working in an office is good experience," Pugh said.

The most difficult thing in teaching is encouraging the students to continue, she said.

A student of Pugh's said she felt fortified by Pugh's assistance.

"I felt lost and she said just hang in there. She made me feel like I was just one of the girls," Pat Mitchell, a business technology freshman returning to school after 30 years, said.

Figure 10.13 The San Antonio College *Ranger* features large page-one photographs and sans serif typography. Used by permission.

Photo by Gary Fitleberg

Volume 55, No. 9

Woodland Hills, CA 91371

Wednesday, Nov. 18, 1981

Financial aid feels further budget cuts

by MARK PICKERING
Staff Reporter

The burden of financing a college education will be shifted even more heavily onto the shoulders of the student in the 1980s, according to the assistant director of the Congressional Budget Office.

Dr. Nancy Gordon at a Nov. 5 public hearing on "Federal Cuts and Student Financial Assistance," held by the California Legislature Assembly Education Subcommittee on Postsecondary Education at California State University, Los Angeles (CSULA).

Describing the efforts of the United States Congress to reduce the federal deficit and to balance the budget, Gordon said, "The outcome for the future will be more cuts. It is a very gloomy picture to look forward to."

Gordon said there was no likelihood the federal government would avoid cuts in funds for student aid.

"The magnitude of cuts in the federal budget is so large it is very difficult for any one program not to be cut.

"Expenditures for the student aid program have increased from

'The degree to which they suffer will depend on the regulations...'

$600 million to $4.5 billion over the last decade. Any program that has seen this much growth will be looked at to be cut," she said.

Federal cuts are "likely to affect total enrollment and the student's choice of institution," Gordon said.

Pierce President Herbert Ravetch said students at community colleges in California were "fortunate at this time" because tuition is not charged. However, cuts in federal aid were bound to have some effect on the student.

"The degree to which they suffer will depend on the regulations that are established," he said.

One federally funded program being studied for new regulation is the Pell Grant (formerly called the Basic Educational Opportunity Grant) program.

Gordon said the Pell Grant program, which gives grants in aid directly to the student, might be changed in two ways.

Either aid would be targeted more directly to the needy by lowering the maximum family income level for student eligibility, or the maximum grant amount would be reduced across the board, having a "disproportionate effect on the disadvantaged."

The most optimistic expectation for the future of the Pell Grant program is that it would receive funding at the current level in dollars unadjusted for inflation. The least optimistic is that it would be phased out, she said.

Another area likely to see cuts is the Guaranteed Student Loan (GSL) program, she said. Currently, the federal government pays interest on these loans while the student is in school. The student then pays back the principal and the remaining interest when he or she leaves.

Gordon said Congress is looking at the possibility of requiring the student to pay the interest on the loan while attending school, or of adding the interest into the total amount to be paid back after leaving school. Either could save the federal government as much as $1.3 billion in five years, she said.

Much of the growth in the GSL program has been through the Carter administration's efforts to make the loans available to upper- and middle-income students.

Congress is now moving away from that position by their newly enacted annual family-income ceiling of $30,000 for GSL eligibility.

It is also considering a requirement that a student be unlisted as a deduction on his or her parents' income tax statement for three years instead of the current one year to be considered financially independent, she said.

Support for the three-year independence rule, already enacted in California for state aid to students, was given at the hearing by Art Marmaduke, director of the California Student Aid Commission.

'Our role is to be as aggressive as possible...'

"Our role is to be as aggressive as possible for adoption of the California standard of financial independence. That is the best way to reduce the federal financial aid appropriation," he said.

However, eliminating the federal interest subsidy for GSL's "could be a fatal blow" to the program, he cautioned.

Another note of caution was heard from CSULA President James M. Rosser, who said he was concerned at the increasing emphasis on loans instead of direct aid for minority students.

He noted that even after graduation from a university, upon which loan repayment would begin, blacks and other minorities have greater difficulty in finding a job than whites.

"The Guaranteed Student Loan is no panacea for the minority student. Tuition is up 14 percent nationally, yet aid is being cut. One should discourage the reliance on loans for low-income students," he said.

Marmaduke agreed.

"I am concerned about the amount of debt being accrued by students. I don't think we have addressed the question of how many is too many student loans," he said.

Recycling center kicks off drive

by MICHAEL JONDREAU
Staff Reporter

If Pierce's first-ever newspaper drive stacks up response, it may collect itself a spot on the Associated Student Body's (ASB) yearly agenda, according to ASB President Steve Miles.

Miles kicked off the drive at the Nov. 5 meeting of the Inter Organizational Council.

Miles hopes for a strong effort by the clubs in supporting the drive. Individuals are encouraged to participate in the drive as well, Miles stressed.

"A $200 prize is what we're offering for top accumulated weight after the three weighing dates," Miles explained.

The dates are tomorrow, Dec. 3 and Dec. 17—noon to 4 p.m.—at the Pierce Farm livestock scales.

Heather Kriensky, Pierce College Community Recycling Center manager, said there is a chance the drive will have the use of portable scales. The scales will enable the Recycling Center to become a weighing station.

The center is on Victory Boulevard across from the campus just west of Winnetka Avenue.

"Come in," Miles encouraged. "Mention your club or your own name and start a tally sheet. Volunteers are welcome as weighers," he added.

Inspiration for the drive, according to Miles and Kriensky, grew out of need to publicize the center.

"I'm for whatever good the drive will do," Kriensky said.

Kriensky also acknowledged the funds the newspaper drive will generate—about $15 a ton, will be beneficial as well.

Miles, on the other hand, spoke with dismay of that price, which is a severe dip from last semester. "Just rotten luck and timing," he said, shaking his head. "Paper brought $30 a ton last year."

There are, however, benefits above and beyond money, Kriensky pointed out, savings in trees and energy, and reduction in pollution.

"A ton of recycled paper equals 17 mature trees," she said, taking information from a publication of the California Solid Waste Management Board.

Seventy percent less energy is required for reprocessing paper over manufacturing it" she went on, and, "that means 70 percent less pollution in a very polluting industry."

"And," Kriensky added, "streams are spared. Only half the water of new paper is required."

These factors considered, even at the present low rate, which could change during the drive, Miles expressed hope of being, "up to our ears in paper."

"A successful drive could be a legacy to future classes," he said. "The center has been ignored by those in office at Pierce the last couple of years. People have pointed out losses. A successful drive could make them wonder what they were thinking."

Hotline spells relief

by CONNIE DURHAM
Staff Reporter

Ma Bell is the medium, and the message is that there is an English reference service just a jingle away.

By dialing 347-0551, Ext. 497, the Pierce College Business English Hotline, callers can get answers to their questions about correct English grammar and its usage.

The hotline is staffed by 11 faculty members of the Office Administration Dept. who answer calls during their non-teaching office hours from 8 a.m. to 2 p.m. Monday through Friday. Presently there are 5 to 15 calls daily.

The telephone is located in the Office Administration anteroom, Room 2 in the Business Education Bldg.

"The Business English Hotline keeps us fresh as teachers," said Dr. Mary Ellen Guffey, associate professor of business. "We're getting feedback on what we need to emphasize in our classes."

Guffey said the non-funded hotline, which began operation in January 1980, was established as a service to the community by the Office Administration Dept. when members read of similar services across the country.

Professor of Business Joyce Mason said, "Dr. Guffey spearheaded formation of the hotline."

Although she provided impetus for the enterprise, Guffey pointed out, "My colleagues are instrumental in taking calls. I am in word processing most of the time."

The majority of calls are from office workers who are employed in aerospace, electronics, manufacturing, communication, entertainment, education, government, trade and health services, she said.

According to a 1980 department survey over a six-month period, questions about spelling are most frequently the subject of calls. Inquiries about the use of commas, apostrophes and capitalization follow close behind.

"Many of the calls to the hotline involved questions which could have been solved by using a dictionary or a complete reference manual," Guffey said.

"Numerous persons don't know how to use the dictionary. One caller asked, 'Why can't I find the word "ranches"?' She didn't know that the plural of regular nouns isn't shown.

"I recommend the American Heritage Dictionary of the English Language. It shows all forms and usage labels. The Merriam-Webster Dictionary doesn't prescribe usage, it just describes the language."

However, the dictionary doesn't have all the answers. Last semester Dr. Lyn Clark, professor of business, was asked to spell the word Maria.

"The caller thought it was the name of a wind god," Clark said. "There was no reference to the word in the dictionary, and Pierce's reference librarian could find no trace of such a god. We finally discovered the word came from a song title in the 50s, 'Maria,' a contrived name."

Clark commented on another question that came in. A caller asked how you make words such as TELEX (a new type equipment) plural. Would it be with apostrophe "s" or "es"?

"Since these are such new terms, there is no reference source to answer the question specifically," she said.

"There are two philosophies: 1.) When you have letters used as letters, the plural is formed by adding apostrophe "s", consequently, TELEX'S. 2.) A newer school of thought doesn't use apostrophe "s" for forming the plural of letters unless clarity is needed, therefore, TELEXES," Clark said.

Reflecting the current consciousness of women in business, several callers how to address organizations of men and women.

Teresa Caruana, associate professor of business, said, "The correct salutation for a business letter today, when man and women are in management of the company, is 'Ladies and Gentlemen.'"

Last semester Leo Sirakides, professor of business, was asked

(See Hotline, page 3)

ANNOUNCEMENTS

Due to the Thanksgiving holiday, school will be closed Thursday, Nov. 26 and Friday, Nov. 27. The next Roundup will be published Wednesday, Dec. 2.

****

The Roundup notes that certain events have been covered though the sponsors have not been named, including the following Associated Student Body sponsored events: Dr. Jerry Buss speech, Autumn Festival.

We recognize the necessity of attributing events to their sponsors and will, in the future, make every effort to include this information.

Earthquake readiness

Campus is safe —Lewis

by STEVE ELZER
Asst. Opinion Editor

What's shakin'?

According to state officials a major earthquake in Southern California is inevitable.

Presently, Pierce officials are working to bolt bookshelves to walls and anchor any materials that might fall in the event of a quake.

According to Dean of Students William Lewis, "The campus is absolutely safe. We (Pierce) meet all the earthquake requirements in California law."

Lewis is taking the possibility of a major quake very seriously. "There is no doubt in my mind one will hit. Now it's a question of how prepared we can be."

Lewis is planning a disaster drill. During the drill procedures will be followed which are specified in "A Plan for a Major Emergency and Disaster Preparedness," authored by both Lewis and Campus Police Captain Joe Holts.

During the disaster drill, injuries will be simulated and campus officials will survey potential damage.

According to Holts, a hospital in the San Fernando Valley will be utilizing the campus football field as an emergency shelter both during the drill and in the event of an actual quake.

"Many outside agencies will be looking to Pierce for help and shelter. The campus is very stable and can withstand a disaster," said Holts.

Lewis said a major problem in the event of a quake could be the control of livestock.

"If one of the fences fall in a quake, the animals could be a danger to the community or themselves," he said.

At an earthquake preparedness discussion held in the Campus Center Oct. 15, State Earthquake Education Officer Jeff Sampson said that a major earthquake would strike the valley area anytime between "now and the next decade."

Sampson said the likelihood of an earthquake, 8.3 or larger on the Richter Scale, occuring in the next 10-15 years is great.

Sampson stressed the need for citizens of California to be prepared.

"Chances are you will not be able to receive basic emergency help for at least three days," he said.

He said that families should know how to turn off the gas and water. A three day supply of food and water should be kept in the house.

Basic provisions should be kept on hand, a first aid kit, radio, flashlight and plenty of spare batteries.

"Keep your batteries in the refrigerator, they will last longer. Recycle them about once a year," Sampson said.

Earthquake information is easily obtainable, said Sampson.

"Anyone who has a telephone book has directions on how to prepare yourself in an earthquake," he said.

On Oct. 23 several tremors roared through the southland. Although no injuries or damage were reported, it was a reminder that Southern California is earthquake country.

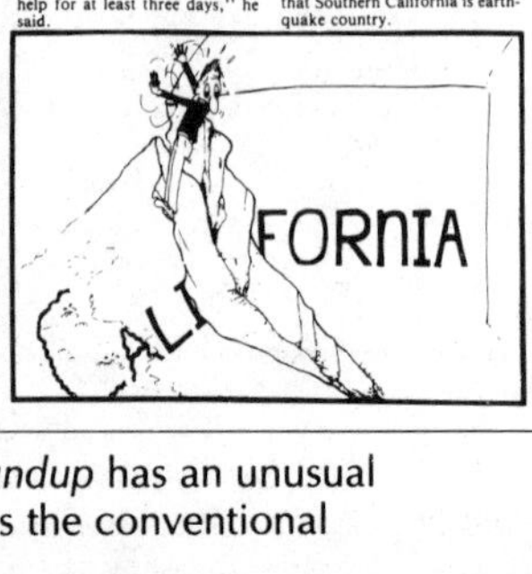

Figure 10.14 This issue of the Los Angeles Pierce College *Roundup* has an unusual vertical nameplate. At other times the *Roundup's* nameplate has the conventional horizontal format.

or more, consider running it wide enough to avoid having more than about five consecutive inches of type in one column. For a 16-column-inch story, a 4-column by 4-inch spread is much more appealing than a 2-column by 8-inch display. Don't be afraid to run a story all the way across the page, either boxed or unboxed. If such a module can include artwork, all the better.

Another design technique to consider is running a boxed story with wider-than-normal columns. Wider columns tend to be more readable than narrow ones, and if there is additional white space between columns, that makes the story even more readable. A boxed story with three wide columns of type where there might normally be five columns is an excellent display device.

To compute the column widths for such a display, you'll need to do a little simple math. Suppose your columns are normally 15 picas wide, with a 1-pica *gutter* (of white space) between columns. That means 5 columns would be 79 picas wide (5 times 15 equals 75, but there are four 1-pica gutters in a 5-column spread, for a total of 79 picas). If you wanted 3 wide columns with wider-than-usual gutters (for a more open look), you might use three 24-pica columns (for 72 picas of type) plus two 3½-pica gutters (for a total of 79 picas).

Common Makeup Errors

In designing pages, there are a couple of pitfalls to avoid. One is a classic error called the *tombstone*. A tombstone occurs when you have two similar headlines side by side. The reader may not notice that there are two separate stories: the two may look as if they run together as a single headline. Try to avoid this problem by using art between headlines or by boxing one story and using considerable white space beside the headline. If you must have two headlines side by side, make one small and the other large, and be sure the type styles are different: perhaps one could be bold while the other is condensed.

Another potential problem is a lack of balance. Newspaper designers once thought every page had to be pretty evenly balanced from side to side. The rules on balancing pages are much more flexible today, but it's still not considered good makeup to put all the weight (that is, art and headlines) on one side, with most of the gray areas of type on the other. If you have a large photograph on one side of the page, something heavy (perhaps a large headline) should go on the other side.

Another related problem, of course, is gray areas of body type. Be careful not to create large areas of gray matter—they aren't very readable. There are various ways to break up a large story. For instance, small photos or drawings may be interspersed with the text, or key quotations may be pulled out, set in larger type and given top and bottom borders. Subheads may also be used to break up gray areas, provided your design style permits subheads. Some newspapers have stopped using subheads except under unusual circumstances.

You should also remember that there are some rules about the placement of photographs. As you begin to make up pages, you may wish to review those rules (in the previous chapter).

All of these rules and suggestions are just that—suggestions. The ultimate test of a newspaper page is whether it is aesthetically pleasing to the staff and the readers. If it meets that test, it is well designed. If not, no amount of faithful adherence to the rules of makeup will rescue it.

Special Section Design

So far we've talked mainly about front pages. Much of the challenge is to come up with attractive designs for special section pages and for ad-heavy inside pages.

On a page with heavy advertising the problem is to come up with a news display that can compete with the strong visual effect of the ads. If the ads are arranged in the traditional pyramid fashion (as shown in Figure 10.15), the best bet is often to place the strongest visual element of the news display in the corner *diagonally opposite* the visually strongest advertising. In any case, it is usually unwise to place a news or feature photograph adjacent to a well-illustrated ad: the result is often aesthetically unappealing and may lose readership for both.

Some college papers are now adding a *second front page,* following an example set by many larger professional papers. Such a page follows the same design principles as the front page, since it, too, is an open (that is, ad-free) news page. Figure 10.16 shows an inside front page from the San Antonio College *Ranger*. It reflects the same vigorous design as the *Ranger's* front page, but with an added feature. It has a standing column called "F.Y.I.," which provides a place for the many small items a newspaper must carry.

Newspapers were once full of separate little stories about all of these items. The result, of course, was a cluttered page with as many as 20 different stories. With contemporary modular makeup that would be out of the question, but by putting all of the items in one column, the need to carry these items is met.

Most college newspapers also have special-purpose pages or sections that focus on a different topic each issue. Figure 10.17 shows such a spread from the Fort Hays State *Leader*. Note that, although the paper is full-size, this spread is set up in tabloid fashion: the reader must turn the paper 90 degrees to read it. The result is the appearance of a two-page-wide horizontal display instead of a single-page vertical presentation. This device makes it possible to produce a more visually appealing display.

Another feature carried by many college papers is a one- or two-page photo series. Figure 10.18 shows such a two-page display from the Pepperdine *Graphic*. Not all college papers have enough space to set aside two full-size pages for such a photo series, but if you have the space, the result can be dramatic.

Most college papers today carry sports, entertainment and editorial pages or sections. Often the sports section has some of the best photography and the boldest headlines to be found anywhere in the paper. The editorial page, on the other hand, is typically the most restrained part of the paper, with smaller headlines and a grayer display than is found elsewhere.

Jeff Brown, Bonner Springs junior, relaxes in his studio apartment in Hanover Place.

Studio housing offers privacy, but loneliness is a drawback

By JANICE GUNN
Staff Reporter

Jeff Brown, Bonner Springs junior, gets up, gets dressed and goes to his classes every day, as most students do.

But, unlike many students, he is reluctant to go home at the end of the day.

It's not that he's not relieved to be finished with that daily routine, it's just that he likes to stay on campus and talk to friends rather than return to his studio apartment at Hanover Place, 200-1 Hanover Place, to have a lonely dinner.

"That's the worst thing about living in a studio apartment—having to eat dinner by yourself," Brown said last week. "I like to look across the table and see someone sitting there, not an empty chair."

BUT, DESPITE THE drawbacks of not having a dinner partner or companion for other home activities, Brown and other studio apartment dwellers say they'd rather give up the companionship for privacy.

Of all the studio apartments in Meadowbrook, Trailridge, Alvamar Quail Creek, Cedarwood and Heatherwood apartment complexes,

apartment managers said there were no vacancies.

Mark Graham, Lawrence junior and assistant manager of Cedarwood Apartments, 2414 Ousdahl Road, said that at the beginning of the semester, there was a bigger demand for studio apartments than Cedarwood could accommodate. Four of the complex's 122 units are studio apartments.

"It's very unusual that they're full," Graham said. "People try to get the best buy they can and a one-bedroom apartment is only $20 more a month than a studio."

BUT STUDENTS SAID they had to sacrifice the extra space of a one- or two-bedroom apartment to save money.

Because they don't have a roommate with whom to split food, telephone and utility costs, many said that studio living was more expensive.

Several students said the extra cost was worth having a place to themselves where they could entertain, eat or sleep whenever they wanted to, without disturbing other people.

All of the students interviewed had lived in organized living groups either at the University of Kansas or other

universities and said they studied more when living alone.

KEITH HARRISTON, Washington, D.C., graduate student, said he had neither the time to deal with another person in his apartment nor time to keep up a large place, he said.

His studio at Meadowbrook Apartments, 15th and Crestline streets, is 15 by 12 feet.

"I just like to live by myself," Harriston said. "It's just the right size for me, since I don't have the time to put up with personality conflict that you might have to if you lived with somebody."

Although he said he had lived with roommates before as an undergraduate and had no disagreements with them, he was a private person and believed in "preventive medicine."

He said he would like to live alone in a bigger place, but because of the cost and lack of time to maintain such a place, the studio was just right.

But Brown said that he liked to work on his apartment and when he moved in, he arranged and decorated it.

Senate meets for changing of guard

By MICHAEL ROBINSON
Staff Reporter

It was goodbye to the old and hello to the new last night at the final Student Senate meeting of the year.

In a joint meeting of last year's Senate and the newly-elected senators, Bert Coleman and Bren Abbott, former student body president and vice president, bid their final farewells to the group they had directed during the past year.

"I think we had a really good year," Coleman told the old Senate. "I think we worked very, very hard to accomplish what we did."

DURING THEIR administration, Coleman and Abbott had to contend with severe dissension on several issues and criticism about Coleman's performance in office.

Detroit auto sales lowest since 1959

By United Press International

DETROIT—Domestic auto sales in November were the lowest for the month since 1959, down 16.4 percent from a year ago, with one analyst blaming the drop on consumers' economic fears.

Ford suffered the biggest decline—a 20.2 percent drop—with General Motors falling 18.1 percent from a year ago. Chrysler's sales were 15 percent for the month, but the company managed to keep its sales for the year more than 14 percent above 1980.

Domestic automakers sold 431,726 cars in November, down from 529,288 a year ago. This was a daily rate of 17,988 cars, the lowest since the rate of 15,995 recorded in November 1959.

Overall, the industry recorded sales of 561,726 cars last month, down 16.4 percent from the 696,050 sold in 1980. The combined daily rate of 24,439 was the industry's lowest since 1974.

Imports grabbed a 25.8 percent share of the market.

A Ford analyst said that the figures were better than expected but that customers were still too worried about their economic futures to make major investments, such as car purchases.

Coleman warned the new Senate that federal budget cuts and rising education costs would make its job more important and more difficult.

"I think the future is going to be difficult for students," he said.

"Just work really hard and don't get frustrated. Perseverance will get you farther than anything else."

Abbott told the incoming senators to go to David Adkins and David Welch, the newly elected president and vice president, for advice and ideas.

"Utilize David and David to the greatest extent possible," he said. "Nothing will be changed until you start utilizing those two."

He also told the senators to accept victories and defeats as they came.

"And don't be afraid to speak out," Abbott said.

BEFORE GIVING up the lectern to Welch, his successor, Abbott told the old Senate, "I think it's been a good year."

For the new, he added, "Work hard for your constituents."

The outgoing Senate also selected Loren Busby, Hutchinson junior; Mollie

Mitchell, Hutchinson junior; and Staci Feldman, Wichita sophomore, as holdover senators.

Each year, the outgoing Senate selects three of its members for the holdover positions, meaning that they will be in Senate during the next term.

Busby was an unsuccessful candidate for student body president and Mitchell and Feldman were defeated for re-election to the Senate.

The new Senate, in its first action, chose Sarah Duckers, business senator, and Jim Cramer, Nunemaker senator, to serve on the University Council for the coming year.

WELCH ENCOURAGED the senators to participate actively in Senate and the committee activities.

Adkins, in his first speech to the senators since his election, called on them to discard the competitive feelings of the campaign.

"My first order of business tonight is to proclaim the campaign over," Adkins said. "I would think we would like to look beyond whatever divisions we've had in the past."

He said his new administrations would be based on teamwork, communications and enthusiasm.

Figure 10.15   This page from the *Daily Kansan* shows advertising in a pyramid to the right, with the most prominent editorial display in a diagonally opposite position. Used by permission.

Soviet student likes America; says Russian schools difficult

Would you pay $100 for a pair of jeans? How about $50 for a Stones album? Unbelievable, huh? That's exactly what Inna Abzel, a student here from Russia, has done.

"I paid $100 for the only pair of jeans I ever had through the black market," she said.

Abzel, a computer programming major, left Leningrad, Russia, with her parents and grandmother two years ago. After living in New York City nine months and Monterrey, Calif., seven months, Abzel and her family moved to San Antonio where her parents are Russian language instructors at Lackland Air Force Base.

Abzel and her family lived in "common apartments," where two or three families share an apartment, for three years.

"We had two rooms and there were three for the others, and one bathroom. We were constantly fighting.

"America is very beautiful, but sometimes I miss my friends," she said.

What Abzel says she does not miss is the Soviet way of life. Everyday conveniences Americans take for granted are considered luxuries by Soviet standards, she said.

"We waited 20 years for a telephone and did not have one the day we left. In New York, we had one installed in 15 minutes," she said.

There is at least a six-year waiting list to buy a car, she added.

Abzel said Russian children boil erasers and add sugar to make chewing gum because it is not sold in Russia.

The government regulates the radio, theater and television. Because of the strict moral code, no sex is shown in movies. Most movies are about the communist way of life and show factories and people at work, she explained.

Abzel said the Soviet government believes rock 'n' roll is a product of American immorality; therefore, it is not played on Russian airwaves.

Russian schools are different from American schools, Abzel said.

Beginning in the fifth grade, Abzel studied English, physics, chemistry, astronomy and many other subjects that are considered college level in the United States.

"American schools are very easy," she said.

As for partying in Russia, the computer programming major said that is where Americans and Russians are alike.

"We love to party," she said.■

SECTION B

THE RANGER
Dec 4, 1981

Martha Ward, activities secretary, illustrates the need for students to claim lost articles. *Photo by Bobby Sanchez*

Lost items go unclaimed

Underwear. A lost crutch or cane. A false leg with a shoe brace. These may seem unusual, but they are some of the unclaimed items in the lost and found department in the student activities office of Loftin Student Center.

Other unclaimed items in the office are books, glasses, wallets, jewelry, calculators, keys, checkbooks and clothes.

Martha L. Ward, secretary of student activities, said in an interview the reason items go unclaimed is that students come into the office immediately after losing an item.

Ward said, "It takes time for the item to get turned in."

"Valuable items such as watches, calculators and expensive jewelry are kept in a safe until claimed. Items of less value are kept up to six weeks," Ward said.

The office donates unclaimed glasses to a Lion's Club where they are given to the underprivileged. The hundreds of unclaimed keys are given to the maintenance department.

"All the other unclaimed items are given to a club that would like to sponsor a lost and found sale. Half of the money goes to the sponsoring club and the other half is given to the student activities office," Ward said.

The Cheshire Cheese Club sponsored a sale Oct. 1 and raised more than $200.

"Many, many books get turned in daily without any identification. The students are the losers in this case because we cannot give the student the books unless his or her name is on it, or unless some kind of mark appears in the book so the student can identify the book," Ward said.

Another problem the lost and found department faces is items being kept at circulation desks in other campus buildings for weeks or even months, Ward explained.

"Items will sometimes stay at the circulation desk for three or four days in the building where you have lost an item. Most students do not know this. After the three or four days it is supposed to be turned in at the student activities office, but sometimes it never does," Ward said.

Senior rings are a popular item in the lost and found.

"In the spring, when the principals and counselors from different high schools come, I find out what schools have come and bring out the corresponding rings so they may find out what student it belongs to by the year and date," Ward said.■

Two say papers inform voters

By Bettie Cross
Staff Writer
Second of two parts

When the average voter stands inside a voting booth pulling a lever beside the name of his favorite candidates, his choices are largely determined by the information he has received from television and newspapers.

But are television stations and newspapers providing the voter with the necessary information to make an educated choice at the ballot box?

Editors from the San Antonio Express-News and San Antonio Light say newspapers do, but television stations do not.

Two local television news directors agree.

The four interviewed were Jim Dolan, managing editor of the Sunday Express-News; Joe Rust, associate editor of the Light; Bill Church, KSAT-TV news director; and Jay Solomon, KMOL-TV news director.

"Newspapers generally will present much more information on political candidates than people will ever be able to absorb," Rust said.

Dolan agreed saying that the Express runs "acres of newsprint" on campaigns and elections.

However, he added, "Television has ended up being nothing more than a headline service that runs stories about 24 hours after the newspapers."

Church agreed television news is superficial. "TV news has to be superficial. We don't have the time to be anything but."

Solomon said with the exception of documentaries and series, television is not able to provide in-depth reporting on political candidates because the medium is not conducive to detailed information.

"I will accept the criticism that we have been generalists because that is what time permits," he added.

Other than the limited time of newscasts, Solomon also cited their quick pace and the lack of good interesting visuals to back up political stories as the reasons for the superficial approach to campaigns and elections by television.

Both news directors also said they think they have a responsibility to their audience to cover major political events. They, however, do not see it as their responsibility to educate the public on political issues.

"I cannot say the media have the responsibility to educate the public. I can say the public has the reponsibility to help educate themselves," Solomon said.

Church said people who are getting all of their news from television are shortchanging themselves.

"Sixty-four percent of the people get their news from television and that's nothing to be proud of. Actually that's a knock on the citizenry of America," Church said.

"If a person wants to know where a candidate stands on all the issues all the time and what his/her voting record has been, the person will have to turn to newspapers and magazines for that kind of information," he continued.

Rust agreed that for a person to come up with a complete picture of a candidate or issue, he/she must read the paper daily.

"Newspapers in any kind of an election will present much more material than people will ever read," Rust said.

He added the problem is that it's usually presented over such a long period of time people do not realize the volume of material that is being presented and keep up with it.

Rust also said by the time newspapers compile all of this information into an election section which is published a few weeks before the election, most people already have made up their mind who they are going to vote for.

"Newspaper election sections are almost a complete waste of time because of when they're put out," he said.

Both newspaper editors and television news directors agreed reporters who specialize in political science would provide more in-depth coverage of political candidates and issues.

However, Dolan stipulated that the specialized reporter also would have to be a good communicator in order to be effective as a journalist.

Church, Rust and Solomon agreed, though, that the higher salaries these specialists would require curbs the tendency to hire them.

"You cannot increase and specialize the news staff without spending more money," Church said. "This is a free enterprise, and everybody is out to make money, not spend it," he concluded.

However, Dolan said, "Every station in this town makes a higher rate of return than any newspaper in this town, but they're just sitting there making the profits and not spending it to increase and improve their news staff."■

F.Y.I.

Department to sponsor workshop

The drafting department will sponsor a workshop for junior college drafting teachers May 17-21 in Nail Technical Center.

Norman Neundorf, chairman of the department, said the purpose of the workshop, which is sponsored by the Texas Education Agency through a grant from Southwest Texas State University, is to train teachers from other schools to use computer-aided drawing.

"We are trying to help other schools that are beginning to use computer graphics to reach the level we have reached," he said.

"Computer-aided drawing is when a computer is programmed to draw to the drawings we need made," Neundorf explained.

The workshop will run from 8 a.m. until 4:30 p.m. and an open lab will be available from 6 p.m. until 10 p.m.

"We will divide the participants into two groups. While the first group is getting a lecture, the second group will have a chance to use the machines," Neundorf said.

Representatives from 20 junior colleges throughout Texas were in attendance at the workshop held last May, and the drafting department is preparing for an equal turnout this year.

"We are programming the machines with an orientation for the schools that did not attend last year's workshop," he said.■

Faculty elects committee members

The faculty elected May O'Neal, history professor, to the faculty hearing committee in a runoff Nov. 25.

O'Neal received a majority vote of 80 to Robert Brown's, psychology professor, 56 votes.

O'Neal joins Robert Bryant, mathematics professor; Lewis Fox, economics chairman; Jessie Cox, foreign languages professor; John Igo, English professor; Dr. Douglas Johnston, history professor; and Dr. Kenneth Shumate, chemistry chairman, on the committee.

The committee meets by request of tenured faculty involved in dismissal. The committee description and function is outlined in Board Policy 73-1.■

Professor to discuss relaxation

Melodie Olson, nursing professor, will present a program in relaxation techniques at noon Monday for the Women's Company: In for Lunch group.

Olson, who wrote her doctoral dissertation on relaxation, will provide a relaxation experience for the participants. Special clothing is not required.

"The joy of relaxation is whatever is comfortable," Olson said.

The group meets at the women's center at the United Methodist Student Center, 102 Belknap Place.■

Group to review dental accreditation

The Commission on Dental Accreditation will meet in May to review and evaluate the status of this college's dental assisting program.

The commission awards the dental program provisional approval, conditional approval, full accreditation or loss of accreditation.

Dr. James L. Wyatt Jr., chairman of dental assisting, said the accreditation team evaluates the program every seven years. It was fully accredited on the last evaluation.

"I feel the accreditation program is helpful because it lets some outside expert look at our program. We need someone to see the program with other than our own eyes," Wyatt said.■

Thorogood considers three for chair

The director of technical education is considering three nominees for data processing department chairman.

Alvin J. Stehling, data processing professor, has resigned as chairman of the data processing department. His resignation becomes effective Dec. 31.

The nominees were considered in an advisory capacity by selection committees of Department Chairman's Assembly and the dean's council, Dean Truett Chance said.

"Their recommendation of one of the three nominees went to Nellie Thorogood, director of occupational education and technology," Chance said. "She is currently preparing her final recommendation to me."

If Chance approves Thorogood's selection, he presents it to Chancellor Byron McClenney, he said. "At that point, under the current administration, I am uncertain who actually appoints the new chairman," he said.

The chancellor appoints the chairman, Dr. Frank Thomas, vice chancellor for academic affairs, said.

"In effect, the dean makes the choice and we just approve the selection," Thomas said.

The district board of trustees must approve the new chairman's contract, Thomas said.

"The chances of the dean's selection being overturned are almost nil," he said.

Both Chance and Thorogood declined to name the three nominees.

Homebuilders set committees' duties

Members of the San Antonio College Homebuilders Association discussed the responsibilities of five of the organization's committees at a recent meeting.

The business cooperative committee's main concern is obtaining discounts for homebuilding members, Pete McMahon, homebuilding instructor and club sponsor, said.

"The program committee brings programs into the club for the benefit of the club," McMahon said.

The public is informed on the association through the publicity committee.

The fund-raising committee is to "raise funds for the various activities we plan to do for the club," he said.

"The membership committee is designed to attract more members in the club and also for the alumni and honorary members," McMahon said.■

Library will close Dec. 21 for holidays

The library in Moody Learning Center will close from Dec. 21 to Jan. 2 because of the Christmas and New Year's holidays.

Students and faculty may check books out until Dec. 10; however, all books are due Dec. 11. The circulation desk will receive books and clear records from 8 a.m. until 4 p.m. Dec. 19 and from 8 a.m. to 4 p.m. Jan. 4-8.

Students also may return books and clear records from 8 a.m. to 5 p.m. Jan. 11 and from 8 a.m. to 9 p.m. Jan. 12-14 and from 8 a.m. to 4 p.m. Jan. 15.

Regular hours and services will resume Jan. 16.■

International club plans banquet

The International Students Association will have its scholarship and awards banquet Dec. 11 instead of today.

"We feel that more students will be active in Las Posadas if we have the banquet later," Marina Villanueva, club president, said.

The banquet will be at 12:30 p.m.-3 p.m. Dec. 11 in the Madrid Room of Loftin Student Center.■

Figure 10.16 Like many professional dailies, many college papers have a news-oriented second front page such as this one from the San Antonio College *Ranger*. Used by permission.

Leader Focus

Select few chosen for upcoming drama production

by Kenton Kersting

"All the world's a stage, all the men and women merely players" — Shakespeare.

Of the billions of the world's players, a select few were chosen to perform in the upcoming Fort Hays State production of *A Streetcar Named Desire*.

Of the 16 persons who auditioned in February, 12 were selected to play the roles in Tennessee Williams' classic. The casting process should not be taken lightly since it is far from simple and is described by the director as "agonizing."

"Casting is the single most important element over which a director has control," Dr. Stephen Shapiro, director, said.

When scheduling auditions and subsequently selecting the cast, Shapiro follows several guidelines.

It is the policy of FHS that auditions for plays and productions are open to the community, not just students. Shapiro makes the scripts available to interested persons before audi-

tions. With the advance availability of the script, people do not need to go into auditions while still unfamiliar with the play and the characters, Shapiro said several people checked out *Streetcar* scripts and studied the show before auditions. "It's a wise thing to do," he said.

At the audition, Shapiro looks for several features among potential cast members. These include vocal quality, physical requirements and good speech and intelligence in interpreting lines. An actor's stage presence and how well he relates to other actors on stage are also considered.

Shapiro tries to avoid typecasting. "I, like every director, have certain concepts and ideas about the physical and emotional aspects of a character, but I try not to cast according to type," he said.

Stage experience is also important. Certain parts require greater levels of experience. He noted that almost everyone in the *Streetcar* cast has had some acting experience, though not necessarily at FHS. "This is the type of play where you would not want to have a majority of novices," he said.

Shapiro describes the next step as "agonizing." After reviewing the actor's emotional appeal, control of the stage, line interpretation and other factors, the director then completes "the single most important element over which he has control," selecting members of the cast.

The decision is made, parts are assigned and the cast list is posted. Announcement of the cast might elicit squeals of delight and excitement from those who made it or talk of "there's always next time" from those who did not.

After choosing the cast and having that load taken off his shoulders, Shapiro does not look back. He goes with his decision and makes it work. "If time and effort are put into making the decision, the director won't look back and say, 'Oh, if only I had cast differently,'" he said.

In speaking of *Streetcar*, Shapiro said, "The cast exhibits a real spirit of team work. The feeling of ensemble and cooperation is stronger than I've ever experienced in a show."

If Shapiro's feelings about the cast hold true, Williams' classic could be well on the way to becoming a classic production at FHS.

Performers reap experience, applause

by David Clouston
Senior Staff Reporter

As an extracurricular activity, a play has to be ranked as one of the most time-consuming. A great deal of effort goes into putting on a first-rate production. One might wonder what makes a student want to be involved in this area of theater.

David Clark, Oakley senior, plays the role of Mitch in the upcoming Fort Hays State production, *A Streetcar Named Desire*. He said, "I get a kick out of being on stage. Vanity's a part of it." Lex Reisig, Hays senior, and Carol Davidson, Russell senior, agreed.

"It has to be," Davidson said. The three also compared their work in *Streetcar* to their experience in other productions. Davidson is playing the role of Stella, while Reisig is portraying the nurse.

"The hardest thing about this show is that we haven't had as much rehearsal time," Clark said. "We usually get five weeks, and we only had four this time."

Reisig also thought that timing is a factor. "It was hard because it fell so close to mid-terms," she said.

Clark said this compared with many FHS productions. The current production will mark Clark's 14th appearance on the Felten-Start stage. Davidson has been in several plays, "usually two a year," she said. For Reisig, this will be her first time before the footlights.

The three said they enjoy what they are doing, anyone who puts in three or four hours a night, five days a week, for two or three weeks working to perfect what will be over after four two-hour performances, must have some extra incentive.

Yet Clark said, "Usually you get more credit than they deserve."

What is it that keeps a performer at the personal satisfaction; it is a release," Davidson said. It is also true most college thespians are theater majors in search of ex-

perience that will help them land a job later. Davidson, Clark and Reisig are all aiming toward this end.

Reisig said she wants to be a drama director. But she also enjoys the time she spends on stage. "That's why I auditioned for this show, even if it's just for five minutes on stage."

Davidson wants to combine an acting and directing career, while Clark said he would be happy with any theater job. "Working in the box office all the time might get boring, however," he said.

In regards to their most recent effort, the three say they have not encountered any major problems. "Williams gives you a lot of dimension," Davidson said.

"The characters have a lot of dimension," Davidson said. Reisig agreed. "They're real people."

It would seem that the rehearsal process would become boring after awhile. In reality, boredom is replaced by a sense of

tachment, the three said, Clark said, "I've become detached from rehearsal when I'm off stage." Davidson said she thinks about the play sometimes during the day.

In the same way that boredom is replaced by detachment, so perfection is replaced by the reality of unfulfilled expectations. "I'm always thinking I should have done this, or

brought that out just a bit more," Davidson said.

Clark said, "I've never reached the point where I was entirely satisfied with any production. There's a point where you begin to sense a balance, though."

The three described *A Streetcar Named Desire* as a release. More than any they had ever been in.

"There's a lot of sex and violence and it's a lot more body-oriented," Reisig said.

The play is the thing for these FHS performers. The audience's entertainment is the result of their work. Their reward? Experience and participation, as well as the applause of the crowd if it draws the audience's "trade." Perhaps. But considering the amount of work put in, the members of the cast deserve a great deal of credit.

From left: Terry Weber, Virgil Scott, Brenda Meder and David Clark.

Long-range planning required
Staging, sets, costumes chosen

by Sherryl Province
Staff Reporter

Have you ever wondered what is involved in preparing for a play production at Fort Hays State? You may be surprised at the amount of time spent planning the play long before it is performed on the stage.

Steve Larson, technical theater director using *A Streetcar Named Desire* as an example, explained what his duties are in preparing for the production.

Plans for *Streetcar* began in November, while *Dracula* was still being performed. Larson said he began by reading the script twice to single out technical elements of the play. Next, he determined the number of sets the play requires, costumes needed and problems of staging, if any.

After completing these, Larson set out the basic cast of the play. Having this basic cast of the play, from backdrops to the paving of the actors, is essential.

After completing these steps, Larson will sit down to plan his ideas, such as to why the director chose the play and what he wants to get across to the audience. This enables Larson to prepare the play so that the people involved with performing the play

prior to the opening of the play so the actors can get the feel of their surroundings and work out any problems that may arise, Larson said.

Lighting the show is next on the agenda. In *Streetcar*, a ceiling fan in the bedroom scene presented a problem with hanging the fan from the ceiling of the theater. Larson said he handles this type of problem.

"Practical lights — inside and outside lamps on the sets — are tested at this time."

The prop crew then begins looking for items essential to the era of the play, which in *Streetcar* is 1947. A few items that fit into this category are beer bottles, coke bottles and a telephone. People of the community have been good about donating furniture, clothing and so on to the theater, Larson said. *Streetcar* prop crew members are still looking for men's suits with padded shoulders. Antique shops in Hays have also helped by having merchandise to be used in the production.

Much goes into preparing for a play. Seeing six efforts utilized for the entertainment of others remains more to the crew than anything else, Larson said.

A Streetcar Named Desire performances will be 8 p.m. Saturday and at 2 p.m. Sunday at Felten-Start Theatre in Malloy Hall. Tickets may be purchased at the Student Service Center or Malloy Hall box office. Prices are $3 for adults and $2 for students.

Sound effects are being worked on to depict the authenticity of the part of New Orleans where two of the play's characters live.

Much research is then done on the play location, people, sights and sounds give the effects of reality to the audience. Larson is a large research library that he has obtained over the years. If he does not have the necessary materials in his files, he goes to the library to research further.

The floor plan is then executed. A map of the interior and exterior sets are taped on the floor of the stage to show the amount of space available for action. Wall plans are next in bringing the actors to their stage.

Larson said he pores over the 10 pages of blueprints for the play, then gives them to a construction crew of about four people who work to get ready. "These people are the ones that help build the set," Larson said. "I usually about 40 people help with the entire show.

A storehouse of flats some flats beings 10 years old or more, provide flats to be used in producing scenes. Some of the flats are used in many productions and others are not used at all.

Because Felten-Start Theatre is shared with the music department, preparing sets for plays may be different. This constraints the restriction of the theater 10-14 days

The Rock Stor

If you decide to take a drive along Mulholland Highwa
any weekend, you could be in for quite a surprise.

As you round one of the sweeping curves a few miles
Malibu Canyon, you might think that you are driving int
Angels rally.

Actually this is the site of a small store tucked into the
mountain. The Rock Store, owned by Ed Savko, is a gene
from Monday through Friday. On the weekends, howeve
into a gathering place for just about every type of motor
rider.

Some riders are there to see friends, to have a drink and to check out other bikes.
taking time out from cruising Mulholland to get some refreshment or rest. The people
the Rock Store include doctors, lawyers, construction workers, senior citizens and eve
between.

Even celebrities have visited the store, and are pictured on the walls: Ronald Reaga
Cosby, Clint Walker, Lee Majors, Farrah Fawcett and Lassie. But the real stars are th
cycles, which include custom Harley Davidson's, lowered turbo Cafe Racers, dirt bike
mopeds.

Photography

by Rick Ha

Figure 10.18   This photo series, covering two full-size pages, is from the Pepperdine
Graphic. Used by permission.

Figures 10.19 and 10.20 are examples of two-page sports sections from the *Falcon Times,* the seven-time Pacemaker-winning newspaper at Miami-Dade Community College-North in Florida. The *Falcon Times* has long been noted for its attractive design, a look that is evident in these sports sections. By using modular news packaging and by offering columns of brief items along with longer stories, the *Falcon Times* offers readers good reporting, first-rate photography and design that consistently wins praise from competition judges.

Figures 10.21 and 10.22 are editorial pages, from the Pepperdine *Graphic* and the *Daily Kansan.* There is an old taboo about editorial pages, which both of these newspapers—and most other college papers—follow. More than any other page in the paper, the editorial page should be free of advertising. Because the editorial page is where the newspaper expresses its own opinions and welcomes readers and columnists to do the same, it is a sacrosanct place: there should never be even a hint that any space on this page is for sale.

However, space on most other inside pages is very much for sale, because even most state-supported school newspapers depend on advertising for a substantial portion of their revenue. The challenge in making up many of these pages is, as noted earlier, simply to come up with a news display in the face of dominant advertising. If the page consists entirely of advertising except for a few inches per column running across the top of the page, a single story under a banner headline is an obvious possibility. On such a page, several small stories will produce a cluttered look and will probably make tombstones inevitable. Alternatively, two stories may be placed on either side of a photograph. When the entire page is advertising except for a single vertical column, the best bet may be to use the open space for a series of short stories that would create a cluttered look if used on an open page. A single long story could be placed there, but a long uninterrupted column of type isn't very readable.

Dummying the Pages

After you've considered the overall design policies of your newspaper and looked over the material available, it's time for the final step in the design process—actually dummying the pages. Figure 10.23 shows a blank-page dummy that would be suitable for a five-column full-size page. The dummy has vertical rules for the columns, with the depth (in inches) shown on both sides.

Because advertising is often dummied toward the right and is measured from the bottom of the page upward, the inches on the right side are numbered from the bottom up. On the left side the inches are numbered from the top down.

If the page is to carry advertising, the ads are dummied in first and the editors are responsible for filling the remaining space. In both college and professional newsrooms, editorial and advertising departments quarrel about what appears on the dummies the editors receive from the ad staff. On some papers the editors never feel they're given enough space to cover the news, while the ad staff doesn't think the editors fully appreciate who pays the bills.

Figure 10.19   Sports pages from the Miami-Dade Community College North *Falcon Times*. Used by permission.

With or without heavy advertising, there never seems to be enough space, so the editor's job is to make the most of the available space.

The mechanical process of dummying is straightforward: headlines, body type and art are indicated by appropriate symbols. Figure 10.24 shows a finished page dummy for the front page of the San Antonio College *Ranger* that appears in Figure 10.13. When you compare the two, you'll see that the dummy matches the actual page. Experienced editors will tell you that things aren't always this tidy. The dummy is the original plan for the page, the designer's worksheet that tells the pasteup production staff how to arrange the page. However, adjustments often must be made during the production process. Perhaps a story comes out longer or shorter than planned, or possibly a late-breaking story must be squeezed in.

Because of these uncertainties, some perfectly capable editors don't even

Figure 10.20   Sports pages from the *Falcon Times*. Used by permission.

make a page dummy. Although this isn't the recommended procedure, especially for beginners, some editors simply form a mental picture of the stories available and do their own page pasteup—designing as they go. To everyone else's astonishment, the page usually comes out looking acceptable, although there might have been a few moments of panic along the way. Professional designers would point to this as a classic example of expedience rather than aesthetics determining the page design.

Of course, some daily newspapers now have *pagination systems,* which eliminate the need for both the dummy and the pasteup process. A pagination system uses a computer for page design and makeup. The page is displayed on a large video screen, and the makeup editor types commands to place various stories on the page. The computer complies, continuously displaying the result. When the editor is satisfied with the appearance of the entire page, he types in the command for the entire page to be electronically delivered to the press room, where a printing plate is made using other electronic techniques.

editorials

Tuition blues reborn

Another year, another dollar. Well, not quite. Remember we're at Pepperdine, seaside.

Tradition is a strong point around here and for the last quarter of a century college have have each year had to dig deeper into their pockets to those tuition dollars. A tuition in a year of buil gasoline, rising uti $700 an ounce gold, i

The *Graphic* reco tuition mu everything must admit that the inc the national inflat administration mended on r student cost down in overwhelming

The *Gra* administrati notification of the tion schedule fective in the fall of 19 jor policy chang magnitude require planning by student ministrators alike.

The *Graphic* is still unfamiliar with all the advantages

and drawbacks of such a tuition policy, so it cannot yet judge the full merit of the change.

However, *the Graphic* does this change, like all Pepperdine, must be in relation to whether it rely beneficial to the there is no other scale be used, no other ack to go by.

out of our tuition be carefully it is for the nd improvement of our faculty, the above-stated the spending is for of the library then plies with the re-

other hand, our nneled into half-costly enterprises no payoff to the then this does not the demands of a niversity for the students."

If the trustees of our dollars are able to spend them wisely on the students, then *the Graphic* grudgingly supports the tuition rise.

A worthy beginning

The *Graphic* staff stands in favor of the recently approved media committee. Although still in its embryonic stage, the committee has excellent potential to develop into a good appellate outlet for both students and advisors.

However, we do have some reservations. The document containing the committee guidelines is both too restrictive and too general in parts. The mass media representative qualifications are restrictive without any apparent reason.

The committee guidelines state that the mass media representative must not hold the positions of editor-in-chief, managing editor or news editor in student publications.

The broadcasting departments are also restricted preventing the station manager, news director, program director and production manager from being allowed to serve.

The *Graphic's* question is; why these restrictions? University officials' stock answer is, "to avoid conflicts of interest," but we see it as overly confining.

Other than the section dealing with membership qualifications, the document is too general, especially section five relating to professional standards. We recommend that the committee act quickly to delete and revise the ambiguous legalese that dominates much of the document.

The guidelines state "All the media committee's decision-making processes will be informed by a continued effort to maintain the twin ideals of freedom and responsibility."

The *Graphic* believes this aim is a step forward, but we would also endorse the caution of one media advisor who said, "This committee's time has come and I'm looking forward to it as long as it is used properly."

Cheers for what?

Mark Penticuff

After last Friday night's basketball game against the University of San Francisco (USF) Dons, I sat in the stands not believing what I had witnessed for the third time in as many games played at home this season. What finally irritated me enough to sit down and compose this column was not really the loss itself, nor the ineptness of the referees, nor even the play of Brett Barnett. What really galled me to the point of taking some sort of action was the seven cute female members of what is supposed to be our cheerleading squad.

First of all I would like to say that the following in no way refers to all of the Pepperdine cheerleaders, just a chosen two or three that succeed in bringing the whole group down from a respectable cheerleading squad to one of literal disgrace.

This disgracefulness seemed to culminate during the USF-Pepperdine basketball game "half-time show" of the Pepperdine cheerleading squad in which several of our cheerleaders made numerous mistakes, after each of which they would smile that cute cheerleader smile and shrug as if to say, "Oh well, it's only a basketball game." Other members of the squad just laughed and continued to mess up what I'm sure was supposed to be a precise dance routine.

The fact is, they performed about as far from a university cheerleading squad as one could imagine. More than once I heard the comments of people sitting next to me saying how much better their high school cheerleaders were.

Let us be fair in acknowledging that it is indeed difficult to cheer to an audience that doesn't want to cheer. But take San Francisco's cheerleaders for

example. They had no crowd at all backing them yet they continued to take advantage of the music provided by our fine jazz band by doing their dance routines and cheers. Throughout the game they were together as a group, a unit doing what they should be doing; keeping their attention on the game and cheering their team on to victory.

Mark Penticuff is a freshman journalism/political science major.

Meanwhile, on the other side of the court the situation was, unfortunately, extremely different. At one point in the game our cheerleaders were situated in the following way: two girls on the end were sitting down on their behinds stretching their legs out while at the other end a cheerleader was busy talking to a male fan. Another girl was sitting in the bleachers looking completely dazed while the one next to her was squatting on the floor in the proper cheerleader position. Finally, the remaining two girls were up either messing around or dancing to music being played by our jazz band. Boy, if that is not working together I don't know what is.

The main reason I am taking the time to comment on this situation is that I feel not only the basketball team represents Pepperdine each time it takes the court, but our cheerleaders do as well. I shudder to think what kind of impression our girls leave at other schools.

As I am currently a freshman, I have no idea what Pepperdine's past cheerleading squads have been like, but I am sure this group of girls ranks high

in the most apathetic of groups ever to have represented our school.

The problem may lie in the fact that out of this year's seven cheerleaders, four of them were on the team last year. Maybe all of the cheerleading is getting to be too dull and boring for these beautiful young ladies. This seems to be the case as it appears half of them just don't seem to care.

To remedy this problem of tired blood, maybe at the beginning of each basketball season there should be three or four extra girls kept on the squad to replace those who seem not to care any longer. They should take up the attitudes that sports teams go by, namely, when one person is not performing up to par he or she is taken out and replaced with someone else.

I have a funny feeling there would be alot more enthusiasm and a lot less sitting on the bleachers by various cheerleaders if they had the threat of being replaced by someone else hanging over their heads.

Once this season I would love to see a group of seven, not four or five, but a group of seven wildly enthusiastic cheerleaders working together as a team, rooting our basketball team on to victory. After all, it's not like it can't be done.

I think these girls should take a serious look at themselves and re-evaluate the reason they are out on the court wearing the name of Pepperdine. They should take a good look at what they are supposed to be doing and representing. Sure it should be fun, but come on girls, we're not in high school any longer. Let's have some cheerleading along the likes of USC's or UCLA's squads. We may at times lose on the courts, but that is no excuse for losing off the courts as well.

Between the lines

Randall Bemis

A few weeks ago, in the wake of a United Nations resolution calling for a release of the American hostages in Iran and a condemnation of the Soviet Union's invasion of Afghanistan, I was told by a student on campus that the problems of the middle East are a fulfillment of Biblical prophesy. Apparently, this true-believer sees a day of judgment in the very near future and predicates his view on the book of Revelation.

Unfortunately, I've heard arguments along these lines before and am always dismayed.

For years there have been Bible-based predictions which are about as accurate as the inane California earthquake forecasts. Those who vainly predict in the earthquake ballyhoos fall into immediate disrespect; I wonder

why the scriptural soothsayers aren't put out of business just as expeditiously.

To make things worse, these stargazers are always smug in their confidence which can be paraphrased as follows: "My religion predicted this confrontation. When the world finally crashes down upon us all, I'll know that I chose the right faith. I must be right . . . mustn't I?"

Randall Bemis is a senior journalism major and is perspective editor of the Graphic.

To hear people speak this way is a real let down since it can only cultivate a lack of sincere concern over international affairs—at a time when deep

concern and active participation in world affairs is imperative.

Instead of constructively doing what they can to influence the statesmen of our nation regarding international issues, they idly sit by counting their blessings as their long-awaited Armageddon approaches.

To assert that the Bible has predicted what is today happening in the Middle East (or anywhere at anytime) constitutes a stroke of naiveté unsurpassed in the modern age. Conformance to a belief system that predicts its own demise, as this one does, is utterly absurd.

An attitude of this sort is, essentially, a subverting of the meaning and purpose of religion. If religions can have any verbalized purpose, it's certainly got to be more than just the foretelling of the future.

---

letters from readers

Freedom abridged

Editor, the Graphic:
I just came back from listening to Landon Saunders talk about relationships among people. One of the most important things he emphasized was that each person is unique and that we should look upon each other as individual human beings and accept each other for what we are.

I can't help but relate these thoughts to what is happening to one of our teachers here at Pepperdine. I relate the fact that this teacher happens to be an "individual, a unique person, a human being," as Saunders would say. According to Saunders, we shouldn't become like institutions and completely forget the human qualities of people. In this case, the institution is taking priorities over humanity and the freedoms of man; one of which is the freedom of speech. Needless to say, this teacher has not been treated the right way. Just because he stands up for what he believes in and tries to be

fair with his opinions, which don't happen to be the opinions of others, the renewal of his contract has been refused.

As a Christian, as being a part of a Christian university, as a student and most of all as a human being, I ask those that seem to not understand this teacher's opinions to think and reconsider their position. Let's think about all the things that this teacher can give as a human being.

Mari Rodriguez
graduate, public relations

Bye, bye Blue

Editor, the Graphic:
Recently, Pepperdine suffered a major loss felt acutely by those of us who frequent the barn. Blue, the Australian shepherd who roamed our campus and lived at the barn, died of injuries resulting from someone's inconsiderate actions.

Over this past Christmas vacation two young ladies thought they would

be helpful by taking Blue home and feeding him. After vacation, when school reconvened, they brought him back and redeposited him at the barn. Blue, not realizing that the girls did not want him anymore, attempted to return to their residence. On his way back he was hit by a car and was taken to the vet where he later died.

We, at the barn, miss our trusted, furry friend and are sure that our grief is shared by others on campus. Interference on the part of do-gooders who do not realize that these animals are loved and well taken care of can only end in grievous results. Animals are too trustful and we need to realize it's our responsibility to prevent them from developing habits that are hazardous to them.

We speak not only for our remaining pets but for others who may follow students home looking for a handout. Don't start something you can't finish.

Joene Conley, Melessa Bernstein
Nancy Franks, Theresa Guy
Gina Merz, equestrian education
majors

Figure 10.21   This is an editorial page from the Pepperdine *Graphic*, which sometimes publishes a full-size "op ed" page as well. Used by permission.

Opinion

Fun in the desert sun

War games must be a good time indeed. Just like chrome and plastic six-shooters and rat-a-tat-tat submachine guns in the backyard. Not real war, mind you. No deaths, no mutilations, no destruction—just practice, in case.

Military maneuvers, the less colloquial term for the complex logistics and exercises that take place regularly all over the world to mimic war, seem to be in vogue lately.

Particularly in the Middle East, where the Reagan Administration has been busy demonstrating American military oomph behind the tough talk from Washington.

The Georgian did the talking. Now the Californian is wielding the big stick in gunboat diplomacy worthy of T.R. himself. Unfortunately, America's ability to intimidate with armed might has waned since Roosevelt's day, and since the post-war Pax Americana.

First in Egypt, Sudan, Somalia and Oman last month, U.S. forces held a trial run of a tiny forerunner of the full-fledged Rapid Deployment Force in the Bright Star '82 exercises. Then this week, the U.S. announced plans for formal military cooperation with Israel against a Soviet threat in the Middle East, including joint maneuvers with the Israelis.

There is justification for such activities if they are needed for practicing what must be avoided at almost all cost—a direct confrontation with the Soviets. In other words, total war.

But danger supersedes the fun of war games if their principal purpose is a flashy display of power. They might serve only to inflame and fuel the fires of paranoia that burn brightly in the Soviet Union, and cause that nation to respond with a few flashes of its own.

Semester's end brings pain to KU's many procrastinators

Thanksgiving for many students is the most suspect of holidays. Invariably it is situated before the crucial week that, for procrastinators, determines grade-giving. And the cautious mind is reluctant to offer thanks until its ability to grind out a semester's work in one week has been tested.

After a number of semesters, one improves. This year I drifted into Wonder Week with confidence. When I walked into the newsroom on Monday (all columns are due two days before

KEVIN HELLIKER

publication), I found a note in my mailbox: It was mandatory that my column be submitted on time today—something I hadn't managed all semester.

An hour before deadline my column was typed.

Then someone read it and directed my attention to one of last week's papers.

"Did you read this column?" she asked, pointedly.

I hadn't.

"It's the same as yours."

She was right. My column, in essence, had already been written, published and responded to with letters to the editor: the price one pays for neglecting to read one's own paper. I had one hour to try again.

I've found that on such occasions, when one should move quickly, the mind becomes obsessed with time. I had in my back pocket a schedule detailing the academic activities with which I would occupy myself every hour of this week.

But I had not planned to write this column twice. Now every item on the table was necessarily pushed back, spilling a crucial asignment into next week when it would no longer be accepted. Undeniably, I thought, one assignment was lost.

The first fatality of Wonder Week has an awakening effect. Reality evokes a feeble "Oh . . ." from those of us who doubt it.

A semester, in particular, does not seem real until the first loss is suffered. Then the past wasted weeks become as mentally structured as a poem about the unhappy fate of a procrastinating man.

He moans that he grows old. He agonizes over weeks spent watching MASH, Benny Hill, the comings and goings of women on campus.

Echoes of his old delusion torment him, "And indeed there will be time."

"Why do I do it—semester after semester?" he wonders. Because he loves it. There is nothing so exciting as pressure, and nothing so trite yet irresistible as handling it with grace.

By the time this metaphorical mosaic had passed through my head, deadline was upon me. And I still hadn't the vaguest idea what I would write about.

I recalled then one of my teachers reading to the class this message he'd received just hours before a paper was due. A student had written, "The rabbit is dead."

The message made reference to an article by Hunter Thompson in which the author compared his procrastinating tendencies to "whatever instinct it is that causes a jackrabbit to wait until the last possible second to dart across the road in front of a speeding car."

This instinct, Thompson thought, was born out of boredom with rabbits' daily routines: "Eat, sleep, +¼&%, hop around a bush now and then . . ." Add "study", and the routines of students and jackrabbits are much alike, I thought.

Always willing to look on the bright side, I viewed my present predicament as exciting—a cheap thrill. My columns had always been late before. Why change now? Semesters, unlike speeding cars, don't kill.

Granted, my timetable for the week was messed up, but that was no matter. Tonight I would sleep less, work harder and by Friday the road would be crossed.

"When a jackrabbit gets addicted to roadrunning," Thompson added, "it is only a matter of time before he gets smashed . . ."

A fear of this fate ruins many Thanksgiving dinners.

Why hasn't someone done something?

The end of another semester. Everyone is busily studying for finals and finishing term papers. And here's a few things to think about while you're studying . . .

Why is the HOPE award—the only teaching award given solely by students—presented to the alumni side of the football stadium instead of the student side? It seems the University has forgotten that although alumni money keeps a university going, without students there woud be no university.

Will there ever be "good" dorm food? When you are serving 600 people there is no way the food will be as good as if you are serving four, but somehow cold french fries and liquid eggs just don't make it. In fact, a friend of mine who attends the University of Missouri has found that living in a dorm provides her with a sure-fire way to lose weight. Unfortunately, she didn't need to lose any.

While I'm on dorms, how about those pipes that run through the rooms? Will anybody ever come up with a way to insulate the holes they run through, or will dorm residents continue to listen to every word their neighbors say?

Three snickers for Parking Services' latest feeble attempt to operate KU parking lots efficiently. To cram more cars into an overflowing parking lot, Parking Services last year designated certain rows of the dorm lots for compact cars only. They put up signs to that effect and then stopped. I have yet to see a Parking Services employee get out his or her little ruler to find out whether a car parked in those exclusive rows is within the six-foot-wide limit.

Then there are the drivers. I always wonder why people are so stubborn and lazy that they have to park in spaces reserved for handicapped drivers. Walking a few extra feet won't kill anybody, and it doesn't take that long, either. I know, "I'm only going to be here for a minute," although more likely it will be five or 10 miuntes. But what if a handicapped driver comes along during that minute?

Also in contention for the most obnoxious driver award are the people who are too cheap to

BRIAN LEVINSON

pay 50 cents to park in the O Zone, the big parking lot south of Robinson Center. Instead, these people consider it their right to park in the free stalls on the east side of the lot that are reserved for people who need to go to Watkins Hospital.

On to academics. Is anybody else worried about being overlooked when the time comes to interview for jobs because he or she went to college to learn instead of to get a 4.0 GPA? That's not to say that everyone who has a 4.0 took only "pud" classes. Nothing could be further from the truth. Rather, colleges should provide employers with some way of evaluating the classes listed on a transcript so that a student who challenged himself and took tough classes isn't punished for not having a 4.0.

And let's give students a fair chance to evaluate classes and their abilities to perform in them before it is too late. Specifically, professors should be required to give an exam or assign a paper and have it graded before the last day to choose the credit no credit option, or before the last day to drop.

I'm sick of taking classes that seem interesting from the course descriptions in the catalog only to find out too late that they are duds or that the prerequisites listed in the catalog were inadequate and I'm unprepared for the class. Not all students have the time to see an adviser in each department they want to take a class in.

How about Watson Library? Why is it so stuffy? Where are the nice big easy chairs like those they have in the Union? Students need to be comfortable to study. I have yet to meet anyone who is really comfortable in those horrid wooden things the library calls chairs.

Finally, someone should remind professors that there is more to college than just classes. The workload they give their students is likely multiplied five times because most students take five classes, a fact they seem to have forgotten.

I always get a big kick out of professors who ask whether anyone watched the great documentary on television last night or read the latest best seller. Who has got time to watch TV? One of the saddest parts of college is that for four years many students stop reading for fun. They are so sick of reading when they get done with their textbooks that the last thing they want to see is another book. Too bad. I'm sure that after not reading for fun for four years, many people find it a hard thing to do again.

Someone once told me that in addition to learning and getting a degree, college was the last chance I would have to have so much fun and freedom. It would be four years without many responsibilities but with many opportunities. Somehow that doesn't go along with having so much homework that one never does anything but go to class, study and work.

Letters to the Editor

West Campus crowd eschews 'Salina Piece' sculpture

To the Editor:

The following is an open letter to Robert Cobb, executive vice chancellor:

A story in the Nov. 24 Kansan stated, "The dispute over the location of the 'Salina Piece' abstract sculpture should be effectively laid to rest when the sculpture is moved to West Campus." This sentence must have been based on the assumption that the only ones who would disagree with this new location are also laid to rest—in Pioneer Cemetery.

We, the living residents of West Campus, would like a voice in this matter to air our objections to the location of "Salina Piece" in our environs.

Precedent has been set in the area of hideous art on West Campus with the presence of "Icarus" in front of Nichols Hall and the "outhouse roof" look at Moore Hall. However, our concerns transcend artistic and architectural taste into the area of safety.

We urge that the safety study of this monstrosity include conditions of dynamic rather than just static loading for reasons of earthquake safety. If students or other people were climbing around on this piece during a moderate earthquake of the type that occurs every few decades in Kansas, the campus could incur a tragedy of the "Hyatt Regency West" variety.

Lastly, we on Campus West believe that we are entitled to the same safety considerations as the main campus. We take the liberty of pointing out that there are at least two safe installation sites on West Campus. One is in the bottom of the pond west of Parker Hall. The other possibility is to include "Salina Piece" as part of the structural steel in the framework of the new Moore Hall annex.

Another possibility that would still allow Mr. Simpson to have his tax write-off would be to have him take it back and donate it to the Kansas School for the Blind.

Don W. Steeples
Chief of environmental geology and geophysics section and
James R. McCauley
Research associate

An unfair approach

To the Editor:

In response to your Nov. 19 article, "Fraternity lines drawn out in black and white," we feel that certain points need to be clarified.

First, the "member" of our fraternity on which many of your allegations are based, Dave McQueen, was never initiated as an active member of Phi Kappa Sigma. In the article, McQueen said that there had been a meeting to discuss stripping Mike McGlothen of his membership (McGlothen was also not an active member) but that we did not because "it would have looked racist." This topic never arose at any meeting of the members of Phi Kappa Sigma. If Connie Schallau would have attempted to confirm this, she would have discovered such.

Secondly, it was stated that we pledged McGlothen "sight unseen." Every prospective member is discussed and voted on. If Schallau would have talked to an active member, this too would have been made clear. Mike McGlothen was not asked to pledge over the phone, only to attend a rush party scheduled for the next day.

Mike's letter to the editor stated that he was both misquoted and quoted out of context. He repeatedly told Schallau that he did not leave the house because of racism. Schallau obviously had no concern for the facts in this article. We have felt you have blown the entire situation up, trying to find something that is just not there. It is our hope that in the future the Kansan will check its "stories" more closely and try to maintain a professional attitude. But now we know how Carol Burnett must have felt.

Steve Sherman
Overland Park junior
for the men of Phi Kappa Sigma

Remember 'silent doer'

To the Editor:

The passing of Dean Alderson is a great personal loss to me, as I know it is to many other members of the Jayhawk community.

Part of the sorrow I feel is the realization that only in death has he received recognition, and even that has been inadequate. But perhaps that's because the qualities he possessed were so elusive, and in trying so hard to bring others' qualities out, he purposely left himself behind.

Alderson was a gentle man with an indomitable spirit, always more interested in his students' advancement than his own. While an accomplished administrator, he carried the notion of perseverance, courage and commitment beyond his office.

It was simply through the constructive manner in which he lived his life that he had the greatest impact on others. He took time to notice the little things that made life special, and in doing so, made others feel special as well.

He was a listener, a giver, a responder, a silent doer—a friend. He will always be a reminder to me throughout my life of what a man can be.

I hope the entire Jayhawk community recognizes its loss, and in doing so, will reach out to one another in his memory. It's the only recognition Dean Alderson would have wanted.

John Best
Evanston, Ill., senior

Alum a bit displeased

To the Editor:

I have just watched the highlights of the KU-MU football game, thanks to the University of Missouri football highlights program, and I'm bitter.

A disgruntled MU grad? Hardly. I'm a Jayhawk (C'42), as is my wife, to whom beating Crybaby U. constitutes a successful season. I'm bitter because, for the first time in my life, I'm ashamed of my alma mater.

Item: partial jerseys. Even the most notorious "tough guy" schools have stopped such dishabille years ago. It's strictly brown-shoes-with-a-tuxedo stuff.

Item: Tearing down goalposts at any time is also old-hat kid stuff that went out with rumble seats. But it transcends childishness when benighted students do it well before the game ends, thereby jeopardizing their team's victory by causing penalties that result in a touchdown for the opponent. Egregious stupidity.

Both of these things prompt me to reconsider my contributions to KU. Any school that tolerates such hick shenanigans and wanton destruction obviously doesn't deserve my loyalty or need my financial help.

Richard P. Trubey
Bella Vista, Ariz.

Lesson in history

To the Editor:

I find it fascinating that Connie Schallau, in researching her three-part menagerie on the history of black participation in sorority rush, could find so many alumnae ready to malign their former chapters and so few who could give accurate interpretations of rush procedures.

Many of the procedures and practices quoted from former members of sororities were mendacious, to say the least. But perhaps the most descriptive word for Schallau's story is, as I have said, history.

Incidents that occurred between 1977 and 1979 should be regarded as such. They should not be treated as barometers for present or future sorority polices, as the Nov. 18 headline, "Black women find many sorority doors shut," indicated.

Having written this letter before the article on present conditions, I would like to justify this early opinion by saying that Schallau's first article, in printing specific sorority names and prevaricated rush practices, was in itself damaging to those sororities at a crucial time, just before spring formal rush.

Anne Cortopassi
St. Louis junior

The University Daily
KANSAN

Kansan Telephone Numbers
Newsroom—864-4810
Business Office—864-4358

(USPS 650-640) Published at the University of Kansas daily August through May and Monday and Thursday during June and July except Saturday, Sunday and holidays. Second-class postage paid at Lawrence, Kansas 66045. Subscriptions by mail are $15 for six months or $27 a year in Douglas County and $18 for six months or $35 a year outside the county. Student subscriptions are $3 a semester, paid through the student activity fee.

Postmaster: Send changes of address to the University Daily Kansan, Flint Hall, The University of Kansas, Lawrence, KS 66045

Editor — Scott Faust
Business Manager — Larry Leibengood
Managing Editor — Robert J. Schaad
Campus Editor — Tammy Tierney
Editorial Editor — Kathy Brussell
Associate Campus Editor — Ray Formanek
Assistant Campus Editors — Kate Pound, Gene George
Assignment Editor — Cynthia L. Currie
Art Director — Scott Hooker
Head Copy Chief — Don Munday
Wire Editors — Pam Howard, Vanessa Herron
Entertainment Editor — Karen Schlueter
Sports Editor — Tracee Hamilton
Associate Sports Editor — Ron Haggstrom
Makeup Editors — Cindy Campbell, Amy Collins
Copy Chief — Jane Bryant, Kathy Maag
Staff Photographers — Bob Greenspan, Mark McDonald, John Eisele, Kurt Jackson, Keith Flanery, Drew Torres, Earl Richardson
Staff Artist — Julie Green

Retail Sales Manager — Terry Knoebber
Campus Sales Manager — Judy Caldwell
National Sales Manager — Marcee Jacobsen
Classified Manager — Laura Menezes
Production Manager — Ann Hornberger
Tearsheets Manager — John Egan
Staff Artist — John Keeling
Staff Photographer — Cory Hoenk
Retail Sales Representatives — Melissa Rader, Jan Johnson, Kelly McCarthy, Beth State, Leslie Ditch, Renee Youree, Susan Cooksey, Diane Thompson, Barb Baum, Howard Shalinsky, Perry Beal, Jane Wenderott, Sharon Bodin

Sales and Marketing Adviser — John Obersan
General Manager and News Adviser — Rick Musser

Figure 10.22 This editorial page is from the *Daily Kansan*. Used by permission.

Five-column page dummy

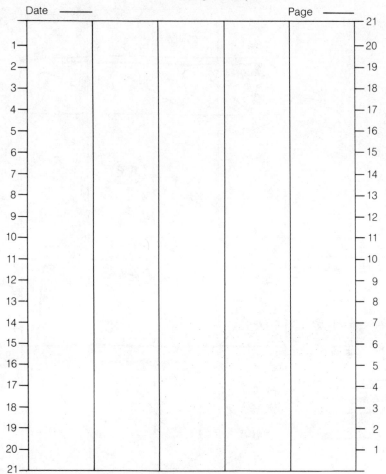

Figure 10.23 This page dummy is intended
for a five-column full-size newspaper page.

That's a terrific process, but few student newspapers will have the hardware
to do it for some time. In the meantime, we suggest that you practice the fine
art of designing your pages well in advance of production, using page dummies.

REFERENCES

1. Arthur T. Turnbull and Russell N. Baird, *The Graphics of Communication*, 4th ed.
   (New York: Holt, Rinehart & Winston, 1980), p. 297.

2. See, for instance, Mario Garcia, *Contemporary Newspaper Design* (Englewood
   Cliffs, N.J.: Prentice-Hall, 1981), pp. 40–43.

Six-column page dummy

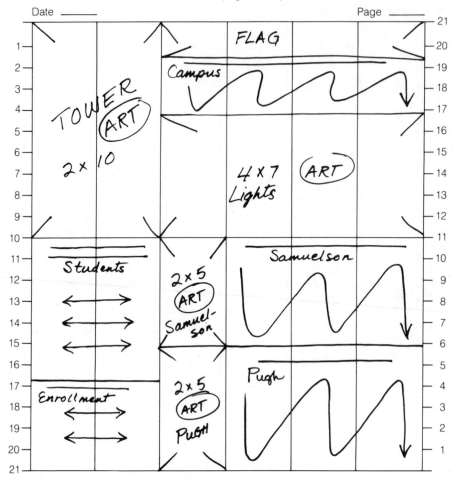

Figure 10.24   This is a dummy of the front
page of the San Antonio College *Ranger* that
is shown in Figure 10.13.

3. For a discussion of the history of typography, see James Craig, *Designing with Type*
    (New York: Watson-Guptill, 1971), pp. 31–84.

4. Garcia, *Contemporary Newspaper Design,* p. 52.

5. Garcia, *Contemporary Newspaper Design,* p. 85.

6. Based on the authors' conversations with Ben Adelson, Mike Cornner, Marv
    Jacobson, Tom Kramer and Bob Scheibel of the Pierce journalism faculty in 1980
    and 1981.

7. Garcia, *Contemporary Newspaper Design,* pp. 40–41.

The Production Process

After standing still for many years, typesetting and printing technology has exploded lately. It has been said that a typographer from Joseph Pulitzer's *New York World* in 1900 could have walked into any large newspaper plant in 1965 and operated the equipment. But if, on the other hand, a typographer left in 1965 and returned in 1980, he would have had no idea how to run the equipment. While that may be a slight exaggeration, the newspaper business is going through a technological revolution today, a revolution that shows no sign of ending soon.

While newspapers still use printing presses, almost everything else has changed, and thousands of jobs in the printing trades have been eliminated in the process. In particular, the typesetting trade has been all but eliminated by technology.

THE OLD WAY

Until recently, the production process began at the reporter's typewriter. The writers typed their stories and editors edited the typed copy with pencils, using scissors and glue to insert additional sentences and paragraphs.

When that job was finished, the typewritten copy was sent to the *back shop,* where a highly skilled typographer, who probably earned a better salary than some of the reporters, would retype the story on the keyboard of a typesetting machine. The machine created lead type for printing, one line at a time.

Once that was done, a *galley proof* would be printed from the lead type, which was placed in a long metal tray called a *galley.* Proofreaders would read the galleys, comparing them against the original copy to find and correct the errors introduced during this retyping process. Those errors would then be corrected by the typesetters, who would retype each line containing an error (or *typo*) and insert the new line of type in the galley in place of the faulty line. New errors often occurred during this correction process. Sometimes typesetters would remove and replace the wrong line from the galley. When that happened, one line of the story would be missing, but another line would appear twice— once with a typo and once in its corrected version. Also, typesetters sometimes would make a new error in the "corrected" line.

After the proofreading and correction process was finished, the galleys were arranged in metal page forms by makeup men (and we do mean *men;* virtually no women were hired to perform these "unladylike" back-shop jobs). Slowly, the pages went together, with the makeup man reading the metal type backward and trying to make as few mistakes as possible. The metal type had to read backward so it would read correctly when it was printed. Think about that for a minute, and see if you can envision why it would be true.

After all of this, sometimes a page proof was made, giving the editor one last chance to correct as many errors as he or she could find under deadline pressure. Then those errors were corrected, and once again new errors were introduced when the old ones were corrected.

At last the metal type for one page (which weighed about 100 pounds by this time) was wheeled out to the *stereotyping* room, where a flexible *mat* was made. The mat would then serve as a mold, and a metal printing plate was cast. Then the plate was mounted on the press, and the actual printing could finally begin.

We wanted to include some photographs of this process, but we couldn't find a newspaper anywhere in our area that was still doing things this way. So you'll have to take our word for it: all of this really did happen, and not too many years ago.

Many retired editors and typographers look back on this process with a certain nostalgic fondness, but the fact is that it was cumbersome, slow and expensive. Even worse, it invited unnecessary errors and resulted in a tremendous waste of time because everything had to be typed twice.

The writers and editors had little control over the production process or the final appearance of the newspaper. However, the old system did have a few advantages along with its obvious disadvantages. For instance, whenever there was a particularly embarrassing typographic error, it was easy to blame the printers and proofreaders. The copy passed through so many hands after it left the newsroom that the editorial staff could hardly be blamed for the typos in the paper.

THE NEW ORDER OF THINGS

The old letterpress printing method we've just described was dominant in American newspapering until about 1970. But it's a totally different world today.

Thanks to the advent of computerized word-processing technology, professional typesetters are about as necessary as stagecoach drivers. At virtually all professional daily newspapers and a growing number of campus papers, the reporter composes the story on a VDT, or *video display terminal* (a device that combines a typewriter-like keyboard and a television screen, as shown in Figure 11.1). As the story takes shape on the screen, the writer has unlimited freedom to move the copy around, inserting and deleting words, sentences and paragraphs at will. Typos? If the reporter sees them, he or she can instantly correct them once and for all with a sweep of an electronic *cursor* across the video screen.

Figures 11.2–11.4 show how electronic editing works. In Figure 11.2, the lead of a news story is on the screen, but with some missing information. In

Figure 11.1   There are hundreds of brands of computer video display terminals on the market. This one is typical of many general purpose VDTs.

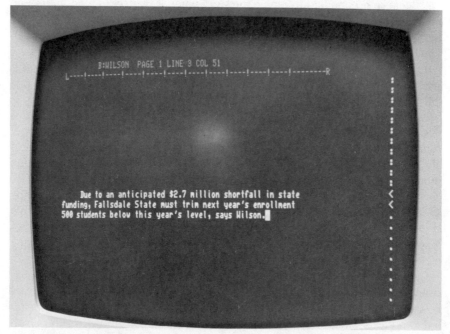

Figure 11.2   The lead here is missing something important: the key person's first name and identification.

Figure 11.3, the type has been spread apart to make room for the addition, and Figure 11.4 shows the story with the addition in place.

Most writers and editors who have used this process say it's faster and easier than composing on a typewriter and editing with pencil, straightedge and glue-pot. In fact, this textbook was written on a VDT. We doubt that we could have met our publisher's deadline without our word-processing system, which consists of a small computer, the video terminal and a high-speed hard-copy printer. Not only does this system make writing faster and easier, but it also eliminates the need to retype the copy after each round of revisions.

If writing on a VDT has advantages for writers, it looks even better from a publisher's viewpoint: it saves a lot of money. Publishers talk about "saving the reporter's original keystrokes," and that is exactly what VDTs do. Since no one has to retype a reporter's stories, an entire step in the production process—and a very expensive step at that, given typographers' salaries—can be eliminated. Sadly, this has eliminated jobs, but so have many of the other labor-saving new technologies of the twentieth century. Typographers, like those stagecoach drivers we mentioned earlier, have had to go into other lines of work.

After the reporter writes the story on a VDT, it goes into a computer for storage, perhaps on a magnetic disk or tape. When the editor is ready to edit the story, he or she calls it up on another VDT screen and makes whatever changes are necessary—again electronically. When the editor is satisfied with the story, it is electronically sent to a computer-driven typesetting system, where the electrical impulses are turned into an image on paper.

Because no one had to retype the story when it was set in type, there's no need for a separate proofreading process. If the writer and editor didn't let any typos slip through, there won't be any typos in the story. Computers do malfunction from time to time, but when they do, the result isn't usually a little typo here or there. Instead, the whole process may come to a halt—which is why most large daily newspapers have more than one computer on line. If one fails, it is usually possible to get the paper out with the others.

After the electronic typesetting, the next step is to arrange stories, headlines (also produced with the help of the newsroom computer) and art on a piece of cardboard. This process is called *pasteup,* a misnomer since the type is almost always secured to the board with wax rather than paste these days. The pasteup process is discussed in detail later in this chapter.

Once the pages are completely pasted up, they are said to be *camera-ready* (ready to be photographed and printed). Each page then goes to a machine that is literally a giant camera—a process camera. It produces a full-size photographic negative of the page, and this negative is used to produce a printing plate, and the page is ready for printing.

At some large newspapers and magazines even the pasteup process has been eliminated by computerization. As we said in the last chapter, there are now pagination systems capable of arranging an entire page—body type, headlines and art—electronically. After the stories are edited, the makeup person simply arranges the entire page on a large video screen, typing commands to tell the computer how to arrange the various elements of the page. Once that

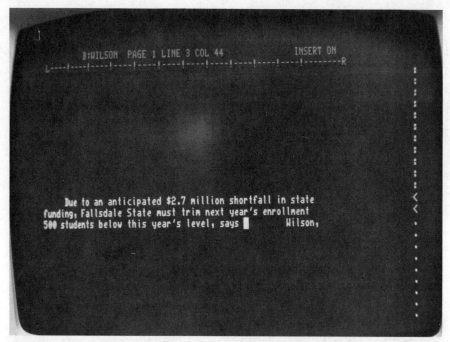

Figure 11.3 Now the text has been opened up to make room to insert the required information.

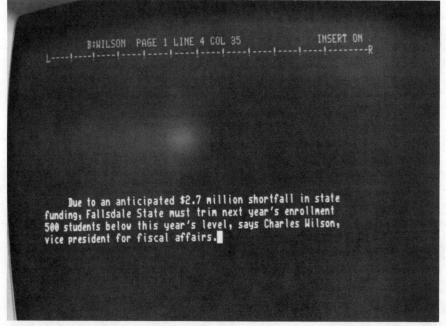

Figure 11.4 The insertion has been made, and the text is closed up. The editing was accomplished quickly—and so neatly that no one will ever know this information was added belatedly.

is done, the entire page can be printed out at once by a large computer-driven typesetting unit.

Full pagination systems are still beyond the budgets of most student newspapers, but it may not be many more years until the pasteup process will also be unnecessary.

Obviously, this entire process is possible because of photo-offset printing. We won't try to explain how offset printing works. Let's just say it is a relatively recent process based partly on photographic principles. It replaced the traditional letterpress method of printing, a process that had been around since Gutenberg's days. That process involved type being covered with ink and then being pressed against paper. The typesetting process for letterpress printing was messy and cumbersome. Someone had to arrange the type to form words, lines and pages. Eventually, of course, machines were developed to prepare complete lines of type, but proofreading and page composition were still cumbersome jobs.

With offset printing, on the other hand, one clean original copy is all that is needed to make a suitable printing plate. There's no need for hot metal type anywhere in the entire process. The new kind of typesetting is called *cold type* because paper with an image on it is all that's needed as a master copy for offset reproduction.

That, in brief, is how the old and new printing processes work. The newspaper production process as you'll probably experience it on campus is our next topic for discussion.

ON-CAMPUS NEWSPAPER PRODUCTION

More and more college newspapers are buying their own typesetting equipment today. Such a thing would have been out of the question for most college papers back in the days of hot metal, but good typesetting equipment is so compact and inexpensive that it hardly makes economic sense not to set your own type and do your own pasteups. Not many campus papers have fully computerized operations in which the reporters write their stories on VDTs just yet, but that too is coming. In the meantime, most college newspapers have some kind of on-campus typesetting equipment.

Why not go all the way and have a complete print shop? A printing press is an enormous investment, and it has to be running many hours a day to be profitable. Few campus dailies generate enough work to keep one busy, although some colleges own newspaper-size printing presses for instructional use in printing technology programs. But for most college papers the logical cutoff point in setting up your own paper is when the pages are camera-ready. At that point the basic creative work is done; the rest is work for technicians, not journalists.

Doing your own typesetting has several advantages. Perhaps most important, you can work on your own timetable—not on an off-campus printer's schedule. Your deadlines can be much closer to press time this way.

If you don't have your own equipment, you have to go through several extra steps that take time. First, you have to send the copy somewhere for typesetting, and then you have to get the galleys back for proofreading. Then you have to wait for the typos to be corrected. Finally, you have to bring the type back for pasteup or else stand by at the print shop while someone else is paid to do your pasteup for you.

There's an old adage that says, "If you want something done right, do it yourself." Nowhere is that more true than in typesetting and pasteup. If you do your own, you can do it exactly how, when and where you choose. In contrast, having an outside shop do your pasteup work can be frustrating. Things never fit exactly right, and tempers always seem to be short just when cooperation is most needed to solve last-minute problems. It sometimes seems to require a presidential proclamation to get that last vital correction set in type if you're depending on an outside shop to do it.

Not only does in-house typesetting and pasteup usually result in better quality control, but it also saves money. It is possible to recoup the initial outlay for equipment within a few years. Modest-size college weeklies report savings of $5,000 to $10,000 or more per year, and the saving may be several times that much for a college daily.

Another advantage to on-campus typesetting is that it allows the staff to experience the production process firsthand. It offers many students their first chance to work with a VDT and do on-screen editing, a skill that is increasingly valuable in the job market.

All right, let's assume you're convinced. Now let's talk about typesetting equipment and the production process.

Setting Up a System

Once a college newspaper decides to buy typesetting equipment, the major challenge is to arrange financing. Many student newspapers borrow the capital outlay money from their college's general fund or student government fund. The money can be repaid from the savings over the cost of off-campus type-setting. Some staffs raise equipment money in various other ways, such as by securing grants from professional newspapers or working out pay-as-you-go lease-purchase arrangements with equipment suppliers. Some colleges are given used but mechanically sound equipment by a local daily that is getting a new system. The donation provides a tax writeoff, of course.

Professional publishers these days are talking about "third generation" and "fourth generation" computerized typesetting systems. While it is clearly profitable for them to keep upgrading their technology, an excellent college newspaper can be produced on the older systems that publishers are now unloading. Under these circumstances, the possibilities for equipment donations should not be overlooked.

If you end up buying an offset typesetting system, how much does it cost? Depending on your bargaining skills, a complete typesetting shop can be purchased for remarkably little, considering the cost of off-campus typesetting. A moderately sophisticated brand-new system with on-screen editing features can be purchased for about $20,000. That cost can be cut considerably by purchasing used equipment or settling for a system without full on-screen editing capabilities.

The heart of a typesetting system is the phototypesetting unit itself. Probably the best bet for a small college daily or weekly is a *direct-entry* editing system such as the one shown in Figure 11.5. This particular unit is a Compugraphic 7500 Editwriter, and it has a keyboard for typing the stories, ads and headlines. As you type, the copy appears on the video screen, and full on-screen editing is possible. It is, in every sense, a VDT.

Several other manufacturers offer similar phototypesetting units with video editing capabilities for about the same price as the 7500 (roughly $17,000) give or take a little depending on which options you specify. As we'll explain shortly, if you are willing to do without the video editing capability, you can get by with a much less expensive typesetting system.

Once the copy is typed, it can be stored on a *floppy disk,* which resembles a 45 rpm phonograph record (see Figures 11.6, and 11.7). The floppy disk is like an audio or video recording tape: a computer can record data on it and read it back later. Typically, a floppy disk will store at least 100 pages of typewritten copy at a time. Of course, an unlimited number of additional floppy disks may be purchased to store additional material. Each disk can be erased and reused, too.

On a system such as the one shown in Figure 11.5, any story recorded on the disk may be called up for additional editing on the video screen. When you're satisfied with the story, you give the proper command, and the phototypesetter prints the story out on photosensitive paper. A small processor unit develops the paper.

The result: you have headlines, ad copy or text matter on a strip of photo paper. The type may be in a wide variety of sizes, styles and column widths. You can tell the machine to give you justified or unjustified text, with any amount of leading you wish (these graphic arts terms were defined in Chapter 10). And if you proofread well on the VDT screen, there will be absolutely no typos on the printed galley. This means your pasteup can be much cleaner than it would be if extensive proofreading and line-by-line corrections were necessary.

Amazing machine, eh? It is, but you need a few other things for an efficient newspaper production operation. Fortunately, most of them are relatively inexpensive.

You will need some *light tables.* These are large tables with glass tops. Fluorescent lighting underneath the glass makes it possible to see how to align the copy during the pasteup process. The typical light table is big enough for two full-size newspaper pages. As a rule of thumb a student newspaper needs

Figure 11.5   This Compugraphic 7500 is a
typical self-contained VDT and computerized
phototypesetter.

one table for each two full-size or tabloid pages; time-sharing arrangements in
which some pages must be completed before others can be started are inconvenient, at best.

The only other major item of hardware needed is a wax-coating machine,
which applies wax to the back of the type and headlines so they will stick to
the pasteup board. Wax is widely used for pasteup because it adheres well
without making it impossible to reposition the copy as needed.

In addition to the equipment, you'll need some supplies to get started. The
basic tools of this trade include border tapes, X-Acto knives, pica rulers, a large
supply of cellophane tape, photosensitive paper for the typesetting machine,
chemicals for the photo paper processor and wax for the wax machine. Graphic
arts supply houses can provide all of these commodities. You will also need
pasteup boards that are ruled in light blue ink (nonreproducing blue) to help
align the type in even columns. The print shop that does your press work can
perhaps supply the pasteup boards. Figure 11.8 shows a student editor placing
the first headline on a blank pasteup board.

Figure 11.6   This is a floppy disk, a magnetic device that works like an audio recording tape to store information in the form of electronic impulses. It goes in the stand-alone editing terminal as shown in the photo in Figure 11.7.

Figure 11.7   A floppy disk is being inserted into an editing terminal.

Figure 11.8   An editor places the first headline on a blank pasteup board. The editorial pasteup process normally begins at the top of the page.

Luxury and Economy

What we've described here is a moderately well equipped in-house typesetting system. However, the extremes of economy and luxury should also be mentioned.

Some college papers use phototypesetting machines that cost less than $5,000. Such a machine will not include a video display terminal, but it will produce good quality phototype. Of course, it probably won't set the larger headline types, so a separate headline machine is needed. Some staffs have relied on press-on lettering for their headlines, but that's probably cutting things a little too close. Still, some quality student newspapers are produced with complete systems that were purchased new for under $10,000. And with donated equipment, the setup cost can be cut to a fraction of that amount. If you want to set up a system but don't have much money, it might not be a bad idea to watch the classified ads in *Editor and Publisher* for used equipment. State press associations and newspaper brokers also may know about bargains in typesetting hardware.

At the other extreme, some college dailies have professional-looking newsrooms, with VDTs on every reporter's desk. At that level the college paper enjoys all the production convenience and efficiency of a big commercial paper. If the system includes more than a few VDTs, the price tag will probably be well into six figures.

Once you have your system up and running—be it the printer's equivalent of a Mercedes or a Volkswagen Beetle—the next step is to get the shop running. That means mastering the pasteup process.

Pasteup Procedures

For many staffs the pasteup process is half fun and games and half slave labor. The job can be completed quickly and efficiently *if all stories, ads, headlines and art are available,* but on many newspapers, the process disintegrates into something that is more like an all-night party than a serious working situation. We'll discuss some ways the process can be made less time-consuming shortly, but first let's look at what has to be done to paste up a college newspaper.

The first step in the pasteup process is to arrange everything conveniently on the light tables. A blank pasteup board for each page should be taped to the glass surface. Next, the standard items that go in every issue (such as standing heads) should be pasted up.

After you've done the pasteup job once, many of the standing heads can be pulled off the old pasteup boards from the last issue and placed on the new boards. Such items can be reused again and again until they become dirty. At that point the print shop can produce new *veloxes* from the original negative (you did save the negative of the paper's nameplate, didn't you?).

Next, the ads should be pasted down, or at least the place where they'll go should be ruled off with a nonreproducing light blue pencil. Some ad staffs steadfastly refuse to put the ads on the pages until all editorial pasteup is finished, and with good reason. The ads are self-contained units, of course, and they can be kept safely somewhere else during the editorial pasteup so they aren't damaged. But to prevent disastrous errors, it's a good idea to place the ads on each page at least temporarily before the editorial material goes on. If there's an error in an ad dummy, it's much better to discover it at this point than later.

Once the ads are on the pages—or their intended positions are marked—the stories should be placed on each page. Using a pica pole as a straightedge, trim the excess photo paper off each story and headline. Many editors position their most important stories first, preferring to cut the lesser stories if it turns out that something has to be cut to fit. Figure 11.9 shows a newspaper page with these steps just about completed.

Early in the process the art should either be placed on the pages or otherwise accounted for. If you do your own halftone screening (explained in Chapter 9), the screened prints should be trimmed carefully and placed on the pages. If the print shop reshoots the photos and strips them in, you'll need windows the exact size of each photo. Windows are usually made of black or dark red construction paper. The most important thing about windows is to get them the right size and make sure they're aligned properly.

Figure 11.9   In this photo, the paste-up of a
page is nearly completed. Note the dummy
on the partition. Ideally, the final page should
match the dummy, but often changes must be
made during pasteup.

At last, you'll have all art, ads, headlines and stories in place. Before you
call any page finished, there are some final steps. First, be sure everything is
straight. Perhaps you'll want to use a T square, or maybe align everything
against the blue lines on the pasteup board, but in any event it's absolutely
essential to get everything straight. No step in the process is more important

than this one, if you want to have a quality product. Another key step is to make sure everything is *clean*. Stray smudges and pencil marks can ruin the appearance of an otherwise attractive page.

Next, make sure everything is really on the page. If last-minute corrections were pasted over the original type, make sure they're all still in place and correctly aligned. And make sure none of the small headlines got stuck on your arm instead of the page. You'll discover little pieces of type stuck everywhere—except where they belong.

Now step back and take one last look at the *content and design*. Are any words in the headlines misspelled? Is the right caption on each photo? Is the type aligned properly? Are the headlines really straight? Is the date correct? What about the issue number? Is there adequate white space, or is everything too crowded? If the page is too tight, it might be worthwhile to take a minute to delete a sentence here or there so everything can be opened up a little—provided you have the time, of course. Figure 11.10 shows an editor giving her page this all-important final review. "Reading out" the pages one last time may prevent some very embarrassing errors.

Once you're sure everything is in order, the final step is to *burnish* the page. Burnishing is the process of briskly rolling the page to secure the type firmly in place. Proper burnishing should create enough friction to actually heat up the type, causing some of the wax to melt onto the pasteup board. Figure 11.11 shows the burnishing process.

When all of the pages have passed their final quality check, they are declared camera-ready and placed in a large box along with all art that must be stripped in at the print shop. When this happens, there is often a little ceremony as someone leaves for the shop with the precious cargo. On many campuses that little ritual occurs sometime around dawn on the day of publication, which brings us to our next point.

Avoiding All-Night Marathons

All-night social gatherings have their place in this world. Probably nothing unites a student newspaper staff more than the late hours that often go into the pasteup process. But unfortunately, the staff that goes through this experience together is also likely to fail a few classes together.

After watching these all-night marathon pasteup sessions for years—but also watching some staffs get the paper out even before sundown—we're convinced the trick is nothing more than establishing realistic deadlines and sticking to them.

That's right, *deadlines*.

If you want to get the pasteup job done efficiently, you need to have all the material ready at pasteup time. An editor with perhaps one semester's experience should be able to paste up the typical full-size page in no more than one hour—if all the materials are on hand.

What makes the job take so long is that there's dead time—maybe hours of it—while everyone waits for that one last story, headline or correction to

Figure 11.10   One of the most crucial steps is to "read out" the pages after they're pasted up. After that, the editors should look critically at each page, checking for such problems as crooked headlines and unsecured correction lines.

come back from the typesetting machine. It's perfectly feasible to produce a college paper—even a small daily—with only one keyboard-driven typesetting system. But if half the stories aren't set in type before the pasteup begins, and if lots of the headlines aren't even written, a huge logjam will develop around the in-basket on the typesetter.

Even worse for everyone's sanity, some staffs have an informal editorial board meeting around the pasteup tables about midnight on the night before publication. The agenda? That should be obvious: it's time to decide what the lead editorial will say, and who will write it (between 1:00 and 2:00 A.M., of course).

When much of the paper is not only pasted up but also *written* during pasteup, the fastest VDT typist in the world can't keep up with the production demands. The only solution to this problem is to develop a work schedule and stick with it. If you have several full-size pages to typeset on a single VDT or other typesetting keyboard, you need paid typists to do the job, and they need to have a specific work schedule. Most important of all, there has to be work

Figure 11.11   At last, the page is finished.
Then it must be burnished with a roller so it
will arrive at the print shop intact.

for the typists to do when they're on duty. That means the copy and headlines have to be there for typesetting. Set firm deadlines, and make *everyone* live by them. If you do, you may be surprised how quickly the pasteup process can be completed.

It would be nice if every reporter could compose his or her stories directly on the VDT; that's certainly an important learning experience. But if you have only one direct-entry typesetter, you probably can't have it tied up this way when the deadline is imminent. The copy has to be written, edited and ready for a fast typist to set on the VDT if you're going to maintain a reasonable production schedule.

If good typists have been systematically setting type all day before the pasteup session—and if someone competent has proofread all the stories on the video screen—there is no reason the bulk of the type can't be sitting there in a basket when pasteup begins. With proper planning it's possible to eliminate almost all of the last-minute typesetting and corrections that snarl the process. It is just a matter of being well organized.

This is not to say you should never hold a place open for a late-breaking story and set it during pasteup. The ability to do that kind of thing is one of the main advantages of having your own typesetting system. But that privilege has to be reserved for stories that are legitimate late-breaking news. It's one thing to typeset a story about the evening's basketball game at 10:30 P.M. so it can be in the paper the next morning, but it's quite another to afford that treatment to a story about last Monday's guest speaker on campus.

Pasteup can be a pleasant experience for a staff, or it can be a nightmare. It depends on what you make of it.

TWELVE

The First Amendment and the College Press

Only 25 years ago, a chapter like this one couldn't have been written. To put it simply, the student press had no First Amendment rights then.

In fact, college students had few legal rights of any kind. College officials adhered to a concept called *in loco parentis,* which, translated from Latin means, "in the place of the parents." College officials were, in the eyes of the law, substitute parents charged with the task of looking after children.

That sort of paternalistic, we-know-what's-best-for-you attitude was challenged by students all over the country during the 1960s. Not only did the students of that era protest racial discrimination and the Vietnam War, but they also declared war on the injustices and indignities they experienced on their own campuses. More than a few colleges were petty tyrannies, run like feudal states by all-powerful administrators. College catalogs said a lot about things like "preparing tomorrow's citizens for democracy," but real democracy was nowhere to be found on some college campuses.

As a result, students turned to the courts in an effort to win the Constitutional rights that other Americans took for granted. By the early 1970s students had won some impressive victories in this struggle. Courts from the U.S. Supreme Court on down had affirmed public school and college students' First Amendment rights. Administrators could never again legally treat their students like mere children or, even worse, pawns in public relations campaigns aimed at wealthy donors.

But even today the battle for student press freedom is far from over. Some college presidents continue to act as if the landmark court decisions of the 1960s and 1970s never happened. In fact, there are signs that the courts may be having second thoughts about some of the stronger Vietnam protest-era rulings. Every year student editors face administrative censorship and faculty advisers have to put their jobs on the line to defend their students' First Amendment rights. (See Figure 12.1.)

Some college officials still think of a student newspaper not as a forum for student opinion but as a vehicle for "good news" to keep everybody happy. New skirmishes are constantly being fought in the battle for free expression on campus. Given the ongoing nature of the problem, all we

THE FIRST AMENDMENT

Congress shall make no law respecting an establishment of religion, or prohibiting the free exercise thereof; or abridging the freedom of speech, or of the press; or the right of the people peaceably to assemble, and to petition the government for a redress of grievances.

THE FOURTEENTH AMENDMENT

All persons born or naturalized in the United States, and subject to the jurisdiction thereof are citizens of the United States and of the State wherein they reside. No State shall make or enforce any law which shall abridge the privileges or immunities of citizens of the United States nor shall any State deprive any person of life, liberty, or property, without due process of law, nor deny to any person within its jurisdiction the equal protection of the laws. . . .

Figure 12.1   The First and Fourteenth Amendments to the U. S. Constitution.

can do in this chapter is summarize the highlights of what has happened so far and offer suggestions for you to consider if you become personally involved in this struggle.

THE *TINKER* DECISION

The starting point for any discussion of First Amendment rights for students is a landmark 1969 Supreme Court decision, *Tinker* v. *Des Moines Community School District.*[1] (Court cases are usually identified by the names of the two sides in the dispute, with a *v.* [for *versus*] between the names.) Because the First Amendment is involved, the legal principles of student press law are based largely on key court decisions.

On the surface, the *Tinker* case had nothing to do with college journalism or even college students in general. But it was a dramatic affirmation of students' rights nonetheless.

The *Tinker* case involved three Des Moines, Iowa, public school students who were suspended for wearing black armbands to protest the Vietnam War. All sorts of other insignia were permitted in the Des Moines schools, including a sort of then-fashionable iron cross that was reminiscent of Nazi symbolism. But the Des Moines school principals quickly met and adopted a policy banning black armbands when they heard of the planned protest. The three students wore their black armbands in a quiet symbolic gesture. No disturbance of any kind resulted from their conduct, but they were suspended anyway.

The students took the school system to court, and their case eventually reached the Supreme Court. The Court agreed with the students' contention that their act was a form of symbolic speech, protected by the First Amendment.

"It can hardly be argued that either students or teachers shed their constitutional rights to freedom of speech or expression at the schoolhouse gate," the Court ruled. The Supreme Court said students in public schools have the same rights as anyone else, except when the exercise of those rights "would materially and substantially interfere with the requirements of appropriate discipline in the operation of the school."

The *Tinker* decision came in 1969. Even before that landmark Supreme Court ruling a few lower courts had recognized students' First Amendment rights. But in the years that followed there was an avalanche of court decisions affirming students' rights: the *Tinker* case was cited as a legal precedent in no fewer than 125 other court decisions by 1980. The courts have repeatedly applied the *Tinker* principle to college students as well as students in the public schools. And the case has been cited often as justification for the idea that student newspapers are protected by the First Amendment.

However, in virtually all instances these court decisions have involved public (that is, tax-supported) colleges. For reasons we'll explain later, the same rules do not apply at private colleges.

THE *PAPISH* CASE

Although the *Tinker* case is regarded as the key Supreme Court decision on student free expression rights, another Court decision in the same era more specifically affirmed the rights of a campus editor. That case was *Papish* v. *University of Missouri Curators*,[2] and it involved a 32-year-old graduate student in art. At least, officially that's what Barbara Papish was. Unofficially, her real love was journalism; she made little progress toward her MA in art during six years on campus, but she produced a little newspaper called *Free Press Underground*, and it put her in the center of attention. The paper often used earthy language to make its point, which was sure to be a controversial one.

The university administration was especially annoyed when she distributed an issue of her shocking paper on a day when high-school students and their parents were visiting the campus. It was definitely bad for recruiting.

Finally, she published an issue with a cartoon showing a policeman raping the Statue of Liberty. There was also a headline with a 12-letter word that college officials considered obscene. At that point, the administration had seen enough. They expelled Papish.

She took the university to court. Ultimately, the case reached the Supreme Court, which ruled in her favor in 1973. First the Court ruled that neither the paper itself nor the 12-letter word was obscene. And the Court decided the expulsion violated the editor's rights under the First Amendment. The university was ordered to reinstate her, although the Court said she could later be disqualified for academic reasons unrelated to her journalistic activities if her performance warranted it. (The administration had argued in court that Ms. Papish's academic performance, or lack of it, would also justify expulsion.)

Ah, some administrators would say, the *Papish* case may have been a very nice victory for student rights, but this was an underground newspaper, not an official campus newspaper. True enough. However, a number of cases involving official campus newspapers had also been decided by then, and student editors who faced administrative censorship were consistently winning.

THE FEDERAL COURTS AND STUDENT PRESS FREEDOM

Even before the *Tinker* decision, in fact, some federal courts had recognized students' First Amendment rights. In the years immediately after it, many more student press decisions were handed down. Before we summarize them, we should explain a little about how the nation's courts are organized. (See Figure 12.2.)

The nation's highest court is, of course, the U.S. Supreme Court. Its decisions set *legal precedents* that apply to all lower state and federal courts. When there is a legal precedent, other courts must decide similar cases in the same way.

Below the Supreme Court, there are federal *circuit courts of appeals*. Each of these courts serves a region of the country (a circuit), and its decisions establish legal precedents that are binding only on lower courts within the circuit. At the bottom of the federal court system are the federal *district courts,* which are primarily trial courts rather than courts of appeal. This is an important distinction because trial court decisions do not normally establish legal precedents: another trial court is free to decide a similar case differently. Only a few federal district court decisions are *published,* which means they appear in law books and become legal precedents. Unpublished court decisions do not normally establish binding precedents; rather, they have little legal significance.

There are numerous instances of student press censorship every year, and some of them inevitably end up in court. Along the way, they may generate considerable publicity, but that does not necessarily mean they have much legal significance. Only the few cases that produce decisions by an appellate court (or a published decision of a district court) establish legal precedents. Except where otherwise noted, all of the cases described in this chapter are precedent-setting court decisions.

Each of the 50 states has its own courts, usually with a state supreme court at the top of the system. However, student press cases are usually handled in federal courts because they involve the First Amendment to the U.S. Constitution. Thus, we'll be discussing federal rather than state court decisions in this chapter.

The *Dickey* Case

One of the earliest published federal court decisions on student press freedom came in a case named *Dickey* v. *Alabama State Board of Education*.[3] The case involved an editor who was expelled from Troy State University but who got a court order reinstating him in 1967.

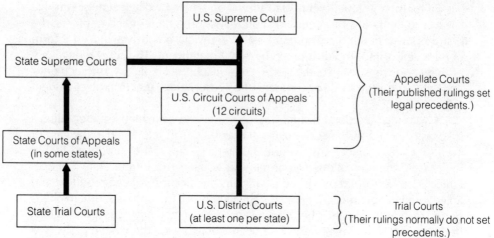

Figure 12.2 The structure of the U. S. court system.

Gary Dickey, editor of the Troy State student newspaper, attempted to publish an editorial criticizing the Alabama governor. The faculty adviser spotted the editorial and urged Dickey not to run it, offering instead an item called "Raising Dogs in North Carolina" for the editorial column. The college president was also shown the editorial and agreed it could not be run because it criticized the governor, and the president felt the campus paper was owned and published by the state.

Dickey chose to run the word *censored* across the editorial column rather than print the essay about raising dogs, and he was expelled from school as a result. He sued the university system—and won.

A federal district court ruled that Dickey's First Amendment rights had been violated. The administration's argument that it—and the state—were the publishers got nowhere. The court said the school didn't have to create a student newspaper or make Dickey its editor, but once those things happened, attempting to control the paper's editorial content was unconstitutional.

The *Antonelli* and *Trujillo* Cases

The *Dickey* case foreshadowed many others that were to follow in the next few years, as students all over America refused to accept the old in loco parentis rules. The courts repeatedly said that student editors were protected by the First Amendment, and that their newspapers could not be arbitrarily censored by school officials.

In the 1970 case of *Antonelli* v. *Hammond*,[4] a federal district court in Massachusetts said a prepublication review board was unconstitutional. At Fitchburg State College, President James Hammond had established a board to make sure nothing obscene was published and to guarantee "responsible freedom of press in the student newspaper."

Editor John Antonelli refused to submit an article by black activist Eldridge Cleaver to the board for prepublication review, and he resigned to protest the board's power to censor. The court said the review board was indeed a form of prior censorship, in violation of the First Amendment. The court didn't flatly prohibit prior censorship of the student newspaper, but it did say any such prior review would have to be accompanied by strict safeguards to protect student rights.

A year later a federal district court in Colorado overruled another editor's suspension for publishing controversial materials. This happened in the case of *Trujillo* v. *Love*,[5] and it involved a "laboratory" newspaper produced within the Mass Communications Department at Southern Colorado State College. Editor Dorothy Trujillo published a cartoon attacking the college president and an editorial criticizing a local judge. The faculty adviser and department chairperson decided to suspend her for this, and she went to court. The federal court said her First Amendment rights had been violated even though the paper was a laboratory teaching tool. However, the court did say that the paper's status as a teaching device (rather than a forum for student opinion) could have been spelled out more clearly. If that had been done, the faculty would have had the right to control the content and discipline defiant editors, the court said.

Joyner: Rights in Conflict

Sometimes newspaper editors exercise their First Amendment rights in ways that seem to threaten other people's rights. In 1973, a U.S. circuit court of appeals had to deal with such a situation—a case that pitted racial integration against freedom of the press. The case, *Joyner* v. *Whiting*,[6] resulted from the strident anti-integration posture of Johnnie Joyner, editor of the *Campus Echo* at North Carolina Central University, which had been an all-black school. The university president, Albert Whiting, said he was afraid Joyner's editorials might cost the school its federal funds, so he cut off funding for the paper until Joyner agreed to moderate his views. As well as opposing the school's integration in general, Joyner had said white students would be unwelcome on the paper's staff and that no ads would be accepted from white-owned businesses.

Joyner hauled Whiting into court, charging that his First Amendment rights had been violated. This created a problem for the federal appellate court. Here was an editor using one constitutional right (freedom of the press) to attack another constitutional right (school desegregation).

In the end, the court came down firmly on the side of the First Amendment. The court noted that Joyner's editorial posture had not caused any actual disruption of the integration process and said he had a constitutional right to express his opinions on the matter. The court took some care to point out that the administration didn't have to create a student newspaper in the first place. However, having established a paper, the college officials could not then shut it down just because the content displeased them.

The *Bazaar* and *Schiff* Cases

Two key court decisions on college press freedom in the 1970s came from the Fifth Circuit U.S. Court of Appeals, which serves several southern and south-western states. One ruling came in the 1973 case of *Bazaar* v. *Fortune;*[7] the other was a 1975 case, *Schiff* v. *Williams.*[8]

The *Bazaar* case arose when the chancellor of the University of Mississippi, Porter Fortune, tried to censor the campus literary magazine, *Images.* One issue of the magazine contained two short stories on racial themes, and both included earthy language. Sponsored by the English Department, the magazine was scheduled for on-campus printing. However, the superintendent of the print shop spotted the language and held up the printing while he contacted Fortune. Fortune ordered the magazine censored.

Editor Eugene Bazaar sued the university, and the federal appellate court agreed that the literary magazine was protected by the First Amendment. The court ordered the university to allow the magazine's publication, although school officials were allowed to add a note on the cover pointing out that the magazine was not an official publication.

In the *Schiff* case two years later, the same court once more affirmed students' First Amendment rights. Kenneth Williams, the president of Florida Atlantic University, dismissed three student editors, contending that "the level of editorial responsibility and competence has deteriorated to the extent that it reflects discredit and embarrassment upon the university." He accused the editors of publishing rumors and engaging in name-calling instead of "accurately reporting items likely to be of interest to the university community."

In court, Williams' decision was overruled. The court said Williams would have to show that the editors were causing a substantial disruption on campus to justify their firing, citing the *Tinker* decision of the Supreme Court. Williams accused the students of putting out a paper full of spelling errors and bad grammar, but the court said that would not likely cause a disturbance on campus and thus was not a sufficient reason to fire the editors.

Once again, a high federal court had refused to allow college officials to control the content of a student newspaper. In almost all of these cases the publications in question were produced in a classroom setting with college financial support. But even so, the courts have said they were protected by the First Amendment. Mere financial support and ties to the academic program are not, in and of themselves, sufficient to strip a school newspaper of First Amendment protection.

Open Forums and Laboratory Newspapers

Like the *Joyner* ruling and several others, the *Schiff* case illustrates the unusual status of student publications at many colleges. The administration may pay the bills, but that doesn't necessarily mean the administration is the "publisher," with powers analogous to those of a private newspaper publisher. A school paper is usually a First Amendment forum, more or less comparable to a speaker's platform in a city park. Once a government agency sets up such a place as a free speech area, officials can't limit its use to those with acceptable ideas. As a First Amendment forum it has to be open even to unpopular and controversial ideas.

From a college president's point of view, then, a student newspaper may be a little like Dr. Frankenstein's monster: you don't have to create it, but once you do, it's pretty hard to control.

However, we should make it clear that the open forum theory of the student press doesn't always apply. In recent years there has been a growing trend for colleges and universities to set up a campus newspapers with ground rules that clearly place the final authority in the hands of someone other than the student editors. For instance, a faculty member may actually be given the title of "publisher," with authority to match the title.

A newspaper organized in this way may not be a First Amendment forum. The *Trujillo* case involved such a situation, although the ground rules weren't spelled out clearly enough to establish the paper's "laboratory" status before the controversy arose. But at this writing no appellate court has ever ruled that publishing a student newspaper under a laboratory teaching arrangement inherently violates the First Amendment.

The laboratory arrangement is sometimes called the "Missouri Plan" because journalism students at the University of Missouri have traditionally produced the *Columbia Missourian* under close faculty supervision. Those who favor the Missouri Plan often point out that under an open forum theory school officials may be held responsible if the paper commits a libel, although they do not have the right to prevent the libel from occurring in the first place. In at least one instance a costly libel suit caused an insurance company to insist that nonstudents be given the final say over student newspaper content. This happened at Michigan State University (see Chapter 13).

Just when a student newspaper ceases to be a First Amendment forum and becomes a laboratory teaching tool is unclear. This is one of the questions about student press law that the courts have not fully resolved.

THE TREND FOR THE 1980s

A decade has now elapsed since the major court decisions on college press freedom. This doesn't mean there aren't any disputes over college press freedom today, but it does suggest that most of the cases are being resolved elsewhere than in the nation's appellate courts. Because so few cases have produced legal precedents lately, it is difficult to predict how the courts will rule in future cases.

However, the era of student activism that spawned the landmark cases is over, and in this new era students tend to be more career-oriented and less inclined to take controversial political stands than they once were. Perhaps there are fewer student press freedom cases reaching the courts today than there were in the early 1970s because students are less outspoken today—and also less likely to go to court if their work is censored. Or maybe college officials have a little more respect for student rights than they did in the highly charged atmosphere that prevailed on campus in bygone days.

One thing that is also apparent, though, is that the courts are becoming less sympathetic toward students who make waves. While few college press freedom cases are reaching the appellate courts today, a fair number of high-school press cases are still showing up. Like their older colleagues, high-school journalists won a series of stunning victories in the nation's federal appellate courts in the early and middle 1970s. But today high-school editors aren't doing so well in court. In recent years high-school students have lost several precedent-setting press freedom cases that they would almost certainly have won in the early 1970s.

In some cases, courts have allowed school officials to justify prior censorship by simply pointing to their unsubstantiated fears that a publication might cause a campus disruption.[9] One appellate court allowed high-school officials to fire a student newspaper editor because his paper criticized the football coach.[10]

In another high-school case, the Fourth Circuit U.S. Court of Appeals (the court that decided the *Joyner* case and several others favorable to student press freedom) affirmed a vague policy forbidding the distribution of information "dangerous to the health and safety of students."[11] Thus, the court allowed the censorship of an unofficial student newspaper carrying a "head shop" ad, even though it seemed apparent that the paper was really censored not because of the ad but because of a cartoon that ridiculed an administrator.

These recent defeats for high-school press freedom could be isolated incidents. But they could also foreshadow a new trend for the 1980s and beyond, a trend toward less judicial support for college press freedom as well.

THE DILEMMA AT PRIVATE COLLEGES

Near the beginning of this chapter we said that the First Amendment applies to public schools and colleges but not usually to private ones. This distinction between public and private schools is based on a legal concept called "state action."

State action simply means an act of any government agency, federal, state or local. In most cases, the Constitution only protects the people from actions in violation of their rights by government officials, not from acts by private individuals. The First Amendment says, "Congress shall make no law . . . abridging the freedom of speech, or of the press." Thus, initially the First Amendment applied only to the federal government and not even to the states.

However, the Fourteenth Amendment was added to the Constitution after the Civil War, forbidding the states to "deprive any person of life, liberty or property without due process of law." In 1925, the Supreme Court ruled that the concept of "liberty" in the Fourteenth Amendment includes the free expression guarantees in the First Amendment. As a result, the First Amendment now applies to the states and their subdivisions (that is, local governments) as well as the federal government.

Thus, all governments and their employees must now obey the First Amendment, but private citizens and private organizations are still under no such obligation. When a state university chancellor or community college president tries to censor a school newspaper, that is a clear case of state action because the institution is a government agency. The chancellor—and lesser administrators—are government officials.

However, the courts have repeatedly ruled that most private university officials are not engaged in state action and hence need not obey the dictates of the First Amendment. Even where a private institution receives substantial government money, courts have refused to find state action in most cases. For instance, a federal court once ruled that Stanford University, with millions of dollars in government financial assistance, was not engaged in state action and thus did not need to extend basic constitutional rights to its students.[12]

There have been instances when courts found state action present in the conduct of private university officials, but these have been unusual cases. Probably the most notable instances of state action at private universities involved the University of Pittsburgh and Temple University in Philadelphia, two institutions that accepted so much state control and state money that the courts decided they were in effect no longer purely private institutions.[13]

However, a 1982 U. S. Supreme Court decision raises doubts about whether there is state action even under these circumstances. In *Rendell-Baker* v. *Kohn*, the high court said there was no state action (and thus, no First Amendment rights) at a private school receiving 90 percent of its revenue from the state. Although this case involved free expression by faculty members and not students, it is not likely the Supreme Court would have ruled differently if student journalists had been involved. With this decision, the Supreme Court has all but ruled out state action as a basis for asserting free-press rights at private schools.

Private Colleges as Public Places

Even without state action, there is one way a private college may find itself subject to the First Amendment. Courts have occasionally ruled that private shopping centers are quasi-public places and thus must allow people to distribute controversial literature or circulate petitions. The California Supreme Court so ruled in 1979, and the U.S. Supreme Court affirmed that decision but made it applicable only to California.[14] In 1981, the New Jersey Supreme Court ruled that Princeton University, like a shopping center, was a quasi-public place and had to allow literature distribution even by nonstudents.[15]

While these court decisions created a right to distribute literature (including unofficial newspapers) in quasi-public places, they do not protect official student newspapers from censorship by private college administrators, even in New Jersey.

Alternatives to the First Amendment

Does all of this mean student newspapers at most private colleges and universities have no First Amendment protection?

Until the courts change their definition of *state action,* that's what it means. However, other possible safeguards may protect students at some private institutions. For one thing, firing student editors is usually bad public relations for a college. Baylor University won national notoriety in 1980 when the editors of the *Lariat* were fired for editorially defending the right of Baylor students to pose for *Playboy* magazine. *Playboy* was doing a photo spread on "Women of the Southwest Conference," but Baylor officials said any Baylor student who posed would be disciplined. After they published an editorial unsympathetic to the administration's position on this issue, the *Lariat* editors were told not to cover the growing controversy. When they continued to cover it, several were fired and others resigned, along with two journalism professors. Before it was over, Baylor was condemned by journalistic organizations (and lampooned by stand-up comedians) from coast to coast.

In the interest of good PR if nothing else, many private colleges voluntarily respect their student newspapers' editorial independence. Heavy-handed censorship just isn't fashionable in modern America.

Moreover, many private schools are committed to the American tradition of academic freedom in the broadest sense, and they recognize that they should afford their students full freedom of expression. Such institutions often have publication policies or codes that provide safeguards for freedom of expression.

Where there is such a policy, students may have a right to go to court if it is violated. Once an institution establishes policies and rules, it cannot arbitrarily ignore them. Under the law of private associations, the courts will enforce an institution's rules when someone can prove they are being arbitrarily violated.[16]

Still, a private college is under no obligation to guarantee its students any free expression privileges at all. Unfortunately, administrators at a few private institutions still live by the old in loco parentis policy. They view their students as fair game for regimentation. Blatant censorship and dismissals of student editors who challenge authority must be widespread in that setting. If there is a written publication code on such a campus, it is likely to declare that the institution is the publisher and has the final say over content. Therefore, even the law of private associations won't help a censored editor there. Moreover, those who run such institutions may not be very concerned about condemnation by the professional media either. They may not care what the general public—or the mass media—think, as long as their primary constituencies (such as wealthy donors and specialized publics) are happy.

Student journalists who find themselves in such an environment have two choices: (1) accept the restrictions and produce the best publication they can without offending those in power; or (2) transfer to an institution where there is more journalistic freedom.

ADVERTISING PROBLEMS

One problem often encountered by student newspapers is advertising censorship. It is not unusual for college officials who wouldn't dare tamper with a student newspaper's editorial page to prohibit ads for cigarettes, alcoholic beverages, contraceptives, abortion referrals and the like.

Is that legal?

Although advertising censorship is one of the most common censorship problems encountered by student journalists, there is no simple answer. At public institutions, the law would seem clear, especially regarding contraceptive and abortion referral advertising. The Supreme Court has specifically ruled that governments may not prohibit advertising for such things as contraceptives and abortion referrals.

Supreme Court Rulings

In a well-known 1975 decision, *Bigelow* v. *Virginia*[17] the Supreme Court said governments may not prohibit abortion referral advertising. And two years later in *Carey* v. *Population Services International,*[18] the Supreme Court similarly overturned a state law against contraceptive advertising. In so doing, the nation's highest Court made it clear that commercial messages about such products and services provide valuable information to consumers and that consumers have a First Amendment right to receive this information. These commercial messages are protected by the First Amendment, the Court said.

Therefore, it would seem that officials at public colleges may not prohibit such advertising in the student newspaper if the staff chooses to publish it. However, college officials routinely forbid tobacco, alcoholic beverage and abortion referral ads on some campuses, and they get away with it—perhaps because no one is prepared to go to court to challenge them.

Many college newspaper advertising staffs are supervised directly by college employees and do not have the same policy-making independence as the editorial staff. Advertising policy decisions may be made by a professional business manager, or even the administration, with little or no student input.

Commonplace as it is, the courts have had little to say about this sort of practice. During the Vietnam era, federal courts twice ruled that administrators could not arbitrarily ban political material from campus newspaper advertising columns, but those decisions said little about nonpolitical materials.

In a 1969 high-school case from New York and a 1971 decision involving a Wisconsin state university campus, federal courts gave individuals wishing to place political ads a right of access to the campus press.[19] In both cases administrative policies forbidding the ads in question were ruled unconstitutional.

However, a federal appellate court more recently upheld the right of the *student editors* of a university newspaper to reject advertising from a homosexual group.[20] The court said the editors had total discretion over newspaper content under the First Amendment. However, the court did *not* say whether the result would have been the same if the *administration* rather than the student staff had prohibited the advertising in question.

The *Portland* Case

In 1981, a federal judge in Oregon addressed that question, and ruled that no college official—not even the newspaper adviser—could bar advertising by a group offering abortion referrals. However, this case, *Portland Women's Health Center v. Portland Community College*,[21] did not produce a published opinion. As we explained earlier, this means it produced no legal precedent and has little legal significance.

Nevertheless, the *Portland* case is interesting. The case arose after the women's health center was refused advertising space in the *Bridge,* the Portland student newspaper, even though the paper carried ads from an anti-abortion group. The adviser rejected the ad without first consulting any students, but he later informed the editors and they said they agreed with his decision.

The court ruled that the *Bridge* is a public forum, protected by the First Amendment, even though it is produced in a laboratory setting by students in journalism classes. Thus, no government official (including the faculty adviser) could deny the women's center access to its advertising columns, the court held.

This case caused considerable alarm among journalism instructors. However, there were some extenuating circumstances. First, the issue was control of a First Amendment forum by a government employee, not by the student staff. Further, the paper had carried ads promoting one view on a controversial issue, but the other side was denied the same right.

If the paper had treated both sides equally—and if the policy decisions had been made by the student staff members (who are themselves protected by the First Amendment)—the *Portland* case might have been decided differently.

Granted, the problem of advertising access is a very unsettled area of student press law at this writing. The Supreme Court has held that there is no right of access to newspapers in general,[22] and it would appear that a college newspaper staff has the right to accept or reject advertising as it pleases. However, when *government officials* deny access to a newspaper that is a public forum, there is a serious First Amendment problem. Nevertheless, officials on many campuses routinely prohibit student newspapers from accepting various kinds of advertising, and they will surely continue to do so until the courts order them to stop.

It is disquieting when there is no clear answer to a legal question, but that is where we stand in this area. No court has yet handed down a precedent-setting decision in any case involving a dispute between administrators and a student staff over advertising acceptability. The cases have all involved outsiders who wanted to advertise and had been turned down.

If a newspaper staff's legal right to prevent administrative control of advertising content is unsettled, another aspect of advertising law that affects student newspapers is very clear: the advertising that appears in student newspapers, like the ads appearing in professional media, must be truthful and not deceptive. Under both federal law and the laws of virtually every state, publishing fraudulent advertising is illegal.

These anti-fraud laws usually exempt publishers who don't know about the fraud, and aim directly at those who place dishonest advertising. However, such laws almost always also say that a publisher who knowingly carries a false or fraudulent ad can be held accountable right along with the advertiser. And an ad need not be outright fiction to be illegal: ads that mislead people are also forbidden in most states. If you are an editor and you have reason to believe that a particular ad is false or misleading, you have a legal duty—as well as an ethical duty—not to run the ad.

PRACTICAL SUGGESTIONS FOR CRISIS TIMES

So far, we've been talking about the law and student press freedom in the abstract: in an ideal world administrators are not supposed to censor student newspapers, at least at public institutions.

But what happens if a college official simply ignores all of this nice legal theory and impounds an issue of your newspaper? What if the college president calls and tells you quite clearly that you will *not* publish a certain story? Or what do you do if you get to your newsroom one day and find a letter telling you you've been fired? Before you even think about filing a lawsuit, there are a number of things you should do.

First of all, if you have a faculty adviser, you should discuss the situation with him or her. Was he or she involved in this decision? How does he or she feel about it? Despite cases like *Dickey* v. *Alabama*, where the adviser was part of the problem, in most instances the faculty adviser is just as committed to freedom of the student press as you are. Advisers put their jobs on the line to defend their students dozens of times every year. Advisers are fired or given other teaching assignments at least as often as student editors are fired for the editorial content of a publication.

If you've been removed from your position, one of the painful things you have to ask yourself is why it happened. Was it really because you wrote a well-documented editorial urging the college president to resign? Or was it because you missed so many deadlines the adviser didn't think you were dependable?

Here's another thing to think about: if the problem was something you published (or wanted to publish), was it something of which you're really proud? Regardless of how morally right you feel, you still have the practical problem of convincing other people who aren't journalists of the rightness of your cause. A well-reasoned editorial or column of opinion is one thing, but a personal vendetta is quite another. Likewise, using a four-letter word in a quote that is important to a story is entirely different from using the same word in a column just to prove you know what it means. The courts have said journalists have a constitutional right to be irresponsible, but your chances of winning the support you'll need to fight your battle are much better if you have been both responsible and ethical.

If you really were fired (or censored) because of the content of the newspaper and your faculty adviser can't help you, your next recourse is probably to a campus-wide board of some kind. On most campuses there is a policy-making board designed to hear just such cases as yours. It may be a student-faculty publications board or maybe a student disciplinary grievance board. Take your case there if your First Amendment rights have been violated.

If going through all of these channels doesn't solve the problem, you are at a turning point. You may have a good potential lawsuit, but it's going to take some time and perhaps cost some money to pursue your claim. It is an unfortunate fact of life that justice is sometimes available only to those who can afford to fight for their rights in court.

At this point you may need to consult an attorney, and that could cost a lot of money. But then again, it might not. If you have a good First Amendment case, a local lawyer for the American Civil Liberties Union may be willing to help you—without charge. Volunteer ACLU lawyers have handled many student press freedom cases on a no-charge basis, often with resounding success.

Perhaps there are other places to turn for help. The Student Press Law Center in Washington, D.C., is one possibility. It probably can't actually provide you with a lawyer, but perhaps the SPLC staff can give you some legal advice via telephone. And possibly the SPLC can refer you to an attorney in your area who will take your case at no charge. Also, local bar associations (groups of lawyers) have sometimes helped student editors win their First Amendment rights on a no-charge public service basis.

In short, it is not necessarily a hopeless situation if you're not rich but have a good First Amendment case. In the last two decades, student journalists have won a series of decisive victories in the battle against censorship. Those victories were possible only because student journalists fought for their rights.

Most disputes over freedom of expression on campus can be settled without anyone resorting to lawyers and lawsuits, but there are times when justice can't be won short of a federal court. The great breakthrough of recent years is that the courts now recognize that students have rights and judges will often intervene when those rights are violated.

REFERENCES

1. *Tinker v. Des Moines Community School District,* 393 U.S. 503 (1969).
2. *Papish v. University of Missouri Board of Curators,* 410 U.S. 667 (1973).

3. *Dickey* v. *Alabama State Board of Education,* 273 F. Supp. 613 (1967).

4. *Antonelli* v. *Hammond,* 308 F. Supp. 1329 (1970).

5. *Trujillo* v. *Love,* 322 F. Supp. 1266 (1971).

6. *Joyner* v. *Whiting,* 477 F. 2d 456 (1973).

7. *Bazaar* v. *Fortune,* 476 F. 2d 570 (1973).

8. *Schiff* v. *Williams,* 519 F. 2d 257 (1975).

9. For an example of this, see *Frasca* v. *Andrews,* 463 F. Supp. 1043 (1979).

10. This happened in a California Fourth District Court of Appeal ruling, *Ortega* v. *Anaheim Union High School District,* 4 civ. 25504 (1981). Note: although this is a ruling of an appellate court, it is unpublished and cannot be cited as a precedent under California law.

11. See *Williams* v. *Spencer,* 622 F. 2d 1200 (1980).

12. See *Furumoto* v. *Lyman,* 362 F. Supp. 1267 (1973).

13. For a discussion of the unique quasi-public status of these institutions, see *Isaacs* v. *Temple University,* 385 F. Supp. 473 (1974); and *Braden* v. *Pittsburgh University,* 552 F. 2d 948 (1977).

14. See *Pruneyard* v. *Robins,* 23 Cal. 3d 899 (1979); 100 S.Ct. 2035 (1980).

15. See *Princeton University* v. *Schmid,* 423 A. 2d 615 (1980).

16. Paul Delaney of Westmont College presented a paper on this issue, "The Law of Private Associations: A New Legal Doctrine for Freedom of the Press at Private Colleges and Universities," at the California Journalism Conference, San Luis Obispo, 25 February 1978.

17. *Bigelow* v. *Virginia,* 421 U.S. 809 (1975).

18. *Carey* v. *Population Services International,* 431 U.S. 678 (1977).

19. The two cases recognizing the right of access to student newspaper advertising space are *Lee* v. *Board of Regents,* 441 F. 2d 1257 (1971); and *Zucker* v. *Panitz,* 299 F. Supp. 102 (1969).

20. *Mississippi Gay Alliance* v. *Goudelock,* 536 F. 2d 1073 (1976).

21. *Portland Women's Health Center* v. *Portland Community College,* civ. no. 80-558 U.S. Dist. Ct. (Ore. 1981).

22. See *Miami Herald* v. *Tornillo,* 418 U.S. 241 (1974).

Staying Out of Legal Trouble

The legal system can be a friend or an enemy to a journalist. The law can protect a student newspaper from administrative censorship, as the last chapter indicated. However, the legal system also protects other people's rights. When a newspaper publishes a story that wrongfully damages someone's reputation, invades someone's privacy or infringes a copyright, the paper may be sued.

These days lawsuits are a big worry for professional newspapers: more than ever before in our history, Americans are looking to the legal system to right real and imagined wrongs. While this book was being written, no fewer than six newspapers and magazines were slapped with million-dollar judgments in the nation's courtrooms, sometimes with catastrophic results.[1] For instance, a relatively small daily newspaper in Illinois was forced to begin a bankruptcy proceeding because it could not pay a judgment totalling $9.2 million.[2]

Because major newspapers and magazines are so often involved in lawsuits, most of them carry insurance policies that protect them against lawsuits stemming from what they publish. Unfortunately, student newspapers have not escaped this flood of lawsuits, and few student papers have insurance protection.

No one really knows how many lawsuits have been filed against student journalists in recent years, but the number must be substantial. Even worse, the danger of lawsuits is sometimes used as justification for administrative actions that strip student editors of their freedom. More than one student newspaper has lost some or all of its autonomy because of a lawsuit.

A classic example of this occurred at Michigan State University, where the editors of the *State News* lost the final say over their paper's editorial content after a $1.7 million libel suit was settled out of court in early 1980. The case began when the *State News* published a story based on an eyewitness account of a police shooting incident. Two police officers shot and killed a suspect, and a witness signed an affidavit (a statement sworn to be true) claiming that it was a wanton killing—an unprovoked and unnecessary shooting.

The editors chose to publish the story despite warnings by the paper's lawyer and its professional business manager that it would probably lead to a lawsuit. (The *State News*, a large campus daily with no official ties to the university, is self-supporting. Students fill most of the staff positions, but the paper is professionally managed by a full-time executive.)

Sure enough, the two officers and the police chief sued for libel. When the case went to trial, the eyewitness was unable or unwilling to back up his earlier charges. Clearly, the paper was in trouble. However, the trial was aborted because of a legal technicality, giving the *State News'* lawyers a chance to negotiate a settlement. The lawsuit was settled for about $60,000.

Fortunately, the *State News* had libel insurance, and the insurance carrier covered all but $5,000 of the settlement. However, the insurance company then took a tough look at the bylaws under which the *State News* operated and decided to cancel the insurance unless the professional business manager was given a veto power over the student editors' decisions. The bylaws were amended, and now the student newspaper is less of a student-run newspaper than it was before.

The student editors lost their final say over the paper's contents because they were determined to run a questionable story even after a lawyer warned them about its potential legal danger. "The writers attempted to build a story rather than report a story," says Gerald Coy, the *State News'* general manager.[3]

Something like that could happen to almost any student paper in America. Clearly, if you're going to write for any newspaper, you need to know something about the legal pitfalls you may encounter along the way.

LIBEL AND SLANDER

Of all the legal dangers that await unwary journalists, certainly the most serious problem is libel. A *libel* is any defamatory statement in written form, while a *slander* is a spoken defamation. There are some technical distinctions between the two that are rooted in the history of the English common law, but for our purposes, the two may be considered identical.

Basically, a libel suit is a legal action in which someone whose reputation has been damaged sues the party responsible for the injury (typically a newspaper or broadcaster). If the person whose reputation was hurt (called the *plaintiff* in legal parlance) wins, a court awards monetary "damages" to compensate for the injury.

Elements of Libel

In explaining how libel suits come about, perhaps we should begin by describing the three elements of a libel (or slander) lawsuit. For a libel to occur, three things have to happen: (1) there must be a defamatory statement; (2) it must identify someone; and (3) it must be published, broadcast or otherwise communicated. Let's look at each of these things briefly.

Publication is just what the name implies. There's no libel until you publish it. Any publication in a newspaper, magazine or a variety of other media is sufficient. However, libel suits also have been based on such things as personal letters that were passed around to people other than the recipient. Also, a poster or billboard is "publication" enough for a libel suit. If a third party—someone other than the perpetrator and the victim—sees it, this element of a libel case is present.

Identification can be tricky. If you name someone in a news story, the identification is obvious. But you can also identify people in other ways. Generally the courts hold that whenever a reasonable number of people know whom you're talking about, there's identification—with or without a name. You can also libel groups of people, but you risk losing a lawsuit only if the group is small enough that the defamation hurts the reputation of the individual members. For instance, if you were to write a story saying some or all members of the college board of trustees accepted kickbacks on a construction contract, each of them could probably sue you. Why "probably"? The rules on group libel vary considerably from state to state; some states would not allow such a lawsuit unless your story clearly referred to a specific member of the board. In any case, only the individual trustees and not the organization itself could sue you. Individuals, nonprofit associations and corporations may sue for libel, but not government agencies (such as the college itself).

The third element of libel is so obvious that people sometimes have trouble remembering it: there has to actually be a defamatory statement. A statement is *defamatory* if it tends to hurt someone's reputation in any way.

There are two kinds of defamatory statements: *libel per se* and *libel per quod*. A libel per se is one that is defamatory in just about any context. To call a person a murderer, a cheater, a child molester or hundreds of other things of that sort is libel per se.

Libel per quod, on the other hand, depends on the *context*. For example, it's not normally libelous to report the birth of a child in a newspaper. But suppose it turns out the mother is not married and that she belongs to a devout religious group in which childbirth outside wedlock is considered immoral. When you add these facts to the situation, an otherwise routine birth announcement can be libelous.

Libel: A Daily Occurrence

At this point you may be wondering why there aren't hundreds of libel suits filed against every newspaper in America. Obviously, many news items published every day meet the three-part test for libel. Newspapers are forever reporting the fact that people are accused of crimes, for instance. Sports columnists often say damaging things about professional athletes, and gossip publications are forever telling tales about the alleged extramarital adventures of celebrities.

How can they do it?

They can do it for several reasons. For one thing, there are several libel defenses which we'll discuss shortly. But there's also another reason why the media sometimes get away with publishing libelous material, particularly about celebrities: lawsuits cost money for both sides. Very often someone who has a good libel suit against the media won't bother to sue because of the expense and trouble it involves. It typically takes several years and costs thousands of dollars in lawyers' fees even to get into court these days. Even then, you may be years away from an ultimate legal victory. The case can be appealed by the losing side, something that further runs up the cost and delays the day when justice will finally be done.

Another thing that prevents some libel suits is the potential adverse publicity and embarrassment that may result. Suppose a supermarket tabloid claims a celebrity is having an extramarital affair. Perhaps only a small percentage of the public will read the story, and even fewer people will believe it. But if the celebrity sues for libel, then all of the major newspapers and television networks will cover the story. Millions of additional people will hear about this juicy tidbit of gossip if the celebrity sues. To avoid that, many celebrities prefer to ignore scandalous stories in certain publications.

Others choose to stand up and fight, of course. Actress Carol Burnett sued the *National Enquirer* for libel after it reported that she was ill-behaved in a Washington, D.C., restaurant. She eventually won an $800,000 libel judgment, although she said it cost her about half that much in lawyer's fees and court costs. And the case was appealed, further escalating the costs. Burnett made it clear she was fighting for a moral principle, not just suing in the hope of collecting some money.

However, if you libel someone, you can't count on the high cost of a lawsuit protecting you. The fact is that the media face hundreds of lawsuits every year, and one of them could have your name on it someday. In fact, the media are sometimes sued by people who know they have little chance of winning a libel suit. These cases are harassment lawsuits, often filed by people seeking revenge. They may be willing to pay the price of hiring a lawyer and going to court just to make the media suffer too. Even if you have a good defense and eventually win, it may cost thousands of dollars to defend a libel suit.

Libel Defenses

You can't do much about harassment lawsuits, but you should be sure you have a good defense before you publish anything that could lead to a legitimate libel suit. There are three classic libel defenses: (1) truth; (2) fair comment and criticism; and (3) privilege. In addition, the U.S. Supreme Court has given the media new protection from libel suits in recent years. First, let's look at the defenses one at a time.

Truth is recognized as a complete libel defense in every state. If you can prove the truth of what you publish, you have a solid defense. You should be aware, however, that it is not always easy to prove something, even if it's true. Suppose, for example, that you got your information from a confidential source. Perhaps you promised not to reveal the person's name, no matter what. Many important stories are based on information gained from people who would be in trouble if their names were used. Sometimes a whistle-blower inside a company or a government agency would be fired if the boss knew he or she had told a journalist about some shenanigan in the company or agency.

Be that as it may, courts aren't always sympathetic about confidential sources. If you can't produce the source, you may not be able to prove the story was true.

Another problem about the truth defense is that truthfully reporting the news isn't necessarily enough. Suppose someone accuses a public official of taking a bribe and you accurately report the story. It isn't enough to prove you reported the quote truthfully and accurately. If the substance of the charge turns out to be false, the person who made the charge can be sued—but so can you. You are responsible for the content of everything you print, including letters to the editor, advertisements and direct quotes. If there's an untrue and defamatory statement anywhere in your publication, you could be in for a lawsuit.

But maybe not. Other defenses may help out if you can't prove the truth of a statement you publish. Another excellent defense is called *fair comment*. It gives wide latitude to the journalist who expresses an opinion about the performance of anyone who stands before the public as a performer—be he or she a politician, athlete, movie celebrity, rock star or whatever. You can be as critical of the performance as you wish, as long as you stick to the performance and don't get into the person's private life. If you want to discuss his or her private life, you had better be ready to prove the truth of what you say. The Supreme Court has gone a long way toward protecting expressions of opinion that are clearly labeled as such, but if you start stating facts that aren't correct, you may be in trouble.[4]

For example, you could call a politician a "bumbling bureaucrat" or a "pompous fool" without much risk of losing a libel suit. Those are value judgments in the best tradition of American political rhetoric.[5] But if, on the other hand, you say someone took a bribe or hangs around with the Mafia, you'd better be ready to prove it's true. Those are allegations of fact, and both of those statements have produced numerous libel suits.

There's still another traditional libel defense: *privilege,* sometimes called *qualified privilege.* It applies to libelous statements that may occur during government proceedings or in public documents. The theory is that in a democracy the media should be free to tell the people what their elected officials are saying, even if it's defamatory. Members of Congress cannot be sued for anything they say on the floor of Congress, and the media can't be sued either, as long as they give an accurate account of what was said and don't quote someone out of context. This defense applies even if the statement is terribly libelous and totally untrue.

The courts have extended the privilege defense far beyond the floor of Congress. Today it applies to virtually all public proceedings down to and including the local city council or—of special interest to student journalists— the board of trustees of a public college or university. It applies to court sessions and to most public records that may be obtained from a court—including those charging people with crimes.

A special concern is the police blotter, which is not privileged in all states, at least not until a person is formally charged with a crime. At that point, the charges become a public record and may be safely reported. Another problem area is government proceedings that are secret. If you somehow find out what happened in a secret grand jury proceeding, for instance, you may risk a libel suit if you print it.

Still, the qualified privilege defense is important in journalism. It permits the media to report an enormous number of government proceedings and public records that are defamatory but that are also clearly within the public's right to know. Without it, the media could never report many important news stories. For example, when a libel suit is filed, the media could not report the substance of the statement that led to the lawsuit if it weren't for the privilege defense. Without it, everyone who reported the story would be guilty of republishing the original libel and could in turn be sued for doing so.

Libel and the Constitution

Until 1964, the basic outline of libel law would have been complete at this point. However, in that year the U.S. Supreme Court introduced a whole new form of protection for the media. In the landmark case of *New York Times* v. *Sullivan*,[6] the Supreme Court said that for a democratic system to work, the mass media needed better protection from libel suits by public officials. The court said a public official could not win a libel suit even if something untruthful and nonprivileged were reported unless there was *actual malice*. The court defined *malice* as publishing a falsehood either with knowledge of its falsity or with reckless disregard for the truth. That definition of malice has been a crucial part of libel law ever since.

The Supreme Court later applied similar rules to public figures—well-known persons who may not hold a public office.[7] They, too, must prove that a falsehood was published either knowingly or with reckless disregard for the truth. But what does *reckless disregard for the truth* mean?

That, unfortunately, isn't a simple question. Lawyers still argue about what those words mean. Generally, though, they mean the journalist suspected or should have suspected that something was untrue but didn't bother to check the facts.

The Supreme Court has followed up its *New York Times* v. *Sullivan* decision with several others that made important changes in American libel law. The most important of these later cases is *Gertz* v. *Welch*,[8] in which the Supreme Court clarified the distinction between public figures and public officials, on the one hand, and private citizens on the other. The *Gertz* case also made it much harder for private citizens to sue for libel.

Before the *Gertz* case, many states allowed private individuals to win libel suits without proving any *fault* on the part of the media. Courts sometimes just presumed that any libelous statement was false, without any proof. The Supreme Court ruled that even private citizens would henceforth have to prove some fault on the part of the media to win a libel suit. The high court said private citizens wouldn't necessarily have to prove actual malice as public officials must, but they would have to prove at least *negligence*. So what's negligence, and how does it differ from actual malice?

That's another tough legal question. *Negligence* is a difficult term to define, but it generally means the failure to do the ordinary fact-checking journalists normally do. It might be negligence to report a criminal arrest, for instance, without double-checking the address of the suspect to make sure an innocent person of the same name hasn't been defamed. It probably isn't actual malice to get two very similar names mixed up in a story written under deadline pressure, but it may well be negligence. What journalists would call sloppy reporting or editing a court might call negligence.

As a result of the *Gertz* decision, it often becomes crucial in libel cases to know whether someone is a public figure or a private citizen. If a person is a private citizen, he or she only has to prove negligence—which isn't terribly difficult to do—to win a libel suit in most states. On the other hand, a public figure has the more difficult job of proving there was actual malice. So who is and who isn't a public figure?

The Supreme Court has decided several cases involving that question. The court said a wealthy jet-set socialite, for instance, was a private person even though she held press conferences to explain why she was divorcing her rich and famous husband.[9] And a mental health researcher with a huge government grant was ruled a private person when a U.S. senator accused him of wasting the taxpayers' money.[10] The high court also ruled that a person who was accused of pro-Communist connections by a popular magazine was not a public figure.[11] In general, a person becomes a public figure only when he or she seeks publicity or voluntarily becomes involved in a matter of public concern.

Students and Libel

What does all of this mean to you as a campus journalist?

It has been said that there are a hundred libel suits lurking in the mind of the college president—and ten in the mind of the faculty adviser—for every real libel suit a college newspaper faces.[12] Still, college newspapers *are* sued now and then, and you have to take some precautions.

Any defamatory statement that can't be proven true and wasn't taken directly from a public record or government proceeding has to be considered dangerous. Be especially careful when you identify the people involved in any criminal matter. First of all, be sure you have the names correct. And because there may be more than one person on campus with the same name, try to use more than just the name for identification. Complete and accurate identification prevents many libel suits.

Another point: make sure the story is as fully qualified as the facts require. If someone has been detained for questioning, don't say he has been charged with a crime. If the person has been charged but not yet convicted, don't say anything that implies guilt. In our system, the accused is innocent until proven guilty, no matter how compelling the evidence. More than one libel suit has occurred because a newspaper prematurely convicted someone in print—and the person was later acquitted. Words such as *alleged* and *accused* may seem trite and unnecessary, and they do not provide absolute protection from libel suits, but if the person is only an alleged rapist and you don't use a qualifier such as *alleged* or *accused*, you're asking for trouble.

Another common problem is a headline that doesn't match the story. The story may have all the needed qualifiers to prevent a libel suit, but the headline writer may drop them in the quest for brevity. If you're dealing with charges of any kind of crime or other wrongdoing, get the qualifiers into the headline even if it means changing the typeface or the layout to do it.

Student publications seem to have more than their share of problems with another potentially libelous situation: reversed captions on photos. If you publish a picture of a senator dedicating a new building and a photo of a suspected arsonist being led away and the captions somehow get transposed, you may need a good lawyer! Photo captions produce a surprising number of lawsuits—perhaps because pictures have so much impact and the reader naturally turns to the caption for names and details after looking at a striking photo.

Retractions and Corrections

If, despite all precautions, a libelous item slips into your newspaper by error, what should you do?

In almost every state, printing a correction or retraction of the error—in as prominent a place as the original error—will reduce the likelihood of a lawsuit. In about half the states, a prompt retraction makes it so difficult and unprofitable to sue for libel that very few people will bother. In other states, the retraction can be used as evidence of your good faith and your absence of malice.

Also, there are some extralegal ways you can protect yourself if you let a libelous statement slip through. Perhaps some diplomatic negotiating will help. College newspapers are sometimes sued (or threatened with a libel suit) when all the injured party really wants is another story that puts things in a different light. If the original libel was the result of an error or oversight, perhaps a second story that goes well beyond a mere retraction will prevent an expensive lawsuit.

Another way some student newspapers protect themselves from libel suits is by buying insurance coverage, as we said earlier in describing the *Michigan State* case. Like Michigan State, a number of other large collegiate dailies and a few weeklies now have libel insurance. Any newspaper that belongs to the American Newspaper Publishers Association is eligible to buy libel insurance from Mutual of Bermuda, a firm that works in cooperation with the ANPA. Several other companies are willing to underwrite certain student newspapers as well as professional ones, including Employers Reinsurance Company, whose ads may often be seen in *Editor and Publisher* magazine.

Libel insurance isn't cheap, but it may be a form of protection worth considering, especially if yours is a large campus paper that covers a lot of hard news. You can also buy "First Amendment" insurance, which will protect you from some of the other legal hazards discussed in this chapter and in Chapter 14.

Libel and Autonomy

Sometimes when a libel suit is threatened, the student editors suddenly find themselves with another problem besides an imminent libel suit. The administration or someone else outside the staff may try to take control of the paper, at least temporarily. You should understand that if a lawsuit is filed, the institution, its administrators, your faculty adviser and perhaps outsiders who have little or nothing to do with the newspaper may be named as defendants.

Even though you have the First Amendment on your side and the board of trustees may not have the legal right to control your editorial content, that won't prevent them from being sued on your account. If the case were to go to court, of course, the trustees and administrators would try to get themselves dismissed from the lawsuit by showing that they had no responsibility for the paper's content. However, they may also try to negotiate a settlement in which they promise that you'll publish something you are not prepared to publish. As a result, you could have a second legal hassle on your hands, this one over freedom of the student press.

Here's an example of how that can happen. In the late 1970s the *State Hornet* at California State University, Sacramento, published a story about the Church of Scientology, a religious sect that followed a policy of suing almost everyone who wrote anything negative about the group. The Scientologists threatened a lawsuit, and attorneys for the Associated Students organization—who had no right to dictate content to the newspaper—worked out a settlement that involved the paper's publishing an apology. The staff was prepared to stand by the original story and refused to publish the apology, but the Associated Students then attempted to force the paper to carry it. When the staff stood firm, a compromise was reached in which the paper did an additional story about Scientology, but without an apology.

Of course, another related problem is that college officials may use the threat of a lawsuit as justification for stripping student editors of their autonomy. The *Michigan State* case, mentioned earlier, didn't involve an administrative takeover (since the paper is independent), but it does illustrate the problem. On some campuses, lawsuits or threats of lawsuits have prompted college officials to turn once-independent student newspapers into laboratory publications with close faculty supervision.

While legitimate arguments may be made for a laboratory newspaper as opposed to an independent one, if your campus is to switch from one to the other, it should not be because the student staff has abused its freedom by being cavalier about libel. It is often said that freedom and responsibility go together, and that is nowhere more true than here.

INVASION OF PRIVACY

Another kind of legal problem for the media, occasionally including student newspapers, is invasion of privacy. In fact, many persons who sue the media for libel also sue for invasion of privacy, hoping to win one way or the other.

Four different kinds of invasion of privacy have been recognized over the years. They are—

1. intrusion into a person's physical solitude;
2. public disclosure of embarrassing private facts;
3. placing a person before the public in a false light;
4. commercial exploitation of a person's name or likeness.

It's not hard to explain what kinds of situations lead to these problems, any one of which may produce an expensive lawsuit. Here are examples of each type.

Intrusion

An intrusion may occur when a journalist (often a photographer) surreptitiously gathers revealing personal information by, in effect, trespassing or spying. Lawsuits have occurred where a journalist got into a person's home under false pretenses and secretly took pictures, and where photographers with telephoto lenses took intimate pictures of persons in seemingly private places.[13] One photographer was placed under a court order requiring him to stay a certain distance away from Jacqueline Onassis (the widow of President John F. Kennedy) and her children.[14]

This sort of thing isn't a problem if you want to take news photos in a public place, but when you have to go on private property without permission to get the picture, it could lead to legal troubles. An exception to this rule is the scene of a disaster: a news photographer is usually safe in going on private property along with law enforcement personnel to cover one.

Also, if you want to photograph celebrities for news purposes and you can take the picture from a public place, you are within your legal rights in so doing, unless you become such a pest that you're consistently in the way. However, the rules are different if the picture is used for something other than news, a point discussed later.

Private Facts

The second kind of invasion of privacy, public disclosure of private facts, is only rarely a problem for the news media because the courts recognize "newsworthiness" or "public interest" as a defense, a point we'll return to shortly. It involves presenting intimate personal details of a person's life. One lengthy lawsuit resulted from a magazine article revealing a well-known surfer's idiosyncracies, such as a penchant for eating insects.[15] The magazine eventually won, but only after a very expensive legal battle.

A few states allow invasion of privacy lawsuits based on the idea that a former criminal has a right to be rehabilitated and start a new life. In California, for instance, a criminal who is rehabilitated and makes new friends who are unaware of his past may sue if the media reveal his past.[16] This kind of private facts lawsuit is only rarely successful, but it is a legal danger to be aware of.

False Light

One of the most dangerous kinds of invasion of privacy is the false light variety. A major newspaper once faced a lawsuit that went all the way to the Supreme Court when it implied a reporter had interviewed a woman whose family suffered financial duress after her husband was killed in a bridge collapse.[17] (The reporter never talked to her.) And a student newspaper was once threatened with a lawsuit for illustrating a story about poverty with a photo of a charming black child at a preschool. The child's father (an electronic engineer) and mother (a teacher with a master's degree) weren't pleased when the caption implied the child came from an impoverished home.[18] A public apology prevented a lawsuit.

Commercial Exploitation

The fourth kind of invasion of privacy, commercial exploitation of someone's name or likeness, is a problem mainly in advertising and the entertainment media. Whenever a person is recognizable in an ad (or his or her name is used), that person must give permission before publication. Celebrities earn a significant part of their income through product endorsements; you can't use their names or pictures in an ad without paying them.

Even nonadvertising photos can lead to such a lawsuit. It is standard procedure to get a signed *model release* when you have someone pose for a feature photo (such as a magazine cover). If the photo is clearly newsworthy, you don't need permission to use the picture, but it's best to get a signed release whenever there is any doubt. The form can be very simple: it should say the person posing gives his or her permission for the picture to be used in return for the free publicity that may result.

To be valid, the release must be a legally binding contract. A contract must be supported by *consideration*. The consideration can be money, but it can also be anything else of value, such as free publicity. Still, if you're paying the model, the release should clearly indicate it. The model signs and dates the form, and the publication keeps it on file. If the model is under the age at which one may legally enter a contract (usually 18), the parent or guardian must sign.

Privacy Defenses

As in libel law, there are often potential lawsuits for invasion of privacy that don't materialize because a defense applies. The two most important defenses in privacy suits are newsworthiness (or public interest) and consent.

Public interest or newsworthiness will protect you in many situations where you've used someone's name or photo for news purposes or where you've revealed intimate private facts. Nearly everything that appears in most newspapers can be defended as newsworthy, and the courts will rarely go along with someone who seeks to second-guess a publication about the newsworthiness of a straight news, feature or sports story. Even innocent bystanders at the scene of a news event have little chance of winning a lawsuit if their picture appears in print.

The consent defense, on the other hand, is not quite so automatic. You need a contractual arrangement to show consent, as in the use of model releases for nonnews photographs. Sometimes a photographer claims there was *implied consent*. "But she posed for me," the photographer will say when the editor asks to see the signed consent form. While it may be possible to prove there was consent without having the signed form, there's rarely a good reason to take the chance. Whenever you set up a picture and have a model pose, it is best to have a signed consent form. That is especially true when the photo will be used for advertising purposes.

Comparing Libel and Privacy Lawsuits

In comparing libel and privacy lawsuits, you should remember that you can have one legal problem without the other—or you can have both. Truth is not always a defense in invasion of privacy cases even though it is in libel suits. Newsworthiness, on the other hand, is not in and of itself a libel defense. Something that may be perfectly safe from a libel standpoint can be a potential invasion of privacy, or vice versa.

The U.S. Supreme Court has recognized something of a "public records" defense in privacy cases as in libel,[19] and the Court has also ruled that public figures must prove malice to win certain kinds of privacy lawsuits.[20] However, in some circumstances neither absence of malice nor absolute truthfulness will prevent a lawsuit for invasion of privacy. When you do a story that reveals embarrassing or intimate facts, they must be newsworthy or you're risking a privacy lawsuit.

COPYRIGHT PROBLEMS

Another legal question that sometimes troubles student journalists is copyright law. If something is copyrighted, you generally may not republish it without permission. Even when there's no valid copyright, plagiarism raises ethical questions.

Most literary, artistic and other creative works may be copyrighted, regardless of whether they are published or unpublished. If a work is copyrighted, no one else may copy it or perform it in public (as in musical and dramatic works) without consent from the copyright owner. A copyright is normally valid for the author's lifetime plus 50 years.

Generally, if a work has a *copyright notice* (for instance, "Copyright 1984 by Fred Freelance"), that means it's copyrighted. Even if there isn't any copyright notice, the federal copyright law provides a way that the work can be copyrighted. If there's no copyright notice, *innocent infringers* (those who don't know the work is copyrighted) cannot be penalized for using the work, but once an infringer is informed of the copyright, the infringement must stop.

If a work is *not* copyrighted, it is said to "fall into the public domain" as soon as it's published. That means anyone may copy or perform the work without permission. There is still the ethical (and possible legal) problem of fraudulently presenting someone else's work as your own, but there is no copyright problem if a published work is in the public domain. However, an unpublished work belongs to its author, even if it isn't formally copyrighted.

Even if a work is copyrighted, some limited copying is permitted. Under a legal concept called the *fair use doctrine*, it is permissible to copy brief excerpts from lengthy works (books, for example), as long as the copying doesn't cut into the potential profit of the original work. Under the fair use doctrine, most noncommercial single-copy photocopying is a fair use, as is quoting a brief passage of a copyrighted work in a review or a news story.

For journalists, perhaps the most important point about copyright law is that the news itself cannot be copyrighted, although a *description* of a news event can be. Therefore, if a daily newspaper in your area publishes and copyrights an important story concerning your campus, you may take the information from the story and use it in the campus paper—as long as you rewrite it completely.

Some journalism teachers continue to tell their students it is illegal to use any information from a published source in their stories, but that is clearly not true in the United States. If it were, the first reporter to publish a story about a major disaster could deny the story to everyone else.

However, there is another potential legal pitfall in using published information. If one systematically gets all or most of his or her information from a published source instead of doing original newsgathering, that may be what is called *unfair competition*. The Supreme Court recognized that legal concept long ago.[21] Nonetheless, it is perfectly legal—and in fact a standard practice among professional journalists—to take information from a previously published story, rewrite it and run it. If you rewrite completely, you're on safe ground in using previously published information now and then. No one may lock up factual information and deny its use to others by copyrighting a description of the facts.

There is, of course, a closely related ethical issue here. Consistently using someone else's research instead of doing your own is a form of plagiarism. No ethical journalist does it.

Securing a Copyright

Should a student newspaper be copyrighted, and if so, how is it done?

In general, there is little reason to copyright most student newspapers. The copyright system was intended to prevent commercial theft of the profits from one's creative endeavors. The fact is, of course, that very little of what is published in a student newspaper—or any newspaper, for that matter—has much commercial value after the date of publication. Very few fortunes have been made by republishing yesterday's news stories. And the facts themselves cannot be copyrighted anyway. Generally, copyrighting a student newspaper is a waste of time and money.

Nevertheless, there may be a time when you develop a story that is significant enough that you want to copyright it. If so, the procedure is fairly simple. You include a copyright notice with the story (the notice simply says "copyright" or uses a c inside a circle, followed by the year and the name of the copyright owner). That's all you have to do to establish copyright protection.

There are formal copyright registration procedures, but the 1976 Copyright Act says these formalities are "permissive"—you don't have to follow through to have a valid copyright. If you do decide to register a copyright, you first obtain the proper forms from the U.S. Copyright Office, Washington, D.C. 20559. For a newspaper or any other written material, you'll need Form TX. Once you have the form, you fill it out and mail it back along with two copies of the work and a $10 fee. For a newspaper, a separate registration is required for each edition.

Given the cost and inconvenience of registering, it is not unusual for a newspaper staff to include the copyright notice and do nothing more unless an infringement occurs. That is normally legal: it is never mandatory to follow through with the registration process unless the federal copyright office asks you to do so (which isn't likely), and even then you have another 90 days to finish the job.

However, if you complete the registration before an infringement occurs, you have more legal remedies available in the event of a lawsuit. Before you can sue an infringer, you still have to register the work, but if you didn't register prior to the infringement, you generally cannot collect your attorney's fees or statutory damages. Statutory damages are a sum of money that may be awarded in a copyright infringement lawsuit without proof you suffered any losses or that the infringer made any profits. Even if you didn't register before the infringement occurred, you can still sue for your actual losses and recover the infringer's profits, but that may not amount to much money. And you still have the right to have all pirated copies of your works impounded.

Obviously, the copyright law was written this way to make copyright infringements unprofitable and to encourage people to register their copyrights without actually making it mandatory.

OBSCENITY LAW AND JOURNALISM

Since few student editors set out to practice pornography in campus newspapers, little need be said of obscenity law except to provide some guidelines on what is and is not legally obscene, since student publications are sometimes forbidden by a campus policy to publish anything "obscene."

As a result of Supreme Court decisions over the past 30 years, many subjects that were once considered obscene are no longer so under the law. No longer is mere nudity—even frontal nudity—legally obscene in America. For a photograph to be obscene, the people in the photograph must generally be doing something more than sitting there passively posing for a picture.

This is not to say that nudity is necessarily always in good taste in a campus newspaper: that's a policy decision for each publication's editors to make with due consideration of the prevailing climate on campus. It's just that nudity is not legally obscene.

If nudity isn't obscene, what is? In the *Miller* v. *California* decision, the Supreme Court offered a broad, general definition. To decide whether a work is obscene, one determines:

Whether the average person, applying contemporary community standards, would find the work, taken as a whole, appeals to the prurient interest; whether the work depicts or describes, in a patently offensive way, sexual conduct specifically defined by the applicable state law; and whether the work, taken as a whole, lacks serious literary, artistic, political or scientific value.[22]

This is a vague definition, written in "legalese." Let's just say that materials far more sexually explicit than most student editors would ever consider for a general campus publication are not legally obscene under this definition.

Moreover, mere four-letter words do not constitute obscenity either. Again, they may or may not be appropriately used, and they may not be in good taste; but none of your favorite or unfavorite four-letter words is legally obscene. In fact, the Supreme Court has specifically ruled that everyone's favorite four-letter sexual expletive is not obscene as it is normally used.[23] Nor does putting *mother* in front of it make it obscene, according to the Supreme Court (that was decided in the *Papish* v. *University of Missouri Curators* decision, discussed in Chapter 12).[24]

Sometimes profanity and obscenity are confused, often by administrators who see the campus press mainly as an off-campus public relations tool. The term *profanity* refers to disrespectful references to deity, not to sexually oriented materials. There are few laws still on the books today that prohibit the use of profanity in print; those that still exist would not likely withstand a constitutional challenge if tested in court.

Again we should emphasize that there is a difference between what the law allows and what may be vulgar or in bad taste. We are simply summarizing the law of the land, not suggesting what your standards of good taste should be. But if someone tells you not to use a particular four-letter word because it's obscene, he or she hasn't been keeping up with the U.S. Supreme Court.

REFERENCES

1. There were at least six libel judgments with awards of over $1 million in the United States between 1979 and 1981. They were—

    $4.6 million against the *San Francisco Examiner* for reporting that two police inspectors and a deputy DA pressured a witness to lie in a murder case;
    $39.6 million (reduced to $4 million by the judge) against *Hustler* and Larry Flynt for a cartoon showing *Penthouse* publisher Robert Guccione engaged in a homosexual act;
    $9.2 million against the *Alton Telegraph* for sending a memo to the Justice Department accusing a developer of financial improprieties;

$26.5 million (reduced to $14 million by the judge) against *Penthouse* for a fictitious story about a beauty contest winner who excelled at oral sex and who resembled a real "Miss Wyoming";

$1.6 million (reduced to $800,000 by the judge) against the *National Enquirer* for saying actress Carol Burnett was boisterous and unruly in a restaurant;

$2 million against the *Dallas Morning News* for saying a prominent citizen had threatened a state college president.

2. The *Alton Telegraph* filed for bankruptcy after the libel judgment mentioned in reference no. 1. The case was eventually settled for $1.4 million and the paper avoided bankruptcy.

3. Telephone interview with Gerald Coy, 30 November 1981.

4. In *Gertz* v. *Welch*, 418 U.S. 323 (1974), the majority opinion said, "Under the First Amendment there is no such thing as a false idea. However pernicious an opinion may seem, we depend for its correction not on the conscience of judges and juries but on the competition of other ideas."

5. For an example of a case in which a court ruled that tough political rhetoric was constitutionally protected, see *Desert Sun* v. *Superior Court*, 97 Cal. App. 3d 49 (1979).

6. *New York Times* v. *Sullivan*, 376 U.S. 254 (1964).

7. See *Curtis* v. *Butts*, 388 U.S. 130 (1967).

8. *Gertz* v. *Welch*, supra.

9. *Time, Inc.* v. *Firestone*, 424 U.S. 448 (1976).

10. *Hutchinson* v. *Proxmire*, 443 U.S. 111 (1979).

11. *Wolston* v. *Reader's Digest Association*, 443 U.S. 157 (1979).

12. This was a remark by Reuben Mehling, professor of journalism at California State University, Hayward, during a seminar at the California Journalism Conference in 1971.

13. *Dietemann* v. *Time, Inc.*, 449 F. 2d 245 (9th cir., 1971).

14. *Galella* v. *Onassis*, 487 F. 2d 986 (2nd cir., 1973).

15. *Virgil* v. *Sports Illustrated*, 527 F. 2d 1122 (9th cir., 1975); 424 F. Supp. 1286 (S.D. Cal. 1976).

16. See, for instance, *Briscoe* v. *Reader's Digest*, 4 Cal. 3d 529 (1971); *Conklin* v. *Sloss*, 86 Cal. App. 3d 241 (1978).

17. *Cantrell* v. *Forest City Publishing Co.*, 419 U.S. 245 (1974).

18. This incident arose from a photograph published in the *Daily Titan* at California State University, Fullerton, in 1969.

19. See *Cox Broadcasting* v. *Cohn*, 420 U.S. 469 (1975).

20. *Time, Inc.* v. *Hill*, 385 U.S. 374 (1967).

21. *Associated Press* v. *International News Service*, 248 U.S. 215 (1918).

22. *Miller* v. *California*, 413 U.S. 15 (1973).

23. *Cohen* v. *California*, 403 U.S. (1971).

24. *Papish* v. *University of Missouri Curators*, 410 U.S. 667 (1973).

FOURTEEN

Newsgathering and the Law

S uppose you're covering a meeting of
your college's board of trustees and the
chairperson suddenly asks everyone
in the audience to leave the room. "We're
going into an executive session to discuss
personnel matters," he says.

Is that legal? Don't reporters have a
right to cover the news, personnel session
or not?

Over the years, a variety of laws have
been enacted to deal with situations such
as this one. Every state now has an open
meeting law, a law that tells government
agencies when they may hold secret meetings and when they must allow the public
to attend. And almost every state has a
public records law—a law giving the press
and the public access to many kinds of
government documents. Meanwhile,
Congress has enacted several laws that
protect your right to obtain federal records
and attend meetings of federal agencies.

If you are on the news staff at a public
college or university, many of these laws
apply to you. In fact, some of the federal
public records laws even apply to private
colleges. Thus, if you're going to be an
effective reporter on campus, you will need
to know something about the laws governing public records and public meetings.

In addition, you may need to know a

little about another aspect of newsgathering law. Suppose a nontenured professor
finds out that a close friend of the college
president has been getting college construction contracts and has been funneling
money back to the president in return. If it
could be documented, such a charge would
be very newsworthy: that's called a kickback, and it is both unethical and illegal.
Now suppose this professor comes up with
solid documentation and presents it to you
but insists that you cannot use his name in
your story. After all, he isn't tenured, and
he could lose his job if the president knew
he was the whistle-blower.

Professional journalists often encounter situations such as this one. Many
important news stories could never be
reported without the use of confidential
sources. This kind or reporting obviously
raises ethical questions.

But there are also potential legal problems. Suppose you do the story about the
alleged kickback to the college president.
Since taking a kickback is a major crime,
law enforcement officials and perhaps a
grand jury would be very much interested
in your story. What could you do if you
were called before a grand jury and ordered
to reveal your source of information? If you
refuse to cooperate, you can be cited for

contempt of court and might land in jail. However, if you comply, you'll be breaking your promise to your news source—and he may be fired. What do you do?

In many states, *shield laws* have been passed to deal with that kind of situation. A shield law exempts journalists from having to reveal their confidential sources, at least under some circumstances. In addition to a shield law, there may be another legal solution to your dilemma. In some states whose legislatures have never passed shield laws, the courts have recognized a concept called *reporter's privilege*. Like a shield law, the reporter's privilege doctrine allows a journalist to keep his or her sources confidential—sometimes. If you're protected by either a shield law or reporter's privilege, you may not have to reveal your source for the kickback story. If not, you may have a problem.

Because campus newspaper reporters are often trusted by people who would never talk to law enforcement people, they often come up with information of interest to the authorities. When that happens, student newspapers sometimes find themselves caught in situations where the only two choices are jail and breaking a promise to a news source. Obviously, you need to know if your state has a shield law or recognizes the concept of reporter's privilege, or perhaps both.

In this chapter, there's no way we can describe the law of newsgathering in all 50 states. To do that would take an entire book, and such a book would be out-of-date almost before it could be printed. All we can do is summarize the basics of the law concerning open meetings, public records and confidential sources. Under these circumstances, it is inevitable that some of the generalizations and examples we use will not apply in your state. That's why we explain how to find out the specifics of your own state's laws in this field.

ACCESS TO PUBLIC RECORDS

At last count, every state except Mississippi had a law giving the public a right to inspect and copy at least some kinds of public records. Many of these laws were patterned after the federal Freedom of Information Act, a law enacted by Congress to open up the federal bureaucracy to public scrutiny. Perhaps our starting point should be the federal FoI Act.

The FoI Act was passed in 1966 and extensively amended in 1974.[1] It gives the public a right to see records kept by many federal agencies. Hundreds of thousands of documents have been made public because of the FoI Act. Thanks to this law, we've learned about the FBI's policy of harassing civil rights leader Martin Luther King, Jr. And we learned the military conducted experiments with dangerous drugs in the 1950s, using civilians who had no idea they were "guinea pigs" as subjects. Historians have learned vital details of the American government's clandestine activities in places like Chile, Iran and Cuba by using the FoI Act to get information that would never have been made public otherwise.

Journalists consider the FoI Act to be a cornerstone of their right to gather information. The act covers almost the entire federal government, except for Congress and the courts. It applies to the executive branch, independent regulatory agencies such as the Federal Communications Commission, government-controlled corporations such as the post office, and just about everything else in the federal bureaucracy.[2]

Without the FoI Act, the federal government would be far less accountable to the public. That's why journalists are so alarmed about a package of proposals before Congress that would weaken the act. At this writing, the proposals have not been approved, but if they are, they will deny the public access to many key documents.

Meanwhile, the government processes thousands of requests for information under the FoI Act each year. Here's how the act works. The person seeking information files a formal request with the agency that has custody of the desired documents. How do you know who has the documents you want? That's a difficult problem, but most federal agencies publish lists of the documents they possess. The lists appear in the *Federal Register,* a voluminous but well-indexed publication that is available at many large libraries.

Once a FoI request is made, the agency has ten working days to comply (or deny the request, if the documents in question fall within one or more of nine exemptions to the law). The government almost never meets the ten-day deadline, and there's not much a citizen can do if the bureaucracy is a little slow.

However, if the documents aren't provided within a reasonable time, the citizen has a right to go to court. If the resulting lawsuit is successful, the government must pay the citizen's legal expenses. In deciding the case, the judge has the right to privately inspect the requested material to decide if it properly falls into the exemptions.

FoI Exemptions

The exemptions are often crucial in FoI cases. Here are the kinds of documents that are exempt from public scrutiny under the FoI Act:

Documents that might endanger national security if made public

Documents relating to the "internal personnel rules and practices" of federal agencies

Materials that are specifically exempted under some other law

Trade secrets and certain other financial and commercial information

Some internal government memoranda

Personnel and medical files of individuals

Law enforcement investigatory files

Reports involving financial institutions such as banks

Oil and gas exploration maps

Obviously, some of these exceptions create giant loopholes. Every year about one-half million documents are declared secret for national security reasons alone. And journalists say that perfectly harmless documents are often so classified—not to protect national security but to keep the public from finding out that the Pentagon wasted the taxpayers' dollars by paying too much for something or other.

But despite the loopholes, the FoI Act has made the federal government much more accessible to journalists. This federal law is especially important because it has served as a pattern for so many of the state public record laws—laws that are much more likely to affect you directly as a campus journalist.

Privacy Laws and the Buckley Amendment

While Congress was moving to open up the federal bureaucracy to public scrutiny, it was also moving in another direction: toward closing certain records to public inspection to protect individual privacy. The Privacy Act of 1974 was a major step in that direction.[3] The Privacy Act set strict limits on the way federal agencies may use the information they gather about individuals. Generally, it says that if an agency collects personal information for one reason, the information may not normally be passed along to other agencies to be used in different ways. There are, however, exceptions to this rule for such things as law enforcement. Significantly, the Privacy Act gives individuals a right to inspect many of their own records that may be held by federal agencies, and it allows individuals to sue government officials who wrongfully release personal information about them.

Although the Privacy Act is important—and has resulted in journalists losing access to some sources of information about individuals—another federal law in the privacy field is of more immediate concern to campus journalists: the Family Educational Rights and Privacy Act, often called the "Buckley Amendment."[4] It gives the parents of students under age 18 the right to inspect their children's school records, and it gives students over 18 the right to inspect their own school (and college) records. The Buckley Amendment also places limits on school officials' authority to release personal information about students to anyone else but the student or his family. Anyone who wrongfully releases information may be sued for damages. School systems that violate the Buckley Amendment may be denied federal funds. It applies to both public and private schools and colleges.

As a campus journalist, you may find the Buckley Amendment to be both an asset and a nuisance. It does, of course, give you the right to see most of your own school records. There are times when that can be a valuable right. And like many other rights, it's a right you can waive (that is, voluntarily give up). For instance, in order to secure a more candid (and thus credible) letter of reference to a graduate school from a professor, you may choose to waive your right to see the letter if you ever exercise your right to inspect your own student files.

However, the Buckley Amendment can also be a real nuisance for campus journalists. School officials sometimes use it as an excuse to withhold information that really isn't the least bit private. Some school officials have been known to withhold such routine information as the heights and weights of athletes involved in intercollegiate sports. And school officials tend to regard almost all disciplinary proceedings involving students (and often faculty) as private under this law or similar state laws.

Thus, student and faculty grievance and disciplinary proceedings are typically held in private unless the individual chooses to "go public" with his or her case. The result, of course, is that much that is newsworthy goes on behind closed doors, and you either have to forget about reporting it or resort to investigative methods, some of which may raise ethical questions.

State Public Record and Privacy Laws

Among the 49 states with public record laws there is such a wide variation that we cannot describe all of their provisions here. But in general, these laws follow the pattern set by the federal FoI Act. In fact, more than half the states have enacted such laws—or greatly strengthened existing ones—since Congress acted in this area in 1966. Generally, the state laws provide public access to the records maintained by state and local government agencies, with exemptions for most of the same things that are exempted from the federal law and usually a few others.

However, long before state public record laws were commonplace, some state and local records were open to public inspection as a matter of custom. For example, real estate ownership records have traditionally been public, as have been most court records. However, many states keep records of court proceedings involving juveniles confidential, and many also keep divorce and adoption records secret. Some states also deny public access to records that would identify victims of sex crimes.

State public record laws generally apply to numerous records of interest to campus journalists. At public colleges and universities, budgets and salary schedules are almost always public records. So are many records of construction projects and other matters involving the expenditure of public monies. However, the exemptions can be a major obstacle to newsgathering. As already indicated, personal records involving individuals are usually confidential. Moreover, law enforcement investigatory records are almost always excluded from public record laws.

From a college journalist's point of view, the exemptions for law enforcement records can be a problem. Professional reporters in almost every state are allowed to inspect the actual *police blotter* (a record of daily police activities), but often that is a matter of courtesy and not a legal right. Just before this book went to press, California adopted a law giving the public access to much police blotter information, but many states still lack such laws.

Don't be too surprised if the local police turn you away while routinely allowing reporters from the downtown daily to check the police blotter. Unless your state has a law making the police blotter itself a public record, there is not much you can do if the police won't extend you the same courtesy they routinely extend to the professionals. Obviously, some before-there's-a-crisis negotiating may be in order.

On the other hand, the actual fact of a booking and the filing of criminal charges are almost always public records. When charges are filed in court, you have as much right as any professional journalist to go down and read the record. Sometimes it is a good idea to read the public record on a criminal case involving a newsworthy campus official, even if you don't intend to cover the story extensively. You may discover something far more newsworthy than the criminal charges.

A story obtained from police and court records obviously requires careful handling. As a matter of ethics you may choose not to publish all the brutal facts you unearth by reading court records. However, whatever privacy an individual otherwise has is usually lost when he or she is charged with a major crime. Most states try to protect juveniles from heavy media exposure, but sometimes even juveniles face extensive publicity if the case is sensational enough. In fact, if you learn the facts of a newsworthy case involving a juvenile, you will usually have a First Amendment right to publish those facts even if your state makes such information confidential. The Supreme Court has ruled that a state may not prevent the media from publishing the facts, as long as they were lawfully obtained (from eyewitnesses, for instance).[5]

While court records are usually open for public inspection, many other records involving individuals are confidential. Like the federal government, most states have privacy laws as well as public records laws. Some states give them other names, calling them "information practices" laws or something of the sort, but the result is the same. Such laws restrict the release of personal information about individuals—information that might otherwise be a matter of public record. They rarely affect court records as such, but they do affect other kinds of records kept by state and local government agencies. As we noted earlier, privacy laws usually require that records of student disciplinary proceedings be kept confidential, unless the student waives his or her right to confidentiality.

The specifics of public records and privacy laws vary so much from state to state that generalizing is difficult. Again, the best advice we can give is for you to look up the laws of your own state, using the methods described later in this chapter.

OPEN MEETING LAWS

Every state has some kind of open meeting law, as does the federal government. However, the federal government was by no means the leader in this field: at least 46 states had such laws before Congress finally got around to enacting the federal Government-in-the-Sunshine Act in 1976.[6]

The federal law is much narrower than many state open meeting laws. It only applies to about 50 federal agencies, such as the Federal Communications Commission, the Federal Trade Commission, the Nuclear Regulatory Commission, the Civil Aeronautics Board, and the Equal Employment Opportunity Commission.

The governing boards of these agencies must generally hold open meetings. However, the federal open meeting law has all of the same exceptions as the FoI Act, plus one more: discussions of pending lawsuits.

The federal Sunshine Law does require these boards and commissions to announce their meeting times and invite the public to attend unless a specific item of business falls within one of the exceptions. And citizens who are wrongfully excluded from agency meetings may sue in federal court, with the court authorized to require the agency to pay their legal expenses if they win.

Moreover, the law requires most agencies to keep detailed records of what goes on in secret meetings and to publicly announce any action taken. The way each commissioner or board member voted must be reported.

Journalists like those provisions, but they also see a major problem in the Sunshine Law: it doesn't have any teeth in it. Unlike many of the state open meeting laws (to be discussed shortly) the federal law doesn't provide any criminal or civil penalties for violations. Nor does the law allow a court to invalidate any action taken at an illegal secret meeting. A federal agency can knowingly violate the law without fear of anything worse than a judicial hand-slapping.

Nevertheless, most journalists think the federal open meeting law is better than nothing. It could be much stronger, but it has opened many previously closed meeting-room doors to the public and press.

State Open Meeting Laws

As in the area of public records laws, there is wide variation among state open meeting laws. Most such laws apply to both state and local governments, including public school and college boards of trustees. These laws generally require open meetings of elected and appointed policy-making boards while allowing closed meetings of administrative staffs and advisory committees.

Like the federal law, the state open meeting laws almost all have exceptions, allowing secret meetings for a variety of reasons. Certainly the most common exception is the one for personnel matters. When a board or commission wants to discuss hiring or firing one of its officers, it is almost always legal to do that in private.

Another very common exception is one allowing government agencies to exclude unruly people from meetings and to bar everyone when public safety or the security of public facilities requires it. Also, there are almost always exceptions for discussions of legal strategy in pending lawsuits and for strategy sessions to plan salary negotiations with employees.

On the other hand, some state open meeting laws have almost no exceptions at all. For example, Florida's Government-in-the-Sunshine Act (not to be confused with the federal law of the same name) has no stated exceptions.[7] It says state and local governments must hold open meetings—period. However, there are loopholes even in Florida. The courts have ruled that government agencies may meet in private with their lawyers to map legal strategy, for instance. And some preliminary labor-management negotiating may be done in private under the Florida law.[8] But in general Florida's law is short on loopholes. Even decisions to hire and fire executives are supposed to be discussed in public under the Florida law, a rule found in few other states.

Social gatherings of government officials present a touchy problem under some state open meeting laws. Some such laws are so broad that they even make it illegal for a quorum (more than half) of a city council or school board to gather socially (or ride somewhere in the same car) without inviting the press and public to join them. Obviously, laws written in that way invite abuse. But on the other hand, some state laws are like Pennsylvania's, which is a broad law with only a few exceptions, but which applies only to formal meetings, not to informal gatherings or even "study sessions" where government officials may debate the issues and decide how they're going to vote at a later public meeting.[9]

Many state open meeting laws do have some teeth in them, something the federal law lacks. In about half the states, actions taken at illegal secret meetings may be invalidated by the courts, and public officials who participate in unlawful secret meetings may face criminal penalties. Ohio even has a provision allowing a court to remove a public official from office as a penalty for taking part in an illegal secret meeting.[10]

New York and Connecticut both have official "watchdogs" whose job is to see that government officials obey the law. In Connecticut, for instance, there is a Freedom of Information Commission that hears citizen complaints about secrecy in government and has the power to act against government officials guilty of unlawfully excluding the public from their meetings.[11] New York has a government official with somewhat similar responsibilities.[12]

Many states have comprehensive open meeting laws. Others have their open meeting provisions scattered all over their statutory laws. Indiana has a comprehensive law, called the Indiana Open Door Law, that requires open meetings of state and local governments.[13] Similarly, Texas' open meeting law covers most agencies of state and local government, with exceptions for only a few things (for example, to discuss lawsuits; hiring, firing and discipline; land negotiations; and labor negotiations).[14]

California, on the other hand, has no fewer than four different open meeting laws covering various government agencies.[15] In fact, the provision requiring community college boards of trustees to hold public meetings is in one law (a local government open meeting law called the Ralph M. Brown Act), but the provision requiring student governments at community colleges to hold open meetings appears in a different law, a law that generally applies only to state agencies.

Incidentally, while virtually every state requires public college boards of trustees to hold open meetings, California is one of only a few states with similar provisions applying specifically to student governments. In many states, student governments, faculty senates and similar bodies are free to hold closed meetings—except when they voluntarily admit visitors under their own rules. If that's the case in your state, there may not be much you can do if such a body votes to close the meeting-room doors just when things become newsworthy.

However, several courts have recently ruled that open meeting laws *do* cover advisory bodies on college and university campuses. For instance, an Illinois court ruled that the intercollegiate athletic board at Eastern Illinois University had to hold public meetings under that state's open meeting law.[16] And in Texas, a state attorney general's opinion ruled that the University of Texas Athletic Council was covered by the open meeting law.[17]

Since public university trustees have to hold open meetings, the courts are increasingly taking the position that the bodies that advise the trustees—or make important decisions on their behalf—must also hold open meetings. This is an unsettled and rapidly changing area of open meeting law.

FINDING YOUR STATE'S LAWS

We've repeatedly said you may need to look up your own state's open meeting or public record laws. How do you do that?

In some states journalistic organizations have prepared pamphlets describing the open meeting and public record laws. If such a publication exists in your state, you can obtain a copy at little cost. If there is no such publication, you may have to check out the law for yourself.

Looking up a state law isn't very difficult. Your college library almost certainly has a complete set of volumes with the text of your state's laws. In many states, the *statutory laws* (that is, the laws enacted by the state legislature) are collected in a set of volumes called "annotated statutes" or "annotated codes." The word *annotated* simply means the law books include not only the text of the law itself but also summaries of court decisions interpreting the law.

Once you've found your state's collection of statutory laws, check the last few volumes. You will find a lengthy and detailed index. In that index, you'll see references to everything from murder and armed robbery to meat inspections and welfare payments, although perhaps not under those terms. Once you've found the index, the trick is to find the right key words. If you're looking for open meeting laws, look under "meetings," "open meetings," "freedom of information," "public meetings" and similar headings. Sooner or later, you'll find the heading under which your state's law or laws is indexed. If all else fails, check under "records" or "public records." Even if you're looking for open meeting laws rather than public record laws, the state public records law may help you, because there is often a cross-reference to the open meeting law in the public record law. And in about twenty states, the two laws are consolidated and will be found in the same place anyway. If you live in California, Connecticut, Florida, Illinois, Indiana, New York, Ohio, Pennsylvania or Texas, check the appropriate footnote at the end of this chapter. It will lead you directly to your state's open meeting law.

After you've found your state's law, read it. Don't let the legalese stop you. Take it slowly and perhaps outline it as you go. Ask yourself some key questions. Does the law say it applies to college trustees? (If not, don't panic; the college or university system is surely a state or local government agency anyway.) Does it mention student governments? What are the exceptions? What enforcement provisions are there? Is it a crime to knowingly take part in an illegal secret meeting? What other loopholes do you see? You may want to photocopy the law for class discussion.

When you're reading the law, take a look at the court decisions, which may be summarized in fine print after the law itself. They are only brief summaries, but do any of them appear to apply to your institution? Do the court decisions generally close the loopholes or create new ones?

Once you've looked up the law, you may want to consult someone with experience under your state's open meeting and public records laws. Perhaps there's a local government reporter at a nearby daily newspaper who knows the open meeting law well and who would be willing to discuss it with your news staff. Or maybe there's a local lawyer who's willing to give a guest lecture on the subject.

PRACTICAL CONSIDERATIONS

So far, we've been talking about laws that assure public access to government meetings and records. Such laws are valuable, but they create all sorts of practical problems for journalists, both on and off campus.

For one thing, the law only works if you know your rights and are prepared to fight for them. Unfortunately, it is not at all unusual for government officials to be ignorant—or contemptuous—of these laws. Some officials routinely tell people they have no right to see records or attend meetings that are clearly covered by an open meeting or public record law.

Sometimes the only way to win your rights is to threaten a lawsuit—or actually file one. But often you can win access to public records or meetings by appealing to higher authorities. If a clerk tells you a record isn't open for public inspection when you know or suspect that it is, ask to see his or her supervisor. If you have a copy of the open meeting or public record law with you, your chance of prevailing at this point is much better.

If you're attending a public meeting of your college board of trustees and a closed session is announced, your first step is to decide whether the closed session is permitted under your state's laws. If it is, you'll have to leave, although you should first make arrangements to contact someone who will be present at the closed meeting so you can find out what happened there. The campus public information officer may be willing to help you with this. Or you may prefer to interview several people who attended the closed meeting to be sure you get a balanced perspective if something controversial is discussed.

However, if the closed meeting appears to violate the state open meeting law, you have a dilemma. If you refuse to leave, you may invite disciplinary action or even criminal prosecution for trespassing. If you're right, you may eventually win your point, but you could still be guilty of trespassing. Are you prepared to pay that price? Who will back you up if you decide to stand up for your rights? These are things you will have to decide for yourself after consulting your faculty adviser.

Another practical problem with all open meeting and public records laws, of course, is that they only work when public-spirited government officials want them to work. If the board of trustees says it's going into a closed session to discuss "personnel matters" and then the discussion turns to another topic, how will anyone outside ever know? Public officials bent on doing the public's business in private can always find a way, even if it means meeting quietly over lunch out of town.

Public records laws are even more difficult to enforce when government officials are determined to keep secrets. Among the thousands or millions of records sitting in file cabinets, how can you ever be sure a certain record is there? Unless you know exactly what to ask for, government officials can always tell you the record doesn't exist. Like the federal FoI Act, many state laws require government agencies to publish lists of the major records they keep as a service to the public. But even if you locate one of these lists, it may not be possible to identify the exact record you need.

A growing problem today involves the retrieval of computerized records. Even if a certain public record isn't in a computerized data bank, it is easy for government officials to insist that it is and then say the cost of retrieving it would be prohibitive. The FoI Act and almost all other public record laws allow governments to charge a fee for locating and duplicating records. Thus, a government official can legally make a record inaccessible by setting a fee so high that no one can afford to pay it. The fees are supposed to be reasonable, but if a computer is involved, who is to say what is and is not a reasonable retrieval charge?

SHIELD LAWS AND REPORTER'S PRIVILEGE

So far, we've been talking about ways to use the legal system as a crowbar to pry open government file cabinets and meeting-room doors. But when that doesn't work, a good reporter will look for other methods of getting a story, and that sometimes means working with confidential sources of information.

As we said at the outset, many important news stories could not be developed without the use of confidential sources. Some people with an important story to tell simply cannot talk on the record lest they jeopardize their careers or vital friendships. The Watergate story, which led to the resignation of Richard Nixon as president of the United States, is a classic example of such a situation. *Washington Post* reporters Robert Woodward and Carl Bernstein have not yet revealed the identity of their key source, an informant they call "deep throat" in their book on the Watergate affair.[18]

You may never cover a story as filled with intrigue (or as significant) as the Watergate story, but you may nevertheless have to promise someone that you won't use his or her name in order to get important information. Or you may have a situation where the information itself is confidential. Student newspapers occasionally stumble onto evidence of a crime that they feel they cannot disclose to the authorities. Few reporters—professional or student—are willing to turn their notes or unpublished photographs over to the police, regardless of the circumstances.

If you find yourself in a situation where it is necessary to promise confidentiality to a news source or if you possess confidential information of interest to the authorities, you'll need the protection of a shield law or at least the reporter's privilege.

At this writing, 26 states have shield laws. They are Alabama, Alaska, Arkansas, Arizona, California, Delaware, Illinois, Indiana, Kentucky, Louisiana, Maryland, Michigan, Minnesota, Montana, Nebraska, Nevada, New Jersey, New Mexico, New York, North Dakota, Ohio, Oklahoma, Oregon, Pennsylvania, Rhode Island and Tennessee.

These laws vary almost as much as state open meeting and public record laws. Some were intended to be weak when they were approved by various state legislatures, while others have been weakened by the courts. In New Mexico, for instance, the state Supreme Court has virtually abolished the shield law; in that state, journalists have little protection when ordered by a court to reveal confidential information.[19] In California,[20] New York[21] and New Jersey,[22] the courts have weakened the shield laws, although not as drastically as in New Mexico.

In general, when a court faces a situation in which a journalist appears to have information that could affect the outcome of a criminal case, the court tends to look for a loophole that could be used to force the journalist to reveal what he or she knows. From a judge's viewpoint, it is the court's responsibility to find the whole truth, and a journalist, like any other citizen should step forward when he or she has relevant evidence. Nevertheless, if you're in a state with a shield law, you have at least limited protection if you are ordered to reveal confidential information.

However, there are other problems for campus journalists. Many state shield laws define the term *journalist* so narrowly that the definition excludes student journalists and sometimes even foreign journalists. If you face a confidential-source situation, it may be time to find out exactly what your state's shield law says—if your state even has a shield law.

If your state doesn't have a shield law, then the only real hope for protecting your sources lies in the concept of reporter's privilege. At this writing, Supreme Courts in five states (Iowa, Wisconsin, Kansas, Virginia and Vermont) have recognized a reporter's privilege in the absence of a shield law. However, in every instance so far, this privilege has been limited. It may protect you from an overzealous district attorney's "fishing expedition," but it may not be much help if a judge really believes you have information that would affect the outcome of an important case (especially a criminal case).

In general, as a campus journalist you should probably not rely on either a shield law or the reporter's privilege doctrine to protect you if you promise confidentiality to a source. You should use that reporting technique only when it is absolutely necessary to get an important story, and even then you should use it only if you're prepared for the consequences (which may well include a stay in jail if you keep your promises).

NEWSROOM SEARCHES

A few years ago, the *Stanford Daily* at Stanford University became entangled in what was probably the most famous legal dispute ever for a student newspaper. The case began when *Stanford Daily* photographers covered a sit-in demonstration at the Stanford University Hospital. The demonstration was forcibly broken up by law enforcement agencies, and a number of people were injured when the situation became violent.

Two days later, the *Daily* ran a photo spread on the incident. The local district attorney's office got a search warrant and the police then searched the newspaper's office in an effort to find more photographs that could be used as evidence.

That newsroom search angered journalists all over America. The *Daily* had done nothing wrong; its staff was merely covering a major news story. If a newspaper office can be searched whenever the police think a reporter has useful information, the First Amendment means nothing, journalists contended. The Stanford students took their case all the way to the Supreme Court, arguing that the search of their office violated the First Amendment. In an important 1978 decision (*Zurcher* v. *Stanford Daily*), the Supreme Court ruled that police searches of newspaper offices did *not* violate the First Amendment, even if no one on the staff was suspected of any crime.[23]

In the aftermath of the *Stanford* case, there were several other well publicized searches of newspapers and radio and television stations. Media representatives began lobbying in Congress and various state legislatures for laws prohibiting newsroom searches. As a result, several states banned newsroom searches, except when a member of the staff was suspected of a crime. More importantly, Congress eventually passed the Privacy Protection Act of 1980, sharply limiting the circumstances under which newsroom searches are permitted by either federal, state or local law enforcement officials.[24]

The Privacy Protection Act allows newsroom searches, but only when journalists are suspected of a crime, when they might otherwise destroy the evidence, when someone's life or safety is in danger, or when the journalists involved have refused to obey a court order requiring them to turn over the materials in question.

This law was obviously a compromise measure; it didn't make everyone happy on either side of the issue. Nevertheless, it effectively overrules the *Stanford Daily* Supreme Court decision and makes it less likely your newspaper will be subjected to a surprise search by the police.

CONCLUSION

Whether you're covering a college campus or the highest levels of government, newsgathering has legal ramifications. As a journalist, you have extensive rights, but you may also face serious responsibilities. In general, the better you do your job, the more risk you run that a court will someday want you to reveal your sources of information. If you never cover anything more provocative (or important) than school spirit and keeping the campus clean, you probably won't need to use a public records or open meeting law. Nor will you need to fear court orders requiring you to reveal your confidential sources. But if you do a good job, the price you may have to pay is a few legal skirmishes as you gather the news. Sloppy reporting produces an abundance of libel suits, but good reporting may land the reporter in jail for refusing to reveal confidential (but important) information.

REFERENCES

1. 5 U.S.C. 552.

2. "How to Use the Federal FoI Act," available from the Reporters Committee for Freedom of the Press, 1125 Fifteenth St., N.W., Room 403, Washington, D.C. 20005.

3. 5 U.S.C. 552a.

4. 20 U.S.C. 1232g.

5. See, for instance, *Smith v. Daily Mail*, 443 U.S. 97 (1979).

6. U.S.C. 552b.

7. *Florida Statutes Annotated*, chap. 286.

8. See, for instance, *Bigelow v. Howze*, 291 So. 2d 645 (1974).

9. *Pennsylvania Statutes*, 65-261 to 269.

10. *Ohio Revised Code Annotated*, sec. 121.22.

11. *Connecticut General Statutes Annotated*, sec. 1-15 to 1-21k.

12. *New York Public Officers Law*, sec. 95-106.

13. *Indiana Statutes*, 5-14-1.5-1 to 7.

14. *Texas Revised Civil Statutes Annotated*, sec. 6252-17.

15. See the Grunsky-Burton Open Meeting Act, *California Government Code*, sec. 9027–9032; State Agency Open Meeting Act, *California Government Code*, sec. 11120–11131; the Ralph M. Brown Act, *California Government Code*, sec. 54950–

54960.5; and open meeting provisions for the University of California Board of Regents in *California Education Code*, sec. 92030.

16. See *Illinois Annotated Statutes*, chap. 102, sec. 41–45.

17. See Texas Attorney General's Opinion no. H-438 (1974).

18. Robert Woodward and Carl Bernstein, *All the President's Men* (New York: Simon and Schuster, 1974).

19. See *Ammerman* v. *Hubbard Broadcasting, Inc.*, 551 P. 2d 1354 (1976).

20. See, for instance, *Farr* v. *Superior Court*, 22 Cal. App. 3d 60 (1971).

21. See, for instance, *WBAI-FM* v. *Proskin*, 344 N.Y.S. 2d 393 (1973).

22. See *In Re Farber*, 349 A. 2d 330 (1978).

23. *Zurcher* v. *Stanford Daily*, 436 U.S. 547 (1978).

24. 94 Stat. 1879.

FIFTEEN

Ethics and College Newspapers

I n the last three chapters we've been talking about the legal rights of the student press. The question has been, "Legally, what *can* you do?" In this chapter we go a step further and ask, "What *should* you do?

The ethical questions that face journalists are often controversial and troubling—and they rarely have absolute right and wrong answers. You need to go no further than the nearest drugstore magazine rack to see that journalists set a wide variety of ethical standards for themselves.

This is true because ethics are an individual matter for American journalists; there is no government agency that forces journalists to be ethical. Granted, the Federal Trade Commission may act when an advertiser deceives the public, and the Federal Communications Commission still has rules requiring broadcasters to present more than just one point of view on controversial issues. But for the most part, ethical behavior is voluntary.

It is also true that unethical journalists may face a certain amount of social pressure. Media critics regularly write magazine articles about journalists' misdeeds. The *Columbia Journalism Review,* for instance, often carries such articles. However, journalists are free to ignore the critics and go about their business. In fact, some of the most successful journalists in American history were perennially criticized for practicing sensationalism, for taking liberties with the truth and for blatant editorializing on their news pages. In a media history course, you'll meet a number of shady characters who prospered in journalism without worrying much about the ethics of what they did. Journalistic ethics are a matter of integrity and professional honor, and nothing more.

Journalistic ethics are based mostly on an honor system on college campuses, too. Your faculty adviser undoubtedly does critiques of your newspaper and has a professional obligation to discuss ethics as well as misspelled words. Higher authorities may do more drastic things—like trying a little censorship—if they think the paper is flagrantly violating their concept of ethics. But if that happens, you'll probably have the First Amendment on your side, because the First Amendment protects irresponsible as well as responsible journalism. In a famous 1974 decision, the U.S. Supreme Court put it this way: "A responsible press is undoubtedly a desirable goal, but press responsibility is not mandated by the Constitution and like many other virtues it cannot be legislated."[1]

In a free society, then, journalistic ethics are a matter of conscience for journalists. You will undoubtedly hear from various people who want you to follow their ethical standards, and some of these people may have very legitimate concerns. But because of the First Amendment, you will have a lot of freedom to make up your own mind. In this chapter, we'll outline some of the dilemmas that you may have to face.

CODES OF ETHICS

Although ethical behavior is an individual matter, journalists have discussed ethics for many years, and several journalistic organizations have adopted codes of ethics. One of the best known is the code of the Society of Professional Journalists, Sigma Delta Chi (see Figure 15.1).

The SPJ-SDX code outlines the responsibilities of journalists in various areas, including some we've already discussed in this book. For example, the code emphasizes the importance of accuracy, of writing objectively and of separating news reporting from expressions of opinion. The code also addresses such issues as journalists accepting free gifts, the use and abuse of confidential sources in news reporting, and conflict of interest problems.

However, the SPJ-SDX code and others like it are purely voluntary. In that respect, journalists' codes of ethics differ from the ethical codes in such professions as medicine and law. Errant doctors and lawyers may be punished for their unethical conduct, and they may ultimately lose the right to practice their professions if their misconduct is sufficiently flagrant. However, journalists need no license to practice their art, and no one has the authority to make an unethical journalist stop writing and publishing. In short, journalistic codes of ethics have no teeth in them. Journalists are free to ignore their provisions.

Another problem with any such code is that it must by nature be broad and general—it cannot cover all of the specific situations that journalists may face. For example, the SPJ-SDX code says, "Nothing of value should be accepted." However, journalists routinely accept small freebies from the organizations they cover. Just how big a gift is too big?

Moreover, the code says, "The media should not pander to morbid curiosity about details of vice and crime." But major media report the details of vice and crime stories daily. At what point do those details become morbid?

Obviously, many matters of journalistic ethics must be decided on an individual day-to-day basis. A code of ethics can do no more than suggest broad principles of right and wrong. It remains up to each journalist, guided by his or her conscience, to apply the principles.

With that background, we will explore some of the specific ethical problems that college journalists often face.

Figure 15.1   The Society of Professional
Journalists, Sigma Delta Chi, Code of Ethics.
Used by permission.

The Society of Professional Journalists, Sigma Delta Chi

CODE OF ETHICS
(Adopted by the 1973 national convention)

The Society of Professional Journalists, Sigma Delta Chi, believes the duty of journalists is to serve the truth.

We believe the agencies of mass communication are carriers of public discussion and information, acting on their Constitutional mandate and freedom to learn and report the facts.

We believe in public enlightenment as the forerunner of justice, and in our Constitutional role to seek the truth as part of the public's right to know the truth.

We believe those responsibilities carry obligations that require journalists to perform with intelligence, objectivity, accuracy, and fairness.

To these ends, we declare acceptance of the standards of practice here set forth:

Responsibility   The public's right to know of events of public importance and interest is the overriding mission of the mass media. The purpose of distributing news and enlightened opinion is to serve the general welfare. Journalists who use their professional status as representatives of the public for selfish or other unworthy motives violate a high trust.

Freedom of the Press   Freedom of the press is to be guarded as an inalienable right of people in a free society. It carries with it the freedom and the responsibility to discuss, question, and challenge actions and utterances of our government and of our public and private institutions. Journalists uphold the right to speak unpopular opinions and the privilege to agree with the majority.

Ethics   Journalists must be free of obligation to any interest other than the public's right to know the truth.

1. Gifts, favors, free travel, special treatment or privileges can compromise the integrity of journalists and their employers. Nothing of value should be accepted

2. Secondary employment, political involvement, holding public office, and service in community organizations should be avoided if it compromises the integrity of journalists and their employers. Journalists and their employers should conduct their personal lives in a manner which protects them from conflict of interest, real or apparent. Their responsibilities to the public are paramount. That is the nature of their profession.

3. So-called news communications from private sources should not be published or broadcast without substantiation of their claims to news value.

4. Journalists will seek news that serves the public interest, despite the obstacles. They will make constant efforts to assure that the public's business is conducted in public and that public records are open to public inspection.

5. Journalists acknowledge the newsman's ethic of protecting confidential sources of information.

Accuracy and Objectivity   Good faith with the public is the foundation of all worthy journalism

1. Truth is our ultimate goal.

2. Objectivity in reporting the news is another goal which serves as the mark of an experienced professional. It is a standard of performance toward which we strive. We honor those who achieve it.

3. There is no excuse for inaccuracies or lack of thoroughness.

Figure 15.1 *(continued)*

4. Newspaper headlines should be fully warranted by the contents of the articles they accompany. Photographs and telecasts should give an accurate picture of an event and not highlight a minor incident out of context.

5. Sound practice makes clear distinction between news reports and expressions of opinion. News reports should be free of opinion or bias and represent all sides of an issue.

6. Partisanship in editorial comment which knowingly departs from the truth violates the spirit of American journalism.

7. Journalists recognize their responsibility for offering informed analysis, comment, and editorial opinion on public events and issues. They accept the obligation to present such material by individuals whose competence, experience, and judgment qualify them for it.

8. Special articles or presentations devoted to advocacy or the writer's own conclusions and interpretations should be labeled as such.

Fair Play Journalists at all times will show respect for the dignity, privacy, rights, and well-being of people encountered in the course of gathering and presenting the news.

1. The news media should not communicate unofficial charges affecting reputation or moral character without giving the accused a chance to reply.
2. The news media must guard against invading a person's right to privacy.
3. The media should not pander to morbid curiosity about details of vice and crime.
4. It is the duty of news media to make prompt and complete correction of their errors.
5. Journalists should be accountable to the public for their reports and the public should be encouraged to voice its grievances against the media. Open dialogue with our readers, viewers, and listeners should be fostered.

Pledge Journalists should actively censure and try to prevent violations of these standards, and they should encourage their observance by all newspeople. Adherence to this code of ethics is intended to preserve the bond of mutual trust and respect between American journalists and the American people.

MAJOR ETHICAL PROBLEMS

What Is News?

Chapter 3 discussed the pros and cons of covering off-campus news in college newspapers. Sometimes off-campus events may seem far more controversial, exciting and relevant to students than the routine doings of campus groups and organizations.

The *Mustang Daily* at California Polytechnical State University in San Luis Obispo faced this dilemma recently. There were major demonstrations at a nuclear power plant a few miles away, and hundreds of people were arrested. The paper covered the story lavishly, but in the process the editors weren't as enthusiastic about covering their own campus as they might have been. Compared to such a big issue, a lot of campus news seemed mundane.[2] As a result, many students, faculty and administrators—who didn't consider their own activities to be all that mundane—became disenchanted with the paper.

Obviously, off-campus news is of vital concern to students. Probably no one would contend that a college newspaper should completely ignore major off-campus stories. But shouldn't a college paper cover its own campus thoroughly as well? If the campus newspaper doesn't cover campus news, who will?

Sometimes the answer to that question is simple: another newspaper. At a number of colleges and universities a second newspaper has been created precisely because of dissatisfaction with the job the original paper was doing in covering campus news.

Student governments chronically complain that campus activities are poorly covered in student newspapers. Meanwhile, some newspaper advisers think college newspapers devote *too much* space to the deliberations of student governments themselves but *too little* space to the activities sponsored by the student governments. Student leaders themselves have sometimes become so frustrated about the poor coverage of campus activities that they have created rival newspapers with a specific mandate to cover the campus and nothing else.

In debating the merits of covering the campus as opposed to covering the world at large, it is easy to overlook the interests of readers. The readers have many alternative sources of world and national news, but they may have no other source of campus news.

Most student newspapers try to strike some kind of balance between covering the campus and covering the world. How you strike that balance is one of the most important decisions you'll face.

What Is Good Taste?

As a result of court decisions in recent years, student newspapers at tax-supported colleges and universities have broad freedom to cover the news, including news that may shock or offend some readers.

The courts have made it clear that mere four-letter words and frontal nudity do not constitute obscenity. But under what circumstances should nudity or potentially offensive language appear in your paper?

The answer to that question depends very much on the nature of your institution. You have many diverse publics to think about, including the students, faculty and staff, trustees and donors, and the community at large. When is a story important enough that you should run it even if it offends one or more of these groups?

Perhaps the answer should be, "when the offensive words or pictures are clearly newsworthy." Some—but not all—professional newspapers will publish once-verboten four-letter words when they are part of an important quote by a public official or celebrity. When the quote itself becomes so controversial that it jeopardizes someone's job, it's difficult to cover the news without using the quote.

Let's illustrate with the Earl Butz case. Butz was the secretary of agriculture when Gerald Ford was president of the United States. Butz had a habit of making controversial off-color remarks, sometimes mixing vulgarisms with racial slurs.

Finally, he made a statement—in front of several witnesses—that was so offensive he lost his job.

It is difficult to discuss the ethics of publishing a statement such as the one Secretary Butz made if you don't know what he said. In order to foster a full discussion of the issues involved, we're presenting Butz' infamous quotation.

Butz was asked why so few black Americans are Republicans, and he replied by asking the questioner if he knew what blacks wanted. Then Butz answered his own rhetorical question: he said blacks want "first, a tight pussy, second, loose shoes, third, a warm place to shit."

Is that statement too vulgar to use in a family newspaper? Remember, a major public official lost his job over it. Some newspapers carried the quote, but with the two vulgarisms deleted and paraphrased. A few unblushingly published it in full on the ground that its newsworthiness was the overriding issue.

Would you have used it? Suppose the football coach on your campus was about to be fired for saying something like that. Then would you print it? Or suppose the quote appeared in a guest column that you had solicited in order to present an alternative viewpoint on the editorial page. Would you delete it from the column? The columnist would scream "censorship!" if you did. But some readers would surely be offended if you didn't.

These are difficult questions, and your answer would depend not only on your definition of news but also on your sense of the prevailing standards of good taste on your campus.

Are There Private Facts?

An issue closely related to good taste is individual privacy. The SPJ-SDX code says, "The media must guard against invading a person's right to privacy." But when does a story invade someone's privacy? When is a story newsworthy enough to publish despite the fact that it may invade someone's privacy?

Suppose the dean of students is having an affair with a student. Is that news? Or is it nobody else's business?

On some campuses, that might be a major scandal. On others, almost no one would care. If yours is a large, public university, you may well conclude that the story is nobody else's business.

However, would your answer be different if it were a professor having an affair with a student and you had evidence the professor gave the student an A in a class the student didn't attend? Or suppose you learned that a professor had been arrested for shoplifting at a store some distance from the campus. Is that newsworthy?

Suppose instead you learned that the professor had been convicted of a crime long ago and that he had served his prison time. Would you report that?

On the other hand, suppose you learned that a college administrator who handles state funds was once convicted of embezzlement. Would knowing that alter your news judgment?

A story that is clearly newsworthy in one context may be an invasion of privacy in another. The problem is deciding when a story is so newsworthy that the public's right to know outweighs the individual's right to privacy. It's a question you must decide with sensitivity for the individuals who may be hurt—but also with sensitivity to your obligation to cover the news.

Is There Enough Documentation?

Everybody loves a good news story, and few things are more frustrating than waiting to run a story while someone painstakingly verifies the facts. But a single incorrect story could ruin someone's career or cause a libel suit that would bankrupt a prosperous newspaper.

If a news source gives you a hot tip, how thoroughly should you document it before you run a story? Remember the movie *Absence of Malice?* Did the reporter violate journalistic ethics by publishing unverified rumors as news? How much additional checking should she have done before publishing the stories that turned out to be so wrong? What does the SPJ-SDX Code of Ethics say about the kind of reporting depicted in the movie?

In their coverage of the Watergate scandal, *Washington Post* reporters Robert Woodward and Carl Bernstein waited until they had independent documentation from two sources before they published any story based on confidential information. Are two sources enough? And how reputable must the sources be before you trust them? Should you ask yourself what might be the motives of your sources?

Obviously, secret-source reporting can be abused. It's easy for a reporter to be exploited by a source who is out to get someone, as *Absence of Malice* so well illustrated. But on the other hand, many important investigative news stories could never be reported without relying on inside sources, people who might lose their jobs if they were identified. In any given situation, you have to weigh the reliability of the sources, the social importance of the story and the amount of damage the story will do if you're wrong.

As we've said before, accuracy is extremely important if your newspaper is to maintain its credibility. Double-checking is always vital to good reporting, but when the story accuses someone of wrongdoing, meticulous fact-checking could make the difference between a Pulitzer Prize and a libel suit.

Are the Quotes Correct?

Like facts, direct quotations are sacred to journalists. Longtime student newspaper advisers often say that one of the most serious shortcomings of the campus press is a cavalier attitude toward quotes.

When is it ethical to change a direct quote? Some journalists would say "absolutely never." Others might say it is acceptable to change a little word like *is* to *are* in the interest of good grammar. But to that, some reporters would respond, "If somebody makes grammatical errors, the readers should know it."

In any case, generally accepted journalistic ethics do not permit any change in a direct quote, however slight, that changes the meaning or context of the statement.

Likewise, it is generally agreed that a quote should not be taken out of its context. To be accurate and fair you have to include enough of the surrounding statements that the context is clear. The quotation from Earl Butz earlier in this chapter was placed in its context by the explanation that preceded the actual quote. Without that explanation, the quote would have been out of context.

Is It Fair and Impartial?

The editors of college newspapers have a lot of power, and the temptation to use that power for personal ends is sometimes irresistible.

No newspaper and no reporter can be completely objective. It is inevitable

---

THESE PEOPLE MAY TEST YOUR ETHICS (AND YOUR PATIENCE)

Almost every campus has certain individuals who pose problems for student newspaper staffs. Any resemblance between these characters and people on your campus is intended.

Weasels   Weasels equivocate. They occupy middle management positions, neatly sandwiched between students and higher authorities. And they are probably as high up in the system as they're going. Don't waste a lot of time interviewing them, because they will do everything possible to avoid saying anything significant. If you do quote one, don't expect support. Since they don't know what part of a story might get them into trouble, they always claim they have been misquoted. Sometimes if you contact them long after a story appears—when the whole thing has blown over—they may admit your quotes were accurate. But probably not.

William Tells   William Tells aren't on the staff, but they love to edit copy—your copy. They're "just concerned about accuracy," of course. Some may have a legitimate gripe, particularly in the hard sciences. Both college and professional journalists are notorious for botching stories about technical and scientific subjects. But more often, it's their own posterior they are trying to protect. There may be times when you should show a technical story to a news source to verify its accuracy, but generally William Tells should be invited to edit someone else's copy.

Protectors   These people are cheerleaders for the institution. They're afraid of all sorts of sinister outside forces, and they appeal to your sense of loyalty. If you see no evil, hear no evil and speak no evil—in other words, ignore that personal biases will sometimes slip into anyone's writing or editing. But journalists generally try to keep those tendencies in check, perhaps deliberately including *more* information reflecting opposing viewpoints than they include representing their own view.

A newspaper has a right—in fact a duty—to present its own views in the editorials, but nowhere else. If a newspaper is to serve all of the varied interests on a college campus, it should be open to all viewpoints. The editorial page should offer a variety of opinions, including those contrary to the editorial board's own views. And the news columns should be open to everyone, too. They should not be a vehicle to publicize the activities of an editor's friends or to blackball enemies.

On some ethical issues, there is wide disagreement among journalists, but impartiality is not one of them. While there is a place for advocacy journalism in America, a general student newspaper is not the place.

---

everything except the good news—they'll love you. But a reporter can't always be a cheerleader; sometimes you have to ignore the dire warnings of the protectors and go ahead with a story.

Inside Dopesters   Inside dopesters may catch you off guard. They seem friendly and may actually be friends. They may be faculty members or student leaders, and they seem like good people to bounce a story idea off. They may even have good story ideas from time to time. But if you confide in them, you're forgetting something important: they are just as glib when they're somewhere else.

Bloated Egos   These people may be real space-grabbers. They drop by the office often, usually with news of their own marginally newsworthy achievements. Many are professors who publish a lot (just ask 'em if their work is important), but these types also gravitate toward student government. They should be treated politely, but firmly. Cover their "news" only if it's really *news*.

Prudes   All colleges have prudes, but some have more than others. They're self-appointed warriors in the struggle to save the world from immorality. Unfortunately, their definition of immorality includes almost everything that's newsworthy. It usually doesn't help to tell them other people have a right to their own opinions, but that is about all you can say in defense of your policy of covering all sides. To them, balanced reporting is nothing more than giving equal time to the devil himself.

Gadflies   Gadflies love a good controversy or scandal. Their story ideas aren't as self-serving as the suggestions of the bloated egos. In fact, they may want to remain personally anonymous, but they've always "got a great story for you." Sometimes it really may be a good story, but don't run it without checking adequately.

Was It a Free Gift?

Freebies have bothered journalists for many years. As a journalist you have the power to confer great benefits, and your friendship will be cultivated by people who hope to gain these benefits.

As we noted earlier, the SPJ-SDX code flatly forbids taking anything of value. Few journalists would defend the practice of accepting large gifts such as new cars or expensive clothing. But what about free tickets to plays, movies and ball games? And what about free record albums and books? These are borderline cases, and not all journalists agree here. Some say a journalist shouldn't accept *any* gift from a news source. Some professional newspapers insist on paying their sports reporters' admissions to athletic events. Others don't go that far, of course.

The problem you have to deal with when you accept any freebie is whether it will affect your objectivity. Can you go to an event as a guest of the sponsors ıd still write an impartial review? Can you be objective about an athletic team if you've been given free travel accommodations, and you want to be given the same treatment next time? These are some of the difficult questions journalists must answer about freebies.

What Will the Advertisers Think?

If you have to ask what the advertisers will think before you do a story, you have an ethical dilemma on your hands. Nevertheless, advertiser pressure is a fact of life in journalism; both student and professional papers must deal with it. What do you do if a major advertiser—someone whose advertising is really needed to make ends meet—wants to get a story in the paper, or keep one out?

The problem can vary from trivial to serious. You may encounter an advertiser whose son is on the football team and who wants his son's name in the paper. That's a petty matter, but it may have to be dealt with. At the other extreme, suppose a big advertiser is running for public office in the area and demands a good press. Then what do you do?

An ethical absolutist would say there's a simple solution: tell the advertiser where to go. But in the real world, college newspapers are dependent on advertising to stay in business, so the answer isn't always that simple.

Are You Loyal in Battle?

We've talked about a journalist's ethical obligations to the readers, to the people whose names appear in print, to news sources and to advertisers. But a journalist also has an ethical obligation to his or her fellow staff members and to the newspaper as an institution.

For example, suppose someone not on the staff criticizes the newspaper. You may agree philosophically with the criticism: rarely does everyone on a news staff agree with every decision another staff member makes. Should you tell an outsider what an incompetent you think the current editor is? Or should you say you disagree with the paper's basic policies?

Whatever may be the internal friction on the staff, a staff member owes some loyalty to his or her colleagues. Few people respect someone who chronically backstabs fellow staff members. The time may come when a staff member who honestly disagrees with the paper's policy must resign. Even short of that, it may be appropriate for a staff member to write a column disagreeing with a staff-written editorial. However, the staff has a right to expect a little personal loyalty from each member. Internal squabbles should generally remain internal matters.

This is especially true in the context of campus-wide politics. Student newspapers are often caught up in bitter feuds with administrators, faculty members or student leaders. In the campus political arena, student newspapers risk losing everything from financial support to editorial freedom. The last thing the newspaper needs at such a time is to have its position undermined by disloyal staff members.[3]

Another aspect of this problem is the matter of counting your chips before playing the game. Machiavellian power games go on at colleges just as they do in the outside world. Before you take on the people who have real power on your campus, it is important to ask yourself whether the battle is worth fighting—and whether you have a chance of winning.[4] As we pointed out in Chapter 12, you may find that you have strong support from the professional media and civil liberties groups—but only if your cause is a defensible one.

There may be a time when you have to decide a particular battle for freedom of expression simply cannot be won—or wasn't worth the trouble in the first place.

CONCLUSION

In this chapter, we've posed a lot of questions and offered only a few answers. In fact, many of these questions have no clear-cut answers. A few do have clear-cut answers, but they are answers that journalists sometimes forget. In almost all of these areas, your ethics are a personal matter. Only you can decide what kind of journalism you want to practice.

REFERENCES

1. *Miami Herald* v. *Tornillo,* 418 U.S. 241 (1974).

2. This information was obtained in a telephone interview with James Hayes, faculty adviser to the *Mustang Daily* at California Polytechnic State University, San Luis Obispo, on 19 January 1982.

3. Some of the ideas presented here are based on conversations with Ben Adelson, professor of journalism emeritus at Los Angeles Pierce College.

4. Some of this material was inspired by a presentation by Vicki Bortolussi of Ventura College at the 1980 Journalism Association of Community Colleges Faculty Retreat at Morro Bay, California.

INDEX